SCIENCE
and the
PARANORMAL

SCIENCE
and the
PARANORMAL

PROBING THE EXISTENCE OF THE
SUPERNATURAL

EDITED BY

GEORGE O. ABELL and BARRY SINGER

CHARLES SCRIBNER'S SONS · NEW YORK

"Plant Sensitivity and Sensation," by Arthur W. Galston and Clifford L. Slayman, first appeared as "The Not-So-Secret Life of Plants" in *American Scientist* 67 (May 1979), pp. 337-44, and is reprinted here by permission of Arthur Galston.

Some of the material in "Biorhythms," by Tarek Khalil and Charles Kurucz, has appeared in different form in the following articles by the authors: "The Influence of 'Biorhythm' on Accident Occurrence and Performance," *Ergonomics* 20 (1977), pp. 389-98, and "Probability Models for Analyzing the Effects of Biorhythms on Accident Occurrence," *Journal of Safety Research*, vol. 9, pp. 150-58.

"The Subtlest Difference," by Isaac Asimov, copyright © 1977, 1978 by Mercury Press, Inc., from his book *The Road to Infinity*, copyright © 1979 by Isaac Asimov. Reprinted by permission of Doubleday & Company, Inc.; Mercury Press, Inc.; and the author.

"Life After Death," by Ronald K. Siegel, copyright © 1981 by Ronald K. Siegel, is reprinted here by permission of the author and has appeared as "Accounting for After-Life Experiences" in *Psychology Today*, January 1981, pp. 65-75.

Some of the material in "Psychic Healing," by William A. Nolen, has appeared in different form in the author's book *Healing: A Doctor in Search of a Miracle*, Random House, 1975, and Crest, 1976.

"An Analysis of *Worlds in Collision*," by Carl Sagan, is excerpted with permission from Carl Sagan's *Broca's Brain*, Random House, New York, published in 1979, © 1976 by Carl Sagan. This essay first appeared in *Scientists Confront Velikovsky*, Donald Goldsmith, editor, Cornell University Press, 1977.

Parts of "Recasting the Past," by E. C. Krupp, have appeared in "The von Däniken Phenomenon," by E. C. Krupp, in the *Griffith Observer*, April 1974 and July 1977, and are reprinted here with permission.

Some of the material in "UFOs," by Philip J. Klass, has appeared in different form in the author's book *UFO's Explained*, Random House, 1974, and Vintage, 1976.

First Charles Scribner's Sons Paperback Edition 1983

Charles Scribner's Sons
Macmillan Publishing Company
866 Third Avenue, New York, NY 10022

Library of Congress Cataloging in Publication Data

Main entry under title:

Science and the paranormal.

   Bibliography: p.
   Includes index.
   1. Psychical research—Addresses, essays,
lectures.   2. Occult sciences—Addresses, essays,
lectures.   3. Science—Addresses, essays, lectures.
I. Abell, George Ogden, 1927-   II. Singer,
Barry.
BF1045.S33S38   133.8'01'5   81-26839
ISBN 0-684-17820-6

10 9 8 7 6 5 4

Printed in the United States of America

CONTENTS

Believing the Unbelievable:
The Scientific Response—A Foreword   vii
    PAUL KURTZ

Introduction   1
    GEORGE O. ABELL
    BARRY SINGER

1. To Believe or Not to Believe   7
    BARRY SINGER

2. Monsters   24
    DANIEL COHEN

3. Plant Sensitivity and Sensation   40
    ARTHUR W. GALSTON
    CLIFFORD L. SLAYMAN

4. Parapsychology and Quantum Mechanics   56
    MARTIN GARDNER

5. Astrology   70
    GEORGE O. ABELL

6. Moon Madness   95
    GEORGE O. ABELL

7. Biorhythms   105
    TAREK KHALIL
    CHARLES KURUCZ

8. Scientists and Psychics   119
    RAY HYMAN

9. On Double Standards   142
    BARRY SINGER

10. **The Subtlest Difference**   149
    ISAAC ASIMOV

11. **Life After Death**   159
    RONALD K. SIEGEL

12. **Psychic Healing**   185
    WILLIAM A. NOLEN

13. **Kirlian Photography**   196
    BARRY SINGER

14. **Science and the Chimera**   209
    JAMES RANDI

15. **An Analysis of** *Worlds in Collision*   223
    CARL SAGAN

16. **Recasting the Past: Powerful Pyramids, Lost Continents, and Ancient Astronauts**   253
    E. C. KRUPP

17. **The Bermuda Triangle**   296
    LARRY KUSCHE

18. **UFOs**   310
    PHILIP J. KLASS

19. **Intelligent Life in the Universe**   329
    FRANK D. DRAKE

20. **On the Causes of Wonderful Things: A Perspective**   349
    PHILIP MORRISON

Notes and Bibliographies   363

Additional Readings   392

The Authors   395

Index   407

Believing the Unbelievable:
The Scientific Response
A FOREWORD

PAUL KURTZ

A dispassionate observer of the current scene can only be astonished by the rapid growth of bizarre beliefs in recent years among wide sectors of the public. This involves everything from belief in "psychic" forces—clairvoyance, precognition, telepathy, psychokinesis, psychic surgery, psychic healing, astral projection, levitation, plant ESP, life after life, hauntings, and apparitions—to the widespread conviction that our earth has been visited in the past by ancient astronauts in "chariots of the gods" and is being visited today by extraterrestrial creatures in space vehicles. Added to the collage is the fascination with such science fiction as the "Bermuda Triangle mystery," which is explained by a secret underwater UFO base (or a "black hole" or a "time warp") from which unsuspecting ships and planes are snatched. Included in the upsurge of strange views is a revival of many ancient occult beliefs: demonic possession, reincarnation, astrology, palmistry, fortune telling, monsters of the deep, auras, and pyramid power.

These phenomena are often called "paranormal," especially by their proponents; the term is applied to anomalous data that supposedly transcend the limits of existing science and are due to unknown and hidden causes. The paranormal world view that seems to be emerging contravenes the model of the universe derived from the physical and behavioral sciences. It is fed by the mass media: books, articles, TV, quasi-documentaries, and movies all herald the new paranormal "frontiers" of knowledge. Countless millions of people are intrigued by the realm: they are convinced that ESP is a proven fact, that there is conclusive evidence for life after life or life before life, that psychic healing can cure physical ailments, that there have been close encounters of the third kind with intelligent beings from outer space.

What should be the response of scientists to the current outbreak of irrational beliefs? Until recently, many scientists have chosen to ignore them, attributing their persistence to gullibility and superstitition, hoping that they would eventually dissipate. Yet others are disturbed by their continued growth. Does this portend the end of the Enlightenment and the Age of Science, which began in the sixteenth and seventeenth centuries, they ask? Perhaps it points not to the end of technology but only of the scientific outlook in which knowledge is based upon careful methods of inquiry and verification. Some have assumed that a new Apocalypse of Unreason is about to descend upon us. The symptoms of this, they say, can also be seen in the proliferation of numerous cults and sects that offer salvation, abandon objective standards of truth, and manifest a dread of technology and science. If in earlier periods people looked to science and reason as the great promise of the future, today there is often great fear of science and technology as harmful and destructive. The classical periods of Greek and Roman civilization, in which philosophy and the arts flourished, were fairly brief—and were eventually engulfed by the Dark Ages. Some warn that the same "failure of nerve" may be repeating itself, as future shock and cultural breakdown overtake us. Such doomsday forecasts are probably overly speculative, for there are still millions of educated people who believe in the uses of science and require hard evidence to establish truth claims. Fortunately, there are also a number of scientists who have recognized that they have a responsibility that goes beyond their own specialties: to apply the methods of science to the scrutiny of claims of the paranormal and thus contribute to public information and education.

In 1976, I was instrumental in founding the Committee for the Scientific Investigation of Claims of the Paranormal, whose explicit purpose is the evaluation of paranormal claims. We believe that scientists should not simply reject unorthodox claims out of hand, however fanciful they may appear, but rather should submit them to careful investigation. Although in the present day there is a strong antiscientific and antitechnological mood that recoils from the scientific method of inquiry, there are also many proponents of the paranormal who attempt to co-opt the mantle of science, claiming that their work is supported by science. The term *pseudoscience* has sometimes been applied to many such fields: fields of inquiry that claim to be based upon scientific research, yet lack coherent or consistent theories, have no clearly definable conceptual framework, do not use rigorous methods to test their hypotheses, and make claims of discoveries that are not substantiated by the evidence. This is the case today with biorhythm theory and astrology, for example, as it was with phrenology in the nineteenth century.

Nevertheless, scientists cannot commit the fallacy of a priori negativism—that is, they cannot reject new areas of knowledge antecedent to inquiry. The history of science is full of radical breaks with established theories, however unexpected they were—the Einsteinian modification of classical physics, the germ theory and Simmelweiss's battle with the medical fraternity, the concept of shifting continents, and so forth. On the other hand, not every claim to truth from any source is responsible or deserves an equal hearing. The concepts and hypotheses introduced must be meaningful and must lend themselves to some verifiable tests.

Certain areas of the paranormal have been examined by scientific investigators in the past. This is particularly true of "psychical research." The Society for Psychical Research, for example, founded in 1882 by a number of distinguished scientists and philosophers, was dedicated to the investigation of "spiritual" and "psychic" phenomena. This was superseded by the emergence of parapsychology in the 1920s and 1930s, which marked an effort to use experimental methods to investigate psi phenomena.* Unfortunately, surrounding these fields are a large number of unproven claims, extrapolated beyond the narrow confines of the laboratory. Many investigators in these fields are biased by an a priori commitment to the belief that a specific phenomenon exists and can only be given a paranormal explanation. Often ranged against them are the uncompromising skeptics who reject the very

---

* Psi is defined here as an alleged general psychic ability that manifests itself in precognition, psychokinesis, clairvoyance, telepathy, and other alleged paranormal phenomena.

possibility of phenomena such as ESP, arguing that they contradict the existing principles of science. Unfortunately, both postures are mistaken. Science must always be open to novel departures in thought and receptive to new theories—even though they may overthrow the existing framework. Most of the claims that new paradigm models have been discovered in the paranormal realm have not been substantiated by the evidence. Merely to proclaim a "discovery" does not validate it; there is a difference between a constructive skepticism that is based upon careful inquiry and analysis and suspends belief until it is confirmed experimentally, and one that prejudges a subject matter without inquiry. It is only the former that is defensible and makes a contribution to scientific progress.

Two problems that confront science today are especially serious: First, there has been some confusion in the public mind in distinguishing between science fiction and truth. This is the Age of Science Fiction, where the human imagination outstrips present reality. Isaac Asimov, a contributor to this volume, is a brilliant author of science fiction, yet he is skeptical of the truth of the paranormal. He is well aware that an idea's being plausible or possible does not necessarily make it true. Human creativity can construct ideal worlds, but we should not accept them as true until there has been independent confirmation.

Second, there has been an evident breakdown in the consensus concerning the standards or criteria for judging truth claims. Some of this may have its source in recent philosophy of science, where positivistic criteria of scientific validation and confirmation have been questioned. Some of it may also emanate from the new frontiers of physics and astronomy, often difficult for laymen to understand or translate into common-sense terms. Unfortunately, many people have apparently concluded—and this is especially true of numerous undergraduates today—that there are no standards of knowledge, that all knowledge is subjective, and that any one belief is as true as the next. Subjectivism contests the epistemological foundations of science: the controlled uses of objective methods of inquiry, the criteria of logic, and the use of experimental tests to verify hypotheses. In the last analysis, it is *evidence* that can decide the truth of one claim rather than another—and this evidence must be available to scrutiny by independent observers and capable of being replicated under test conditions in any laboratory in the world. Regrettably, most of what goes under the name of the paranormal is pseudoscience, since it does not satisfy these rigorous standards.

The contributors to this volume are eminently qualified to deal with the many controversial claims made about the paranormal. They have taken the claims seriously; they have not rejected them without examination, but have devoted their energy and talents to investigating their merits. For example, Dr. William Nolen has scrutinized psychic healing first-hand, even visiting the Philippines to be "operated" upon by a "psychic surgeon." Carl Sagan has devoted a good deal of his attention as an astronomer to the theories of Immanuel Velikovsky, and he helped to initiate and plan a special controversial session of the American Association for the Advancement of Science to discuss his theories. Martin Gardner has spent years examining the "fads and fallacies" of the day, with special focus on parapsychology, as have Ray Hyman and James Randi. George Abell, a noted astronomer, is an expert on astrology and has actually sought out, worked with, and debated astrologers about their claims. Philip Klass, one of the leading authorities in UFO research, has even gone into the field to examine alleged sightings. Larry Kusche has painstakingly analyzed the data concerning the Bermuda Triangle. Other contributors to this volume are similarly qualified.

Unfortunately, all too many recent books have extolled the paranormal: there have been numerous best sellers on astrology, biorhythms, the Bermuda Triangle, ghosts, the superpsychics, and other such topics. Here at long last is a different kind of book, one that critically and dispassionately analyzes such claims—and finds them wanting. It is long overdue for the public to have a more balanced appraisal of the paranormal.

SCIENCE
and the
PARANORMAL

Introduction

GEORGE O. ABELL

BARRY SINGER

Science was relatively simple in Galileo's day. At that time a well-educated person had a good chance of acquainting himself with much of what was known about natural philosophy—or science, as we now call it. There was no quantum mechanics, no nuclear physics, no biomedicine, no immunology; mathematics was pretty well limited to algebra and geometry, and physics consisted of some rather simple rules about the way bodies in motion seem to behave.

It is superfluous to say that science exploded in the last century. As the world population increased manyfold so did the number of scientists, each building on the advances of the previous generations of scientists. As the number of scientists and disciplines and subdisciplines has increased, the latter becoming ever more complex, science has become increasingly remote from the lay person, making it more and more difficult to learn what is known about even a limited subject. As an example, consider the *Astrophysical Journal*—just one of several international sources dealing with modern astronomy. All the issues of the *Journal* published in the fifty-five years from its founding in 1895 until 1950 occupy fourteen feet of shelf space; those published in the eleven years from 1968 to 1978 fill seventeen feet of shelf space! The frontier of knowledge in astronomy has become so specialized that astronomers in one field often cannot understand the papers in another; to do so would require months, often years, of study. Each subarea of each discipline has developed its own jargon, and even scientists in the same general field often cannot communicate with those in different subdisciplines.

Those scientists who work at the frontier of knowledge in a particular subdiscipline often disagree with each other, sometimes vehemently. Generally, though, as more information becomes available on a subject, the investigators begin to find out which ideas are right and which wrong by the success of their predictions, and gradually the scientists in that discipline reach a consensus. Then the frontier moves on to new areas, where new disagreements emerge. Meanwhile, scientists in other subdisciplines, even of the same general field, may frequently misunderstand hypotheses recently accepted by those in a different subdiscipline. For example, astronomers who are expert in the study of the structure of stars may have quite a wrong idea about the confidence with which their colleagues estimate the distance to a particular cluster of galaxies.

If even scientists within the same discipline are often in the dark about an aspect of their discipline not in their own field of specialization, how can the public hope to interpret strange-sounding claims that purport to apply at the frontier? The very language spoken by scientific experts is alien to many of their colleagues; how much more foreign it must sound to those outside science altogether.

Yet many of those fields at the very frontier of science are of tremendous interest to all of us. What is the age of the universe? What started it expanding? Will it expand forever? What defines consciousness in a living organism? How does the consciousness of animals differ from that of plants? What is intelligence? What is the fundamental difference between living and nonliving organisms? How did life come to be in the first place?

Unfortunately, the news media cannot always be trusted to provide reliable information on these issues. In a free society there is quite rightly no requirement that everything published or presented in the media be true; unfortunately, a great deal of it is balderdash indeed. Bookstores contain many times as many volumes on pseudoscience as they do on science; so do the best-seller lists. Television programs and motion pictures with the format of documentaries carry demonstrably false accounts of ancient astronauts, psychic healing, strange monsters, and children who allegedly bend metal with their minds. The public's good faith and willingness to believe the media are mercilessly exploited, and fortunes are being made in the process.

How then can nonscientists inform themselves about a particular area of science? The best strategy for obtaining an objective evaluation is to do what scientists themselves do: ask those who best understand the subject. Thus, scientific journals regularly commission review papers on particular subjects to acquaint those in other subdisciplines with knowledge at the frontier. Scientific meetings and symposia are regularly scheduled to share and evaluate new data and new ideas. Those who are most expert in the subject—who are closest to the field—are the ones selected to prepare these summaries and reviews.

Of course the experts are sometimes wrong, even when there seems to be a consensus among them. It is not unusual for one or two dissidents to argue vigorously and alone, and once in a while they will turn out to be correct. Galileo is a classic example. In his time, the traditional view was that the earth was immobile and at the center of the universe, but he (and a few scientific colleagues, like Kepler) argued that the earth rotates and revolves around the sun. But it is rare that a dissident is right, and even then the dissident is almost always himself an expert in the field. Galileo was not an outsider; his learning and experience placed him at the very forefront of the field he was investigating.

Even though erroneous scientific ideas may be held for a time, in the long run they will be rejected because science is a self-correcting discipline. It is guided by rigorous rules, and constantly and continually rechecks its hypotheses; each is taken seriously only to the extent that it successfully predicts the results of new research. Where mistakes are made, or when the consensus of those in a particular discipline turns out to be wrong, the error is usually found out before long and the mistakes put right.

Meanwhile, far behind the frontier is a well-trodden region which has become very well understood indeed. Main ideas in that region are very unlikely to be proven wrong. The system of Newtonian mechanics, for example, works extremely well for the motions of objects in the solar system (consider the brilliant success of the Voyager mission to Jupiter!), as well as for material objects on the earth. Indeed, Newtonian mechanics is the basis of much of our modern technology. It is true that it is not absolutely and finally correct; both quantum mechanics and relativity theory extend our understanding into realms where Newtonian theory does not apply. But quantum mechanics and relativity do not show that the Newtonian system is wrong in the regions where it has been well tested. In fact, when we deal with objects that are not at the submicroscopic level, or moving at speeds near that of light, quantum mechanics and relativity theory predict exactly what Newtonian theory does.

The subjects discussed in this book are those in which dramatic claims and speculations, usually made by nonscientists, have aroused considerable public interest. The claimants typically assert that they have made discoveries beyond or in contradiction to traditional science; hence the term *paranormal*, where the Greek prefix *para* means "beyond." The term *pseudoscience* is often used by scientists to describe such topics and claims. The reason scientists have rejected most of them is not that their practitioners do not pay dues in the scientific "establishment," but because the claims cannot withstand rigorous scrutiny and are not consistent with what has been well documented and what is well understood.

Where there is a conflict between scientists and those outside of science, we have already suggested that it would be a reasonable strategy to give more credence to the experts—the scientists—than to those outside the relevant discipline. Unfortunately, however, it is often difficult for the public to know which scientists are most qualified to speak for that discipline. Moreover, while many people respect the opinions of scientists in most areas, they do not perceive scientists to be as authoritative when they criticize the area of the paranormal, perhaps because they suspect that scientists are uninformed or biased about paranormal subjects. This book is designed to deal with these problems.

First, all the authors in the book are recognized experts in the fields they are writing on, eminent scholars who are widely acknowledged to be scientists or science writers (frequently both) of exceptional merit and integrity.

Second, and most important, our authors have not just asked us to take their word for their positions, but have tried to explain the mainstream scientific viewpoint on each paranormal topic thoroughly and simply. They do not merely debunk, but look at each topic through the lens of science, and by minimizing technical terms and simplifying theories they invite us to share that microscope with them, to follow the details of their reasoning. We believe that our readers will enjoy the process, and come to understand and agree with the systematic logic of the conclusions reached.

For we are less interested in debunking than in presenting a sound scientific perspective. In fact, the topics of this book span the range of degrees of credibility. Some authors speculate on subjects at the scientific frontier where not a great deal is known but where the paranormal view does not at this time seem plausible. Others deal with subject matter in well-trodden territory where the pseudoscientific view is clearly incompatible with what is well understood. Still other speculations discussed here, however, might very well prove to be correct: there is a slight chance, for example, that there does exist a large species of animal in the Himalayas or in Loch Ness that has not been classified by zoologists. And, as Frank Drake shows, many scientists today consider the chances that intelligent life exists elsewhere in the universe to be very high indeed.

Third, not only have our authors attempted to be open, clear, and detailed in their reasoning, but the charge of scientific prejudice or double standards with respect to the paranormal is explicitly addressed in the chapter by Hyman and the essay on double standards by Singer that follows it.

The authors of this book have taken time from busy professional lives to prepare careful analyses because they care deeply what the public thinks, and how it regards science. The human race is facing many crises: overpopulation, pollution of the environment, exploitation of resources and their eventual exhaustion, the growing stockpile of nuclear weapons, racial intolerance and economic deprivation, and a host of other problems, all of which threaten our very existence as a species. If we are to survive even over the next few decades, let alone for hundreds of thousands of years, we must somehow face the problems that confront our society with all of the intellectual capacity and rationality at our disposal. We are lost if we pin our hopes instead on pseudoscientific speculation or on the murky occult beliefs of past millennia.

1

To Believe or Not to Believe

BARRY SINGER

How do we know what we know? For all of us, our beliefs about the world are a complex combination of common sense, intuition, faith, and what we have been told is scientifically true. In many instances we accept the scientific point of view even though it contradicts our intuitions and ordinary senses. We accept that the light from stars in the night sky is thousands or even millions of years old, even though that concept contradicts our intuitions; we believe those same stars are unimaginably huge balls of glowing gases whose light is maintained by nuclear fusion on a scale that reduces hydrogen bombs to sparks from a flint, even though they look like tiny, pristine jewels. We believe that this book we are holding is solid, even though at the atomic level we know that it is almost 100 percent empty space. Historically, it was not always easy to convince people of these counterintuitive facts, but today we accept them and live comfortably with the paradox that these scientific descriptions are true even though they wildly contradict our common-sense impressions of stars and solid matter. Perhaps we have learned to accept these paradoxes because they are so universally agreed upon in our culture, and we have been taught to accept them ever since we started elementary school.

Is it ever valid to trust one's own personal experience with the world instead of trusting scientific opinion? This is a difficult question, and a particularly important one when it comes to the paranormal, where phenomena like ESP can be so intuitively compelling. To help clarify conflicts between scientific and intuitive approaches to belief about the paranormal, psychologist Barry Singer has written on the psychology of knowing. He describes recent discoveries about our knowing processes, provides tests and examples to allow the reader to assess the degree to which he or she is subject to the biases and deficiencies psychologists have discovered, and shows how some of these biases and deficiencies can lead us into error in forming beliefs about the paranormal. To deny the validity of any bit of heartfelt knowledge, even though it is contradicted by objective evidence, is very difficult; and it also can be one of an individual's most sophisticated achievements in the process of personal and cognitive growth.

As a scientist skeptical about most paranormal phenomena, and as a psychologist interested in people, I've wondered for some time why paranormal beliefs are so prevalent. Upon investigation, I found that most paranormal beliefs spring from two sources: the popular media and personal experience. This essay will deal only with the latter source. I shall examine reasons why paranormal beliefs seem natural and compelling when we depend on our intuitive experience alone, and further examine reasons why intuitive experience can be profoundly misleading when forming such beliefs. In my classes I have my students take the following powers-of-observation test (the answers are given following the questions). I ask them not to do any experiments to help them find the answers, because the point is to help them check their intuitive perceptions. Answers are on page 10.

1. What causes islands to float in the ocean?
2. In Diagram A on page 9, a glass half full of water is shown resting on a tabletop. The bottom of the glass has zero degrees of tilt with respect to the tabletop, the sides of the glass have 90 degrees of tilt (i.e., are perpendicular) with respect to the tabletop, and the surface of the water has zero degrees of tilt with respect to the tabletop. In Diagram B the glass has been rotated through 45 degrees of tilt. What is the degree of tilt now of the surface of the water with respect to the tabletop?

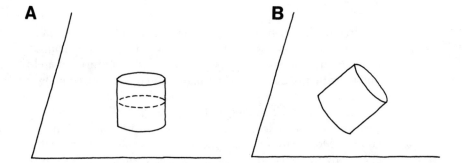

3. From what direction or directions does the moon appear to rise in the evening sky?

4. In the diagram below a four-pound weight and a two-pound weight are being dropped from a height of sixteen feet to the floor. Approximately how long will it take each to reach the floor, in seconds?

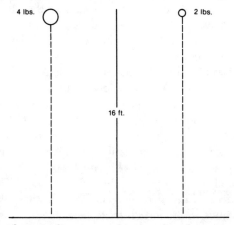

5. How long is the average human female menstrual cycle?

6. When traffic lights are arranged vertically, is the green light on the top, or the bottom?

7. Think about your best friend of your own sex. What color are his or her eyes?

8. What is the probability (expressed either in terms of odds or a number between zero and one) of at least two people in a class of thirty having the same birthday?

Answers:

1.   Islands do not float in the ocean. Rock and earth will not float in water. Islands are the tips of submerged mountains, reefs, or land masses. Many people are unaware of this fact and will assert that islands are lighter than water or are buoyed up by ocean currents.

2.   Zero degrees. Standing water is always level, at zero degrees, unless it is being agitated (e.g., twirled around in a bucket). Most males, but not all, understand this basic principle of our physical environment. Only half of the female population is aware of it. Filling a glass with water and slowly tilting it to various positions will enable you to verify the principle for yourself.

3.   Always in the east, like every other astronomical body. Only a minority of people are aware of this fact. Many people, probably because they occasionally discern a faint image of the moon during the daytime, believe that the moon does not rise and set like the sun, but always floats around in the sky until it's dark enough to see it. But the moon does in fact rise in the east and set in the west, and the daily time of moon rise is probably given in your local newspaper.

4.   The weights hit the floor simultaneously, which is the most important point, taking one second to fall sixteen feet. Many people believe that the heavy weight falls faster than the light one. And some people guess that the weights take five or ten seconds to fall, apparently envisioning them floating down like paper airplanes. You can easily experiment with falling weights by dropping, say, a paper clip and a notebook from a standard height and observing when they hit the floor. They will strike simultaneously unless one object, like a feather, offers very great air resistance in proportion to its weight.

5.   The menstrual cycle is twenty-eight days on the average. Most females are well aware of this fact. Most males will guess thirty days, and male guesses in my experience have ranged from five days to thirty years.

6.   The green light is always on the bottom. A few people (like me) are usually confused or wrong about this fact.

7.   Check it out. You probably had trouble remembering. When I cover my face and ask my students to write down what

color they think my eyes are, the most common answer given is blue. My eyes are green.

8. The probability is .71. That is, the chances are seven out of ten that at least two people in a class of thirty will have the same birthday. Almost everyone estimates the chances to be much less, on the order of one in a thousand or smaller. It does not seem intuitively correct that the probability is so high. The mathematical proof is too complicated to explain here. But you can verify the accuracy of the .71 probability figure by surveying various groups of approximately thirty people. You should in fact discover that about seven out of ten of them contain two or more people with the same birthday.

Students seldom achieve a perfect score on this test and are often annoyed with themselves for their poor performance, but their experience is normal for all of us. We have all seen the moon rising, water remaining level in a tilted glass, the arrangement of traffic lights, or the color of our best friend's eyes almost every day, so that the average adult has observed these events ten to twenty thousand times.

Unsystematically observed them, that is. Events that are not personally important for us to notice or remember can occur thousands of times under our noses (literally under our noses, in the case of tilting a glass of water) and still remain below our level of conscious awareness. This does not occur because we are stupid. It is a human characteristic. Every time I administer this test I have to look at my notes to discover the truth about traffic lights, and I can hardly recall the color of my own eyes, let alone anyone else's. If I had asked you, before attempting the test, to make some pertinent *systematic* observations, you would have had little trouble discovering the truth. It would have taken you five seconds of experimenting with tilting a glass of water to discover the principle that unagitated water is always level; a single conscious observation would have disclosed the color of your friend's eyes; and so forth. Systematic observation is characteristic of science, and this demonstration illustrates one reason why science is often a better judge of reality than unsystematic intuitions.

How does this point apply to interpretations of paranormal phenomena? Some UFO reports originate from ambiguous stimuli, such as lights or glowing balls, which are often interpreted as large objects several miles away moving very fast. Yet quite frequently such objects turn out to be meteors hundreds of miles away, or reflections from raindrops slowly being blown across a car window. This should not surprise us, for psychological research shows that our brains often play perceptual tricks on us, and our powers-of-observation test reveals that we are such poor natural observers of our physical environment that sometimes we hardly know which way is up.

Clairvoyant dreams provide an excellent example of our failure to notice and consciously observe events that occur countless times but are not usually important. Clairvoyance is often inferred from a dream about a loved one or a relative dying, or some other catastrophe which, some short time later, turns out to correspond with reality. Perhaps the fact that dreams are such private and mysterious events lends a convincing sense of awe to such coincidences. The person claiming a clairvoyant experience will assert that such dreams are not typical occurrences, and that every time they do occur they come true. The results from our powers-of-observation test might, on the other hand, lead us to suspect that such dreams have occurred for this person hundreds of times before, but when they *didn't* come true, they went unnoticed and unremembered.

And in fact we do have good scientific evidence to this effect. From current research on sleep and dreams we know that dreams correspond roughly with the rapid-eye-movement (REM) stage of sleep, that everyone dreams, that we experience REM sleep and dreaming about two hours a night, and that most dreams are negatively toned. That is, if we monitor eye movements and wake people up whenever they are dreaming, they will usually report that the dream they are having is a disturbing one, involving accidents, deaths, or impending crises. In other words, we experience a solid hour or so of bad dreams every night, most of which we don't remember or take note of. It is predictable that a small percentage of these dreams must come true, since death, taxes, and misfortune claim us all. When a real-life catastrophe does occur, and we have dreamed about a similar event in the recent past, it seems that we have a tendency to recall that particular dream and to mistakenly experience the coincidence of dream and reality as a remarkable event. I am not arguing that there is no such thing as clairvoyance or prophetic dreams. I am arguing that we clearly cannot trust our everyday observations and interpretations of our experiences to infer clairvoyance, and would be much more likely to obtain a reasonable perspective on these experiences by using a systematic and objective approach.

A problem closely related to our tendency to misobserve our every-day environment is our difficulty in estimating the probabilities of ordinary occurrences. Research has shown that all of us, including trained scientists, are prone to certain predictable biases when estimating probabilities. Consider this problem. An unbiased coin has been flipped for a series of five tosses for six different series. The results (in heads or tails) of the first four tosses in each series are given below. Before reading further, fill in the blank in each series with your estimate of whether the final toss was a head or tail.

1.	HHTH _____		4.	HTTT _____	
2.	TTTT _____		5.	HHHH _____	
3.	HTTH _____		6.	HHTT _____	

The fact is that the probability of a head or a tail in each case is 50 percent. It does not matter what has occurred before a single toss; the probability of a head on any given toss is always 50 percent. Most people, however, bias their guesses depending on previous events, a habit known as "the gambler's fallacy." In the coin problem, people tend to guess an "H" for series 2 and 4, a "T" for series 5, and so forth, in a quite predictable but statistically incorrect fashion.

The mathematical probabilities of *rare* events, in particular, often run counter to intuition, but it is the mathematics, not our intuition, that is correct. For instance, if a bridge player was dealt thirteen cards of the same suit, he might think this a remarkable event, worthy of surprise and much comment. But being dealt a hand of all clubs has the same probability as being dealt any other specific bridge hand that is named in advance. A bridge hand of all clubs has a very low a priori probability of occurring (less than one chance in ten billion). But any other specified bridge hand is equally unlikely to occur. A hand of thirteen clubs is no more unusual than a hand comprising the jack of spades, three of diamonds, five of hearts, etc. It is the rules of bridge and our associated habits of mind that make the event *seem* remarkable. The remarkable quality does not lie in the event itself.

We also tend to underestimate the frequency with which rare events, such as being dealt a particular bridge hand, do in fact occur. Suppose that the probability of an event's occurring on any given trial is only one in a thousand. In the long run, however, in a thousand trials, the probability that the event will occur *at least once* is .63, or a little better than six chances in ten. In the very long run, say ten thousand trials, the event is virtually certain to occur (probability of occurrence = .99995). In the same way, the chance correspondence of a dream with a real-life event may be rare, yet stating that it is rare is really equivalent to stating that in the long run, over the course of a lifetime, a dramatic correspondence of dreams with real-life events will undoubtedly occur several times just by chance.

One conclusion to emerge, therefore, from this brief survey of the psychology of probability estimation is that most of us are quite poor at estimating how often events occur by chance and at assessing coincidence. Very often someone will tell me that a particular sequence of events has to involve psychic forces because it is too unlikely to be simply a coincidence, or, as it is sometimes phrased, "it is too big a coincidence." *Coincidence* means the joining of two chance events in time or space in ways that happen to strike us as dramatic. But we have just seen that most people are poor at judging probabilities and are likely to attribute drama to everyday unsurprising correlations of events. It is impossible to tell whether something is more than "just a coincidence" without the aid of careful statistical analysis.

For example, suppose that in every class you took, from kindergarten through high school, there were at least two people with the same birthday. This fact might strike you as peculiar, even "fated." In fact, however, it is not really unexpected on the basis of chance, since we know that the chances of its occurring in each class are about seven in ten, and that its occurrence in any one class does not diminish the chances of its occurring in the next. Or suppose that your astrological sun-sign description asserts that "you are a person who got married for convenience or sensible reasons rather than for love, and you secretly detest parties, but go anyway"—and that these descriptions are true. The facts are, myths to the contrary, that most people do not get married out of romantic love but usually have more practical motives, and that most people secretly feel uncomfortable about parties. Or suppose a psychic or "reader" takes your watch, holds it in his or her hands, and declares it was "given to you by a loved one"—and that this is true. No psychic powers need be involved, however, for very few people buy their own watches. They are usually gifts, and since they are often expensive they are purchased by loved ones rather than casual acquaintances. The psychic, in such cases, may just be a better judge of probabilities than you are.

Amos Tversky and Daniel Kahneman are two psychologists who have recently investigated common fallacies in probabilistic reasoning. They have found that psychologists, mathematicians, and other scientists are as subject to these fallacies as anyone, if the scientists are interviewed under circumstances in which they cannot readily use their professional training.

One of the fallacies Tversky and Kahneman have identified is called the "representativeness" fallacy, and I believe it is responsible for more mistaken paranormal beliefs than any other single factor. For example, imagine a male in his thirties, slight of stature, with poor eyesight, who is shy and likes to read. Is this person more likely to be a librarian or a farmer? Most people immediately answer "librarian," but that is not the best guess. The category *librarian* is apparently chosen because the description fits or "represents" our stereotype of male librarians and certainly does not fit our stereotype of a farmer. However, the fallacy here is in thinking only in terms of the representativeness of an event with respect to a given category, without considering the number of such events possible in alternative categories. That is, we fail to take into account the fact that there are many more farmers than librarians. Suppose as a reasonable estimate that one out of five librarians is a male who matches this stereotype, and that there are fifty thousand librarians in this country. We might estimate, on the other hand, that only one out of one hundred farmers fits the above description, *but* over five million people in this country are farmers. Thus, fifty thousand farmers would fit the stereotype, as opposed to ten thousand librarians who fit it, and therefore a person matching this stereotype would be five times as likely to be a farmer as a librarian.

Although the concept of the "representativeness fallacy" seems a bit complex, it is well worth considering, to clarify how we think about paranormal phenomena. We are, I believe, apt to immediately interpret a mysterious event as representative of a mysterious cause and to overlook ordinary causes simply because ordinary causes are not usually associated with that event. It may be, however, that there are many opportunities for ordinary causes to combine in unlikely ways and bring about the event, as we would realize if we systematically thought about it.

Suppose, to take another example, the medium-sized brig *Mary Celeste* is found floating and abandoned in the area of the ocean known as the Bermuda Triangle. The brig is in perfect condition; meals are left half-eaten in the galley; the weather has been mild for weeks. What has caused this?

The event is dramatic and spooky, and we succumb to the representativeness fallacy if we look immediately for dramatic and spooky explanations. We might imagine, for instance, that the sailors had been zapped by a death ray from Atlantis, kidnapped by a flying saucer, or sucked into a magnetic vortex created by the Triangle. We would admit, perhaps, that these paranormal hypotheses seem unlikely, but we tend to reject the alternative hypotheses of ordinary causes because the event does not resemble or represent anything produced by an ordinary cause.

But wait. Consider the possible number of such events produced by ordinary causes as opposed to paranormal causes. We have already conceded that paranormal hypotheses seem very unlikely, but we feel we are forced to them. What could an ordinary cause be? Perhaps all the occupants were swimming by the side of the ship and encountered a whirlpool or shark attack. Or perhaps the ship's bread became moldy, producing lysergic acid, and halfway through the meal a mass paranoid psychosis took place, causing the occupants to jump overboard or abandon ship. How often might such circumstances be estimated to take place? Certainly very infrequently . . . perhaps once every million times a ship embarks on a journey, as a not unreasonable guess. But if approximately four million boats and ships enter the Triangle area every year, also a reasonable estimate, then we would expect that such rare combinations of natural causes would result in an average of four structurally sound abandoned ships every year. The case of the *Mary Celeste* is now seen as much more likely to fit into the category of natural cause than the category of paranormal cause.

I do not wish to push this example as an explanation of actual events in the Bermuda Triangle. I do want to illustrate the fact that a complex but common bias in reasoning, the representativeness fallacy, can easily get us into trouble when we attribute paranormal causes to mysterious events and do not think about the opportunities for ordinary causes to bring them about.

Closely related to our problems in accurately perceiving probabilities is our tendency to make too much of coincidence, to confuse feelings about coincidence with facts. After all, the word *coincidence* was made up to describe two events happening together by chance in such a way that meaning only *seems* to be inherent in their occurring at the same time. In a true coincidence, where no causal or other connection relates the two events, it is the *observer* who subjectively perceives meaning in their juxtaposition. When coincidences happen, we often get feelings of drama, strangeness, significance, puzzlement. These feelings do not mean that the joining of the events is itself strange or needs explaining. Nothing ever really "needs explaining"; the need to explain is internal to the observer. But sometimes our strong need tricks us into believing that there really is something mysterious about a coincidence that requires explanation.

Consider the following example. A young man named Brad is lying in bed, nostalgically thinking about a woman he has not seen or heard from in seventeen years, and feeling that it was a serious mistake they ever broke up. At that very moment Brad receives a long-distance phone call from the woman, who tells him she has just been thinking about him in the same way, and would like to see him. The next day Brad comes racing to my office to tell me about the episode and exclaim, "How can you possibly explain *that?*" (Meaning, "Hah! I got you this time! There's *no* way you can explain this except as a psychic event!")

Here we see a stark contrast between scientific and intuitive modes of thought. I feel no need to explain the incident. In fact, if the story gets too detailed, I'll probably get bored by it. After all, it didn't happen to me and I can't easily share Brad's feelings of drama, elation, and puzzlement. It strikes me, in fact, as just the sort of chance event we have made up the word *coincidence* to describe. As a scientist, I have no interest at all in coincidences. I am interested in laws of nature, in cases where A follows B with regularity under conditions X and Y. If Brad told me that *every time* he lay in bed and thought about a former friend that friend immediately called him, I would be quite interested, but for an isolated episode—no. What strikes *me* as needing explanation about this event is Brad's need to explain it.

I think, as do B. F. Skinner and other psychologists who have investigated the matter, that our puzzlements and dramatic feelings about coincidence have evolutionary significance for us. Most of our environment is causally structured, and when personally significant events happen it is adaptive for us to feel impressed by them and to think about possible underlying causes. We can then better predict and control such events in the future. When a hungry rat presses the lever for the first time in a Skinner box and receives a food pellet, the animal is quite impressed and will press the lever an extra fifty times without further receipt of food. When one of our ancestors wandered too far from the cave campfire at night and was threatened by a saber-toothed tiger, it was adaptive for him to be struck by this incident and to think about the possible relationship between night and the presence of large carnivores. Our capacity to be impressed by personally significant events and to conjecture about their causes is obviously adaptive most of the time. But it gets us into trouble when such personally meaningful events *seem* to be connected, but in fact only occur together by chance. From a rational or objective point of view, we should be impressed only when such events occur with predictable regularity.

Our problem in jumping to conclusions is exacerbated by our enormous capacity for rationalizing or defending whatever we conclude. Numerous psychological experiments on problem solving and concept formation have shown that when people are given the task of selecting the right answer by being told whether particular guesses are right or wrong, they will tend to do the following:

1.   They will immediately form a hypothesis and look only for examples to confirm it. They will not seek evidence to disprove their hypothesis, although this strategy would be just as effective, but will in fact try to ignore any evidence against it.

2.   If the answer is secretly changed in the middle of the guessing process, they will be very slow to change a hypothesis that was once correct but has suddenly become wrong.

3.   If one hypothesis fits the data fairly well, they will stick with it and not look for other hypotheses that might fit the data better.

4.   If the information provided is too complex, people will cope by adopting overly simple hypotheses or strategies for solution, and by ignoring any evidence against them.

5.   If there is no solution, if the problem is a trick and people are told "right" and "wrong" about their choices at random, people will nevertheless form all sorts of hypotheses about causal relationships they believe are inherent in the data, will believe their hypotheses through thick and thin, and will eventually convince themselves that their theories are absolutely correct. Causality will invariably be perceived even when it is not present.

It is not surprising that rats, pigeons, and small children are often better at solving these sorts of problems than are human adults. Pigeons and small children don't care so much whether they are always right, and they do not have such a developed capacity for convincing themselves they are right, no matter what the evidence is.

Adults usually seem to be much better problem solvers than pigeons or children in the real world. This is not because adults are naturally more open-minded, however, but because they are more intelligent and experienced and can think more abstractly and, more important, because they have evolved an efficient method for solving problems and forming concepts as part of their social institutions. The method involves thinking of all the possible hypotheses to explain a puzzling event; listing the hypotheses in order, from most to least probable; attempting to eliminate some hypotheses by looking for evidence that contradicts them; and, finally, deciding which of the remaining hypotheses has the most supporting evidence and the least negative evidence, and choosing it as the best bet, always being open to the possibility that new evidence may give cause for a change of mind.

This method seems sensible and we are all familiar with it. It is used by our doctor every time we present him with a set of symptoms he must diagnose and treat. It is used by police detectives in solving crimes. (An excellent example of this was created by author John Fowles in his story "The Enigma.") It is used in courts of criminal law to decide guilt or innocence. And it is also the general methodology used by science. Notice that we tend to use it especially when a question or problem is crucial, a life-or-death matter; or, as in science, when we want to be as honest and careful as possible about the answer. But, unless this methodology is woven into institutions such as science, law, police work, and medicine, I think we tend not to use it because, as the above psychological research shows, it does not come easily or naturally to us.

In showing how biases in problem solving cause trouble in thinking about paranormal phenomena, I'd like to first illustrate by an analogy. Suppose I assert that the moon is made out of cheese. What evidence do I have? Well, the moon is yellowish in color, much like aged Swiss cheese; it has various-sized dark spots which look like Swiss cheese holes; it is round, like the imported balls of Swiss cheese I see hanging in the market. The cheese has been perfectly preserved over the millennia by the vacuum and bitter cold of outer space. The belief that the moon is a ball of cheese, furthermore, is an ancient one. Innumerable cultures throughout the world's history have held this belief. "But," you might say, "we have actually sent astronauts to the moon, and all they have seen is dust and rock." "Ah!" I counter. "That's no problem. We would expect such a large body of cheese to acquire a layer of dust and rocks from meteor showers over the years. Also, the astronauts left seismographic equipment on the moon, and we found that moon tremors are quavery and reverberating. This seismic pattern is unlike tremors associated with bodies of rock, as on the earth, but is characteristic of a tremor pattern in a giant ball of cheese." After enough such "evidence," if I am clever enough with my arguments, you might actually start to wonder about the edible qualities of the moon.

The problem with my moon-as-cheese argument is not that it's indefensible—I can produce some evidence for it and can explain away negative evidence. The problem is that in ignoring the hypothesis that the moon is a sphere of rock and metals roughly similar to the earth, a hypothesis that has much stronger evidence in its favor, I am being biased to the point of absurdity. By ignoring competing hypotheses I can make a convincing-appearing case for any idea whatsoever: that President Eisenhower was a Communist, that the earth and the life forms on it were suddenly created in a divine burst of inspiration only ten thousand years ago, that the sun is hollow, that the inner earth is populated by Munchkins. If you would like to build a case for our civilization's having been started by a colony of ancient astronauts, you have only to leaf briefly through illustrated archeology texts to find dozens of ancient technological marvels, and primitive pictures that look like spaceships. The problem with such a theory is not that the theory can be proved wrong, or that no evidence can be found for it; the problem is that the theory is absurd. It is arbitrary, biased, and contrived. The competing theory that civilization developed organically and sequentially as the result of a social evolutionary process has thousands of times as much supporting evidence and much less contradicting evidence. We need to guard carefully against becoming trapped by our tendency to support our pet hypotheses and overlook more reasonable alternatives.

One of the most astounding examples of our tendency to overlook reasonable alternatives is the difference between the way we perceive "psychics" and the way we perceive magicians. That is, when an alleged psychic reads minds, psychokinetically bends small metal objects, dematerializes ashes, or teleports a compass needle, many of us become very excited and impressed by this apparent demonstration of psychic abilities. But if a magician performed these same stunts, we'd think the performance stale and old hat. If we were being thoroughly reasonable and methodical about our beliefs, we would look at a psychic's performance and ask, "Could a magician do that? If so, could this performance actually be a magic trick?" But, perhaps because belief in psychic abilities is so exciting and we need to have our beliefs confirmed, we often look at a psychic's performance only in ways that tend to confirm our beliefs.

Recently, several colleagues and I did an experiment in which we asked a student named Craig to develop a standard magic routine to present to our college classes. In it he read three-digit numbers through his fingers while thoroughly blindfolded, teleported ashes through the hands of a volunteer, and bent a thick brass rod by gently stroking it with his index finger. All the tricks we used were simple and standard amateur ones that take only minutes to learn, and which may even be found in children's books of magic.

At no time during his performance did Craig call himself either a psychic or a magician; he merely performed. Craig appeared in six different college classrooms. In half the classes the professors introduced Craig by telling the students that Craig said he was psychic, although the professors themselves were skeptical. In the other classes the professors explained at length that Craig was an amateur magician who would be using simple stage trickery to simulate psychic performances. In these classes the professors asked the students to write down and interpret this introductory statement to make sure the students had heard and understood it. After he had finished his performance, Craig asked the students to write down any reactions they had.

We ascertained what the students believed about Craig by analyzing their response sheets. In the classes informed that Craig believed himself to be psychic, about 80 percent of the students clearly also believed that he was. Only a few students in these classes expressed any real skepticism. We expected a high percentage of belief, but we were surprised by the intensity of it. Many students gasped or screamed faintly during Craig's performance and were visibly agitated. On their response sheets many students wrote such comments as "Fantastic! I wouldn't have believed it if I hadn't seen it with my own eyes. Can anyone develop such powers?" And about a dozen students became seriously disturbed or frightened, filling their papers with exorcism rites or warning Craig against trafficking with Satan. We were disturbed by how easily we had triggered such profound reactions, and we all went back to the classes the next day to explain that the performance was a fake.

We found two interesting results in the classes told that Craig was an amateur magician. First, the number of students who believed he was psychic was about one-third lower than in the classes told he *might* be psychic. Although they saw the same performance as the other classes, these students often commented, "Nice trick!" instead of "How did you develop such powers?!" Some people in these classes offered guesses as to how the tricks were done, sometimes correctly.

Second, even though the level of psychic belief was lower than the 80 percent shown in the other classes, over 50 percent of the students in classes that were emphatically told that Craig was an amateur magician who would only pretend to demonstrate psychic powers *nonetheless believed he was psychic!* Some of them even commented that although their instructor had told them otherwise, they thought there was no way Craig's performance could be stage magic. If our results can be generalized, they indicate that over half the student population will ascribe psychic powers to a vaudeville routine, no matter how amateurish it is and no matter who tells them the truth about it. This strikes me as a remarkable state of affairs.

In summary, psychological investigations have shown us that we are saddled with serious flaws in our everyday reasoning processes. We are poor observers and cataloguers of our natural environment, and we underestimate probabilities and find it difficult to reason accurately about them. We too easily attribute mysterious causes to mysterious events, and we too easily confuse our feelings about those events with their reality. We tend not to look at all possible hypotheses when faced with a problem, but to pick one that feels good and then look only for evidence to support it.

Science may look awesome, with its mathematics, jargon, and technical apparatus, but basically it is nothing more than a sensible, systematized method of reasoning that has been deliberately constructed to compensate for our natural reasoning deficiencies. Thus, the rules of science dictate not letting feelings and wishes interfere with interpretations; observing the environment carefully and systematically, using instruments where possible instead of human observers; using mathematically correct probabilities; considering all alternative hypotheses; and looking for negative evidence against favorite hypotheses, instead of just trying to support them. There is nothing too technical or complex about this set of rules. Science has accomplished more than our unaided intuitions in understanding the world, not because it is such a miraculous system—it is obviously not infallible—but because unaided intuition is so likely to err.

There are many areas where we automatically acknowledge that science is right and our intuitions are wrong when the two are in conflict. Thus, we all believe that the earth is round, even though it looks flat to us. We believe that the earth is round in spite of the fact that our intuition tells us that people in China would therefore be walking upside down and would fall off. We believe that the earth rotates around its axis and orbits around the sun, even though it is intuitively obvious that we are stationary and the sun revolves around us once every twenty-four hours. We believe that the chair in which we are sitting is composed of atoms and in that sense is mostly empty space, even though it looks quite solid to us. But, somehow, when scientists tell us there is no good logic or evidence to support a belief in astrology or ESP, we "know" they are wrong. Why?

Science is not always better than intuitive knowledge, and science is not always right. However, the most remarkable advances of science are characterized by science's reaching beyond or even contradicting our ordinary senses and intuitions. And science has clearly proven better than intuition so often in the past that when our intuitive experience of the paranormal contradicts scientific opinion we would do well to look closely at our own reasoning to see whether we haven't been deceived by the biases that are just part of human nature.

> "The human understanding, when any proposition has been once laid down . . . forces everything else to add fresh support and confirmation. . . . It is the peculiar and perpetual error of the human understanding to be more moved and excited by affirmation than negatives." Francis Bacon, *Novum Organum* (1620).

2

Monsters

DANIEL COHEN

Monsters, both real and legendary, seem to haunt the imagination. The world has certainly known an abundance of awesome creatures— dinosaurs, saber-toothed tigers, gigantic sharks—and the discovery of some, like the giant squid and the gorilla, have been genuine surprises to science. Thus, the existence of creatures such as the Loch Ness monster and Bigfoot cannot be dismissed out of hand, and these hypothetical latter-day monsters have aroused intense interest.

Possibility, however, is not probability. Daniel Cohen shows why it is reasonable for science to take an open-minded but conservative attitude toward the existence of these monsters. The central issue is, to what extent can belief be based on marginal evidence? How strong a case can be made from fleeting glimpses, legends and myths, and indistinct photographs? While such evidence may excite our interest, we should remember that the same sort of evidence has been used to support claims for the existence of fairies, dragons, giants, and unicorns. Further, when we investigate monster sightings thoroughly, we often find hoaxes.

As Cohen explains, some scientific investigations have been made of present-day monsters, so far with negative or ambiguous results. The most reasonable position, then, would seem to be one of uncertainty, one at least slightly on the skeptical side. Uncertainty can be an uncomfortable and frustrating feeling, and monsters like Nessie and Yeti are so interesting and attractive that most of us wish they were real. But wishes do not a monster make, and science is not in the business of letting wishes interfere with realistic appraisals. Cohen explains why the evidence isn't convincing yet, and what evidence scientists would need to convince them.

Is the world populated by a host of large, strange-looking creatures quite unknown to orthodox science? To the readers of certain popular books and magazines the answer would be a resounding yes. Not only are there well-known creatures such as the Loch Ness monster, the great sea serpent, Bigfoot, and the Yeti, there are also accounts of an enormous number of lesser-known but even stranger large creatures that we lump under the term *monster.* Monster tales are attached to practically every large or medium-sized body of water in the world. Monsters have been reported in remote jungles, dense forests, snow-capped mountains, and barren deserts, and there have even been a surprising number of monster reports from more populated and accessible areas.

Every year the cumulative file of monster sightings grows fatter. Often the reports are accompanied by photographs, or even motion pictures. Can all of the witnesses (some are of very high caliber) be lying or hallucinating? Are all the pictures and other physical evidence faked? Why do most scientists blindly continue to ignore, and occasionally even ridicule, this body of evidence?

There is undoubtedly an enormous amount of material relating to the existence of monsters in today's world. But the question that is rarely asked or adequately answered by those who believe in monsters is, "How good is this material as evidence?" A whole roomful of old newspaper clippings and photos of dubious origin counts (or should count) very little as evidence.

Let's put the best case first: that for the Loch Ness monster. In the whole realm of strange phenomena there is probably none that has received more careful scrutiny than the thing (or things) supposed to dwell in the dark waters of Scotland's Loch Ness.

Loch Ness is located in the Scottish highlands. It is an area that was, until recent times, remote and difficult to reach. The loch itself is about twenty-two miles long, but only about a mile wide. Still it is by volume the largest freshwater lake in the British Isles, and the third largest in Europe.

To those familiar only with North American lakes, Loch Ness is a strange and rather ominous body of water. It is extremely deep, seven hundred feet over most of its length, and reportedly over nine hundred feet deep in some spots. At most places along the banks of the loch the sides dip sharply into the water. The water is extremely murky, owing to a heavy suspension of peat particles. Underwater visibility, even with a strong light, is limited to a few feet. The waters of the loch are very cold, maintaining a constant temperature of approximately 42° F year round.

The highlands were once full of legends of monsters that dwelt in the waters of its various lochs. The oldest surviving written account of the Loch Ness monster, or at least *a* Loch Ness monster, appears in a biography of St. Columba, the Christian missionary to Scotland, who lived in the sixth century. This account is a traditional miracle tale in which the saint saves a soul from being devoured by the monster.

Over the centuries there were a few additional sketchy accounts of "something" in the loch, but the modern era of Loch Ness monster sightings really began in 1933, when a road was completed along the western shore of the loch. Though Loch Ness had been a tourist haven for the rich in Victorian times (the queen herself journeyed up the loch in a paddle steamer in 1873), it was the road that really opened the area to large numbers of visitors.

The story generally credited with starting the modern interest in the Loch Ness monster appeared in the *Inverness Courier* of May 2, 1933. It described how an unnamed local businessman and his wife watched a strange creature while it "disported itself, rolling and plunging for fully a minute." The businessman was John Mackay, owner of a hotel near the loch, a fact not missed by skeptics. The man who wrote the article was Alex Campbell, the young water bailiff of the loch. Campbell, who served as water bailiff until his retirement in 1966, always remained an active supporter of the monster. He said that he had seen it several times himself. He also claims to have given it the title "monster" not because there was anything fearsome about it but simply because he didn't know what else to call it.

The first known photos of "something in the Loch" were taken in November 1933, but they were too unclear to attract much attention. The most celebrated Loch Ness monster photo was taken in April of the following year. The exact circumstances under which the picture was taken have never been entirely clear. The man who took it, Lt. Col. Robert K. Wilson, a London gynecologist, was extraordinarily publicity shy. For many years even the name of the photographer was not generally known, and the picture was referred to simply as "the famous London surgeon's photograph." Actually, Wilson took two shots that seem to show the monster. The famous one (below) shows what appears to be the silhouette of a long neck and small head of something emerging from the water. Unfortunately, there is nothing in the photo that can be used to judge the size of the object, and skeptics contend that the object could be quite small—the head of a bird or the tail of a diving otter, rather than the head and neck of a large creature. In any case, the "surgeon's photo" matched the descriptions of witnesses who said the creature had a long neck and small head.

After that the popularity of the Loch Ness monster rose and fell regularly. During the war years there were few sightings, but interest began to build again after the war. In April 1960 an English aeronau-

The 1934 surgeon's photograph of the Loch Ness monster. Courtesy Associated Newspapers, London.

tical engineer and monster buff named Tim Dinsdale took a brief film of what he said was the monster moving across the surface of the loch. Dinsdale was standing on one side of the loch, the "thing" near the other shore. The moving object in the film is tiny and indistinct, but photo reconnaissance experts from the Royal Air Force examined the film and declared that it probably showed an animate object that might be as much as ninety feet in total length. Not everyone agreed with that assessment, however; some thought the film showed a speed-boat. In any event, the Dinsdale film opened a new era of investigation, and during the warmer months regular and often well-equipped expeditions as well as innumerable free-lance monster hunters flocked to Loch Ness.

Another important milestone was reached in 1972. An expedition sponsored by the Academy of Applied Science used an underwater camera to obtain two pictures that appear to be the diamond-shaped flipper and part of the body of a large animal. Again, in 1975, an academy expedition obtained a number of dramatic underwater photos, one showing what might be a long-necked, small-headed creature, another showing a rough, knobby object that has been called a close-up of the monster's head. On the strength of this encouraging development the *New York Times* aided the academy in sponsoring the largest and best-equipped monster-hunting expedition ever, in 1976. This expedition turned up nothing of significance, though, and interest in the creature has been declining since. But, given the past history of the Loch Ness monster, it is safe to predict that interest will rise again.

In addition to the photos and films, there have been some intriguing but inconclusive sonar readings possibly indicating the presence of large unknown creatures in the loch, as well as hundreds of sightings by people who think they have seen "something" in the loch.

Speculation over what the monster might be has long been a popular sport. Possible candidates have ranged from a long-necked seal to some sort of giant invertebrate, but over the years the leading candidate has always been the plesiosaur, a huge sea-going reptile from the time of the dinosaurs. Sir Peter Scott of the World Wildlife Fund has even given the monster a scientific name, *Nessiteras rhomboptery,* which translates roughly as "the Loch Ness marvel with a diamond-shaped fin."

When totaled, the evidence for the existence of large unknown creatures in Loch Ness is good, and in the world of monsters it is very good evidence indeed. Yet it is impossible to escape the conclusion that it is not as good as it should be. For nearly half a century, Loch Ness has been the subject of careful scrutiny. Many of those who have gone searching for the monster have been dedicated and competent observers, and in recent years they have often used sophisticated equipment. Yet all that these investigators have been able to come up with is a handful of pictures that might show a large animal or might show something else, and some intriguing but ambiguous sonar readings. No scrap of physical evidence of the monster has ever been found. Surely these creatures are not immortal. Why haven't remains ever turned up? On rare occasions the creatures have been reported coming on shore, but no authentic footprint (or flipper print) has ever been found.

Yes, the loch is long and deep. Yes, the water is unusually dark and cold. Yes, there are innumerable difficulties connected with mounting an expedition at Loch Ness. But could a group of large creatures have escaped conclusive detection for so long in such a limited area? While some eminent scientists have gone on record as supporting the existence of a monster in the loch, most remain open-minded but highly skeptical.

If the Loch Ness monster pops up in front of motion picture cameras for a good close-up, or if the carcass of one of the creatures washes ashore, the problem of the Loch Ness monster will be solved. If not, the tantalizing question will remain and people will continue the search no matter how hopeless the situation may appear to skeptics.

The evidence for the existence of a sea serpent or sea monster is not nearly as good as the evidence for the existence of the Loch Ness monster. Yet the chances of finding one or more large unknown sea creatures are far better than the chance of finding Scotland's elusive monster, for the seas are vast and not well explored when compared with Loch Ness.

Large unknown sea creatures of one sort or another have been reported by sailors for centuries. Indeed, they may once have been considered one of the regular hazards of long-distance navigation. Some of these sightings can be accounted for by known sea creatures: whales, the ribbon fish, the giant squid, and so on. Others may be mistakes or pure invention. And finally, some may have been genuine sightings of large sea creatures as yet unknown to science.

Sea-monster sightings have declined markedly in modern times. Monster buffs quite reasonably suggest that sea creatures are less likely to surface near the large power-driven ships of today than near the wooden sailing ships of old. Even so, there have been sea-monster sightings from modern ships.

There are, however, no good sea-monster photographs. A few photos of what are reported to be sea monsters have popped up from time to time, but these are generally considered to be fakes.

On the other hand, an abundance of reputed sea-monster remains has either washed up on beaches around the world or been fished out of the sea. Unfortunately, these remains fall into two categories: Either they were washed out to sea or otherwise lost before they could be carefully examined by competent authorities, or they were examined by competent authorities and have turned out to belong to a known sea creature.

The single exception is a large pinkish mass that washed ashore at St. Augustine, Florida, in 1896. Photographs, drawings, and measurements made by people on the scene indicated that the mass might be the remains of a gigantic octopus, many times larger than any known octopus. Others thought it was a whale carcass. The mass was washed out to sea before it could be examined by biologists, but a few tissue samples were sent to the Smithsonian Institution. There the bottles containing the specimens gathered dust until the late 1950s, when scientists took a new interest in them. Microscopic examination of the samples indicated that they did indeed come from an octopus, so there is a very real possibility that an octopus with tentacles up to one hundred feet long may live undetected in the depths of the ocean.

A more typical story, however, is that of the New Zealand monster. In April 1977 a Japanese fishing ship trawling off the coast of New Zealand snagged a large rotting carcass at a depth of nine hundred feet. The thing was thirty-two feet long and its estimated weight was four thousand pounds. It smelled awful and oozed a slimy whitish substance all over the deck. The fishermen feared that the carcass would contaminate their catch. One of the crewmen took some photographs, made measurements, and clipped off a few tissue samples. Then the carcass was tossed overboard.

When the photographs were developed they became a sensation in Japan. A variety of authorities quickly offered guesses as to what the thing might be: a whale, a basking shark, an elephant seal. But by far the most popular guess was that the thing was the remains of a plesiosaur. The photographs and a drawing made by the crewman indicated that the thing had a distinctly plesiosaurlike shape: small head, long neck, thick body with four flippers, and a long tail. There is no known large sea creature alive today that has such a shape.

Very few of the scientists who commented on the New Zealand monster at all would give tentative support to the plesiosaur theory, but newspapers around the world adopted it with enthusiasm. However, in addition to the photos and drawing there were the tissue samples. These were subjected to a variety of tests—which indicated that the chemical structure of the tissue was identical to that of a shark.

The shark identification should have come as no surprise to anyone familiar with the history of sea monsters. On many other occasions the decayed body of a large shark, particularly the giant basking shark (which may grow to a length of over forty feet), has been mistaken for a plesiosaur's remains. This happens because of a peculiarity of the shark's anatomical structure. The shark's most notable feature, the huge jaws, are only loosely attached to the backbone. When a basking shark carcass begins to rot, the jaws fall away easily, as does the dorsal fin, another shark characteristic. Since the shark's backbone runs only into the upper half of the shark's two-lobed tail fin, the lower lobe may also disappear. What remains is a small cranium attached to a long backbone, a thick body with lower fins but no dorsal fin, and a long pointed tail: a perfect pseudo-plesiosaur. A carcass exactly like this washed up on the beach at Scituate, Massachusetts, in November 1970, but this one was not tossed back into the sea and was conclusively identified as the remains of a shark.

Still, it would be rash to conclude that the oceans hold no more surprises, and we may yet discover one or perhaps several different types of sea monsters.

Even more popular today than the Loch Ness monster and the sea monster are two manlike, hairy giants, Bigfoot and the Yeti. Here we sometimes leave the realm of reasonably careful investigation and speculation and enter the realm of fantasy—and, all too often, fraud. While a small number of responsible scientists find the case for the existence of these creatures impressive, if not conclusive, the evidence is not nearly as good as it is for the Loch Ness monster.

We'll start with the Yeti. It is an article of faith among monster buffs that belief in the hairy, manlike Yeti is widespread among the people who live in the Himalayas. Yet one Indian scholar[11] concluded that all of the alleged references to the Yeti in Himalayan folklore are in reality references to bears or to entirely mythical mountain spirits that don't resemble the popular image of the Yeti at all. In truth, no one knows how widespread the belief in the Yeti is among the native population of the region it is supposed to inhabit, because there has never been a thorough study of the folklore of the area.

A second article of faith among monster buffs is that there are a large number of good first-hand sighting reports. This is simply untrue. The late Ivan Sanderson, who was an enthusiastic supporter of the Yeti, was able to list only nine Yeti sightings of any kind between 1887 and 1960, and most of these were second- or third-hand reports of extremely dubious authenticity.

The earliest, and still the best, eyewitness account of the Yeti comes from N. A. Tombazi, a Greek photographer serving as a member of the 1925 Royal Geographical Photographic expedition. He was camping at an altitude of some fifteen thousand feet in the mountains of Sikkim when his porters pointed to something odd moving across the lower slope. The glare was intense, but Tombazi finally spotted the thing about three hundred yards away.

"Unquestionably, the figure in outline was exactly like a human being, walking upright and stopping occasionally to uproot or pull at some dwarf rhododendron bushes," Tombazi wrote. "It showed up dark against the snow and, as far as I could make out, wore no clothes. Within the next minute or so it had moved into some thick scrub and was lost to view."

Later the photographer examined the footprints made by the creature. "They were similar in shape to those of a man, but only six to seven inches long by four inches wide at the broadest part of the foot. The marks of five distinct toes and of the instep were perfectly clear, but the trace of the heel was indistinct and the little that could be seen of it appeared to narrow down to a point." There were fifteen such footprints in all and Tombazi concluded that they were "undoubtedly those of a biped." When he asked his porters what the figure might be they responded with "fairy tales" about demons.

Though Tombazi's sighting was brief and made under difficult conditions, there is no reason to doubt his account.

What was walking around the mountains of Sikkim that day? Of course it could have been the Yeti. But another explanation is possible. Throughout his description, Tombazi stresses that the shape he saw was "identical with the outline of a human figure." Unlike the giant Yeti footprint of legend, the prints seen by Tombazi were similar in both shape and size to the footprints of a human being. Isn't it possible that what Tombazi saw actually was a human being? Back in 1925 he thought so.

"I conjecture then that this 'wild man' may be either a solitary or else a member of an isolated community of pious Buddhist ascetics, who have renounced the world and sought their God in the utter desolation of some high place, as yet undesecrated by the world."

Such ascetics do exist, and they are capable of walking about naked or nearly so in the frigid mountain air.

Long after he made the sighting, Tombazi spoke of seeing the Yeti, but his first guess, that he had actually seen a human being, is probably the accurate one. And his account, it must be emphasized, is far and away the best on record.

Footprints alone are another form of evidence offered to support the existence of the Yeti. One might get the impression that Yeti footprints are a common sight in the snowfields of the Himalayas, but as with sightings of the creature itself, the footprints are far less frequent than commonly believed. In fact, there is only one set of footprints that really count as evidence; they were found by a witness of the highest caliber, and he photographed them.

In November 1951, mountaineer Eric Shipton found and photographed a trail of mysterious prints on the southwestern slopes of Menlugtse in the Himalayas. Shipton followed the trail for about a mile, until it disappeared on hard ice.

Shipton's photos show what look like large, roughly humanoid footprints. But are they? Some experts say they are the footprints of a bear; others contend that they were made by a line of smaller animals all jumping into the footprints made by the leader of the line. Another school of thought holds that the prints were made by a monkey, possibly a langur, jumping with all four feet together. Footprints in the snow are often distorted and enlarged by melting and refreezing. No definite conclusion seems possible; the Shipton photographs are like a mirror, for everyone who looks at them sees his own particular theory reflected back.

There is yet another form of alleged evidence of the Yeti, the scalps, bones, or other pieces of a Yeti supposedly kept as relics in monasteries throughout the region. According to Yeti lore the lamas consider these objects sacred and will not allow them to be desecrated by a close examination.

Interest in the Yeti had grown so intense by 1960 that a major expedition was launched to search out information on the beast. An encyclopedia publisher was the main sponsor of the quest, and publicity was undoubtedly one of the aims. Chosen to lead the expedition was Sir Edmund Hillary, the first man to conquer Mt. Everest, and a genuine celebrity. But Hillary was no misty-eyed monster buff. After tramping around the mountains for a brief period Hillary returned and announced that he had found no evidence of the Yeti. Further, he said that the whole Yeti business was nonsense. To prove his point he brought back one of the "sacred Yeti scalps." It turned out to be an ordinary cap made of goat fur, a type of cap commonly worn by people of the region.[9]

The Hillary expedition did not silence monster buffs. They claimed that Hillary had not searched hard enough, or in the right places, or that he was jealous because he couldn't find the Yeti himself. But they couldn't produce any evidence to refute him. Monster buffs usually get a great deal of mileage out of the claim that the skeptics are armchair critics who have never been out in the wild. Sir Edmund Hillary certainly could not be accused of that. While the Hillary expedition didn't actually kill interest in the Yeti, it weakened it badly.

Perhaps *weakened* is the wrong word—*shifted* would be better. Because as soon as people stopped looking for the big hairy thing in the Himalayas, they started looking for its North American cousin. This creature has been called many things, but is best known under the name Bigfoot in northern California and Sasquatch in western Canada.

Monster buffs claim that there is a strong tradition among the Indians of the western United States and Canada concerning the giant hairy, manlike creature. But this claim is not supported by evidence. The name *Sasquatch* first appeared during the late 1920s and in the 1930s in the stories of a British Columbian writer named J. W. Burns. Burns had been a teacher at an Indian reservation and knew Indian legends, but it is not clear how much of the information in his Sasquatch stories came from Indian tradition and how much from his own imagination. Besides, Burns's Sasquatch was a giant Indian who lived in the wilderness, not some sort of hairy beast. Burns called his Sasquatch hairy because he had long hair on his head, not all over his body.[11]

There had also been a handful of stories about some sort of strange creature or "wild man" in the forests of the American Northwest, but these stories never seemed to generate more than local interest until 1958, when members of a road crew working in a mountainous wilderness area of Humboldt County in northern California reported finding large footprints around their camp. One of the men made a plaster cast of a print and showed it to a local paper. That resulted in a front-page story. In 1958, interest in the Yeti of the Himalayas was high, and the national wire services picked up this tale of "America's abominable snowman." Since the print was so huge, the creature was nicknamed Bigfoot.

The next major burst of Bigfoot publicity came nine years later, when a couple of monster hunters named Roger Patterson and Bob Gimlin produced a film of what they said was Bigfoot walking through a wilderness area northeast of Eureka, California (see page 36).

The film has been widely shown and stills from it have appeared with practically every article or book on the subject. It either shows Bigfoot . . . or a man in a monkey suit. It is not possible to prove that the film was a hoax: "I couldn't see the zipper," said one scientist. On the other hand, it certainly *could* have been a hoax. Patterson and Gimlin were quite frank in stating that they hoped to make money with the film.

Since the Patterson-Gimlin film, other supposedly authentic Bigfoot films have been taken. In some of these you actually can "see the zipper"—or at least the sewn seams of the furry costume.

Neither the footprints nor the film, all of which could easily be fakes, provide adequate proof for the existence of Bigfoot or Sasquatch. What is needed is something more tangible in the way of evidence: a bone, a skull, perhaps even the creature itself. But there has been none of this. Even the number of sightings reported by witnesses who are (or should be) reliable is surprisingly small, considering the area in which these creatures are supposed to roam. While the terrain may be rugged, these areas are hardly inaccessible. Hikers, hunters, and campers as well as rangers and some organized Bigfoot expeditions regularly penetrate Bigfoot's alleged habitat. Monster buffs often pose the question that if the creature does not exist, what are people seeing? A more pertinent question might be, if the creature does exist, why don't people see it more frequently?

But there is at least some justice in the monster buff's question. Why would people falsely report sighting Bigfoot? Money is one possible reason. A good sighting report, particularly if accompanied by pictures, can be worth something, though ghost and UFO hoaxes seem to have been more profitable.

Excitement and the need to be noticed are more common reasons. Typical is the story of a fifteen-year-old Stilwell, Oklahoma, boy who claimed that he had been attacked by a Bigfootlike creature in August 1977. A few days after the initial report the Tulsa, Oklahoma, *Tribune*

The Patterson-Gimlin Bigfoot photograph. Courtesy United Press International.

ran a story saying the boy confessed that there never had been an attack. The whole thing started as a joke, the boy said, but it just got out of hand.

Then there are genuine mistakes. A person sees "something" in the woods or by the side of the road. He doesn't really get a very good look, but he has heard Bigfoot stories and his imagination may build the brief encounter into a Bigfoot sighting. It is, after all, far more exciting and interesting to have met Bigfoot than to have glimpsed a brown bear.

Local newspapers play an important part in building the case for Bigfoot. Very often they will report incidents that they know, or have reason to suspect, are exaggerated or downright false. As a general rule, reporters and editors treat monster stories as feature or entertainment items, not as hard news. They therefore tend to suspend critical judgment on the assumption that it doesn't make much difference if the story is true or not. The television networks appear to hold pretty much the same opinion about monsters and other borderline subjects. Programs on such subjects, although they often have the format of documentaries, are generally handled by the entertainment or features departments rather than the news department. There is little attempt to check the facts or present a balanced view. As a result, the average reader or viewer may be excused if he cannot tell the difference between these entertainment features and serious, hard news.

You may have noticed that the boy who claimed that he had been attacked by Bigfoot came from Oklahoma, which is not traditional Bigfoot territory. In fact, tales of Bigfootlike creatures have come from practically every state in the Union. Often the alleged creatures are given local names, like the giant hairy ape, the skunk ape, the swamp ape, and the Minnesota iceman. And they have been reported in areas in which no reasonable person could believe that a large and strange-looking creature could remain hidden for long.

There is also a tendency to combine mysteries. Bigfoot sightings are often reported in conjunction with UFO sightings. When a rash of mysterious animal mutilations was reported in some of the western states, there were rumors that a hairy, manlike "thing" was seen in the vicinity. The mutilations were also attributed to satanist cults and UFOs, but in fact there seems to have been nothing unusual going on. Most of the animals died of natural causes and the mutilations were caused by small predators.

Most of those who speculate on such matters as UFOs and monsters do not claim that Bigfoot actually came out of a UFO. But some contend that the UFOs, the monsters, and a host of other strange things are part of some grand cosmic scheme or deception being carried out by extraterrestrials or ultraterrestrials. They hint that while people actually see such things, they are not "real" in a physical sense, but some sort of illusion or psychic projection. Such a theory is extremely convenient, for it retains the "mystery" while dispensing with the need for any physical evidence.

Such theories are attractive only to the mystically inclined or to the most radical fringe of Forteans. (The name *Fortean* comes from Charles Hoy Fort, an early twentieth-century American writer who didn't like modern science or scientists and collected a lot of odd facts that he insisted indicated that scientists were wrong about almost everything.) Monsters are among the favorite subjects of modern-day Forteans.

In addition to reports of hairy, manlike creatures from the Himalayas and North America, there have been persistent reports that similar creatures have been spotted in the mountainous regions of the Soviet Union. Unlike the situation in the United States, where Bigfoot reports are generally met with scientific indifference or ridicule, eminent Soviet scientists are supposed to have carefully investigated the reports and have found hard evidence of the existence of these creatures. Similar reports have filtered out of the Soviet Union concerning parapsychology, extraterrestrial life, and a number of other borderland topics. In the cases in which these reports could be checked out, they were always found to be greatly exaggerated or downright fabrications. On a couple of occasions Soviet science-fiction stories were reported in the West as real events. Until the Soviet Bigfoot evidence can be checked more thoroughly, it is prudent to treat it with extreme caution.

Hairy monsters of the Bigfoot type are not the only monsters that are supposed to have worldwide distribution. Loch Ness–type monsters have been reported in other Scottish lakes, and in deep lakes throughout the world. There have been numerous sightings of a creature called Ogopogo that is supposed to dwell in a lake in British Columbia. A monster that according to United States accounts was sighted in Lake Baikal in the Soviet Union turned out to be one of those cases of a Soviet science-fiction story's being reported as fact.

There have been persistent reports of a large and strange creature called the binyip living somewhere in Australia, and rumors that the giant ground sloth still survives in South America. Dinosaurs have been seen in New Guinea, and woolly mammoths have been reported tramping around in Siberia and Alaska. There are tales of giant kangaroos in Illinois, a monster of varying description called the Jersey Devil that is supposed to inhabit the Pine Barrens of New Jersey, and a winged horror called Mothman supposedly seen by numerous witnesses in West Virginia. And this list only begins to scratch the surface of modern monster reports.

Serious monster buffs do not necessarily believe in all of the monsters that have been reported, or even in the majority of them. But they do hold that there is probably something to a considerable number of these reports. Most often they advance what can be termed the coelacanth argument. The coelacanth is a large (five- to six-foot long) fish of a type thought to have been extinct for millions of years. In 1938 one of these fish was caught off the southern coast of Africa. Since that time a number of other specimens of the "extinct" fish have turned up, and scientists have concluded that this fish, while rare, is far from extinct.

So, large and unusual-looking animals can escape the eyes of science for a long time. But a five- or six-foot fish is one thing; a seven- or eight-foot hairy, manlike creature is something else. It is far more difficult to imagine how such a creature could have escaped conclusive detection for so long. The hard and unromantic fact is that no large and singular-looking land animal has been discovered by science since the discovery of the okapi around the turn of the century. In more than three quarters of a century the world—both land and sea—has been more thoroughly explored than ever before, and none of the fabled monsters has turned up.

Despite the overwhelming odds against making such a find, the search will go on, for the search for monsters is not essentially a scientific quest, but a romantic one. There are elements of antiscience in the quest, a desire to show all those Ph.D.'s that they "ain't so damn smart," and to prove that the ordinary guy with muscle and common sense really knows more than the scientists with all their fancy university degrees. But in the main, monster hunting is a harmless, even charming activity. There are, after all, far worse ways to spend a summer than sitting on the shores of Loch Ness looking for the monster, even if you don't find it.

3

Plant Sensitivity and Sensation

ARTHUR W. GALSTON

CLIFFORD L. SLAYMAN

The idea that plants are aware and responsive is an appealing one, since it meshes well with modern ecological consciousness and spiritual philosophies. In the past few years, the purported discovery of plant sensitivity has been widely reported in the popular media, where it has been touted as a major scientific breakthrough revealing both consciousness and emotions in plants.

There is no objective scientific evidence for the existence of such complex behavior in plants. The recent spate of popular literature on "plant consciousness" appears to have been triggered by "experiments" with a lie detector, subsequently reported and embellished in a book called The Secret Life of Plants. *Unfortunately, when scientists in the discipline of plant physiology attempted to repeat the experiments, using either identical or improved equipment, the results were uniformly negative. Further investigation has shown that the original observations probably arose from defective measuring procedures. Awareness and emotional responsiveness of the sort that has been attributed to plants depends, as far as we know, on a complex nervous system*

*organized into a central "brain" structure. Plants possess no organ
resembling a brain.*

*Several plant physiologists have seriously explored and tested the
publicized experiments on plant consciousness. In this essay Arthur
Galston and Clifford Slayman describe the care and thought that have
gone into those experiments, and they particularly underscore the special attention that must be given to technical problems of measurement. This discussion illustrates the point that scientific expertise is not
simply window dressing, but that background and methodological skills
are necessary to make sound scientific observations. Otherwise, it is
easy to misinterpret a faulty measurement as a breakthrough.*

*Galston and Slayman also consider the kinds of observations that
would, in fact, be necessary to produce convincing evidence of higher
sensory behavior in plants.*

In the troubled late 1960s, a wave of antiintellectualism swept through
the United States, accompanied by an antiscientism that still persists
in some measure. Some public hostility toward the methods and products of science was understandable, because certain of the technological applications of science had failed to improve man's condition and
had indeed perceptibly diminished the pleasure and grace of modern
existence. Critics were quick to equate science with antihumanism
and to call for reliance on alternate ways of arriving at an understanding of the universe about us. This appeal found receptive ears in
a world worried about pollution, overpopulation, unemployment,
growing crime, and—perhaps most important—a nasty and persistent
war in which technology played a major role.

Onto this scene, in 1973, burst a book, *The Secret Life of Plants,*[1]
which claimed for members of the vegetable kingdom many mental
capabilities previously regarded as limited to gods, human beings, and
some higher animals. These included the ability to perceive and respond to human thoughts and emotions, as well as to distant traumatic
events, such as the injury or death of other organisms. Quoting from
uncontrolled experiments, random observations, and anecdotal reports, the book fashioned a case for the ability of plants to count, to
communicate with each other, and to receive signals from life forms
elsewhere in the universe. Plants were alleged to respond favorably to
certain forms of music (e.g., preferring Bach to rock); to display conditioned reflexes; to predict storms, earthquakes, and the like; and even
to transmute elements (in order to avoid mineral starvation). Among

many bizarre claims, the most incredible was the assertion that we can rid plants of insect pests, or fertilize the soil in which they grow, simply by exposing photographs of the growing plants to particular frequencies of electromagnetic radiation. Throughout, the book indiscriminately mixed accounts of generally accepted phenomena with unsubstantiated and incredible reports.

The authors of the book, Peter Tompkins and Christopher Bird, are, without question, adept popularizers of scientific and technological topics and are certainly acquainted with some aspects of modern plant research. Moreover, the issuance of the book was shrewdly timed to take advantage of the general malaise about science just noted. These facts, plus a lavish advertising campaign and several book-club selections, made the book vastly popular. (Perhaps the ultimate measure of its success was the spate of cartoons it inspired in the *New Yorker* and in the syndicated strip *Doonesbury*.) Had the majority of readers taken it in with the joy of escape to fantasy that may be accorded a good novel, no damage would have been done. This was not what happened, however. The book catalyzed numerous claims of bizarre observations from "one-man" laboratories, led to widespread lay criticism of professional scientists for not taking account of the purported "facts" of plant existence, and permeated student arguments in university biology classes.

In response to this uncritical acclaim, though perhaps after undue delay, several scientific reviews of the book appeared[2] and the American Society of Plant Physiologists (ASPP) and American Association for the Advancement of Science (AAAS) scheduled sessions to evaluate some of the claims made. One of the most crucial portions of Tompkins and Bird's book is a discussion of electrophysiological experiments on plants conducted by polygraph expert Cleve Backster.[3] In June 1974, at the ASPP meeting in Ithaca, New York, Dr. B. G. Pickard of Washington University (St. Louis) organized a symposium at which independent and well-controlled experiments were described which attempted—but failed—to reproduce Backster's results.[4] Following this, Galston organized a session at the AAAS meeting in New York City in January 1975, which brought Backster face to face with some of his critics, including the two scientists E. L. Gasteiger and J. M. Kmetz, who had gone to great lengths to reproduce Backster's experimental conditions. At that meeting, and in subsequent public debates, Backster appeared uninfluenced by the inability of others to repeat his results—so uninfluenced that he himself has never described repetition or extension of his own experiments on the plants. The hoped-for scientific dialogue has therefore been impossible.

Since it is on the interpretation of electrophysiological data that Backster's case and much of the Tompkins-Bird case rests, the purpose of the present essay will be to reexamine the published experiments and to relate them—from the point of view of both philosophy and technical procedures—to the body of controlled and reproducible electrophysiological experiments that *have* been carried out on plants.

It is common knowledge, reaching back to Galvani in the eighteenth century,[5] that variations in electric potential occur in specialized animal cells and tissues, most conspicuously as the "action potentials" of nerves and muscles. However, the knowledge that related electrical phenomena occur in plant tissues has not been widespread. The impression left by the Tompkins-Bird book, and apparently accepted by a considerable number of its readers, is that the only important early work in plant electrophysiology was done in the early twentieth century by the eminent Indian physicist J. C. Bose,[6] and that that work was ignored for more than forty years, until Backster's report was published in 1968. We shall deal later with the substance of Backster's experiments, but we must first dispel this mistaken historical impression and then develop some fundamental ideas in the modern scientific view of "plant electricity."

In retrospect, Bose certainly does deserve great credit. With vast ingenuity, he designed sensitive and elegant instruments to measure small changes in electric potential and small changes in shape (bending, swelling, and so on) of plant materials. With these instruments he was able to demonstrate withdrawal movements of plant tissues from sites of injury, thus complementing for "ordinary" plants the observation of conspicuous movements in certain plants such as Venus's-fly-trap, sundew, and *Mimosa*. Action potential-like disturbances had already been described[7] in insect-eating plants, and Bose and other workers followed at intervals with similar observations on algae,[8] higher plants,[9] and even fungi.[10] Bose quite properly pointed out *functional* similarities between the electrical/mechanical responsiveness, or irritability, of plant and animal tissues, but his data do not in any way support Tompkins and Bird's conclusion that plants "perceive" their environment in the manner of human beings and other higher animals.

While Bose's thought was very advanced in some respects, it was rather primitive in others. His American contemporaries, chiefly the school of W. J. V. Osterhout, were far closer to a proper physical understanding of electrical events in plants. Drawing on the emerging theory of electrolytic solutions set forth by Nernst, Planck, and other illustrious physical chemists of the late nineteenth and early twentieth centuries, Osterhout reasoned that differences of electric potential between the interior of (algal) cells and the external environment must result from differential diffusion of ions (e.g., of sodium, potassium, and chloride) through selective membranes at the cell surface.[11] This hypothesis, together with suggestions about specific "ion carriers" to facilitate transport across membranes,[12] became an important component of the modern theory of bioelectricity.

The other major component of the modern theory began to emerge in the 1930s, from experiments carried out by E. J. Lund at the University of Texas, H. S. Burr at Yale, and H. Lundegaardh in Sweden. Lund observed that differences of electric potential measured along plant stems and roots (we shall return to the methodology of these measurements later) were sensitive to certain poisons,[13] while Lundegaardh found that the same potential differences, along with the rate of oxygen consumption by the tissues, was closely tied to the intake of negatively charged ions from the medium.[14] The inference was drawn that metabolism could "pump" charges through the cell surface membranes, thus creating an electric-potential difference across the membranes. This idea came to fruition in the late 1960s, after P. Mitchell had realized that it could account for much experimental data on the generation of energy in biological systems.[15]

Bioelectric potentials arise from separation of oppositely charged ions across the surface membranes of individual living cells (hence the term *membrane potential*), but widespread verification of this fact was delayed until the late 1940s and 1950s, following the development of fine glass capillary electrodes that could be inserted into single cells. Most of the early work, therefore, depended on whole-tissue recording techniques. Typically, pairs of saline-bathed electrodes were used, one member of the pair being placed at a reactive spot on the tissue, the other member at a distant—and presumed quiescent—spot. (The most important and familiar example of this technique is the recording of electrocardiograms as the electrical difference between a skin electrode placed over the chest wall and another skin electrode fastened to an arm or leg.) The technique is easier than the intracellular recording technique, but it is also much more treacherous, since it depends on many diverse features of the whole recording circuit: the quality of the electrode-tissue contact; the size of the electrodes relative to the size of individual cells; the presence of "dead" space (cuticles, connective tissue); and the constancy of potential near the quiescent electrode. Thus, the intrinsic variability of whole-tissue recording techniques is large, and the caution required in interpretation is much greater than for intracellular recording techniques.

In both plant and animal electrophysiology, interpretation of data from even the most careful and technically sophisticated measurements has often been vitiated by inadvertent tissue damage. Damage during preparation of the specimen can produce prolonged depolarization, sometimes accompanied by fluctuations. Typically, such responses display a rapid onset, but recovery is delayed for tens of minutes up to several hours. Given the natural impatience of a scientist to "get on" with his work, such artifacts have permeated a very considerable fraction of published experiments. Nevertheless, in careful hands both intracellular recording techniques and whole-tissue recording techniques can yield much important information, the whole-tissue techniques being particularly suitable when scientific interest is focused on electrical gradients that extend long distances, over many cell diameters.

Growth studies on plants provide an excellent terrain for such measurements. Thus, the growing tip of the seedling leaf sheath of oat plants was found by Lund[16] to be about 100 millivolts negative to the base of the organ, and similar electric gradients have been observed along other plant organs, including roots, stems, and reproductive axes.[17] Furthermore, these gradients can be altered by mechanical distortion, and by changes in temperature, light, and ambient salt concentration.[18] While normally no transverse electrical gradient exists across cylindrical plant organs, certain stems, roots, and leaf stalks can be polarized transversely, to 100 millivolts or more, by exposure to light or gravitational fields. And the polarization correlates with redistribution of the growth hormone auxin, and subsequent growth curvature.[19] Electric currents accompanying growth changes in single fertilized eggs of marine algae, such as the familiar rockweeds *Fucus* and *Pelvetia*,[20] have also been measured, with the use of ultrasensitive extracellular electrodes. In this case, calcium ion migration, rather than hormone redistribution, is the chemical event most crucially linked to the electrical change.[21] Finally, it should be noted that various rhythmic "clock" functions of plant tissues are associated with changes in electric potential, which can readily be observed either with intracellular or extracellular electrodes. The best-known of these display roughly twenty-four-hour (circadian) periods, phase-locked to the normal day–night cycle; but they can persist for long periods in the absence of light stimulus and can also be shifted or reset by pulsed light absorbed by a specific pigment called phytochrome. As an example, diurnal leaf opening and closing in plants such as *Samanea* involve periodic depolarization and repolarization of different groups of cells in the leaf motor organ.[22] Although the precise causal relationships have not been worked out for these systems, it is evident that both the cellular swelling and shrinking which produce the leaf movements and the measured changes of electrical potential arise from periodic cellular uptake and release of potassium and chloride ions.[23]

Cleve Backster, whose experiments in plant electrophysiology have been so handsomely reported in the Tompkins-Bird book, is a highly trained polygraph (lie detector) specialist, whose introduction to the method came during service as an interrogation instructor in the U.S. Army Counterintelligence Corps; thence he traveled to the Central Intelligence Agency, where he developed the standard polygraph examination methodology. From the CIA, he became director of a polygraph institute in Chicago, and in 1951 founded the Backster School of Lie Detection. He claims to have served as a consultant to almost every government agency that has used the polygraph and to have made numerous technical refinements aimed at reducing the number of inconclusive examinations. Within his field he is widely recognized, having served on the board of directors of the American Polygraph Association and as chairman of the research and scientific committee of the Academy for Scientific Interrogation.

When used on human subjects, the polygraph records uncontrolled reactions (chiefly sweating) of the autonomic nervous system, which are often associated with lying and other emotional disturbances. It does this by measuring a fall of electrical resistance in the skin between two independent surface electrodes (wire mesh or plate, in saline/agar paste). The phenomenon is known as the psychogalvanic reflex.

Backster's initial foray into plant physiology[24] evidently came almost casually, as he wondered whether the surface resistance of plant leaves might be analogous to human skin resistance, and might reflect variations in the flow of sap following routine watering (of a common potted house plant, *Dracaena*, in his office). It seemed a reasonable question, and the polygraph experience suggested that increased evaporation of water from the leaf should *decrease* the resistance between the upper and lower surfaces of the leaf. As is often the case in any new experiments by electrophysiologists, the initial records were rather unstable. They contained at least two unaccounted-for quasi-periodic variations, at about 1 cycle/second and 2 cycles/minute, superimposed on a slow downward trend, which suggested—if anything—a progressive *increase* of leaf resistance. There was also a segment (of the single record published) which superficially resembled the slow rise-and-fall of resistance that occurs in human polygraph records during verified lying (Figure 1).

At this point we find a totally unscientific discontinuity of logic. Without investigating the recording conditions in order to identify or eliminate the sources of unexpected noise and drift, Backster jumped to the conclusion that *because* the plant record *resembled in a single respect* human records obtained during emotional reaction, *the plant must experience* something like human *emotion.* This is roughly equivalent to arguing that because the face of the full moon displays dark patches resembling a human face, there must be a real man in the moon.

Backster thereupon decided to explore further the possible emo-

Figure 1

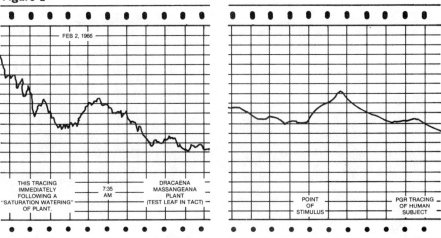

The original recording suggesting to Backster a parallelism between plant response to watering (left) *and the psychogalvanic response* (PGR) *in humans* (right). Courtesy Parapsychology Foundation, Inc., New York.

tional response of his plant by affecting it in ways that evoke strong emotional reactions in human beings: with injury, or threats of injury and death. He reports finding that scalding a nearby leaf (with hot coffee!) was not sufficient to evoke a response on the polygraph, but that when he *thought* about burning the leaf with a match there was a "dramatic change in the tracing pattern." (No methodology has been given for timing the onset of a thought, but the published record, Figure 2, certainly did become erratic.) Similar but undocumented experiments were subsequently carried out on other plant species, "frequently serving to reinforce" Backster's hypothesis. Although no interpretation was given of those experiments that *failed* to reinforce the hypothesis, the author did note that the phenomenon "persisted when the leaf . . . was detached from the parent plant, and even when . . . shredded and redistributed between the electrode surfaces." In view of the spurious behavior of damaged tissue, mentioned above, the latter claim is most remarkable.

Thereafter, Backster refined the format of his experiment in several ways: (1) by devising a constant and remote emotional stimulus in the form of scalding-death of brine shrimp (*Artemia*); (2) by selecting *Philodendron cordatum* as his recording species, its leaves being optimally stiff, broad, and thick; (3) by automating the experiments and

Figure 2

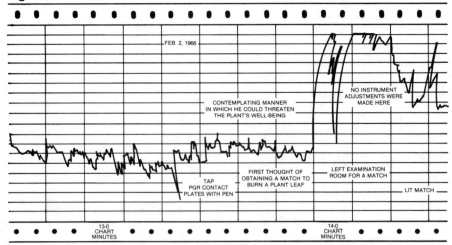

The recording suggesting to Backster that plants can react to thoughts. Courtesy Parapsychology Foundation, Inc., New York.

running them in triplicate; (4) by connecting a fourth recorder to a 100,000-ohm resistor (instead of a leaf) as a control against instrument noise; (5) by isolating the main recording instruments, each plant, and the brine shrimp in separate rooms of the laboratory; (6) by using a blind randomizer, along with controls of sterile brine (no shrimp), so the experimental observer would not know when or whether (during a particular experiment) shrimp had actually been killed; and (7) by keeping light and temperature constant for all plants.

The analysis of data from seven experiments carried out in this manner is as follows. All seven of the fixed resistor tracings were flat, giving no indication of electronic disturbances in the instruments. Of the twenty-one leaf records, two were discarded because of failure in the pen recorders, three were discarded because of "gross overactivity," and three were discarded for "not displaying typical fluidity." This left a total of thirteen usable chart records. Each experimental run was 2½ minutes long, divided into six 25-second blocks. During the first 10 seconds of each block a shrimp killing could occur, but in only thirteen blocks (designated stimulus blocks) out of the seventy-eight total did a killing actually occur. (The remaining sixty-five blocks were designated "control" blocks.) A sudden deviation of leaf resistance was scored as a positive reaction, and this occurred in eleven of the thirteen stimulus blocks, but in only eight of the sixty-five control blocks. No positive reactions were obtained in control runs with the sterile brine alone. Backster subsequently inferred that plant cells must have "a primary sensory system."

This is the sum total of published experimental information underlying the widely publicized claims. The report, appearing in the *International Journal of Parapsychology* (winter 1968), stands today as the only report of such results. It was supplemented, however, during the 1975 AAAS meeting (see page 42). There Backster described new experiments in which the recording organism was *Lactobacillus* (yogurt). Pots of yogurt were said to display changes of electric potential upon addition of oxidizable substrate to nearby pots. This, too, received extensive press coverage.

When confronted with reports that are as weak and logically faulty as this, one is tempted to dismiss them out of hand. Identifying and cataloguing all of the uncontrolled experimental variables is likely to be a very time-consuming task, which—because of probable negative conclusions—seems unrewarding. We are indebted, therefore, to two serious and dedicated researchers, E. L. Gasteiger of Cornell University and J. M. Kmetz, then of the Science Unlimited Research Foundation in San Antonio, Texas, who set about explicitly to confirm or reject the Backster report from solid experimental ground. Verbal advice was given by Backster to both researchers, so that the experimental conditions and layout would be as nearly identical with the original circumstances as possible. Both sets of results were presented to the public (in the 1975 AAAS symposium), and one has been published.

Gasteiger, working in collaboration with two undergraduate students, K. A. Horowitz and D. C. Lewis, arranged experiments with all the seven features listed above in Backster's refined format. Some further improvements of the procedure were also incorporated, including maintenance of the plants in light-tight rooms; ejection of the brine shrimp into the boiling water by solenoid-drive pipettes, whose electrical activating pulse was automatically recorded; videotape monitoring of the entire shrimp-killing operation; careful insulation and shielding of the electrodes, plant preparation, and electric cables; and use of high-gain capacity-coupled voltage amplifiers to measure microvolt changes of potential (rather than resistance) across the leaves. The latter modification has substantial advantages, particularly in its greater sensitivity and lesser vulnerability to extrinsic noise.

As befits the extreme care used in arrangement of the electrophysiological apparatus, the resultant records were much "quieter" than those of Backster and displayed only one feature that could possibly have been construed as a response to the emotive stimulus. That feature was a brief 10- to 45-microvolt deflection that occurred spontaneously and at irregular intervals, but with only about 30 percent of the plants studied. Horowitz, Lewis, and Gasteiger scored the deflections as positive, negative, or null, depending on whether the amplitude of the one immediately following a shrimp killing (or trial with water alone) was larger than, smaller than, or equal to the one (if any) occurring in the immediately preceding control period. A total of sixty randomly sequenced shrimp killings and forty water trials were conducted with twenty plants. Statistical analyses of the data were carried out in several different ways, but no criterion was identifiable under which either the shrimp killings or the water trials could be associated with voltage shifts.

Although the authors did find Backster's reported data to be significant by the same statistical analyses, they could safely conclude from their own experiments that "we matched, and in several instances improved on, Backster's experimental techniques. . . . We obtained no evidence of primary perception in plants. While the hypothesis will remain as an intriguing speculation, one should note that only the limited published data of Backster support it."

Kmetz was even more assiduous than the Cornell group in replicating Backster's experimental conditions, and in particular he returned to the "lie detector" method of recording leaf resistance (Figure 3). But after 168 trials on 42 plants, involving 84 shrimp killings and an equal number of water trials (Figure 4), he could find no significant correlation between resistance shifts and shrimp killing.[26] He also delved into the "yogurt experiment" with the same thoroughness—and with the same negative result.

Perhaps more important, Kmetz carried out the time-consuming and difficult task of ferreting out and documenting the probable source of Backster's results. We have already noted that Backster's chart records from plants were noisy, much noisier than the polygraph record he produced from a human subject. When viewing, for example, Figure 2, in the 1966 article, anyone experienced with practical electric circuits (and particularly anyone experienced with bioelectric recording) would suspect an unstable electrical junction somewhere; and even for the much cleaner record of Figure 5, obtained from Backster's refined experimental format, the low-level irregularity of the trace and the base-line blurs raise suspicions. The problem is to identify the exact point of the bad junction.

Figure 3

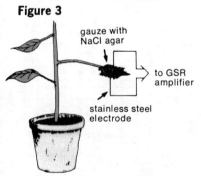

galvanic skin reflex experiment

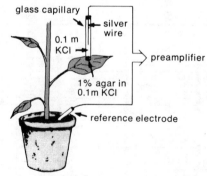

surface-potential change experiment

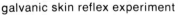

Drawings of Kmetz's reproduction of Backster's setups for monitoring galvanic skin reflex (GSR) (left) or surface potential changes (right) in plants. Courtesy J. M. Kmetz.

Figure 4

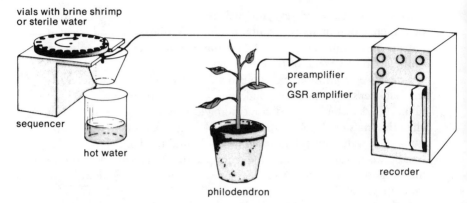

A *drawing of Kmetz's reproduction of Backster's brine-shrimp experiment.*
Courtesy J. M. Kmetz.

Kmetz had noted that the plant records appeared "more active" ini-
tially, after connecting the leaves to the recording system, than they
were later on, and so he carried out one novel and crucial control
measurement: Instead of recording simply from a 100,000-ohm resistor as the control against instrumentational noise, he included a pair
of the Backster electrodes (but still no leaf) in that circuit. The resulting records were every bit as "active" as when a leaf was included, and
they calmed down with time. After studying the electrodes visually in
many experiments, Kmetz wrote the following summary:

Figure 5

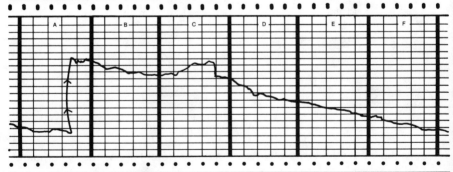

*The recording suggesting to Backster that plants have a "primary sensory sys-
tem."* (NOTE: *Time block A shows recentering of automatic recording device.*)
Courtesy Parapsychology Foundation, Inc., New York.

Immediately after placing a set of electrodes in operation, water begins to evaporate from the agar gel, causing a change in concentration of sodium chloride in the gel. [This change] in turn causes a change in resistance which appears as a pen deflection on the [recorder]. Since . . . the evaporation process is not uniform, rather wide variations in resistance occur. In other words, immediately after the system is set up, it is extremely unstable. After a period of time, a "skin" forms [between the agar and the air]. Although the skin does not completely prevent the drying process, it retards it sufficiently to make the electrode system appear stable. . . . Our observations indicate that the equilibration time is [20–30] minutes. From the description given in his 1968 paper it appears that most of Backster's plant readings were taken during the equilibration period. I would suggest . . . that any readings taken [then] may be invalid.[27]

We can thus state unequivocally that Backster's experiments do not support either his hypothesis or the Tompkins-Bird claims. It seems likely that most of the other experiments purported to reflect human-like emotional or sensory behavior in plants could be debunked with the same precision. The cost, however, would be unacceptably high in both time and scientific distraction. For this reason, and because the notion admittedly does have revolutionary implications, it will surely float around on the fringe of science for a long time to come. Both the logic and the history of science, furthermore, require us to be alert to the possibility—however remote—that harder data may one day turn up; and from this caveat, it seems appropriate to discuss briefly the questions of what identifiable features a bona fide sensory communication process in plants might possess, and how an experimenter might go about demonstrating its presence.

In order to establish that sensory reception is taking place in a plant or animal, the organism, or a specific part of the organism, must be shown to respond in a systematic way to the onset of an external stimulus. For large stimuli, signal shape, amplitude, and delay (between the stimulus and the response) are easily identified, but for small stimuli the major problem is to separate the signal itself from the "noise," which is analogous—in biological systems—to static in a radio. Biological systems can indeed be *very* noisy. For example, most animal sensory receptors spontaneously emit electrical pulses that are identical with bona fide signals, except that they occur randomly and thereby tend to obscure any response to a weak stimulus. Common techniques to distinguish signals from the noise are either to search for pulses with a fixed delay after the onset of a stimulus, or to use computer techniques to determine whether the average signal frequency is higher during the stimulus than in its absence.

Over the past seventy-five years, electrophysiological experiments—frequently using such small-signal discrimination techniques—have in fact identified a number of different sensory processes in plants. It must be pointed out, though, that all such receptor processes display one more essential characteristic: anatomical localization. Not only have proponents of plant sensitivity, as reported in the Tompkins-Bird book, failed to isolate signals from noise (in response to "emotional" stimuli; see pages 47–48) using systematic methods like those suggested above, but they have also failed to identify any plausible anatomical site of such a receptor system. It is this lack of a reasonable receptor structure which, in our view, drives the final nail into the coffin for the Backster, Tompkins, and Bird view of plant "sensory perception." Perception, communication, and emotion are properties of highly developed nervous systems (and perhaps in the near future will be properties of complex computer circuits). Nowhere in the plant kingdom is there an anatomical structure that approximates the complexity of insect, or even worm, nervous systems, much less the mind-boggling intricacies of the cerebral cortex in higher primates.

Throughout this discussion, we have repeatedly invoked two essential operating principles of science: reproducible data collection, and independent verification. Backster's conclusions, as well as many others in the Tompkins-Bird book, collapse under the test of either principle. Fortunately or unfortunately, depending on your point of view, ideas often prove very tenacious in men's minds. Over the past century, large numbers of scientists, perhaps even a majority, have clung to pet hypotheses long past the time when data and other scientists have laid those hypotheses to rest. Eventually, time erases (or at least blurs) our memory of such dead hypotheses, though occasionally one will be resuscitated or even reincarnated in fruitful form at a later time.

But that corpus of fallacious or unprovable claims that comprise "the secret life of plants" is being kept alive in the popular literature by highly efficient mass-media techniques. Its body has been kept breathing despite the fact that its brain is obviously dead. The rationale for this was given by Backster in an interview with the *Christian Science Monitor*:

> The only problem in this kind of research is that Mother Nature does not want to jump through the hoop ten times in a row, simply because someone wants her to. It is difficult to structure repeatable experiments. There are some phenomena that occur that make this kind of thing very difficult. For instance, once you are sure something will happen, it very well may not. I suspect that's because you are communicating to the biological material as long as you keep your consciousness involved in the experiment.[28]

The proposition has been stated slightly differently by Marcel Vogel, another Tompkins-Bird hero:

> Hundreds of laboratory workers around the world are going to be frustrated and disappointed until they realize that empathy between plant and human is a key, and learn how to establish it. No amount of checking in laboratories is going to prove a thing, until the experiments are done by properly trained observers. Spiritual development is indispensable, but this runs counter to the philosophy of many scientists who do not realize that creative experimentation means that the *experimenters must become part of their experiments.*[29] (Emphasis added.)

It is a "no lose" proposition. Negative results must be discounted because the experimenter is not "in tune," and only positive results are accepted. The operating principles of science are set aside, and the arguments become removed from contact with physical reality. The scientific method is excluded, the questions posed quickly become irrelevant to science, and we are left in the realm of Ben Kenobi and Darth Vader.

4

Parapsychology and Quantum Mechanics

MARTIN GARDNER

Watson: "This is indeed a mystery. What do you
imagine it means?"
Holmes: "I have no data yet. It is a capital mistake to theorize before one has data. Insensibly one
begins to twist facts to suit theories, instead of
theories to suit facts."
— Sir Arthur Conan Doyle,
A Scandal in Bohemia

*Much of the public is under the impression that parapsychologists have
produced good scientific evidence for the existence of extrasensory perception (ESP) and psychokinesis (PK). Many people have also heard
about physical theories that explain how ESP and PK work. Sometimes
the promulgators of these theories are people with sound professional
credentials, even in physical science. But too often the hypotheses themselves that are advanced to account for paranormal or bizarre events
are based on ideas dealing with areas of physics that are not yet well
understood.*

*Relatively few research psychologists believe there is any convincing
evidence that ESP or PK even exists, and most physicists regard the
physical theories of ESP and PK as nonsense. Martin Gardner explains
the reasons for these attitudes, illustrating the case with a recent theory*

of ESP derived from quantum mechanics. As is so often true, we find that what passes for science in paranormal research is really bad science—scientific window dressing for ideas and procedures that are unsupportable.

Parapsychologists differ considerably about the "facts" of their trade, but there is a fairly solid core of beliefs on which most of them agree. They are convinced that psi powers (ESP and PK)* are possessed in some degree by everybody, and to a high degree by a few. Almost all agree that psi forces are independent of time and distance.

There is, of course, no way they can be sure that extrasensory perception (ESP) and psychokinesis (PK) are manifestations of a single power. Even ESP (which includes telepathy, clairvoyance, and precognition) may, from their point of view, be a name for several kinds of interactions. However, parapsychologists have always been partial to the notion that a single force is responsible for both ESP and PK. If so, what kind of force is it?

Modern physics recognizes four fundamental forces: gravity, electromagnetism, and the weak and strong nuclear forces. All are field phenomena with strengths that diminish with distance. As J. B. Rhine (the American psychologist famous for his studies of parapsychology) perceived early in the game, there is no reasonable way that any such force can explain the peculiar indifference of psi to distance and time. Moreover, electromagnetism, long a favorite among early researchers, seems ruled out by experiments which show that electromagnetic shielding has no effect on psi. Because extremely low frequency (ELF) electromagnetic waves have strong penetrating power, some parapsychologists continue to think of photons† as carriers of psi, but empirical evidence for this is nonexistent.

Nor is there evidence for theories that other particles, such as the "graviton" (conjectured carrier of gravity), or the neutrino (emitted in certain nuclear reactions), play a role in psi. There have been recent speculations that tachyons, alleged particles that can travel faster than

* ESP is defined here as the alleged ability to perceive or sense by means other than the known physical senses. PK is defined here as mind over matter—the alleged ability to move or alter objects by paranormal means.

† Electromagnetic waves of successively shorter wavelength are, respectively, radio waves, infrared radiation, light, ultraviolet radiation, X rays, and gamma rays. All of these are essentially the same kind of energy and are transmitted in small, discrete packets of energy called photons.

light, may be psi carriers. Unfortunately, tachyons probably don't exist, and even if they did, if they were used for communication their faster-than-light speeds would create logical contradictions with the extremely well-documented results of special relativity. Russian parapsychologists have proposed the "psychon," but this is just inventing a new particle to explain a force that nobody understands—and that may not exist in the first place.

Because psi phenomena seem to disobey all known physical laws, Rhine has always held the sensible view that psi is outside physics altogether. We simply don't know, he says, what psi is. Until more data are in, we had best confess our ignorance and patiently await new developments.

Today's paraphysicists are less patient. In recent years, mainly as the result of speculations by Evan Harris Walker, a paraphysicist now in the department of mechanics and materials science at Johns Hopkins University, the notion that quantum mechanics (QM) may explain psi has become fashionable in many psi circles. Walker's ideas, in modified form, have been loudly championed by Jack Sarfatti, a San Francisco paraphysicist and one-time admirer of Uri Geller.[1] They have received partial and less strident support from Nobel Prize winner Brian Josephson of England,[2] O. Costa de Beauregard of the Poincaré Institute in Paris,[3] Harold Puthoff and Russell Targ of Stanford Research Institute,[4] and other less well known physicists, such as Richard Mattuck at the Ørsted Institute of the University of Copenhagen.

Before summarizing Walker's views it will be necessary to consider a few relevant aspects of QM (quantum mechanics). In QM the state of a particle or system of particles is given by the "wave function." The curious thing about this function is that it does not specify precise values for such properties as position, momentum, spin, polarization, and so on. It gives only the probabilities that each variable will have certain values when the particle is measured. The act of measurement, for reasons which QM does not explain, causes the particle to undergo what is usually called a reduction or collapse of its "wave packet." The particle "jumps" from a quantum state in which the value of the variable being measured is indefinite to a quantum state in which it has a definite value.

The situation seems to be similar to what happens when a rolling die comes to rest, but actually it is radically different. Our inability to predict which side of the die's face will be on top is no more than a reflection of our ignorance of all the physical forces influencing the die. In principle, if we could take into account all those forces, we could correctly predict the outcome of the roll. But an unmeasured particle does not behave like a die or a flipped penny or a roulette wheel or like anything else we are familiar with. In QM the value that a quantum property acquires when measured is the result of *pure chance*. For example, if the wave function says a particle can be spinning either clockwise or counterclockwise with equal probability, there is no way of specifying which spin it has; it's as if the particle actually has no definite spin until it is measured. Both spins are somehow latent in the particle. Nature does not "decide" which spin it will be until the act of measurement captures it.

Many QM experts are unhappy with this "pure chance" aspect of the theory. Einstein himself, one of the early contributors to what became QM, liked to say that he could not imagine God playing dice with the universe. He hoped that some day physicists would find deeper laws capable of restoring classical causality on the microlevel. To dramatize his belief that QM was incomplete, Einstein and two friends, Boris Podolsky and Nathan Rosen, devised a thought experiment that became known as the EPR (for Einstein, Podolsky, and Rosen) paradox.[5]

The paradox can be given in many forms. When an electron and a positron (positive electron) come into contact, they annihilate each other, turning into energy in the form of two photons. Suppose, for example, that an electron–positron annihilation sends off two photons in opposite directions. A photon can be plane polarized with the amplitude of its wave motion in either a horizontal or vertical orientation, or it can be circularly polarized, so that the plane of the wave displacement rotates as it moves through space. The circular polarization can rotate in a clockwise or counterclockwise direction. QM predicts that the two photons produced by the annihilation must have *opposite* polarization. Now each can be measured by a filtering device that allows the photon to pass through one of two channels. If a photon is measured for either polarization, then immediately allowed to pass through a second device of the same type, the type of polarization is unchanged. The first measurement has, in a sense, "forced" the photon into a definite state. According to QM theory, states are not "known"—even to the particle itself—until after the particle interacts with something else. The uncertainty is innate until the polarization is observed, or measured, at which point it is no longer possible for it to be one way or the other.

Two photons, produced by electron–positron annihilation, remain correlated in the sense that they must have (when measured) opposite plane polarizations or opposite circular polarizations. To dramatize the paradox, suppose they become separated by ten light-years. QM tells us that if one photon is measured for either variable, we know the value of that variable for the other photon *even though it has not been measured.*

As Robert Dicke and James Wittke put it in their *Introduction to Quantum Mechanics* (Addison-Wesley, 1960), we cannot conceive how a photon can be plane and circularly polarized at the same time. Indeed, QM asserts that the photons have no definite values for either variable until one photon is measured and its wave packet collapses. Yet when measurement "forces" one photon into, say, a clockwise polarized state, the other instantly goes into a counterclockwise polarized state. They conclude, "The two photons constitute a *single* dynamic system. Any information obtained about the system is information about both photons. Any interaction on a single photon is an interaction on the system and affects the state of the whole system."

Now there would be nothing mysterious about all this if we could think of the two photons as intricate little mechanisms that somehow possess opposite polarizations of both types before they are measured, but it is precisely this that QM forbids. It is not until the act of measurement that the photon's wave packet collapses and nature decides what to do. Dicke and Wittke, like the authors of almost all standard textbooks on QM, simply describe what happens and leave it at that. It may seem to be sheer magic, but QM works very well in that it is extremely successful in predicting how electromagnetic phenomena behave.

Einstein wanted to know how the trick works. It is unthinkable, he argued, that information can go instantly from one particle to another one that is ten light-years away—yet QM seems to demand this. Somehow, when one particle is measured, the other "knows" the outcome of the measurement. In the last few years, actual laboratory tests with correlated photons, together with a deep construct known as Bell's theorem, have confirmed the predictions of QM.[6] The new results based on Bell's theorem leave open two possibilities: One, conjectured by the London quantum physicist David Bohm and others, is that correlated particles may be connected on a subquantum level that is outside the space-time of relativity theory. The other possibility is that widely separated particles may be causally connected in space-time, but in a way that violates relativity theory.

An enormous ferment is now under way among quantum physicists over the implications of Bell's theorem and the new laboratory observations. More experiments are planned, so it is too early to guess how the EPR paradox will finally be resolved. Most working physicists probably belong to what has been called the pragmatic or "no-nonsense" school, which accepts the paradoxes of QM without worrying about what is "actually" going on. A no-nonsense physicist sees QM as essentially a mathematical tool that tells him, with astonishing accuracy, what he will see if he makes certain experiments. It tells him nothing about what goes on between experiments. The no-nonsense physicist is content with this tool, and unconcerned about philosophical interpretations; he will continue to use QM unquestioningly until someone comes along with a new theory that has testable consequences and works better than classic QM.

Einstein was more philosophically minded. He was not content with being told no more than that if you measure a particle here, another particle at a vast distance will abruptly alter its state. He ruled out as too "spooky" the notion that information could go from particle to particle at superluminal (greater than light) speed. That seemed to him as absurd as believing that a needle stuck in a voodoo doll could instantaneously cause pain in a victim many miles away. Now that Bell's theorem and new experimental results have ruled out local hidden variables, the possibility that Einstein considered unthinkable has become so thinkable that a number of quantum experts now favor it.[7] But note that only information of a curious, limited sort is transferred, not energy. No one has actually found a way that particle correlation can be used for transmitting any kind of message faster than light. But there is a possibility that widely separated particles may be connected in some as yet totally unknown way.

A useful metaphor—of course, it is no more than that—is to think of our space-time as the "surface" of some vast hypersphere.* Within space-time no information can go faster than light. But we do not know what laws govern the transfer of information through the hyper-

---

* A hypersphere is the analogue of a three-dimensional sphere in four or more dimensions. It cannot be visualized, but is well defined mathematically.

sphere. On a subquantum level,* perhaps information can travel at superluminal speeds—or even instantaneously.

It was necessary to sketch this background because Walker's theory of paranormal powers assumes the existence of a subquantum level. Walker regards the human mind, like all physical systems, as an ongoing QM process. We possess, he says, a "will" that is continually reducing wave packets in the brain to bring about new mental states. This process, he conjectures, involves "electron tunneling across synaptic clefts." There is no experimental evidence of this, but he believes that such evidence may be forthcoming. Because, in Walker's view, all parts of the universe are connected on the subquantum level, he sees no reason why the human will cannot use this level to collapse wave packets of quantum systems outside the brain—regardless of how far they are away.

That the brain can do this is, of course, pure speculation. In QM it is not the human observer who collapses wave packets but the observing instruments. The human observer simply looks at certain macrostructures, such as photographs and pointer readings, to learn the outcome of microlevel measurements. When particles leave tracks inside bubble chambers, it is what goes on inside the chamber that reduces wave packets and gives to the tracks their precise positions and shapes. It is only after a long chain of macrointeractions (involving events that are irreversible) that a human mind "sees" the tracks in the same way it sees a star or a tree. No one supposes that this observation can alter the track any more than looking at a tree can alter the tree. In brief, there is no support for the notion that the brain can change the state of a quantum system outside itself.[8]

Walker's second assumption is even more staggering. Not only does he suppose that the mind can alter wave packets of distant objects, but he also assumes that it can alter a wave packet in such a way as to bring about a desired value for one of the variables. There is no reliable evidence of any sort for this fantastic claim; indeed, it runs counter to the very heart of QM's formalism, which asserts that the value acquired by a variable, after wave-packet reduction, is the outcome of absolute chance.

It is obvious that if both of Walker's assumptions are correct, a scaffolding exists on which to hang a theory of ESP and PK. In Walker's view, psi action is not a force that goes from brain to brain, or brain to

* A subquantum level is a hypothetical unknown theory or principle that is more fundamental than that of quantum mechanics.

object, or object to brain. There is not even a message that travels from here to there. A psi event occurs when one or more persons unite their quantum mechanical power to collapse wave packets in such a way as to select a mutually desired future state from among all the possible states permitted by the relevant wave functions.

Let us see how this works for telepathy. In classical psi theories a mind sends out a wave of some sort that carries information to another mind. Walker's QM approach is strikingly different. Suppose a sender is turning ESP cards and a receiver is recording guesses. Eventually the receiver's list will be compared to the target list. If both sender and receiver want a successful outcome, their minds will collaborate to alter all the quantum systems involved so as to bring about the mutually desired state.

Clairvoyance may seem different but actually is not. An experimenter selects targets, the subject tries to "see" them, but the overall situation is the same as before. All persons participating in the test, including sideline observers, collaborate to influence the outcome. No information is transferred from target to subject. Rather it is a case of all the participants using their wills to "select" a future state from among the myriads of possible states permitted by the relevant wave functions. Precognition is "explained" in exactly the same way. Thus telepathy, clairvoyance, and precognition are simply different names for essentially the same QM process.

Walker's theory clearly accounts for the seeming independence of psi from space and time constraints. Moreover, it accounts easily for the "sheep–goat" effect so often invoked by parapsychologists. The sheep (believers) are supposed to do better than the goats (skeptics) as both subjects and experimenters. Sheep naturally try to reduce wave packets to get successful results. Goats naturally want experiments to fail. This also explains, says Walker, why the mere presence of a skeptic as an observer may cause a psi test to fail. The skeptic keeps collapsing wave packets the wrong way.

Walker's conjectures become bolder when he speculates on how QM can explain ordinary psychokinesis. Historic PK tests, by Rhine and others, involved testing the mind's ability to influence rolling or falling dice. Although a die is made of billions of particles, it can be regarded as a single quantum system with its own overall wave function.

QM does not give the actual state of a particle (say, its position and velocity), but only the *probability* of various states. With extremely many particles, though, as in a die, the individual uncertainties nearly average out, and the state of the composite die is well determined. Similarly, the lot of an individual gambler in a casino is very uncertain, but if there are thousands of gamblers present, the casino operator has a very good idea what the evening's take will be. Thus, statistically speaking, the die's quantum uncertainty is essentially zero—much smaller than the uncertainty arising from the actions of its individual molecules (called "thermal noise"); nevertheless, its uncertainty is not absolutely zero. Suppose the die does a great deal of bouncing as it rolls down a long runway and falls on a flat surface. If a mind can collapse the die's wave packet at the start of its roll, to throw it into one of its possible states, this inconceivably tiny microeffect will be magnified by the divergent process of bouncing. A minute alteration at the outset will, Walker reasons, have a slightly larger effect after the first bounce, a still larger one after the second, and so on. Such divergent effects are not uncommon in the macroworld; a stray spark from a cap pistol can start a forest fire, for example. As someone has said, the flutter of a butterfly's wings in Brazil could conceivably start a divergent chain of causes and effects that would end with a cyclone in Kansas.

If a die bounces enough as it rolls, Walker reasons, will not a tiny alteration of its position at the start be sufficiently magnified at the end of the roll to bring about a desired macrostate when the die comes to rest? He suggests ways in which this conjecture could be tested. For example, one would expect a stronger PK effect in tests with dice that do a lot of bouncing than in tests with little bouncing. Also, the more dice there are, the more they rattle (bounce) against one another; consequently, the more dice, the stronger the expected PK effect. The basic idea extends to such measuring devices as thermistors, magnetometers, radiation detectors, and so on. If the final readings are affected by any kind of natural noise that stems from a QM process, the noise provides a divergent sequence comparable to bouncing dice. This should improve the subject's chances to succeed in altering such readings by PK.

Walker's theory also accounts for the embarrassing fact that parapsychologists have been unable to detect a PK effect on a delicately balanced needle even when many minds are collaborating on the effort over a long period of time. Moving the needle requires a push proportional to the needle's mass. From Walker's point of view, quantum uncertainty is not strong enough to provide such a push (assuming the subject is not a superpsychic) unless it is magnified by a divergent process. Since no divergent phenomena are involved with the needle, the average subject is unable to work up enough PK power to move it.

To bolster his theory that a single wave-packet collapse can start a divergent process that ends with a desired macroresult, Walker relies almost entirely on the published results of experiments made over a period of some twenty years by a retired Swedish electrical engineer named Haakon Forwald. Most of Forwald's papers were published in the fifties in Rhine's *Journal of Parapsychology*. They dealt not with dice but with unmarked cubes of various sizes, weights, and surface textures, and made of different materials. Forwald allowed his cubes to roll down a long incline onto a walled surface divided into two identical parts. The idea was for the subject to influence the cubes so that more ended up in one region than the other. Parapsychologists call it a "placement effect."

In his lengthy paper "Foundations of Paraphysical and Parapsychological Phenomena," Walker devotes many pages to a detailed analysis of Forwald's confusing results.[9] Walker is firmly persuaded that these results are unique in the literature on PK work with cubes, since they show a correlation between the magnitude of the effect and the nature of the cubes.

When I first learned that Walker relied so heavily on Forwald's work I was astounded. Most parapsychologists today have a low opinion of this work. For one thing, almost all of it was solo—that is, Forwald acted as both experimenter and subject. No photographic records were made. Today, if a researcher submitted a paper to Rhine's journal reporting on placement effects with cubes in which the author was both subject and experimenter, the paper would be rejected. But at the time Forwald did his research, protocols were unbelievably lax.

After publishing many papers on the results of his solo work, Forwald went to Rhine's laboratory in 1957 to conduct rolling-cube experiments under the supervision of J. G. Pratt. Forwald's crusty temperament made it difficult for him to work with others. After a number of unsuccessful experiments, an assistant was finally found who was psychologically compatible with Forwald. The assistant was a twenty-year-old married woman employed in the lab as a secretary. The positive results of this work prompted R. A. McConnell, at the University of Pittsburgh, to repeat the tests in 1959 at his laboratory.

This time a motion-picture record was made and the cubes were individually numbered. "It was hoped in this way," McConnell wrote, "to tighten the evidence for the existence of the placement effect."[10]

Alas, with these simple controls the results were negative. McConnell's opinion is that this failure to replicate was entirely psychological. He noted that Forwald spent eight weeks in Durham in 1957 but only nineteen days in Pittsburgh. And "even had he been able to remain longer, it would have been difficult to create in a biophysics department within an urban university the same air of southern relaxation and hospitality that was characteristic of the Duke University laboratory."

A disappointed Forwald returned to Sweden, where, working all by himself again, the placement effect returned. I know of no PK research, over so long a period, that was so consistently uncontrolled.[11]

Not only does Walker accept the validity of Forwald's sloppy solo work, he also accepts the reality of claims that some psychics can cause macroscopic objects to "translocate" (vanish here and appear there) as well as produce the "Geller effect" (paranormal metal bending). In neither case is there a divergent causal sequence, as with bouncing cubes, so Walker is forced to posit a different mechanism. He distinguishes normal or weak PK, such as we ordinary mortals have, from the "strong PK" of superpsychics.

How does strong PK work? As before, Walker offers nothing resembling a scientific theory. He simply makes another quantum jump from a mere possibility to a wild assumption. The superpsychic, by an "extraordinary" and "sustained" effort of will is able to alter *lots* of wave packets. By altering enough packets, he or she can bring about a "highly improbable state" that is nevertheless one permitted by the macroobject's overall wave function. For example, a Felicia Parise moves a plastic pill bottle from here to there, or a Uri Geller bends a spoon by "translocating" a portion of its metal.

What does all this add up to? It adds up to nothing more than a bare assertion that an intensive, sustained effort of will by a superpsychic can produce translocations and metal bending.

There is more. Walker believes that his "theory" will explain the great miracles of historical religions. At the close of his paper "Consciousness and Quantum Theory"[12] he pulls out all the stops. Copernicus is taken as a symbol of the man of science, devoted to reason and empiricism, and skeptical of religious faith. Luther is taken as an opposite symbol: the man of faith who is skeptical of science. Today, proclaims Walker, religion is entering a new age. Thanks to QM we at last have a genuinely scientific explanation for the great miracles of Luther's faith, and presumably those of other religions as well. "We are at a point in time for which certain knowledge, factual knowledge, can provide a basis for the God concept," he asserts.

His QM theory of psi, Walker goes on, gives "only an inkling" of how the "collective will" of all the consciousnesses in the universe can be thought of as "God," and how this God can interact with history in ways that seem miraculous but which actually are nothing more than the collapsing of many wave packets to bring about desired future states. "It is to be through efforts of this nature that the present basis of acceptance of God, faith, will come to an end, and factual knowledge will become the basis for religion. This is to be the rock on which the new age is to be founded. This is the thesis I come to nail to your door."

The thesis he is nailing to our door! It seems clear that Walker sees himself as a new Martin Luther, nailing his QM theory of consciousness on the world's door to spark a new Reformation—a new age in which hitherto blind faith will be supplanted by certain scientific knowledge. For centuries, Christians have supposed, in their ignorance of QM, that when Jesus walked on the water it was a transcendent god suspending the laws of his creation. Now that Walker has nailed his thesis to the church door, Christians know better. It was Jesus, aided by the collective consciousnesses of the universe, who twiddled billions of wave packets to permit the highly improbable state of his levitation!

To readers unfamiliar with QM, Walker's papers seem enormously impressive because they swarm with equations and scientific jargon that only a physicist could understand. But when it is all translated, and you discover exactly what he is saying, his "theory" turns out to be only a collection of pious hopes. *If* our mind operates by quantum jumps, *if* all parts of the universe are connected on a subquantum level, *if* the human will can alter wave packets of distant objects, and *if* it can alter the packets to bring about desired states, then we have an "explanation" of how Uri Geller can bend a spoon. This is not a theory; it is a caricature of a theory. I am reminded of a letter that Wolfgang Pauli wrote to George Gamow. Pauli and Heisenberg had recently cooked up a hypothesis to explain some new results in particle theory. The hypothesis had been shot down. Pauli closed his letter with a "proof" that he could draw like Titian. The proof was an empty square with the note: "Only technical details are lacking." [13]

Walker has proposed ways in which his theory could be tested, but is it worthwhile to fund the testing of a theory of translocation, metal bending, and placement effects before it has been demonstrated that such psi effects actually take place? So far, the main support for Walker's theory is a series of questionable experiments with rolling cubes, conducted by an experimenter who liked to work alone and whose results are regarded with suspicion even by parapsychologists.

Although the general public remains unaware of it, the overwhelming majority of experimental psychologists around the world do not believe that the existence of ESP and PK has even been demonstrated. Yet for the past hundred years the true believers, in violation of Sherlock Holmes's advice, have been turning to the latest theories of physics in hopes of finding support for the shaky results they are convinced are genuine. It is a sad history. When Maxwell's theory of electromagnetic fields was new, it was fashionable to theorize about how magnetic forces could account for psi. When relativity theory was new, it was fashionable to explain psi by forces in hyperspace that move in and out of our world.[14] Today the big mysteries of physics are on the microlevel. It is not surprising that true believers, eager to underpin psi with science, would turn to QM.

For once I find myself agreeing with Rhine. Paraphysicists would do well to abandon theory and concentrate on devising experiments that can be replicated by unbelievers. At the end of the two-day conference in 1974 on QM and psi[9], there was a roundtable discussion at which the writer Charles Panati, editor of *The Geller Papers*, made a good point. He had been enormously impressed, he said, by Puthoff and Targ's account of how their superpsychic Ingo Swann had altered a magnetometer. This, said Panati, is something "no magician would dare to claim he could duplicate." (Although Panati admits he is totally ignorant of conjuring methods, he is quick to tell magicians what they can't do.) Why not call an international conference of eminent physicists and let them witness Swann perform this miracle? Would it not hit them all like a "sledgehammer blow"?

Arthur Koestler thought the suggestion excellent. But immediately the paraphysicists began to toss cold water on the idea. If any of the observing scientists are skeptics, warned Costa de Beauregard, "the demonstration will come out zero." Walker allowed that Swann's magnetometer feat was closer to being *the* definitive demonstration than any other he knew, but he reminded everybody that he had once seen Uri Geller try to perform for skeptics at Berkeley, and because their wills kept reducing wave packets the wrong way, Geller could do nothing. The final blow to Panati's innocent plan was struck by Targ in a memorable sentence. "Even if Geller walked on the water from Berkeley to San Francisco," said Targ, "skeptics would simply say, Oh, that's the old walking-on-the-water trick."

So the familiar deadlock remains. Believers keep getting sensational results, skeptics keep failing to replicate them, and the believers keep invoking their old Catch 22 to explain the failures. Work like Forwald's, through which loopholes run like holes in Swiss cheese, seems never to fade from the literature. There is no indication that paraphysicists have the slightest desire to train themselves in the subtle arts of deception, or seek the aid of knowledgeable magicians in any significant way. As a result, they continue to act like excited little children every time a new psychic charlatan shows them a trick they can't explain. In the report of the conference on QM and psi, there are numerous favorable references to Geller.[15] Not one person who spoke at the conference, least of all Walker, questioned Uri's psychic powers.

It looks as if Panati will have a long wait for that sledgehammer blow. In the meantime, paraphysicists would be well advised to stop rushing about pretending to be Martin Luther, nailing new paradigms on laboratory doors. They would do better to have Sherlock Holmes's advice that opened this chapter emblazoned on large shields and nailed above their own laboratory entrances.

5

Astrology

GEORGE O. ABELL

In its September/October 1975 issue, The Humanist *carried a statement signed by 186 leading scientists, including 18 Nobel laureates,
expressing concern over the widespread public acceptance of astrology.
Among the many grounds on which astrologers criticized the statement
is the charge that the signing scientists knew nothing about astrology!
Actually, quite a number had studied astrology in considerable depth,
and even those who had not did have enough knowledge of the subject
to challenge its basic assumptions.*

*One signer who has studied astrology for two decades is UCLA as-
tronomer George O. Abell. He has read widely on the subject, written
many articles, and engaged in a number of tests of astrological predictions. On radio and television programs he has frequently met and
debated with astrologers, including Sydney Omarr, Carl Payne Tobey,
Neill Marbell, Carroll Righter, and others. Abell has thus become quite
familiar with the arguments defending astrology and attempting to justify belief in it. In the following essay he reviews what astrology is, how
it works, and the status of its scientific basis.*

Astrology is far more than a harmless recreation; it is big business. In
the United States alone there are an estimated ten thousand profes-

sional astrologers, whose fees for a single session average from twenty-five to fifty dollars, but in some instances run up to hundreds of dollars, and most clients return for many sessions. Add to these "professional" fees the income from mail-order computer-horoscope merchants, newspaper astrology columns, radio and television spots and panel discussions on astrology, courses offered in many colleges and schools, astrology schools and astrologically based churches, and astrology books, to say nothing of charms, souvenirs, T-shirts, and the like, and it is easy to see that Americans spend billions of dollars each year on astrology. Moreover, it influences business decisions, the judgments of many legislators, hiring preferences, and even medical treatment. With such enormous stakes at issue, astrology deserves close scrutiny.

In part the belief in astrology stems from the existence of obvious cosmic influences: Certainly the sun provides our energy and brings the seasons. The moon also gives light and is mainly responsible for the tides. In addition, it is the focus of a wide range of alleged cosmic influences. In the short essay that follows his discussion of astrology, Abell explores a number of popular myths concerning the effects of the moon on human behavior.

I am a Pisces with Scorpio rising. The first part of that statement means Pisces is my sun sign. Almost everybody knows his sun sign, but not necessarily what it means. In my case, it means that the sun was within a sector of the sky called the sign of Pisces. As the earth goes around the sun we see the sun from different directions in our orbit, so that during the year the sun appears to trace out a path in the sky, called the ecliptic. The eighteen-degrees-wide belt around the sky centered on the ecliptic is called the zodiac, which is divided into twelve equal parts, or signs. Pisces is just one of them. During the year the sun passes through all twelve signs, and your sun sign is simply the sector or sign of the zodiac the sun was in when you were born.

The division of the zodiac into twelve signs is a completely arbitrary invention of the Babylonians (the Egyptians, for example, divided the sun's path into thirty-six divisions). The signs have the same names as the twelve star groupings, or constellations, distributed around the sky roughly along the ecliptic. But the positions of the signs do not coincide with those of the constellations of the same names. They did coincide about two thousand years ago when they were named, but because of the arbitrary way the signs are defined, they have been forced to slip westward about thirty degrees since then because of precession, a slow motion of the earth's axis of rotation. Today, the sign of Pisces is roughly aligned with the constellation of Aquarius.

The constellations, by the way, are not groups of stars actually clustered together in space; stars are extremely remote suns, all at different distances from earth. The constellations are just apparent configurations named by the ancients to honor people, animals, or significant objects in their mythology. Most primitive peoples named star groupings in this way, but of course different peoples selected entirely different configurations of stars. So the constellations are just as arbitrary as the zodiacal signs.

To say that "I am a Pisces" does not mean that I was born *under* Pisces, or Aquarius, in the sense that either was overhead at Los Angeles, where I was born, on March 1, 1927. Both Aquarius and Pisces are up in the daytime in early March, but I was born at 10:50 P.M., and they were both below the horizon then.

The statement "I have Scorpio rising" means that Scorpio was the sign corresponding to the part of the sky just appearing at the eastern horizon when I was born. But because of precession, that part of the sky now contains the constellation Libra. Thus, although all signs and constellations contain stars—some bright and some faint—there was nothing particularly special about the stars that were either just rising or just passing overhead at the moment of my birth, and none of them had anything to do with Pisces or Scorpio.

Then what significance can there be to the fact that I am a "Pisces with Scorpio rising"? Those who believe in astrology believe that these are two of the most important factors determining my character and the course of my life. Moreover, according to my polls and my colleagues', about a third of the people in the United States and Western Europe believe in astrology. And at least 90 percent are "open minded," meaning they do not dismiss astrology as outmoded or nonsense, as they would dismiss the idea of a flat earth.

Why, in an age of advanced technology, should so many people still cling to an ancient belief? In part, it must be because astrology purports to tell us something about ourselves, and all of us are interested in ourselves. Many of my colleagues have suggested that acceptance of astrology is also in part a rejection of the traditional scientific disciplines and in part a response to a psychological need for a belief to replace the traditional religions that many people are turning away from. More important, though, I think it is because astrology is presented as if it were a science by its modern practitioners, and many people are misled by this.

In fact, astrology was never a science. It is not a hypothesis or theory developed to describe natural phenomena or the results of experiments or observations, and until fairly recent times there was no attempt to test or verify the predictions of astrology. Astrology developed at a time when the earth was believed to be composed of four elements—earth, air, fire, and water—and the heavens of a different crystalline material, perfect and immutable. The planets themselves were variously thought to be gods, abodes of gods, or at least manifestations of gods. Astrology is the polytheistic religion of ancient Babylonia and Greece and is based on a symbolism—a magical correspondence between the gods and the planets that bear the same names.

Astrology could not, of course, have seemed as incredible to the ancients as it does to us. The role of the sun in influencing our daily and yearly lives is obvious; it was a natural extension to attribute other powers to the other planets as well. It wasn't until the time of Newton that we understood that the laws of nature apply to the celestial worlds as well as to the terrestrial one. During antiquity, however, all great scholars believed in astrology.

Astrology began approximately three thousand years ago in Babylonia with what we call today *mundane* astrology; it was applied to monarchs and kingdoms, but not to individuals. Astrology spread in the sixth century B.C. as far east as India, where it flourishes today. The Egyptians, meanwhile, developed their own kind of astrology. But the astrology now practiced in Europe and America is that developed by the Greeks, who synthesized the ideas of the Babylonians and Egyptians and enriched them with concepts from their own fertile imaginations.

To understand how astrology works, we should first take a quick look at the sky. Although the stars are at enormous distances, they do indeed give the impression of being affixed to the inner surface of a great hollow sphere surrounding the earth. Ancient people, in fact, literally believed in the existence of such a celestial sphere. As the earth spins on its axis, the celestial sphere appears to turn about us each day, pivoting at points on a line with the earth's axis of rotation. This daily turning of the sphere carries the stars around the sky, causing most of them to rise and set, but they, and the constellations they define, maintain fixed patterns on the sphere, just as the continent of Australia maintains its shape on a spinning globe of the earth. Thus the stars were called *fixed* stars.

The motion of the sun along the ecliptic is, of course, merely a reflection of the revolution of the earth around the sun. But the ancients believed the earth was fixed and the sun had an independent motion of its own, eastward among the stars. The glare of sunlight hides the stars in daytime, but the ancients were aware that the stars were up there even as they are at night, and the slow eastward motion of the sun around the sky, at the rate of about thirty degrees each month, caused different stars to be visible at night at different times of the year.

The moon, revolving around the earth each month, also has an independent motion in the sky. The moon, however, changes its position relatively rapidly. Although it appears to rise and set each day, as does nearly everything else in the sky, we can see the moon changing position with respect to the background of stars during as short an interval as an hour or so. The moon's path around the earth lies nearly in the same plane as the earth's path around the sun (it is tilted at only about five degrees), so the moon is never seen very far from the ecliptic in the sky. There are five other objects visible to the naked eye that also appear to move with respect to the fixed background of stars on the celestial sphere. These are the planets Mercury, Venus, Mars, Jupiter, and Saturn. All of them revolve around the sun in nearly the same plane as the earth does, so they, like the moon, always appear near the ecliptic. Because we see the planets from the moving earth, however, they behave in a complicated way, with their apparent motions on the celestial sphere reflecting both their own independent motions around the sun and our motion as well.

Today we know the sun as a star typical of the myriads of others in the sky, and the moon as a satellite of the earth; we know that the other planets are worlds much like the earth. To the ancients, however, the sun, moon, and other planets all had one thing in common that distinguished them from the fixed stars: they changed positions gradually among the stars during the days, months, and years. Thus the sun, moon, and other planets visible to the naked eye were all called planets in antiquity (the word *planet* is Greek for *wanderer*). So there were the fixed stars and the wandering stars. Although the planets, or wandering stars, had independent motions that in some cases were quite complex, even the ancients recognized a regularity in those motions.

The Greek gods were immortal but otherwise had the same attributes of anger, happiness, jealousy, rage, and pleasure as we do. These attributes were assigned to the planets that either were the gods, were their abodes, or represented them. Each god, and thus each planet, served as a center of force, but how that force prevailed depended on how it was tempered by the effects of other gods.

Now, if the gods' whims were capricious, at least the planets were potentially predictable in their movements. Because our own lot in life is so unpredictable, it must be purely at the mercy of the gods. But if the gods are the planets, or at least somehow associated with them, then we have only to learn the rules of the motions of the planets to understand the whims of the gods and how they shape our own lives.

Thus, as the Greek astronomers learned more about the motions of the planets in the sky they felt they were learning more about the ruling forces of their own lives as well. The Greeks had the prophetic wisdom to suppose that the motions of the planets are indeed governed by some precise laws of nature—perhaps transcending even the will of their all-too-human gods—and thus by inference they presumed that our own lives are similarly programed by the predictable motions of the planets. What then can determine our own individual fates? Only the moment when we happen to enter the world and fall into step with the eternal and predestined movements of the heavens.

So the belief developed that each of our lives is preordained by the precise configuration of all the planets in the sky at the moment of our birth. All the motions of the planets thereafter follow the laws of nature, and hence the influence of the planet-gods must similarly be constrained. This is *natal* astrology; it was invented by the Greeks in the first few centuries before Christ.

The key to natal astrology is the map or chart (called a natal horoscope) that indicates the direction of the planets in the sky as seen from the earth at the time and place of one's birth. The first natal horoscope prepared or cast by Greek astrologers was probably not earlier than the third century B.C. It is a simple matter for an astronomer to observe the current directions of stars and planets, but it is usually more difficult to prepare such a chart for some time in the past when an individual was born, or for a time in the future when it might be desirable to know how the ruling forces will then shape his life. In order to do that it was necessary for the Greek astrologers to know how the planets moved—that is, to have some astronomical scheme so they could compute those directions for any time in the past or future. A strong motivation for the development of Greek astronomy was, therefore, the study of the motions of the planets. That study culminated in the elaborate scheme of Ptolemy in the second century A.D. It is beyond the scope of this essay to describe the earth-centered Ptolemaic cosmology, but it was a remarkable achievement and served to predict the motions of the planets as they were observed by the naked eye for hundreds of years. It was not substantially revised until the time of Copernicus. Thus the Greeks had devised a means of preparing horoscopes for times in the past or future.

Two different kinds of measurement are used in a horoscope. The first involves the zodiac, that belt around the sky centered on the ecliptic through which the sun, moon, and planets all appear to move with respect to the stars (see page 77). One reference point in the zodiac is the position of the sun on the first day of spring, when its path along the ecliptic carries it across the celestial equator from the southern half of the sky to the northern half. That point is called the vernal equinox. Obviously, the position of the sun on the ecliptic with respect to the vernal equinox determines the season of the year.

The ancients, as we have seen, divided the zodiac into twelve equal sectors or signs. The first sign begins with the vernal equinox and extends thirty degrees eastward along the zodiac. It is called the sign of Aries. The vernal equinox, at the beginning of this sign, is the first point of Aries. The next thirty-degree sector along the zodiac is the second sign—the sign of Taurus. The subsequent zodiacal signs in order to the east are Gemini, Cancer, Leo, Virgo, Libra, Scorpio, Sagittarius, Capricorn, Aquarius, and Pisces. All but Libra (the scales) are named for animals or people; *zodiac* comes from the Greek word for animals.

At any given time each planet occupies a particular position in one of the zodiacal signs. For example, if the date is between March 21 and April 20, the sun is in the sign of Aries. If you were born during this period your sun sign is said to be Aries. Each of the other planets also has a position that can be specified both by the sign it occupies and by its location in that sign, measured in degrees from the western boundary of that sign. Thus, in the preparation of a horoscope the first task is to assign each planet to its proper position in the zodiac. Today modern astrologers do this by consulting standard tables. Few are able to calculate from theory where the planets should be in the zodiac,

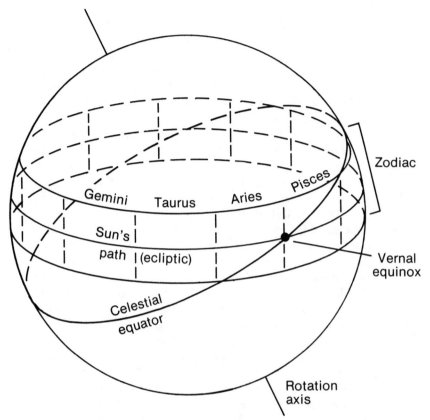

The celestial sphere. The celestial equator (equator of the sky) and the sun's path (ecliptic) are shown. The belt around the sky centered on the ecliptic is the zodiac, and some of its even divisions, called signs, are shown.

but the ancient astrologers were astronomers as well and hence were very competent at this task.

Specifying the locations of the planets in the various parts of the zodiac tells where they are with respect to the fixed background of stars, but does not give their directions in the sky as seen from a particular place, because the sky constantly appears to be turning, due to the earth's rotation. On the other hand, if we know the precise direction of the vernal equinox with respect to the horizon and also the latitude of the place, we can specify the orientation of the zodiac with respect to the horizon, thereby giving the directions in the sky as well. This orientation is accomplished through a knowledge of sidereal time. Sidereal time is simply a measure of how far the vernal equinox has progressed since it passed from the eastern to the western half of the sky—that is, across the meridian, a north–south line running through the observer's zenith. Once the location in the sky of the vernal equinox (or sidereal time) is known, the positions of all the signs and hence of the planets are specified with respect to the horizon.

The second measurement used in astrology has the purpose of orienting the planets and signs with respect to the horizon. It is the system of astrological *houses*, which are zones of the sky fixed with respect to the horizon. As the celestial sphere rotates, all the signs and planets are carried successively through the twelve houses distributed around the sky. The first house is that sector of the sky immediately beneath the eastern horizon; it contains those parts of the celestial sphere that will rise within approximately the next two hours. The second house is the next one below the first; the third through sixth houses are the remaining ones below the horizon, the sixth containing objects that have set within the past two hours. Houses seven through twelve stretch across the upper half of the sky from west to east (see page 79). This description is more vague than it may appear because several precise but different definitions of the boundaries between houses have been used by astrologers throughout the ages, and continue to be used today.

A complete horoscope is usually represented by a circle denoting the center of the zodiac (the ecliptic) with the twelve houses indicated as sectors inside the circle. The signs and their boundaries are also located on the horoscope, as well as the positions of the seven planets. Sometimes the positions of the more conspicuous stars of the zodiac are indicated as well. Page 80 shows my own horoscope. It is a chart of the directions of the planets with respect to the vernal equinox and also with respect to the horizon as they appeared from Los Angeles on March 1, 1927, at 10:50 P.M.

The pie-shaped divisions numbered from 1 to 12 are the various houses. The planet Saturn, symbolized by ♄ , was in the first house. Notice that the eastern horizon intercepted the ecliptic in the sign of Scorpio; thus Scorpio was rising in my natal horoscope. The sun, in the fourth house, was in the sign of Pisces. Also in Pisces were the planets Jupiter (♃), Mercury (☿), and Uranus (♅).

The planets Uranus, Neptune, and Pluto were discovered after the invention of the telescope and thus played no role in Greek astrology.

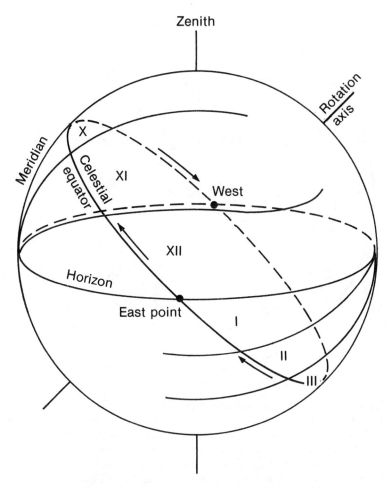

Zenith

Rotation axis

Meridian

Celestial equator

X

XI

West

XII

Horizon

East point

I

II

III

As the earth rotates, the celestial sphere appears to rotate about imaginary points in the sky called the celestial poles. Objects, as they rise, move across the sky and set, eventually rise again, and pass through stationary regions of the sky called houses (here labeled with roman numerals).

Modern astrologers include them in the horoscope with the traditional planets. The alleged influences of the newly discovered planets are just those you would expect for gods of the same name, as their influences are based on symbolism and magical correspondences.

Note that my horoscope shows, in addition to the position of each planet in its sign, the location in each zodiacal sign of the boundary

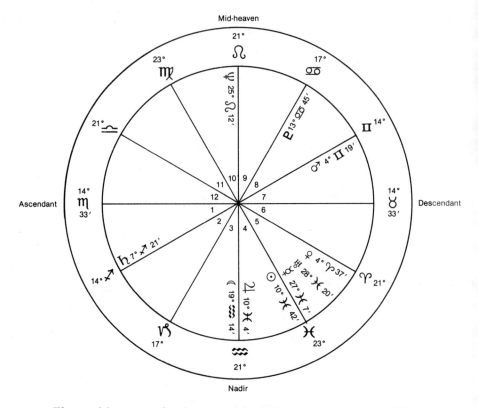

The natal horoscope of a skeptical astrologer born at Los Angeles, California, on March 1, 1927, at 10:50 P.M. The pie-shaped divisions are the houses. The symbols in the outer circle are the signs of the zodiac, and the numbers indicate the positions in the signs corresponding to the boundaries (cusps) between houses. The positions of the planets in their respective houses are indicated by the symbols for the planets, and beside the symbol for each planet is indicated the sign that that planet occupied and its position within that sign. (In this horoscope the house boundaries are calculated according to the system of Placidius.)

between each pair of houses. All of these numerical details give the horoscope a somewhat complicated appearance, but it is straightforward to construct it. (I have used the definition of house boundaries given by Placidius.) The astrologer need only interpret my horoscope to learn about my characteristics, my personality, my friendships, my health, my death, my marriages, and all other events of my life.

According to astrologers, a person's entire horoscope must be examined to analyze his character. Thus the column entitled "Your Daily

Horoscope" that appears in daily newspapers is not a horoscope at all, but simply daily advice based on your sun sign alone. According to astrologer Sydney Omarr, advice based on one's sun sign is about as useful as taking a patent medicine; it may be of "some value" but can hardly be considered "definitive."

In addition to the sun sign, other important things in the horoscope include the ascendant (what is about to rise), what is culminating (what is about to cross from the eastern to the western half of the sky), and a host of other things. Since according to astrology each planet is a center of force, and because each sign is ruled by a planet, the influence of that planet is amplified or weakened according to whether it is in its own sign or in one sympathetic with the sign it rules. *Aspects* are important, too—for example, what planets are trine (about 120° away from each other), or in opposition (opposite in the sky), or squared (90° away), and so on.

In addition, each house plays a certain role in the make-up of a person's character; so the planets (and signs) in the various houses play key roles. For example, the first house (just below the eastern horizon) controls temperament and personality. Mars, the aggressive god of war, in that house might dispose one to an aggressive career (perhaps military or athletic), especially if Aries, the sign that Mars rules, is also rising and hence is in that first house. The second house is supposed to relate to one's wealth and fortune, the third to siblings, the fourth to parents, and so on. The planet in the eighth house, which deals with death, might tell the astrologer how the subject will die.

As an example of how a horoscope might be analyzed, let us again look at page 80 and consider some of the features of my horoscope. Because the sun was in Pisces when I was born, I am a Pisces, which means that I am nebulous, indecisive, and very impressionable. But I am also compassionate and want to relieve suffering; this is why I would make an excellent physician. The first house, which controls my personality and temperament, contains part of the sign of Scorpio (in the ascendant), which indicates intensity and passionateness. Also part of Sagittarius, containing Saturn, is in the first house, and Saturn implies conservatism and limitation. Thus I have the free, open tendency of a Sagittarius in my make-up but am tempered by the limitations of Saturn; all this gives me a great sense of responsibility and a penchant for choosing long-term studies. The tenth house, dealing with my career, contains the planet Neptune, associated with cloudiness and indecisiveness. This would suggest that my career would have many changes during my life, except that the sign of Leo is also there

and Leo brings power and creativity. Thus my career of many voca-
tions should at least be a creative one.

The seventh house of my horoscope contains Mars, and the sign of
Gemini. A characteristic of Gemini is communication, and of Mars,
energy and initiative, and the seventh house deals with marriage.
Consequently I can be expected to be a good talker, writer, and com-
municator, and to have a good attitude toward marriage. (I like this
analysis.) Notice that Venus, in the sign of Aries, is in my fifth house.
Venus is the love goddess and brings harmony and unison; Aries, on
the other hand, is assertive and has a sense of urgency; thus I am ar-
dent in my passions, and because the fifth house deals with pleasure
and sexual affairs, I must be quite a swinger. (I should have read my
horoscope when I was younger.) The fourth house of my horoscope,
dealing with my parents, contains the sun, bringing happiness and
power, and also Jupiter, bringing in addition an expansive characteristic. The sun in conjunction with (in the same direction as) Jupiter
brings optimism and generosity; but these planets are also in Pisces,
which suggests humbleness and compassion. All of this, I suspect,
points to a fine set of family relations. Moreover, the moon, in
Aquarius, in the third house (the house that deals with siblings)
suggests that I will have a good elder sibling (but I was an only child).

Some of the aspects of my horoscope are also interesting. The sun
in conjunction with Jupiter creates optimism and generosity. Moreover, the sun is trine (120° away from) the ascendant, which accentu-
ates all the effects of the sun. Mercury and Venus are also in conjunction, suggesting a charm in my use of language. And—perhaps most
interesting of all—Venus is sextile (60° away from) Mars, which combines the affection and warmth of Venus with the passion of Mars,
making me a very sexy person. Unfortunately, however, Uranus is also
sextile with Mars, which bodes sudden changes; evidently I must be a
pervert.

And so it goes. There is an enormous number of rules for interpret-
ing horoscopes, not all of which are used or even known by all astrologers. Many give conflicting results; that is where the "art" of the astrologer comes into play—weighing the various influences and selecting
those that seem most important.

Needless to say, the analysis is usually most successful when carried
out on the horoscope of a person who is well known. Thus, in various
astrology publications, we can find very enlightened analyses of the
horoscopes of Marilyn Monroe, former President Nixon, and Charles
de Gaulle. But it would be a mistake to suppose that the analyses are

completely random. Although some astrologers do, in fact, completely fabricate their "analyses" from their imaginations, the "legitimate" practitioners really do follow, or attempt to follow, the rules handed down from antiquity. If several different astrologers analyze the horoscope of the same individual (one who is unknown to them), there may be many conflicting, and sometimes rather amusingly different, opinions in various details, but there generally will also be a certain measure of agreement. My own horoscope has been analyzed by nearly a score of different astrologers, and there are indeed certain trends of agreement that run through all the analyses. For example, most of the astrologers agree that I have a penchant for a career in medicine, that my first marriage was at age twenty-four, and that I have a talent for communication. The latter may, of course, have been suggested from the fact that I was known to all of the astrologers as a professor and a person who has published a number of articles and books. But the first two predictions, and others, were based on the traditional analysis of my horoscope. A few, by chance, happened to be correct; I was, for example, first married when I was twenty-four.

As a person goes on living, the earth goes on turning and the planets go on moving through the zodiac. The astrologer, by keeping track of these motions and always relating them to the client's natal horoscope, believes he can foretell times of significant events in the subject's life, what times are happy ones for the subject, what ones good for important journeys, and even when the subject may suffer calamities or death.

Moreover, each sign of the zodiac is presumed to relate to a given part of the body; thus Aries rules the head, Leo the heart, Cancer the stomach, Scorpio the genitals, and Pisces the feet. Mars in the sign of Aries in the natal horoscope might predispose the subject to a tendency toward headaches all his life, and Uranus in Cancer might plague him with stomach cramps. In the Middle Ages most physicians believed in and practiced according to this medical astrology. Even today, astrologer Noel Tyl claims that doctors frequently consult him for help in diagnoses.

The zodiacal signs were also associated with hot and cold, wet and dry, and the assumed elements: earth, air, fire, and water. The planets were associated with various metals—the sun with gold, the moon with silver, Mercury with quicksilver, and so on. Even nations were thought to be ruled by signs and planets. Not only were individual characteristics of people (such as stature, color of hair, and eye color) attributed to details of their horoscopes, but also these characteristics of entire races, according to the signs and planets assigned them.

The rules by which the astrologer analyzes the horoscope—that is, the influences that he must weigh—go back to antiquity. But they are not based on statistical studies of thousands of individuals, as some astrologers would have us believe. Statistics had not even been invented in those days. Rather they are based on symbolism—magical correspondences between planets and gods that bear the same name, and the animals or beings for which those zodiacal signs or constellations are named. To verify this assertion, one need only go back to the principal authoritative document of antiquity—the *Tetrabiblos* of Ptolemy. Ptolemy was one of the greatest astronomers of antiquity and also the most important astrologer. He summarized the astrological knowledge of his time in the four books that are now the primary source of modern astrology. Traditional astrological doctrines are almost entirely based on the *Tetrabiblos* or on subsequent works that were in turn based on it. In the *Tetrabiblos*, we can read of the effect of Jupiter passing through the tail of the lion, or of Mars in Virgo. But Ptolemy himself evidently saw a rationale for some of these influences. Thus we read that the moon, being the nearest planet to the earth, soaks up moisture from the earth and so has a dampening influence. Further, we read that Mars, being the planet nearest the sun (as was thought according to the Ptolemaic cosmology), was hot and arid and so had a drying influence. Saturn, being far from the earth and sun, was cold; it moved slowly and so was mystical in its influence. (Incidentally, we know today that the moon is bone dry but that Mars has a good deal of water—although currently frozen as permafrost or in ice caps at the poles.)

Astrologers do not all insist that one's entire life is absolutely dictated by the motions of the planets. Many modern astrologers say that the stars impel but do not compel. Even Ptolemy acknowledged three influences on people: environment, heredity, and astrology. Yet some of the more orthodox astrologers still argue that the entire course of one's life is dictated in detail by the motions of the planets through the zodiac; if only we understood the influences and laws thoroughly enough, they think, the entire course of one's life could be forecast with precision.

Not only does the earth rotate on its axis and revolve around the sun, but it has other motions as well. As mentioned earlier, one of these—discovered by the astronomer Hipparchus in the second century B.C.—is precession. The earth is not a perfect sphere but because of its rotation is slightly bulged at the equator. This bulge makes the earth's equatorial diameter exceed that through the poles by only twenty-seven miles; nevertheless, the gravitational tidal forces of the sun and moon pulling on that equatorial bulge attempt to alter the direction of the earth's axis of rotation. Under the influence of that pull, the earth acts like a spinning top or gyroscope, with its axis describing the slow conical motion we call precession, described earlier. The result is that the positions of the celestial poles are not fixed on a celestial sphere, but describe circular motions in the sky, taking about twenty-six thousand years for one complete cycle. It is a tribute to Hipparchus that he was able to discover this subtle motion. An effect of precession is to cause the vernal equinox to slide westward along the ecliptic during that same twenty-six-thousand-year period. The result is that the signs of the zodiac are slowly sliding westward with respect to the constellations that bear the same names. That is why the sign of Aries no longer corresponds with the constellation Aries, but with the constellation Pisces. Rather soon now, the vernal equinox will have slid all the way through Pisces and into the constellation Aquarius. That is when the Age of Aquarius is said to begin, although the exact time of this occurrence depends on what boundary one chooses between the several constellations. Ancient charts are noncommittal and the modern constellation boundaries date back only to 1928, when they were arbitrarily assigned by the International Astronomical Union.

It is a mistake to accuse astrologers of being ignorant of precession; indeed Hipparchus, its discoverer, was an astrologer as well as an astronomer, and Ptolemy understood the motion very well (except for its physical cause). Nevertheless, the traditional or classical school of astrology practiced in the West is based not on the fixed constellations but on the moving signs. The rationale, I think, is that the seasons depend on the sun's position in the zodiac with respect to the equinoxes and solstices, which slide westward with the signs, and have nothing really to do with the position of the sun among the various constellations. This conventional school of astrology is called tropical astrology.

There is a school, however, called sidereal astrology, that bases its horoscope upon the constellations and not the moving signs. Sidereal astrology is widely practiced in some Eastern countries, and there is a growing cult of it in the western United States. I suppose sidereal astrologers feel that it is more logical to associate the planets with the constellations rather than with the arbitrary division of signs. Some tropical astrologers counter that the signs remember the influence of the constellations that corresponded with them two thousand years ago. I don't know how they explain why those same signs do not also recall the influence of other constellations that corresponded with them in even earlier millennia.

The Dark Ages saw a decline in the influence of astrology because it clearly conflicted with the Church's view of free will. However, astrology had a resurgence during the Renaissance, and by the time of the Reformation nearly all scholars believed in astrology and many universities had chairs in the subject. The great astronomers Tycho Brahe and Johannes Kepler evidently believed in astrology and both cast and interpreted horoscopes as a major part of their duties.

Following the astronomical discoveries of Kepler, however, science gradually turned away from astrology. We had learned that the planets not only obey precise laws but that these are the same laws that govern things here on earth. We found that the earth and the planets were made of the same stuff—the same kinds of atoms. Science in a sense unified the universe. Moreover, we learned that there were many thousands of times as many worlds, even in this solar system, as had been supposed by the ancients, to say nothing of the countless numbers of planets that must revolve around other stars, planets that we may never know about. We learned of the tremendous distances to the planets, and that many have satellites of their own; that the stars are suns, and that our sun is but one star in a vast galaxy of stars. In the light of this new knowledge of the true nature of the universe, and the truly universal laws that govern its behavior, the belief in the planet-gods of antiquity seemed as incredible as the notion of spontaneous generation—that rats and mice are generated spontaneously in dirty laundry—or that fortunes can be told from the entrails of animals.

Thus scientists turned away from astrology by the time of Newton and never turned back. We would think that in the twentieth century a belief in such an ancient religion would stretch the credibility of even the most gullible among us. And yet, not only do tens of millions of Americans believe in astrology, but many regulate their lives according to it. Why is this so?

Partly it is because of the increased specialization of science. As the frontier of knowledge is pushed forward, science has become more and more complex and scientists themselves increasingly specialized. Every new subbranch of science develops its own jargon, each of which is incomprehensible to the nonscientist and, indeed, even to scientists in other disciplines. Consider the following terms: deceleration parameter, trine, progression, Robertson-Walker metric, rectification, Hubble constant, periastron, cusp, spicule, refraction, ascendant. How is the average person to know which of these terms are scientific and which relate to astrology? How, indeed, can he know what is science and what is not?

Is there any scientific basis for astrology? I have met astrologers in television debates who have claimed that tidal forces exerted on people by planets can influence them. "Consider the lunar tides on the oceans," they say. "If the moon can raise tides of several feet in the waters of the ocean, think what it can do to the fluids in our own bodies." The lunar pull on the oceans is, however, acting over the entire eight-thousand-mile diameter of the earth; on a small object like a human being it is negligible. Planetary forces are enormously smaller yet. The book you are now reading, held arm's length away from you, exerts about one billion times as strong a tidal force on you as Mars does when Mars is at its nearest to the earth.

Astrologers also talk about radiation from the planets. One form of radiation is light. But babies are generally born indoors, shielded from light from the planets. Even all the light of all the planets combined is millions of times less than even subtle variations of the total light output of the sun.

An astrologer once told me that we astronomers only recently learned of the bursts of radio radiation from Jupiter. "Surely," he said, "those radio bursts must exert profound radiation effects on us humans." But those radio waves from Jupiter are very, very weak by the time they reach the earth, and we discovered them only when we had learned to build enormous radio telescopes capable of detecting them. On the other hand, even a small pocket-size transistor radio can easily pick up the waves from a hundred-watt transmitter a hundred miles away. The radiation from manmade radio and television transmitters all around us swamps by many hundreds of millions of times that from the planets.

Magnetic fields similarly play no role. We could not even have known of the magnetism of certain planets until we sent delicate mag-

netometers on space vehicles to the vicinity of those planets. The magnetic field of the permanent magnet in the loudspeaker of that same
transistor radio is enormously strong in comparison with such magnetism.

In short, there is no way in terms of known laws of nature that the
planets' directions in the sky can influence human personality and fortune in the manner predicted by astrology. If the planets were to exert
an influence on us, it would have to be through an unknown force
and one with very strange properties: it would have to emanate from
some but not all celestial bodies, have to affect some but not all things
on earth, and its strength could not depend on the distances, masses,
or other characteristics of those planets giving rise to it. In other
words, it would lack the universality, order, and harmony found for
every other force and natural law ever discovered that applies in the
real universe.

What evidence is there that such a force exists? The astrologers answer, "Astrology works," and I must acknowledge that most people who
have their horoscopes analyzed by an astrologer say that the descriptions they receive of themselves are accurate. However, the descriptions are generally rather vague and sometimes contradictory, and they
almost always reveal a good grasp of human psychology on the part of
the analyzer. Among the many experiments concerning people's surprise at the success of the astrologer, I shall describe only one especially interesting one.

In a test of the computerized horoscope industry, the French psychologist Michel Gauquelin (see the Bibliography) sent ten sets of
birth dates, times, and places to a major advertiser. In order not to
reveal who he was, he used the addresses of various friends. The birth
data were genuine but were not of himself or his friends; they were
the birth times and places of the ten most heinous criminals for whom
he could find records. One of these, Dr. Marcel Petiot, was born in
Auxerre at 3 A.M. on January 17, 1898. He was executed on May 26,
1946, after a spectacular trial. He had posed as an underground agent
promising to help refugees from the Nazis escape occupied France.
When the unfortunates would arrive at Petiot's home, with all of their
money and most prized possessions, he would murder them and dis-
solve their bodies in quicklime in a secret chamber of his house. Although indicted for only twenty-seven such murders, Dr. Petiot, cyni-
cal to the end, boasted of sixty-three. His horoscope said, in part:

As he is a Virgo-Jovian, instinctive warmth or power is allied with the resources of the intellect, lucidity, wit. . . . He may appear as someone who submits himself to social norms, fond of property, and endowed with a moral sense which is comforting—that of a worthy, right-thinking, middle-class citizen. . . . The subject tends to belong wholeheartedly to the Venusian side. His emotional life is in the forefront—his affection towards others, his family ties, his home, his intimate circle . . . sentiments . . . which usually find their expression in total devotion to others, redeeming love, or altruistic sacrifices . . . a tendency to be more pleasant in one's own home, to love one's house, to enjoy having a charming home.

Next Gauquelin placed an advertisement in a Paris newspaper offering: "Completely Free! Your ultra-personal horoscope; a ten page document. Take advantage of this unique opportunity. Send name, address, date and birthplace . . ."

There were about 150 replies. To each correspondent Gauquelin sent the same horoscope—the one he had received for Dr. Petiot. With each he sent a self-addressed envelope and questionnaire asking about the accuracy of the reading. Ninety-four percent of the respondents said they recognized themselves (that is, they said they were accurately portrayed in the horoscope of a man who murdered several dozen people and dissolved their bodies in quicklime), and for 90 percent this positive opinion was shared by their families and friends.

In a recent monumental compendium, *Recent Advances in Natal Astrology*, Geoffrey Dean, of Perth, Australia (who lists himself as an analytical chemist, science writer, and astrologer), surveys more than a thousand books and journal articles on astrology published in the past three-quarters of a century. Dean considers almost every imaginable subject, and many topics only peripherally related to it, related to natal astrology. He was assisted by more than fifty people in the compilation of his book. Dean reveals an excellent background in mathematics, statistics, and practical and spherical astronomy. The technical level of the book is beyond that of any other I have seen by astrologers. It is not intended as an introduction for the lay person but as a resource for astrological investigations.

After reviewing hundreds of experiments and statistical studies, Dean concludes that there is no significant evidence for a single prediction of traditional astrology as regards signs, houses, and planets. Although not precisely intended as such, the book is an effective debunker of traditional astrology. But Dean, like many modern astrologers, is impressed by what he regards to be possibly significant evidence for cosmic influences, especially those suggested by Nelson and Gauquelin, described later. (They are not, however, the sort of influences predicted by traditional astrology.)

First, though, let us consider some obvious cosmic influences on man. The apparent rotation of the celestial sphere gives us day and night, with sleepfulness and wakefulness. The motion of the earth around the sun, combined with the obliquity of the ecliptic, are responsible for the seasons, on which depend weather, growth of vegetation, and other phenomena. The moon, and to a lesser extent the sun, causes the tides. And many organisms have developed biological rhythms related to day and night, the tides, and the seasons. These effects are, however, explicable in terms of well-understood science, without recourse to unknown laws or ancient magic.

There may, of course, be other cosmic effects yet to be discovered, and possibly some may not be understandable within the framework of known physical laws. It would be very exciting to learn of these; indeed, it is for such discoveries that Nobel Prizes are awarded! But unexpected new discoveries, especially bizarre ones, require especially convincing evidence if they are to be generally accepted. The problem is that each year many thousands of experiments and observations are reported in the literature. Some are no doubt sound, but many, even by respected professional scientists, are carelessly performed, have inadequate controls, are carried out with biased techniques or selection of data, or occasionally even are fudged. It is a mistake, I think, to comb the scientific journals for surprising results of experiments of isolated investigators, and then to submit them as evidence that there are cosmic influences that cannot be explained by known scientific theory. Some may eventually be found to be right, but without thorough verification they are no more convincing than much of the astrological research that Dean rejects.

A particular risk is starting out wanting to corroborate a particular idea (say, cosmic influence) and therefore trying to correlate various sets of data in the search for something significant to support it. There is an old adage, "If ye search hard enough, ye shall find." But what is found may be correlations of poor or biased data, or of very few selected results that seem to be significant out of a very large number of trials. Out of every hundred random experiments (say, coin flipping) one can expect three or so results that would occur by chance only 3 percent of the time (say, obtaining only heads in five successive flips). But this is not meant as an argument for rejecting out of hand all possibility of cosmic influences; it is merely a caution that one must look very carefully at new results that seem particularly surprising in light of what is known about the universe.

Two studies that have been widely reported, especially in astrological publications, and that are discussed at length by Dean, are John Henry Nelson's study of the relation between planetary configurations and disturbances in the reception of high-frequency radio signals, and Michel Gauquelin's study of the positions of certain planets in the sky at the time of birth of noted individuals.

The disturbances in radio reception studied by Nelson are caused by charged particles from the sun perturbing the ionized layers in the earth's atmosphere, the particles themselves being ejected in especially large numbers during explosive events on the solar surface, called flares. The occurrence of solar flares has long been known to be correlated with sun spots and other phenomena that are part of the general pattern of magnetic activity on the sun. Nelson believes he has found statistical evidence that the flares are triggered when certain of the planets reach configurations in which they are at or near 0°, 90°, or 180° apart as seen from the sun. As far as I can determine, Nelson's work was brought to the attention of the general public by astrologer Sydney Omarr. In any case, astrologers have made the point that the traditional astrological idea that squares and oppositions between planets are associated with malefic events on earth seems to be verified by Nelson's findings. But the traditional squares and oppositions are geocentric, whereas Nelson's are heliocentric. When two planets are squared (ninety degrees apart) as seen from the sun, they generally *cannot* be squared as seen from the earth.

It is difficult to evaluate Nelson's work. One cannot, of course, prove a statistical correlation by invoking individual examples of success, as Nelson has done in his published papers. While he claims to have maintained an accuracy of almost 90 percent over several years in the predicting of radio disturbances, his forecasts also involve more conventional criteria besides planetary alignments; moreover, it is unclear how he counts a "hit" or a "miss." The forecasting center at the Space Environmental Services Center in Boulder, Colorado, informs me that they had informally evaluated Nelson's forecasts but found his categories of "hits" too broad to verify the accuracy of his techniques and have not found his methods useful.

Michel Gauquelin has personally carried out more statistical investigation than anyone else I know of to test traditional astrological predictions. In the process, he has analyzed the horoscopes of tens of thousands of individuals. In general, he has found no basis whatsoever for any effects on our lives of the positions of planets among the signs or houses and has long rejected traditional astrology as worthless. (His study of the analysis of machine-generated horoscopes was referred to earlier.) Gauquelin has found, however, what he believes to be significant tendencies for certain planets either to occupy or avoid two sectors of the sky at the time of birth of very successful professionals. These sectors are the one just above the eastern horizon and the one just west of the celestial meridian. When he analyzed the birth times of 3,647 scientists, for example, Gauquelin found that Saturn occupied one of the two critical sectors 704 times, as opposed to the 598 that would be expected by chance. For 3,458 successful military men, Jupiter figured in the critical sector 703 times, as against the 572 expected by chance. These differences are significant—although less so than might appear, because there are ten planets (including the sun and moon) and either can be over- or underrepresented in the critical sectors, giving twenty chances of finding the significant relation for each profession.

To date, Gauquelin's results have been critically investigated by others only for sports champions, for whose birth times Gauquelin finds Mars in the critical sectors more often than expected. For brevity, we will call this the "Mars effect." Gauquelin asked the Comité Para, a Belgian committee of scientists who have agreed to investigate apparently anomalous phenomena, to attempt to replicate the Mars effect. He helped the committee obtain data for about five hundred additional sports champions, and the committee obtained the same results that Gauquelin did for his original sample of about fifteen hundred. However, they criticized on technical grounds Gauquelin's procedure for calculating the expected frequencies, and therefore refused to endorse the findings. An independent test on a subset of Gauquelin's sample of two thousand sports champions, carried out by statistician Marvin Zelen, Paul Kurtz, and myself, confirmed that the Mars effect was marginally significant (at the 4 percent level) but that the significance would disappear if those athletes born in Paris were eliminated from the sample, and that the Mars effect did not appear at all for those born in Belgium. Subsequently, an independent sample of several hundred sports champions born in the United States was studied for the Mars effect, and the effect was found to be absent. While these findings are not encouraging, perhaps they are not devastating to Gauquelin's hypothesis.

Most scientists who have looked at either Nelson's or Gauquelin's studies are very skeptical that the results (especially Gauquelin's) can be generally correct, because such effects would be extremely difficult to explain in the context of known scientific theory. But this skepticism is not rejection; it merely means that extraordinary evidence is required to support extraordinary claims. If either Nelson or Gauquelin should turn out to be correct, it would be extremely important and very exciting, for it would suggest unknown effects at work in the solar system. But, and I emphasize this point strongly, even if Nelson or Gauquelin is correct, their studies have nothing whatsoever to do with traditional astrology—as they themselves have emphasized. When people consult astrologers to have their horoscopes cast and analyzed, or seek advice from astrological literature, or even consult daily astrology columns published in newspapers, they are applying traditional astrology based on symbolism, on magical correspondences between planets and gods. That is what is used by professional astrologers who analyze your natal chart, or claim to provide diagnostic help based on astrology to physicians; they are not basing their analyses and predictions on studies by Michel Gauquelin or John Henry Nelson. Any such discovery from an objective modern investigation could not have been the basis of ancient beliefs—unless we are to suppose that certain of our ancestors had a magical wisdom, or that the gods had informed them by divine inspiration. Even Ptolemy makes no such claims as this, and certainly such a hypothesis could not be invoked as part of a "scientific proof" of a religious doctrine.

In conclusion, I believe that for millions of people, astrology can be a harmless recreation. But to the extent that people regulate their lives and even base medical diagnoses on astrology, it may not be harmless. I have recently come across several cases of job discrimination on the basis of astrological sign, even including the job requisition of one congressman looking for a secretary. At the bottom of the form he indicated "No water signs." Some states publicly recognize astrology as a profession and license astrologers or astrological schools. In other states bills are periodically introduced to formally recognize schools of astrology and license individual astrologers. It seems to me that our survival in a world facing severe problems of rising crime, pollution, environmental degradation, depleting energy resources, and above all the tremendous crush of overpopulation requires the utmost of wisdom and rationality that our science can offer, rather than the occult mysticism of an ancient religion that has not changed since the time of Ptolemy.

As Voltaire once put it, "Men will cease to commit atrocities only when they cease to believe absurdities."

6

Moon Madness

GEORGE O. ABELL

"See the moon! How strange she appears, like a woman rising from the tomb!" says Herodias' page near the beginning of Strauss's opera *Salome*. Later, Salome remarks: "How good it is to see the moon! She is like a silver bloom, cold and chaste; yes, as the beauty of a young virgin." And still later, Herod muses, "How strange the moon appears tonight—is she not strange? She is like a mad woman searching for love."

The moon seems able to arouse all manner of imagery, not only in the arts and literature but in folklore and superstition. It has been claimed, for example, that crops fare best when planted just after full moon. Man has associated the full moon with fertility, with the female menstrual cycle, with violence (especially murder and suicide), with romance, with the incidence of epilepsy, with evil spirits, with madness, and even with lycanthropy (the "curse of the werewolf").[1] Accounts of the effects of various phases of the moon are still to be found in magazines, newspapers, books, and even professional journals.

One such account is by Miami psychiatrist Arnold L. Lieber in his recent book *The Lunar Effect*,[2] produced in collaboration with Jerome Agel. Lieber is persuaded that inmates in mental institutions become especially restless at times of the full moon (although he presents no evidence to support this impression). To account for the effect, he theorizes that the moon's gravitational pull produces "biological tides" in men and other organisms. The human body, he reminds us, is 80 percent water, so erratic behavior could well result from tidal action on the bodily fluids, analogous to the action of the moon on the oceans of the earth.

Now, tidal forces are very well understood. Gravitation is an attraction between all material bodies; it is greater in proportion to their masses, and is weaker in proportion to the square of the distance separating them; that is, the gravitational force drops off rapidly with increasing distance.

But tidal forces are differences between gravitational forces, and become weaker even more rapidly with increasing distance between the attracting bodies.[3] The reason the moon produces appreciable tides is that it is relatively nearby, as astronomical distances go, and so pulls on the side of the earth nearest it more strongly than it does on the side of the earth farthest from the moon. The result is that the moon stretches the earth slightly into the shape of a football, with its long diameter pointing toward the moon. (At the same time the earth similarly distorts the moon.)

Although the moon is the earth's nearest astronomical neighbor, this tidal distortion of the solid earth is nevertheless extremely slight— only about twenty centimeters (eight inches). Now, if the earth were perfectly fluid it would give a bit more. But the distortion of the solid earth is not quite enough to bring the tidal forces acting on it into complete equilibrium with the earth's own gravitation. Consequently, the water of the earth tries to flow in such a way as to pile up both under the moon and on the far side of the earth from the moon. But the earth rotates with respect to the moon, so the directions of these tide-raising forces reverse twice each day—far too rapidly for the water to have time to flow significantly over the surface of the earth. But these forces, switching back and forth as they do, set the oceans sloshing back and forth in their basins so that at most places the tides do "come in" and "go out" twice daily.

The heights of the tides produced by the moon have nothing to do with its phase (whether it is new, full, or whatever), but they do depend on the moon's distance. Its orbit is eccentric, causing its distance to vary, and once each month (actually 27.55 days) it is 10 percent closer to us than it is two weeks later. At those monthly times of the moon's nearest approach (perigee) the tides produced are more than 30 percent higher than when the moon is at its farthest (apogee).

The sun also produces tides, but the sun is four hundred times as far away as the moon is. The total gravitational pull of the sun on the earth is actually more than one hundred times that of the moon. However, the sun is so remote that it pulls on all parts of the earth with a nearly equal force. Consequently, the *difference* between its pulls on different sides of the earth—that is, its tidal force—has less than half the effect of the moon. Still, when the sun, earth, and moon are in a line, as they are every two weeks (either at full or new moon), their tidal forces combine and produce. higher than average tides (spring tides), whereas when they are at right angles to each other in the sky (during the first or third quarter) their tides partly cancel each other (neap tides).

Thus, although the moon's pull is no stronger when it is full or new (unless it happens to be near perigee at the time), its tidal force does then join with that of the sun, and slightly higher than average tides result. These are the physical facts that have been used by some to justify the folk belief that the moon's effects are enhanced when it is full. Those, like Lieber, who at least partly understand the situation, also expect enhanced effects at new moon.

To test his theory, Lieber and an associate, Carolyn Sherin, investigated the incidence of violent crime in Miami.[4] In a sample of 1,892 homicides over a fifteen-year period in Dade County, they found a peak in the number occurring on the day of full moon, and another peak two days after new moon. In a second sample, of 2,008 homicides over a thirteen-year period in Cuyahoga County (Cleveland), they found peaks three days after full moon and two days after new moon. Lieber suspected that the time displacement between the peaks in the two samples might be due to a phase lag associated with latitude.

Now, every year tens of thousands of reports of experiments and observations are published. Some are sound, but many are based on poor experimental techniques, on improper controls, on biased or selected data, and others are even fudged. It is not an uncommon practice for those with novel theories to comb the scientific literature for results that seem to support their theses. Among the many thousands of accounts to choose from, it is indeed not rare to find two or three that will serve a cause.

Lieber found what he needed in the studies of the metabolic activity of hamsters by Northwestern University biologist Frank Brown. Brown is himself something of a maverick. He has been studying rhythms of various kinds in living organisms. Brown holds that these rhythms are externally stimulated—say, by the sun or moon—whereas most of his colleagues are of the opinion that while natural selection may have favored evolution of rhythms that are in step with environmental cycles, the actual timing is controlled by internal clocks in the organisms. An example is the familiar jet lag that most of us feel after an air trip from Europe to the United States; for several days our internal clocks keep awakening us in the wee hours until we manage to get those clocks reset to our workaday cycle.

The activity Brown measured in his hamsters roughly matched, in lunar-phase cycle, the Cuyahoga County fluctuations in homicide rate. The correlation between the two is significant, but remember that the hamster study was selected by Lieber because it did resemble the Cuyahoga murder data.

Nevertheless, encouraged by his findings, in late summer 1973 Lieber predicted that "an increase in accidents of all kinds" and "an increase in the number of homicides" would occur in January and February of 1974, when the "Earth, the Moon, and the Sun would be in a straight line . . . with the Moon at perigee unusually close to Earth." He reports, "The murder toll for the first three weeks of the new year was three times higher than for all of January 1973," and he describes several violent events around the world that occurred during "this time of cosmic coincidence." He points out, further, that in Dade County, deaths, psychiatric emergency-room visits, and admissions to the psychiatric institute at Jackson Memorial Hospital were all unusually high during the first three months of 1974.[5]

Needless to say, astrologers have been delighted by the appearance of Lieber's book—not that it confirms predictions of traditional astrology, but because it argues for cosmic influences, which, at least to astrologers, makes their doctrine seem more credible. And on the face of it, Lieber's mass of evidence and statistics seems impressive. It is, therefore, worth a second look.

First, let's consider the actual tidal force the moon exerts on people. The earth's pull on a person is called his weight. The moon's pull on him, on the average, is only three parts in a million of his weight; for a 200-pound man it would amount to only about 0.01 ounce. But the moon's total gravitational pull on a person is not really relevant, because the moon pulls on the earth as well. A more interesting figure would be the amount by which the moon can increase or decrease one's weight—that is, how much your weight in the presence of the moon's gravitational effect differs from what it would be if there were no moon. For our 200-pound man that difference is at most only 0.01 gram, or about 0.0003 ounce, less than the weight of a mosquito on his shoulder.

But what *really* counts—if there is anything to the idea of biological tides—is the difference between the moon's pull on different parts of your body. The moon's influence on the oceans is important only because its tidal force acts over the entire eight-thousand-mile diameter of the earth, which is big compared to a human being. It works out that the effect on your blood—or on any fluid in your body whose flow or circulation could be affected by the moon's tidal force—is about one part in 3×10^{13} (or 30 trillion) of the weight of that fluid. A book that you hold in your hand exerts a tidal force on you that is thousands of times greater than that of the moon.

In short, we would not expect lunar tides to have a significant effect on human behavior, and would, I should think, be very surprised to find a lunar influence of the sort Lieber (and others) proposes. On the other hand, if there is convincing evidence for a lunar effect, we should certainly take a strong interest, for such an effect, if real, could signal new science. So how convincing is the evidence?

Although Lieber does not publish actual figures on homicides in Dade and Cuyahoga counties, I read the numbers, as best I could, from the graphs he displays in his paper. A simple χ^2 test showed that the distribution of Dade County homicides through the lunar cycle does not differ from what one would expect by chance at least 7 percent of the time, and that the actual day-to-day fluctuations are quite in line with chance. Although there was a peak at full moon, I would judge the peak as typical of the random fluctuations that always appear in real data samples, and the second peak was not at new moon, as predicted, but two days later. The Cuyahoga County sample has a distribution that differs from what is expected by chance more often than occurs only 3 percent of the time. Still, that is not overly surprising, and more to the point, the distribution of homicides in Cuyahoga County is very different from that in Dade County. There are *three* peaks in the distribution of the Cuyahoga County sample, the second highest being near third quarter moon, and the third highest two days after new moon. Moreover, the peak near full moon lags three days behind the corresponding peak in the Dade sample, while the peak near new moon has no lag at all. Lieber seems to be changing the rules for what constitutes agreement with his theory.

Other investigators have been unable to replicate Lieber's finding of a lunar effect. In 1964, Alex Pokorny, professor of psychiatry at Baylor College of Medicine, studied the distribution in the lunar cycle of 2,017 homicides and 2,497 suicides in Texas between 1959 and 1961;[6] in 1974, Pokorny and Joseph Jachimczyk analyzed 2,494 homicides in Harris County (Houston), Texas, over the period 1957 to 1970;[7] and Lester, Brockopp, and Priebe, in 1969, checked the distribution with lunar phase of 399 suicides in Erie County, New York, in the five-year period 1964 to 1968.[8] In none of these studies was a significant correlation found between murders or suicides and lunar phase.

Lieber argues, however, that the investigations of Pokorny and others consider only the time of death, while his own statistics are based on the time of initial injury. To verify the relevance of this point, Lieber reexamined the Dade and Cuyahoga counties homicide data, but this time used time of death rather than assault, and he combined these data with a much larger sample of ten thousand homicides in New York City, for which only death times were recorded. He found these death times to have no correlation with lunar phase, and concluded that it is only the violent action that is influenced by the moon.

According to Pokorny, on the other hand, 85 percent of homicide victims die within the first hour after injury. Lieber contends that the 15 percent who die later would destroy the subtle correlation he finds. But even if those 15 percent all died several days later (which is hardly likely), it could only *weaken* the correlation, not destroy it; if the moon at certain phases really triggers violent behavior in men, the 85 percent who die immediately would certainly produce a correlation that would show up in a large enough sample—such as that of the ten thousand New York homicides—unless we are to suppose that *only* those who are attacked at full or new moon do not die at once, but survive for a random number of days afterward.

Lieber's case for violent activity in Miami in early 1974 involves a misunderstanding of elementary astronomy. When new or full moon occurs while the moon is also at its nearest (perigee), the spring tides are especially high. Such was the case at the full moons of January 8, February 6, and March 8, 1974. However, these high tides occur only for a few days; the moon was actually at its farthest (apogee) during the spring tides corresponding to *new* moon on January 23, February 22, and March 23, so those were lower than average spring tides. During a 27.55-day period the moon goes through all its possible distances. To support the theory that tides cause violence in men, one would have to demonstrate that such behavior was significantly increased everywhere, not in just one city, and that the increase occurred only for the two or three days when the moon was near perigee, not during a three-week or three-month period.

A number of investigators have examined hospital records to check for a possible correlation between lunar phase and admission to mental institutions. R. D. Osborn did not find significantly larger numbers of admissions on the day of full moon itself, but he did find higher than average numbers of admissions during the four-day periods following full moons.[9] In an independent attempt to replicate Osborn's study, Pokorny investigated 4,937 psychiatric admissions to a large Texas Veterans Administration hospital over the three-year period 1959 to 1961, but found no relation between admissions and the lunar phase.[10] Two studies suggest a slight relationship between the numbers of admissions and full moon, but in the *opposite sense*.[11] A study of admissions to all Texas state hospitals over a nine-month period showed a slight excess in the number of admissions during the two-week period centered on full moon over the other half of the lunar month, the difference being 2 percent.[12] The remaining studies all gave negative results.[13] In an excellent review paper, Campbell and Beets conclude, "Given the fickle nature of the lunar effect as shown by these studies, it may be appropriate to label the few significant results examples of [statistical] error."[14]

In 1960, Edson J. Andrews, a Tallahassee physician, published a paper in the *Journal of the Florida Medical Association* describing his study of forty-four cases of hemorrhaging during routine surgery on tonsils and adenoids, and reported that 82 percent of the bleedings occurred during the two-week period centered on full moon.[15] He does not publish individual numbers, but only curves representing running averages over seven-day periods, so it is not possible to evaluate the random day-to-day fluctuations in his data. Since on the average there are fewer than two bleedings per day in the lunar cycle, one or two especially "busy" days could well have produced the effect. Andrews's paper has been widely discussed, especially by astrologers, but I know of no published replication. On the other hand, there have been newspaper accounts describing research of Ralph W. Morris, professor of pharmacology at the University of Illinois College of Pharmacy, reporting that he claims evidence of more bleeding and also angina attacks during full and last quarter moon.[16] I contacted Dr. Morris by telephone, and he informed me that these were actually preliminary results of some of his students. He told me that he was currently checking their work, and while he found some of it promising, he had also found errors, and wished to withhold judgment until he had completed his analysis. It would seem, however, that if there were a *striking* relation between lunar phase and medical emergencies, hospitals everywhere would routinely avoid surgery during the "dangerous" parts of the lunar cycle.

One of the most widely believed of lunar effects is that there are many more births of humans at the time of full moon than at other times of the lunar cycle. The belief is widespread among nurses in maternity wards and some gynecologists as well. One astronomical colleague recalls that when his first child was born it was during full moon, and when he arrived at the hospital there were expectant women in the halls waiting for available rooms; the nurses all explained that "it is always this way at full moon!"

There are some published studies that seem to support the idea that the full moon favors a higher than average rate of births. Andrews, for example, reports that in the Tallahassee Memorial Hospital during the period 1956 to 1958 there were 401 babies born within two days of full moon, 375 within two days of new moon, and 320 within two days of first or last quarter.[17] In a study of more than 510,000 births in New York City during a ten-year period beginning in 1948, Menaker and Menaker claim that the birth rate was about 1 percent higher during the two weeks following full moon than before.[18] However, one of those authors later studied another half million births in New York during thirty-seven lunar months from 1961 to 1963 and reported a 1 percent excess in the birth rate during the two-week period *centered* on full moon.[19] Subsequently, Osley, Summerville, and Borst reported on a study of yet another half million births in New York during a later unspecified three-year period showing a 1 percent excess in the birth rate during the two weeks *preceding* full moon![20] In contrast,

Rippmann analyzed 9,551 natural births over a ten-year period in Danville, Pennsylvania, and found no correlation at all with the phase of the moon.[21]

Because even the reports of positive correlations are mutually contradictory, Dr. Bennett Greenspan, of the Wadsworth Veterans Administration Hospital, and I undertook to look into the births at the UCLA Hospital during a period of fifty-one lunar cycles from March 17, 1974, through April 30, 1978.[22] During this period there were 11,691 live births, of which 8,142 were natural (not induced by drugs or Cesarean section). The live births included 141 multiple sets (136 sets of twins, 4 of triplets, and 1 of quadruplets). In addition, there were 168 stillbirths. Thus we had four samples: all live births, natural live births, multiple births, and stillbirths. In no sample was the mean number of births occurring on full moon above average. In fact, in all samples, the distribution throughout the lunar cycle was absolutely random.

These results were a considerable surprise to several of the nurses at the UCLA Hospital maternity ward. To be sure, if one combs through all the data, he can find an occasional lunar month in which there is a greater than average number of births at or near full moon, but these are only random fluctuations; there are just as many months in which there are fewer than the expected number of births near full moon. Probably the nurses simply remember those months in which they noticed there was a full moon during a particularly busy night; it is similar to the tendency to remember those dreams that seem to come true and forget the vast majority that do not.

Perhaps the most widely held of all beliefs about the moon is that its cycle of phases is related to the human menstrual cycle, but I am highly skeptical of that too. The moon's cycle of phases is 29.53 days, while the human female menstrual cycle averages 28 days (although it varies among women and from time to time with individual women); this is hardly even a good coincidence! The corresponding estrus cycles of some other mammals are 28 days for opossums, 11 days for guinea pigs, 16 to 17 days for sheep, 20 to 22 days for sows, 21 days for cows and mares, 24 to 26 days for macaque monkeys, 37 days for chimpanzees, and only 5 days for rats and mice. One could argue, I suppose, that the human female, being more intelligent and perhaps aware of her environment, adapted to a cycle close to that of the moon, while lower animals did not. But then the 28-day period for the opossum must be a coincidence, and if it is a coincidence for opossums, why not for humans?

The moon gives us light, at certain phases, and it has unquestioned influence on ocean tides and other natural phenomena. There may well be undiscovered lunar influences, and some of the alleged influences may possibly turn out to be real. But many of the incredible "facts" concerning the effect of the moon are simply not facts at all.

7

Biorhythms

TAREK KHALIL
CHARLES KURUCZ

The idea of human biorhythms intuitively seems plausible. We are all aware of regular biological cycles in humans and other animals, such as the sleep/wakefulness and menstrual cycles. We are also well aware that our sense of physical and emotional well-being undergoes wide variations from time to time. It may seem to make sense to suppose that variation in these factors is at least in part due to an underlying biological cycle, and it is a comforting idea to think that we could actually chart these cycles and compensate for our "down" days. The recent "theory" of biorhythms is, in fact, based on such an assumption. Almost everyone is aware that some industries here and abroad have used biorhythm calculations as safety indices for their employees. Are biorhythms really a long-awaited scientific breakthrough that can change the conduct and improve the safety of our lives?

Tarek Khalil and Charles Kurucz are professors of industrial engineering. If biorhythms do represent a dramatic new technique for improving industrial safety, it is their business to inform themselves about it. Thus Khalil and Kurucz have done extensive research themselves in biorhythms, and much of their essay illustrates how a careful scientific investigation of such a topic is carried out. They also review evidence for human biological cycles in general, and for the biorhythm theory in particular. Biological systems are almost never as rigidly organized as in the biorhythm theory, though, and certainly not by birth date.

The idea of biorhythms may ultimately have done us a service, nevertheless, if it helped focus attention on valid human biological rhythms. As Khalil and Kurucz point out, there is much we do not yet know about human biological cycles, especially those of mood and alertness. Such knowledge would be exceedingly valuable. The currently popular notion of biorhythm is, though, a commercial exploitation rather than a signpost on the road to such knowledge.

Throughout history man has observed such natural cycles as the rising and setting of the sun, the ebb and flow of ocean tides, and the changes of the seasons. The periodic nature of these events provided people with a measure of security about things to come and gave them reason to reflect on their past and plan for their future. The regularity of such social activities as work hours, meal times, and holiday schedules indicates the extent to which human activity itself is organized in cycles.

Recently, considerable effort has been spent investigating the effects of various biological rhythms in the human body. Certainly interest in these rhythms at least in part results from man's basic desire to predict future behavior.

The human body exhibits a number of repeatable rhythms: heartbeats, breathing rates, brain waves, and other physiological processes within the human machine. In fact, biological rhythms exist at all levels of the hierarchy of biological structures, from unicellular animals that have no neural information systems to that most complex structure, the human brain.

The available literature supporting the existence of biological cycles is extensive and can be broadly categorized into studies focused on cycles that repeat daily or near daily, and studies focused on cycles that repeat over some longer period, such as a month or a year. Cycles that repeat on a daily basis were called diurnal rhythms. However, since living organisms hardly ever repeat a cycle exactly every twenty-four hours, the term *circadian* (from Latin *circa dies*, about a day) is now used to describe cycles that repeat in about nineteen hours to twenty-nine hours. Scientists have shown that twenty-four-hour circadian rhythms in plants and people persist even under artificially prolonged darkness or light.[2,9,24,31]

Scientists studying circadian rhythms in humans have measured sleep patterns and attention spans over periods of several days, and have demonstrated the facts that cycles exist and exert effects on psychological and sociological behavior.[3,6,18,21,25,28,30] A common example of a circadian behavior effect is jet lag. A person's traveling in an east–west direction across time zones upsets his sleep cycle; it may take several days to return to the normal cycle or to readjust to a new one. Other functions exhibiting circadian rhythms include urine production, secretion of enzymes and hormones, blood pressure, heart rate, and physical and mental conditions.

Another class of biological cycles includes those that are approximately one month in duration, such as menstruation in human females. There is growing evidence that men also have similar hormone/mood variations.[20,25] These "circamensual" or "circalunar" biocycles occur about every four weeks, but change from one individual to another and from one month to the next.

Yearly cycles (circannual) are being studied by researchers at the University of Minnesota and at the Rothschild Foundation Hospital in France.[6] These studies show that growth and behavior patterns are affected by the time of year. For example, according to the Paris studies, male sexual activity usually reaches a peak in the autumn.

Cycles of even slower rhythms, such as "population cycles," are also being studied by biologists. These cycles follow the changes in wildlife patterns that may occur over a span of several years.

The scientific evidence in support of the existence of biological cycles is then very strong. Although much research remains to be done on biological cycles, we are convinced that they exist in humans and influence human behavior.

Recently, considerable interest has been revived in a theory of biological cycles in human beings that was introduced at the turn of the century by some European physicians and psychologists. This theory, popularly named "biorhythms," proposes that, starting from the moment of birth, three basic cyclical rhythms occur regularly in human beings.[32] The cycles are a 23-day physical cycle, a 28-day emotional cycle, and a 33-day intellectual cycle, as shown in Figure 1, page 108.

The biorhythm theory claims that these cycles are fundamental to life, are exactly regular, continue involuntarily, and are unaffected by

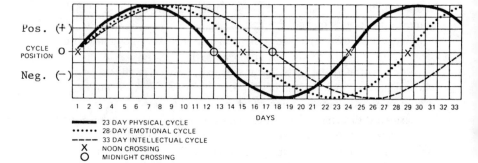

23 DAY PHYSICAL CYCLE
• • • • • 28 DAY EMOTIONAL CYCLE
– – – – 33 DAY INTELLECTUAL CYCLE
X   NOON CROSSING
O   MIDNIGHT CROSSING

The basic biorhythm cycles.

circadian changes. They oscillate between positive and negative, being positive through the first half of the cycle and negative through the second half. A positive state indicates a potential toward strong, vigorous, and good conditions; a negative state indicates a potential toward a weakened condition, low vigor, and poor performance in the respective physical, emotional, and intellectual conditions. The cycles can conveniently be thought of as beginning at a neutral state, climbing to peak positive, then dropping back down to a neutral condition at mid-cycle. At this point, transition is made from positive to negative; in the day corresponding to this point the person (according to the theory) is unstable. The cycle continues through the negative period, at the end of which it is ready, once again, to make a transition from negative to positive.

These days of transitions have been termed *critical days*. It has been suggested that accidents occur on the critical days more often than at any other time.[35] It has reportedly been found that the instability caused by two (or three) simultaneous transitions is much more acute than that with a single transition, with the physical–emotional relationship having the most serious potential of causing instability. The biorhythm theory has recently come to the attention of various industrial firms and researchers interested in its application to accident reduction.[10,19,36] The idea is that during critical periods, the resulting instability tends to cause accidents. Thus, for example, by charting which days the drivers for a trucking company have their respective double- or triple-critical periods, a plan for laying off drivers or cautioning them can be produced. The validity of such an application has reportedly been verified in the case of the Ohmi Railway Company of

Japan, which adopted biorhythms in their driver management. It was reported that "of 212 drivers who had the largest number of accidents, 31% occurred on the critical day and 30% on the pre-critical or post-critical day for a total of 61% over a 5 year period, and that after adopting a biorhythm they enjoyed over 2,000,000 kilometers without accidents."[35]

The biorhythm theory represents an attempt to predict human behavior patterns; however, its approach is simplistic. Public interest in the theory is probably due in part to exploitive advertising about it, since any real predictive power of the theory has yet to be shown. Biorhythm theory offers a simple way to predict biocycles that directly

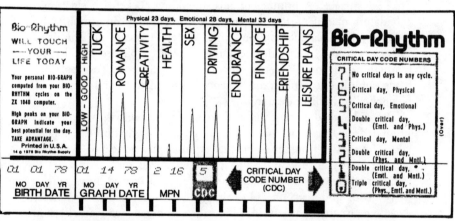

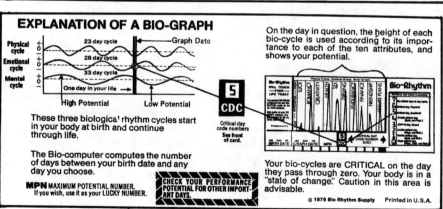

Output from a commercial biorhythm computer. Courtesy Compunetic Devices, Las Vegas, Nevada.

affect human performance, mood, and potential errors. Its calculations are based on repeatable cycles of uniform length and amplitude, thus permitting easy calculation. Commercial enterprises now offer to provide (for a fee, of course) an individual's biorhythm chart to "help plan" his or her future activities. "Bio-computers" are located in many airports, restaurants, and hotels, which, for fifty cents, will inform you how your biorhythms "will touch your life today." Some machines provide a printed output card, graphically illustrating how an individual rates for the day in the categories of luck, romance, creativity, health, sex, driving, endurance, finance, friendship, and leisure plans. High peaks on the graph indicate "your best potential for the day. Take advantage." A number of aids, including pocket-size electronic calculators manufactured by reputable companies, can simplify the tedious job of calculation and immediately indicate critical days. Newspapers and magazines nationwide have published articles on biorhythms and how to get the theory to work for you. Textbooks are being published to explain the "science" of biorhythms and how it can be applied in industrial safety.

The widespread commercial activity related to biorhythm theory has prompted investigations into the validity of the biorhythm fundamentals. The most serious question that is raised in connection with the popular biorhythm theory is that it predicts effects on a rigidly deterministic basis, whereas human beings are characterized by variations in behavior and reaction. One simply would not expect a precise, exact, repeatable pattern in physical, emotional, and intellectual states. And, one would certainly not expect the patterns to be identical for every individual. Finally, we would not expect *any* biological cycles to be predictable from one's birth date, as biorhythm theory claims.

Rushing into applications of the biorhythm theory before it has been scientifically validated is highly undesirable, and could adversely affect the lives of many people who do not have the means or the knowledge to distinguish fact from myth. The burden therefore falls on the scientific community to make all the facts known.

The authors of this essay have conducted several studies that tested biorhythm theory. In these studies we examined actual incidents in the lives of individuals to determine whether those incidents occurred at random or were influenced by biorhythms. We accomplished this by comparing the actual number of incidents (for example, accidents) that occur on "critical" biorhythm days with the number that would be expected by chance if biorhythms had no effect. A significant dif-

Table 1.
Biorhythm Cycle Probabilities
(Critical days are zero-crossing days only)

Cycle	Position	Time of Birth		
		Before Noon	After Noon	Unknown [2]
Physical	Critical [1]	2/23	2/23	4/46
	Positive	10/23	11/23	21/46
	Negative	11/23	10/23	21/46
Emotional	Critical [1]	2/28	2/28	2/28
	Positive	13/28	13/28	13/28
	Negative	13/28	13/28	13/28
Intellectual	Critical [1]	2/33	2/33	4/66
	Positive	15/33	16/33	31/66
	Negative	16/33	15/33	31/66

[1] Critical position = day of zero crossing.
[2] These "unconditional" probabilities assume that before or after noon births are equally likely.

ference between the actual and expected numbers as determined by a formal statistical test would constitute scientific evidence in support of the theory.

Certain probabilities must be calculated in order to determine the expected number of incidents for a statistical test of the biorhythm theory.[12] In particular, we need to know the theoretical probabilities of finding various cycle positions on a randomly selected day in the life of an individual. Some examples of probabilities are shown in Table 1. These probabilities are based on the biorhythm theory and upon a number of assumptions that are common in statistics cited in support of the theory. The probabilities calculated depend upon the exact time at which the individual is born. The first two columns under "Time of Birth" give the cycle position probabilities for the cases where we know whether an individual was born before or after noon. If an individual time of birth is known, the appropriate probability from column one or two can be used. If, however, the time of birth is not known, the "unconditional" probability shown in the last column must be used. For example, if a group of forty-six people was chosen at random (without knowledge of time of birth) one would expect about four of them to have their physical cycle in a critical position. Now if in a group of forty-six people who were involved in accidents twelve had critical physical cycle positions, it could be argued that biorhythms had an effect, since twelve actual critical positions is much larger than the four that would be expected by chance alone.

We carried out a detailed study to determine the influence of biorhythms in practical life and to test the validity of the theory.[9] We were particularly interested in the relationship of biorhythms to accident occurrence and human performance.

For this study we collected two types of data: single events and repeated events. Single events include such things as death and accidents, while repeated events include repeated performances of an activity on different days. Performance at sports events such as swimming meets, bowling leagues, and boxing matches are included in the latter category.

The specific data of the single-occurrence type collected for this study included Federal Aviation Administration aircraft accident reports in which the FAA ruled that pilot error was the cause. We compiled information concerning 63 of these accidents from an area office. We obtained another set of data, comprised of 105 unscreened deaths, from health-department records. A third set of data included 181 traffic accidents where a driver was at fault. For each of these occurrences we recorded the subject's birth date along with the date the event occurred.

We obtained specific data of the repetitive-occurrence type from the records of twenty-three members of a university swimming team. These included the date of the event and the swimmer's birth date. Records of twenty-five members of the university's student–faculty bowling league provided a second set of repetitive-occurrence data. We recorded scores for each bowler for every day that he bowled, together with his birth date.

First, with the use of a computer we calculated the exact positions of all three biorhythm cycles at the time of event occurrence for each person. By giving the computer the occurrence date of the event and the person's birth date, the position of each of the three cycles on the day of the event was identified as either a positive number, zero, or a negative number (corresponding to the three states of the cycles).

We first analyzed the single-occurrence events to determine how many people were in the positive, negative, and critical parts of each cycle at the time the events occurred. Next we analyzed the data to determine how many events occurred at the various combinations of cycle positions: for example, the numbers of events where the three cycles (physical, emotional, and intellectual) were all positive; where two cycles were positive and one negative, etcetera. Similar numbers for event occurrences at single- and multiple-critical days were also obtained. We were particularly interested in answers to questions such as what percentage of occurrences were on critical days, and how many accidents occurred during the negative state of the cycles compared with those occurring during the positive state. As mentioned earlier, in order to determine the validity of the biorhythm fundamentals, we compared the observed numbers for various cycle positions with those that would be expected if events occurred randomly throughout an individual's life (that is, if event occurrence was *not* influenced by the biorhythm cycles).

We similarly analyzed data for repetitive-occurrence events. The performance measure for the swimming team data was the official time recorded for each swimmer for the particular event in which he performed. The best performances as well as the worst performances were recorded, together with their respective cycle positions for each swimmer. We made a count of the positive, zero, and negative states of each cycle for all best performances and worst performances. This provided a useful means of comparing cycle positions for each kind of performance. It also permitted comparison with expected results if a random process was taking place.

We analyzed the bowling-performance data to determine whether cycle positions affect a person's performance relative to his average score. The bowling score on a given day was categorized as above or below average for each person. The cycle positions on that day were also recorded. The number of positive, zero, and negative states of each cycle were then counted for the above-average scores and separately for the below-average scores. All cycle-position combinations were analyzed.

The results of single-occurrence data showed that the total number of the events (accidents or deaths) was evenly divided between the positive and negative portions of the cycles, with only a small percentage falling on critical days. Expected results obtained from probability calculations that assumed random occurrence did not in fact differ significantly from those of the actual data. In other words, the events did not correlate with "biorhythm cycles."

Results of the repetitive-occurrence events (swimming and bowling performance) also failed to show any influence of biorhythm on performance.

In a total of twenty-three swimmers, best performance occurred thirteen times when the physical cycle was in a negative state, compared to eight times when it was in a positive state and two times at a critical day. Worst performance occurred twelve times in a positive state and only seven times in a negative state. These results seem to be running in the opposite direction from what should be expected if the current biorhythm theory is a valid indicator of physical performance, but statistical tests between actual and expected numbers again failed to show any significant differences between the two sets of data. Analysis of the various combinations of cycle positions also showed no statistically significant evidence in support of the biorhythm theory.

The results of our investigations prompted us to follow closely studies of other researchers in this field. A considerable amount of contradiction was observed. Support for the theory came from a number of studies dealing mainly with accident occurrences and their correlation with critical days. Weaver[33] reported that in a sample of one-fourth of the army-aviation accidents over a period of more than two years where the cause was attributed to pilot error, the percentage of incidents occurring on critical days was more than double the expected percentage. However, he does not provide the number of accidents analyzed. A study in the Canadian armed forces[27] indicated a definite relationship between accidents and critical days. A large sample of 7,000 was reportedly used, but methodology and analysis techniques were not detailed. Several other individual studies (usually using smaller samples) reported correlations between biorhythms and accident occurrence. Opposite results were obtained in an evaluation of more than four thousand naval aircraft mishaps involving pilot error.[28] That is, no significant influence of biorhythm on pilot performance was observed. Wolcott et al.[38] also ruled out biorhythms as a causal factor in aircraft accidents, after analyzing more than 8,000 accidents. Brownley and Sandler[4] analyzed the results of accidents fatal to 506 motor vehicle operators involved in single-vehicle accidents. They compared observed occurrence with expected occurrence and found no relationship between accident occurrence and biorhythmic criticality. Their results are in agreement with the conclusions of a similar unpublished study by one of the co-authors of this essay, Kurucz, of 609 single-vehicle accidents. Brownley and Sandler also reported on a study by Sanhein[29] that favorably correlated accidents and critical days, but their personal conversation with Sanhein on a later date revealed that there may have been an error in the original computations, which may change the reported results. *Biorhythms and Industrial Safety*, a recent book by Albert Thumann, published by the Fairmont Press in 1977, has a more detailed discussion of the theory and cites in more detail some of the articles referred to here.

Fewer studies have dealt with effects of biorhythms on performance. Investigators will report an incident in the life of an individual such as Mark Spitz, noting that he won his Olympic swimming medals "on days when both the physical and emotional curves were in perfect synchronization in the positive phase." His intellectual cycle was at a low ebb, but that is considered of little significance to these events. However, when Billie Jean King beat Bobby Riggs in 1974, it was claimed that her intellectual and emotional curves were in a positive state, causing her to play a smart game.[17,36] Similar conclusions have been drawn when other celebrities have been involved in events. Among those often mentioned are Arnold Palmer, Jack Nicklaus, Lee Trevino, Muhammad Ali, Stan Smith, and Harry Truman.

In a more systematic study of biorhythms and long-term performance, Neil and Sink[18] tested three subjects on an information-processing task on a daily basis for a period of seventy days. They measured subjects' reaction time, movement time, and information-processing rate, and attempted to identify periodicities in performance. They identified twelve significant "harmonics," and nine were found to be within one day of at least one of the biorhythmic cycles. They interpreted the results as suggesting the possibility of a biorhythmic influence on the performance of the task.

A major flaw in many of the above studies, particularly those pertaining to performance, is that they reach conclusions from analyses of very small samples. In these cases one suspects that only events in which there was agreement between the biorhythm theory and the outcome of the event have been reported. How many cases that do not support the theory go unreported? In a recent article in *Psychology Today*, Louis[14] reports that a leading biorhythm proponent predicted that Reggie Jackson of the New York Yankees would find it "very tough to get a hit in the 1977 World Series" because his physical, emotional, and intellectual cycles would all be negative. Of course Jackson proceeded to give one of the most spectacular performances in Series history. Louis also reported that he found no statistical evidence to support the biorhythm theory in an analysis of 100 no-hit major-league baseball games and 100 heavyweight title bouts.

Another pertinent observation is that several of the studies that have reported agreement between the commercialized biorhythm theory and reality have been less than complete in reporting methodologies, treatment, or detailed design of the experiments, or in showing strong evidence that would justify reaching the conclusions drawn.

Some of the most comprehensive studies conducted in the area of biorhythms have been undertaken by the Biocron Systems Company of California. They maintain that people do have variations in their physical, emotional, and mental states, as is established by current scientific knowledge. However, each person is said to be different, with a different cycle length and a different effect of his biorhythm.[39] They collected data for about 200 people over a period ranging from a minimum of 70 days to more than 400 days. Results showed a variation in cycle lengths ranging from 2 to 54 days. One subject showed a 2-day physical-cycle length, 21-day emotional-cycle length, and 45-day intellectual-cycle length. However, most people tested showed lesser spreads in cycle lengths. The company reported that it is quite unusual to find cycle lengths in individual data that correspond exactly to the popular theory of biorhythm involving fixed 23-, 28-, and 33-day cycle lengths. Moreover, the data showed that different people are affected differently by their cycles, as indicated by a change in the amplitude of the cycles from individual to individual and possibly from cycle to cycle in the same individual. The Biocron data refute completely the concept of a given cycle that would be exactly the same length for all people and affect them all the same way.

The application of biorhythm calculations to industrial-accident reduction may have produced favorable results in several cases.[20,27,32,35,36] It has not been established, however, that such favorable results arose directly from the existence of a valid biorhythm theory. In some studies psychological factors (for example, the power of suggestion) may have been primarily responsible for producing the observed effects. The influence of such psychological factors can be detected only through controlled studies comparing groups having knowledge of their cycle states with groups unaware of their cycle states.

In an industrial study by Newcomb,[20] which implemented such an experimental technique, foremen were selected and provided with data about their workers. The first group was provided accurate data about the critical days of the workers and foremen were requested to caution them on those days. The second group was given inaccurate information, so foremen were cautioning their workers on noncritical days. For the third group, no information was given and so no warning was given to workers. The accident rates "remained unchanged" for the first group, "rose slightly" for the second, and "climbed a lot" for the third. The results were interpreted to be supportive of the biorhythm theory. Another interpretation of the same results could be that groups one and two were cautioned periodically by their foremen, as opposed to group three, which did not receive any special attention. This periodic safety reminder and the special attention may have resulted in the first two groups' maintaining a lower accident rate than group three. Unfortunately, unavailability of complete data on this study precludes the possibility of performing a comprehensive analysis to prove or disprove the validity of the latter interpretation, or even to reliably evaluate Newcomb's claims.

In 1976, Hirsh[10] reviewed the use of biorhythms in industry and reported that some companies use it to promote safety awareness and not to predict accidents. He also indicated that the widespread claim of biorhythm use by U.S. industry is a definite exaggeration of the facts.

Thus we have seen that there has been a growing interest in the application of biorhythms to programs of accident prevention and performance prediction. Several people have suggested its applicability to medicine, government, business, education, industry, athletics, and military purposes. But in order for biorhythms to be applied on the practical level, its validity and reliability should be established. Serious researchers who have conducted comprehensive reviews of physiological and behavioral cycles of animals and humans have failed even to mention the three fixed-period cycles of biorhythm theory.[8,15]

In our own studies, we analyzed both single-occurrence data and repetitive-activity data. The basic method of analysis consisted of a statistical comparison of actual numbers of occurrence from collected data with those numbers that would be expected if biorhythm had no effect. From the accident and death data, we could detect no definite trend in support of the biorhythm theory. Swimming and bowling data also indicated that performance was independent of the biorhythm-cycle state. None of the other studies that we have found in support of biorhythm theory has provided convincing evidence of the theory's validity. Instead, the existing studies show deficiencies in methodology, sampling techniques, statistical analysis, and/or fail to show a forceful relationship between cause and effect. On the other hand, a number of large sample studies have in fact refuted the biorhythm-theory concept.[4,28,38,39]

Established scientific knowledge indicates that people do indeed show rhythmic biological patterns. However, the failure of biorhythm theory to recognize differences among people and variations in reaction within individuals removes this popular theory from the realm of scientific knowledge. Moreover, the idea of predicting a person's biological rhythms solely from his or her birth date runs contrary to studies that have followed the physical, emotional, and intellectual variations people are subject to over a long period of time. Biorhythm also precludes the changes in a person's own cyclical patterns which scientists have observed.

The much publicized biorhythm theory may serve as a topic of interest and as a focus for social conversation. It may be used by business and industry to promote safety awareness or to motivate employees toward better performance. However, rushing into applications that may be costly and that may affect the lives of individuals based on an unproven theory certainly is not justified. Meanwhile, serious research to reveal the true mystery of biocycles will continue.

8

Scientists and Psychics*

RAY HYMAN

Many people are under the impression that psychic phenomena have been conclusively established by many experiments by reputable scientists. It may seem, therefore, that those scientists who refuse to acknowledge the scientific validity of psychic phenomena are biased and guilty of double standards. The experiments that are reported to the public do seem rigorously scientific, and people have been led to understand that psychic research has been done at prestigious institutions. We often hear the queries, "Doesn't UCLA have a parapsychology department?" and "Wasn't Uri Geller conclusively tested by those famous scientists at Stanford?" Why, then, are we skeptics stubbornly resisting the tide?

In point of fact, UCLA does not have a parapsychology department, and Stanford University (not to be confused with the independent Stanford Research Institute) has not conducted research on Uri Geller. It is true, however, that there are, and always have been (rightly so, we think), a sprinkling of eminent scientists who become involved in psychic

* Work on this essay was supported by a Faculty Fellowship from the National Science Foundation.

research. It is also true that there are several journals and professional associations in parapsychology that occasionally report positive results. How then can the lay person assess the situation?

In the first of two essays on this topic, University of Oregon psychologist Ray Hyman discusses the puzzle of respected scientists who come to believe in psychic phenomena, usually through investigations of famous "psychics." Through both historical and current examples, Hyman documents the fact that scientists have repeatedly been deceived by ordinary stage magic. They have also failed to support their psychic beliefs through normal, standard scientific procedures. The double-standard shoe, in other words, is on the other foot. Hyman then spells out what a truly scientific investigation involves, and provides guidelines for evaluating reports of paranormal phenomena.

In the second essay, Barry Singer addresses the charge that scientifically valid laboratory evidence already exists for psychic phenomena, and that scientists prejudicially ignore such evidence. Once again, a clarification of normal scientific standards suggests that the real inconsistency in applying scientific standards resides in unwarranted claims about evidence for the paranormal, not in mainstream science's repudiation of such evidence.

In 1855, Robert Hare, professor emeritus of chemistry at the University of Pennsylvania, published a most unusual book.[20] Its full title was *Experimental Investigation of the Spirit Manifestations, Demonstrating the Existence of Spirits and Their Communion with Mortals: Doctrine of the Spirit World Respecting Heaven, Hell, Morality, and God. Also, the Influence of Scripture on the Morals of Christians.* In this bizarre mixture of psychic research and theology, Hare relates how he began his inquiry into spiritualism as a nonreligious skeptic and ended up as a completely religious believer. Not only does he describe feats of other mediums, but he even became a medium himself and claims he obtained messages directly from Franklin, Washington, and even Jesus Christ. Indeed, many of his experiments on psychic phenomena were dictated to him by these spirits.

Hare's espousal of spiritualism was met with dismay and anger by his scientific colleagues but welcomed with enthusiasm by the spiritualists. This was especially so because Hare was the first major scientist to support their cause. According to Isaac Asimov, Hare was "one of the few strictly American products who in those days could be considered within hailing distance of the great European chemists."[1]

In spite of Hare's eminence, his scientific colleagues could dismiss his conversion to spiritualism as the result of old age. Hare was already seventy-two years old when he first considered the question of spiritualistic claims and was seventy-four when his book was published.

But such a ready explanation will not do for those scientists who later followed in Hare's footsteps by openly endorsing claims of alleged mediums or psychics. Most of them were at the beginning or in the middle of their productive scientific years at the time they began investigating psychic phenomena. Not many years after Hare's death in 1858, both Alfred Russel Wallace, a codiscoverer of evolution via natural selection, and William Crookes, one of England's greatest physicists, independently began investigations into spiritualistic phenomena. Both became firm believers and staunch advocates of the reality of psychic phenomena. They were followed by other eminent scientists. In England, these included Sir William Barrett, Sir Oliver Lodge, and Lord Rayleigh, a Nobel Prize winner. In France, there was the astronomer Claude Flammarion and Nobel Prize winner Charles Richet. Germany had Professor Zoellner; Italy, Cesare Lombroso; the United States, William James. Most of these eminent converts lived in the late 1800s or at the beginning of this century. Today there is a renewal of interest in, and support of, psychic claims by noted scientists, especially physicists.

The fact that many eminent and obviously sane scientists have openly endorsed psychic claims raises many questions, the most practical and immediate of which are these: How is the interested layman to make sense out of such claims and the arguments they engender? When some scientists report miracles that they have witnessed under "scientifically controlled conditions" and other scientists bitterly dismiss these reports as "superstitious nonsense," what is the layman to believe? If the scientists disagree, how can we expect an outsider to evaluate the competing claims?

I believe some guidance can be given. We can ignore the emotional and irrational excesses of both parties to the quarrels and apply some simple and elementary tests to the assertions. In most cases, these tests will be sufficient to eliminate the claims from the category of *scientific*. The most important consequence, however, of considering such tests is not that we will be able to more accurately evaluate paranormal claims. What is more important, in my opinion, is what the tests can teach us about the nature of scientific investigation and how it operates to protect us from our own follies.

To begin our search for evaluational standards, let us first consider a sample of specific claims made by some well-established scientists.

Alfred Russel Wallace was a naturalist who independently conceived of evolution by natural selection simultaneously with Darwin. When Wallace began his investigations of psychic phenomena in 1865, he was forty-two years old. Wallace was a materialist at that point, but he had already shown a willingness to seriously consider unorthodox phenomena. When he was twenty-one years old he became interested in mesmerism and phrenology. He believed that he had observed clairvoyance in his subjects, especially when a mesmerized subject experienced all the sensations that Wallace, the mesmerizer, was experiencing.[14,41]

Wallace began attending seances in July 1865. He witnessed a number of spiritualistic phenomena that he regarded as genuine and paranormal when his sister discovered the young medium Agnes Nichol (later Mrs. Guppy) in November 1866. Miss Nichol produced phenomena in Wallace's home that the great naturalist considered to be conclusive. In a letter to John Tyndall, dated May 8, 1868, Wallace wrote:

> During the last two years I have witnessed a great variety of phenomena, under such varied conditions that each objection as it arose was answered by other phenomena. The further I inquire, and the more I see, the more impossible becomes the theory of imposture or delusion. I *know* that the facts are real natural phenomena, just as certainly as I know any other curious facts in nature.[41]

Wallace witnessed the standard fare of raps, table tilting, levitations, and musical sounds in his many sittings with Agnes Nichol. He reports that he saw her produce fresh-cut flowers during a winter seance. These included "15 chrysanthemums, 6 variegated anemones, 4 tulips, 5 orange berried solanums, 6 ferns, of two sorts, 1 Auricula sinensis, with 9 flowers—37 stalks in all." Wallace argued that the freshness and coldness of the flowers precluded the possibility that any member of the seance had brought them into the room. Over an hour had passed in a warm room prior to the "materialization."[26] This production of flowers, along with fruit, was repeated in many further seances. Wallace claimed that specific flowers were often produced upon request. "A friend of Dr. Alfred Wallace asked for a sun-flower, and one six feet high fell on the table, having a large mass of earth about its roots." [10]

William Crookes was thirty-seven years of age in 1869 when he began to attend seances with Mrs. Marshall, a medium who was instrumental in converting Wallace to spiritualism. He had already made important contributions to chemistry and physics and was still to make several more. Crookes was later knighted for his contributions to science: the discovery of thallium, the invention of the radiometer, Crookes' tube (which made the electric light possible), radiation effects, and many more. Crookes reported on a series of investigations with the colorful and enigmatic medium Daniel Dunglas Home in the early 1870s. But his most striking accounts of psychic phenomena are of seances that he conducted with Florence Cook during a five-month period beginning in December 1873. [15,16,18,29]

A typical performance would go like this: Florence Cook, the medium, would enter a cabinet (usually a curtained-off section of the room in which the sitters were located) and go into a trance. After a while a white-robed, turbaned female would emerge from the cabinet claiming to be the materialized spirit Katie King. Some skeptics thought the resemblance between Katie King and Florence Cook was rather striking. Crookes admitted that there was some resemblance, but he insisted that there were crucial differences.

> Katie's height varies; in my house I have seen her six inches taller than Miss Cook. Last night, with bare feet and not "tip-toeing," she was four and a half inches taller than Miss Cook. Katie's neck was bare last night; the skin was perfectly smooth both to touch and sight, whilst on Miss Cook's neck is a large blister, which under similar circumstances is distinctly visible and rough to the touch. Katie's ears are unpierced, whilst Miss Cook habitually wears earrings. Katie's complexion is very fair, while that of Miss Cook is very dark. Katie's fingers are much longer than Miss Cook's, and her face is also larger. In manners and ways of expression there are also many decided differences. [29]

One proof that Katie King and Florence Cook were not one and the same person would be to observe simultaneously Katie King and Florence Cook. The skeptics were quick to point out that this was not allowed. But Crookes claimed he had been privileged to make such observations on more than one occasion.

Now we jump ahead 100 years. Two physicists, Russell Targ and Harold Puthoff, investigated the alleged paranormal powers of an Israeli, Uri Geller. The investigations were carried out at the Stanford Research Institute, where Geller visited for six weeks during November and December 1972 and for eight days during August 1973. Both of these scientists have significant accomplishments to their credit in the area of laser physics. Russell Targ did early work in laser development and is the inventor of the tunable plasma oscillator at microwave frequencies. Dr. Harold Puthoff is the author of a standard textbook in quantum physics and holds patents in lasers and optical devices.[38]

On October 18, 1974, the prestigious British science journal *Natural* published Puthoff and Targ's paper "Information Transmission Under Conditions of Sensory Shielding," which reports, in part, on some of the experiments with Uri Geller. One experiment apparently establishes Geller's clairvoyant abilities.

> A double-blind experiment was performed in which a single ¾-inch die was placed in a $3 \times 4 \times 5$-inch steel box. The box was then vigorously shaken by one of the experimenters and placed on the table, a technique found in control runs to produce a distribution of die faces that does not differ significantly from chance distribution. The orientation of the die within the box was unknown to the experimenters at that time. Geller would then write down which die face was uppermost.[33]

The outcome of this simple experiment was impressive indeed. Geller was tested in this manner for only ten trials. On two trials he "passed" (that is, he said that he received no impression, and did not attempt a guess). He was correct on each of the other eight trials. The authors report that the probability of such a result occurring by chance is approximately one in 10 million.

Wallace, Crookes, Targ, and Puthoff were all members in good standing of the scientific establishment when they made their claims for paranormal phenomena public. As recognized and accomplished scientists, these men might be expected to have their claims impartially evaluated by their colleagues. But almost without exception the claims were met with dismay, disbelief, and summary dismissal. Targ and Puthoff in a chapter entitled "The Loyal Opposition" document what they feel are the unfair, unethical, and irrational charges hurled against them and their investigations by incredulous critics and scientists.[38,42]

Although the scientists who have endorsed the claims of alleged psychics have perhaps often been treated unfairly and have had their claims rejected without a fair appraisal of the evidence, this does not, in my opinion, argue for the position that their claims ought to be taken more seriously by orthodox science. Some of the skepticism shown by the scientific community, in fact, has a justification.

With the possible exception of Daniel Dunglas Home, all of the alleged psychics who supplied the phenomena upon which the scientists based their endorsements were at some point in their histories caught in outright fraud or accused of fraud under conditions that at least raise strong suspicions. Just about all of the more than dozen mediums that Alfred Russel Wallace publicly endorsed were caught cheating at least once, and often several times, during their careers. Herne and Williams, who performed effectively for Crookes, were exposed many times. These two mediums trained Florence Cook—who was exposed convincingly both before and after her successful seances with Crookes. (For accounts of mediums endorsed by Crookes and Wallace and subsequently exposed, see notes 8, 10, 11, 13, 14, 15, 16, 18, 26, 32 for this chapter.) By now direct and circumstantial evidence that Uri Geller cheats at least on some occasions is overwhelming.[12,19,23,24,25,28,31,35,36,40]

Of course, the fact that an alleged psychic is caught cheating does not prove that he always cheats or that he or she was cheating when under scientific scrutiny. Indeed, almost from the very beginnings of psychical research, defenders of paranormal claims viewed the tendency to cheat as an occupational hazard of mediums and psychics. Such gifted individuals, so the argument goes, do have genuine paranormal abilities. But these abilities are erratic and not under conscious control. The psychic, whose rewards come mainly from the demonstration of his or her powers, is frequently tempted to supplement these powers with trickery in order to ensure that audiences will not be disappointed.

This belief that true psychic powers and strong tendencies to cheat often go hand in hand is so ingrained within the folklore of psychical research that believers go so far as to blame the skeptics for the presence of trickery.

For instance, Targ and Puthoff present their version of a visit I made to the Stanford Research Institute in December 1972. They write that they suggested to the three members of the visiting committee that we "conduct some experiments" of our own with Geller. The committee

> then spent an engaging couple of hours with Geller in which they observed the informal coffee-table type of demonstration that Uri favors. They tried a number of their own, and from our standpoint largely uncontrolled, experiments. . . . Hyman and Lawrence were not impressed by the results obtained in their experiments, however, . . . and left feeling that Geller was probably simply a clever magician; not an altogether unreasonable conclusion given what they saw and the informal manner in which they chose to interact with Geller.[38]

In other words, Targ and Puthoff seem to be saying that the fact that Geller employed trickery to create the illusion of telepathy and psychic metal bending was the fault of Lawrence and myself. But when *they* take charge of Geller, they control matters sufficiently well to prevent him from cheating, so presumably he settles down and employs his genuine psychic powers!

But even if parapsychologists find it quite plausible that psychics such as Geller have both genuine powers and strong tendencies to cheat,[39] they should not be surprised that skeptics and noninvolved judges are more dubious than otherwise of results that are produced by known cheaters.

In addition to the questionable reputations of the alleged psychics, many indications that suggest a lack of competence or trustworthiness on the part of the investigators further add to the distrust of the paranormal claims. We should try to be clear on this matter. To suggest that scientists such as Crookes, Wallace, Targ, and Puthoff show incompetence in investigating psychics should not be taken as a reflection of their abilities within their chosen fields of science. This unfortunate confusion is continually made by both critics and believers alike. There is every reason to suspect that competence, intelligence, and trustworthiness with respect to one's area of normal science have no connection at all with the ability to produce a trustworthy report on the activities of an alleged psychic. So, in what immediately follows, we will present indications that suggest the given scientist ought not be trusted with respect to his reports on paranormal claims of an alleged psychic.

Even some of Wallace's fellow believers have felt that he was overly gullible with respect to any claims for the paranormal. Hall points out that "Wallace's credulity on psychic matters was traditional."[18] Wallace insisted that S. J. Davey—who was deliberately producing spiritualistic phenomena by trickery to show how difficult it is for well-intentioned investigators to detect trickery—was a medium despite his claims to the contrary.[6,18,21,22] According to Lady William-Ellis, a recent biographer of Wallace, "He had a will to believe, so that over spiritualism he did not exercise the care of weighing evidence that he showed in his scientific work."[18]

Crookes's investigation of Florence Cook has been the center of a heated controversy since the publication of Trevor Hall's *The Spiritualists* in 1963. (For reactions to this book see notes 8, 9, 13, 16.) Hall amassed an array of evidence, some of which had recently come to light, to argue that Crookes was having an affair with Florence Cook and had to endorse the reality of her materializations in order to keep the affair private. But regardless of how one decides the case for this assertion, there is no question that Hall unearthed much material that casts strong suspicions on Crookes's handling of this investigation.

Even more damaging to Crookes's trustworthiness on paranormal phenomena is the recently revealed correspondence between Crookes and Daniel Home with respect to the medium Mary Showers.[16] Home asked Crookes to explain the defamatory accusations that had come to him involving Crookes with the young Mary. Crookes admitted that because of the stories being circulated in the latter half of 1875 about his association with Mary Showers he, Crookes, was "getting the reputation of a Don Juan." Crookes tried to explain how the scandal arose in a series of letters to Home, which he asked be kept in confidence. As Hall reports:

> According to Crookes he had obtained a complete confession from Mary Showers in her own handwriting that her phenomena were wholly dependent upon trickery and the occasional use of an accomplice. Crookes said, however, that

he had undertaken not to reveal the fact that Mary was fraudulent, even to her own mother, because of the very great injury which the cause of truth would suffer if so impudent a
fraud were to be publicly exposed.[16]

Finding evidence to suggest untrustworthiness on the part of the investigator or the alleged psychic is part of the process of "explaining
it away." When a recognized scientist surprises his colleagues with a
report of a supernatural occurrence, the critics are strongly tempted to
jump to the attack by putting forth possible scenarios as to how the
report could be false or misleading. Often they attack the scientist by
implying (without evidence and unfairly) that he or she is temporarily
or permanently incapacitated in some way. Or they reconstruct possible methods the alleged psychic or his confederates could have used to
circumvent the experimental controls. Sometimes they speculate,
without being able to demonstrate, that the seemingly paranormal
findings are due to hidden biases in the instruments, data analyses, or
experimental protocols.

I, along with many of my fellow critics, have often been trapped into
such fruitless attempts to explain things away. Wallace's endorsements
of mediums were dismissed on the ground that he was not an experimenter. Crookes had to defend himself against bitter and inaccurate
attacks on his training, his overspecialization, his election to the Royal
Society, and other ad hominem arguments designed to explain away
his reports on Home and Cook. And Hall argued that Crookes was in
collusion with Cook. The German astronomer Zoellner, who reported
favorably on his investigations of the American medium Henry Slade,
was accused of being of unsound mind at the time of the investigations. Russell Targ has been described by critics of his work with Uri
Geller as being extremely nearsighted. And Harold Puthoff has had
the credibility of his support of Geller's claims questioned because of
his being a Scientologist.

In addition to such ad hominem efforts at discounting the reports,
ingenious and often Rube Goldbergish attempts at supplying a "normal" explanation for paranormal accounts abound. In his attack upon
Targ and Puthoff's research with Uri Geller, for instance, Hanlon
goes into elaborate detail to argue how Geller *might* have had a radio
receiver implanted in his tooth, and how this receiver might have
aided him in successfully performing in both the drawing tests and the
die-guessing experiment.

Now, I do not deny that some ad hominem arguments and some discoveries of possible ways to circumvent the experimental controls are relevant to an evaluation of the evidence. But I believe that on the whole, attempts to explain away cases by these means are badly misguided. They often backfire and actually enhance the original case being made by the supporter of a paranormal claim for the following reasons:

1. The happenings *as described*, of necessity, differ in many ways from the happenings as they occurred. The published account can never be complete and the attempt to account for it by naturalistic means must be a *reconstruction* which has to make several assumptions. Often the assumptions turn out to be ones that the original investigator can easily deny. And because the reconstruction by the critic must be done on the basis of a description that presents the observations in a form that puts ready naturalistic explanations in a bad light, the critic's counterexplanation often becomes highly implausible. It is easy for Targ and Puthoff to show how Hanlon's explanation of Geller's die-guessing is simply ridiculous on the basis of current technology.[35,42]

2. The argument often shifts from the adequacy of the original account to the plausibility of the critic's reconstruction. In Panati's collection of papers to support the "scientific" case for Uri Geller,[30] the only attempt to rebut seriously any of the charges against Geller and his supporters is a report by a dentist certifying that Geller has no radio receivers implanted in his teeth. By focusing on this bizarre and easily dismissed criticism, Panati and other Geller supporters conveniently ignore the less colorful but more plausible objections. Worse, by showing that some of the objections are unreasonable and implausible, both sympathy and support are gained for the proponents of the paranormal, and the credibility of the skeptics is correspondingly tarnished.

3. The hypothetical reconstructions and the counterattacks upon them shift the burden of proof from the original proponents of the paranormal claim to their critics. This again is an unfortunate consequence of trying to provide a hypothetical scenario for the reported event. Ordinarily, most of us would agree that the burden of proof lies with the proponent of an anomalous claim. But when critics put forth hastily conceived

and hypothetical reconstructions, the resulting controversy subtly implies that the burden of proof is now upon the critics.
4. These points are subordinate to what, in my mind, is the most unfortunate implication of our attempts to "explain away" the accounts put forth by Hare, Wallace, Crookes, Targ, Puthoff, and other proponents. This unfortunate implication is that *there is something that requires explaining,* in the first place. But the really surprising consequence of my careful examination of the cases put forth in behalf of paranormal individuals by scientists over the past 125 years is my discovery that they have failed completely to produce anything that needs scientific attention.

The controversies that began with the claims of Hare, Wallace, and Crookes and that are still with us in the investigations by contemporary scientists of such alleged psychics as Ted Serios, Ingo Swann, and Uri Geller create much heat and raise a variety of issues. All of the issues revolve around the question of how to account for the reported results: Can we find a naturalistic explanation, or must we face up to some sort of a supernatural account? If Wallace's account of Mrs. Guppy's levitation is both true and inexplicable by natural laws, then somehow physics and even science as we know it have to be amended or drastically overhauled. The same is true for the accounts put forth by Crookes, Zoellner, Targ, Puthoff, and the other scientists who have related such incidents.

Such controversies assume, however, that there really is some paranormallike phenomenon that needs explaining, an assumption which I question. In normal scientific inquiry, the practice is to follow Mrs. Beeton's procedure in cookbook recipes that begin: "First catch your hare." One documents, within a given scientific context, the phenomena or relationships under controlled and standardized conditions. The data are extracted from observations by procedures and instruments that have been properly calibrated and that are known to be reliable and valid. Furthermore, the phenomena in question have been the subject of systematic scrutiny and have been replicated successfully by the original investigator as well as by independent investigators in other laboratories.

The preceding paragraph lists the minimal criteria that phenomena must meet before they require both attention and explanation on the part of the general scientific fraternity. The history of science demonstrates again and again that anomalous phenomena that fail to meet these minimal standards may justifiably be dropped from further consideration. In the 1930s some Russian scientists thought they had discovered what they called mitogenetic radiation. Some Western scientists also found evidence for this new type of radiation. But many other scientists were not able to replicate the original experiments. Rather soon even Russian scientists could not reliably find evidence for mitogenetic radiation. Biologists no longer feel they have to explain it, nor do they feel it is necessary to account for how the original scientists thought they had established such radiation in the first place. Presumably some unknown factor in the experimental situation misled them. The failure to reliably reproduce the original observation has consigned mitogenetic radiation to the same scrap heap that contains other candidates for scientific acceptance that could not survive continued scientific scrutiny.

In some cases, to be sure, we are fortunate to discover in retrospect a plausible reason for the initial error that led to the false report. In the area of psychical research, the studies in the early 1880s by the Society for Psychical Research on Smith and Blackburn fit into this category. Smith would be blindfolded. Blackburn would be shown a drawing, a number, or some other target that he was to try to communicate to Smith telepathically. Blackburn was able to succeed in such telepathic transmission under conditions that the early founders of the Society for Psychical Research felt were ironclad. In fact, this investigation was one of two that these researchers felt had established telepathy as a fact. Some twenty years after the experiments, when he mistakenly thought Smith was dead, Blackburn publicly confessed how he and Smith had tricked the investigators.[5,17]

If Blackburn had never confessed, the Smith-Blackburn investigation would still be one of those cases in which psychics were investigated under "stringent" conditions, and which cannot be explained away; it was simply a lucky accident that we now can account for the original experiment by natural means. But my point is that even if Blackburn had never confessed, there was no scientific reason for trying to account for the Smith-Blackburn results, because the reports of the phenomena never achieved any of the minimal criteria that I set out.

We should distinguish between personal belief and scientific proof. It is obvious that Hare, Wallace, Crookes, Targ, and Puthoff were all personally convinced that what they reported was truly paranormal.

But the whole point of scientific enterprise is that it deals with phenomena and data that are convincing to the community of scholars. In their own areas, scientists know that their personal beliefs count for nothing. Regardless of how much they are personally convinced, they realize that they have to provide evidence that meets minimal requirements of standardization, reliability, validity, and replicability. The reason for this simple community standard is that the scientific community has learned from bitter experience that personal conviction is a very fallible guide. The essence of science is that personal beliefs are never allowed to substitute for scientific demonstration. Within his own specialty, each scientist is quite aware of this distinction as well as of his obligation to supply the scientific evidence before he can expect his colleagues to seriously consider his claims.

Crookes, Wallace, and the other scientists we have been discussing all have seemed aware of this responsibility in the more traditional areas of science within which they made their reputations. But for some strange reason this important distinction seems to be lost when claims are made for the paranormal. On the basis of observations made under nonstandardized, nonvalidated, and nonreplicated conditions, they stubbornly persist in demanding that their scientific colleagues either provide a naturalistic explanation or admit the paranormal nature of the observations. And their scientific critics obligingly fall into the trap and try desperately to "explain away" the reported observations. If the claims were for something other than the paranormal, I doubt that the claimant would demand explanations prior to ensuring that minimal criteria have been met; and I further doubt that any critics would rush in to explain the data away.

Let's look at just some of the reasons why the reported findings by scientists on their studies of alleged psychics are not "scientific." First, we should realize that an individual, even an accomplished scientist, cannot simply enter a new arena of inquiry and arbitrarily make it scientific. This is not the place to go into all those complicated matters that occupy philosophers and historians of science. But some of the features of the scientific enterprise are that it is a *shared* venture; it is *cumulative*; it is *focused* on problems within a delimited conceptual framework, and individuals in the same field of inquiry share many common properties—similar training, agreed-upon vocabulary, and a consensus concerning the ways to gather data, control for error, analyze the data, report it, and so forth.

So when Robert Hare moves from his field of chemistry to the study of spiritualistic phenomena, he goes from a highly structured and well-developed field of inquiry into a completely unstructured realm with no standardized procedures, paradigms, or concepts. In the pursuit of chemical research, he is accountable to assistants, students, colleagues, and journal editors—all of whom share similar backgrounds, technical vocabularies, standards, and more. This shared context provides a variety of checks and balances. At all stages of inquiry there are clear-cut criteria and evaluative reactions to inform the scientist when he is on firm ground and when he had better recheck or pull back. When Hare insists that he has performed a controlled experiment on some chemical problem, his colleagues in that area know exactly what he means—they know from his training, from his previous accomplishments, and from the general ground rules that prevail within this chemical area.

But when Robert Hare, the accomplished chemist, experiments with spiritualistic mediums, he leaves behind all these safeguards, shared contexts, and checks and balances. His training and expertise are with respect to the tightly knit and highly structured areas of chemistry. Even if he moved to another structured area of science, he would be out of his element until he mastered the new vocabulary, ground rules, paradigms, and the like that characterize the new area. Further, there just does not exist a structured field for testing claims of alleged psychics. There is no shared community of vocabulary, procedures, ground rules, safeguards, and the like. No matter how vehemently Hare might insist that he is being just as "scientific" in this new type of investigation as he has been in his chosen area of chemistry, the claim is meaningless.

The same comments apply with equal force to the cases of Wallace, Crookes, Targ, Puthoff, and all other scientists who claim to have "scientifically" investigated claims of psychics.

The situation is actually worse than I have indicated. All of the reports of achievements by psychics depend upon observing them under conditions that presumably preclude fraud or alternative explanations. Quite often, more than one observer is present, but even this rule is frequently violated. But when multiple observers are present, they do not usually file separate and independent reports. Instead, they simply agree with the report made by the principal investigator. Since everything depends upon the value of these observations, it would seem that a minimal requirement be that the observations meet standards of reliability and validity. (For an elementary and useful discussion of observational methods, see Bickman.[3])

Not one single investigation by scientists of alleged psychics over the past 125 years meets any of the standards that social scientists have found are necessary for trustworthy observation. The observer is a crucial element in any research involving human behavior. When the behavior is complex or extends over time, much preparatory and standardization work must precede the development of an adequate observational system. Decisions have to be made with respect to the exhaustiveness of the system, the level of detail at which the behavior will be observed, the number and types of categories of behavior to be described, how much inference will be allowed at the time of observation, how the data will be recorded (simultaneously with the occurrence of the behavior or later from records), etcetera. Then observers must be trained to use the system. Not all can do so equally well, and inadequate observers must be discarded. The reliability of the system, as well as of the individual observers, must be established.

Furthermore, any system of observation is valid only for the range of standardized settings and situations for which it has been developed. When goals change and when settings and tasks change, the system must be redeveloped and evaluated from scratch. In addition, the reporting of the results of applying the observational system must fall within standardized conventions and vocabularies for a given area of specialization.

I have only scratched the surface of what it takes to make observations of complex behavior "scientific." But even this suggests how difficult and time-consuming the effort must be. If one wants to be scientific about it, there is no alternative. What is striking about every report from that of Hare down to those of Targ and Puthoff is that not even the suggestion of trying to establish a systematic procedure for observation is included. Certainly no attempt is made to train observers, assess their reliability in employing the system, demonstrate that the established system is reliable, etcetera.

Instead of standardized tasks, or even highly similar tasks from one investigation to another, each investigator generates ad hoc tests, often in collaboration with the alleged psychic. As a result, we do not have cumulative data across a variety of settings and situations with which to evaluate the adequacy of the task. And this makes comparing findings from different sessions with the same psychic impossible. The same holds true with comparisons of results from different laboratories. Imagine how orthodox science would have fared if every investigator did experiments of his own devising, each created to fit personal whims of the day and setting, without reference to tasks being performed by other experimenters!

When looked at from a scientific viewpoint, the entire situation is chaotic and incoherent. Often a given investigator will do a variety of different tests with a given subject instead of systematically exploring one or a few tasks over a variety of conditions. Targ and Puthoff, for example, carried out the die experiment with Uri Geller in November and December 1972. Given that this is a very simple and direct test, and given that the results seem so striking (eight correct out of eight attempts), it would have begun to approximate standards for scientific evidence if they had followed through on his next visit and done a few more experiments of the same sort with Geller under more clearly specified and systematically varied conditions. There is nothing wrong with an investigator's trying out a wide variety of tasks to explore the range of effects he might expect from his "psychic." But such preliminary surveys belong to the exploratory stage, which helps the investigator decide which tasks he will later choose for systematic development. The mistake that Targ and Puthoff make, along with the other scientists discussed in this chapter, is to ask us to accept selections from their preliminary canvassing as "scientific" data that somehow require explanation.

But successful replication and systematic exploration of the same task by the same investigator is necessary but not sufficient for a phenomenon to be judged ready for scientific consideration. At least one of two types of replication should be mandatory: either showing that different psychics can produce successful results on the same task, or showing that different investigators in different laboratories can achieve successful results with the same psychic.

Claims, of course, have been made that this latter type of replication has actually been achieved with Uri Geller.[30] But these claims are spurious and completely miss the mark.[23] None of the studies employed observational conditions that meet any of the criteria I have referred to. In addition, rather than being replications, the studies are at variance with one another. The seven or more weeks that Geller spent at SRI were primarily devoted to trying to obtain convincing evidence that he could bend metal and obtain other psychokinetic effects by paranormal means. Targ and Puthoff frankly admit that they completely failed to collect such evidence. Instead, they vouch only for some clairvoyant and telepathic abilities of Geller. However, the physicists at Birbeck College reported success with psychokinetic effects, and John Taylor, at Kings College (both groups are at the University of London but acted independently of one another), observed other sorts of psychokinetic effects. Neither of these two latter groups of scientists even tried to obtain any ESP results from Geller of the type that was observed at SRI.

At the beginning of this chapter I said that we would focus upon the problem of how the interested layman can make sense out of the claims and counterclaims that arise when a scientist reports he has witnessed paranormal phenomena in connection with an alleged psychic. I then gave examples of such claims spanning a period of 125 years, beginning with Robert Hare and ending with our contemporaries Russell Targ and Harold Puthoff. All these claims were met with incredulous outcries from the scientific community. Each of the claimants was attacked on grounds that were in part ad hominem and unfair. On the other hand, the "psychics" who had been tested had dubious reputations and often had been caught cheating in other circumstances. And sometimes circumstantial evidence strongly implied that the scientist's report was untrustworthy for one or more reasons. But I went on to argue that the attempt to explain away these reports because of real or imagined defects was misguided and counterproductive.

The real question is not which of an infinite number of possibilities—which we can never understand with assurance because we can't go back in time to explore the original structure—might have accounted for the original report. But rather, can the reported result hold up and be repeated in the court of scientific inquiry? Has there been a paranormal phenomenon or relationship that was reliably and systematically observed under scientific conditions? Something does not automatically become "scientific" just because an eminent scientist does it or proclaims that what he observed was under scientific conditions. In addition to a community of shared concerns and paradigms with respect to a given problem, the observations must be made with standardized and proven procedures, the observers and their instruments must be reliable, the data must be reported according to conventional categories and attributes, and the settings and tasks must be ones in widespread use or ones that have gone through preliminary checks and standardization. In addition, especially if the reported results are anomalous or at variance with current theories and presuppositions, they must be systematically studied under a wide variety of conditions, and they should be repeatable by investigators in independent laboratories.

The preceding paragraph sums up a minimal set of criteria for deciding if an anomalous result justifies further consideration and attempts at explanation. But the reader might still feel somewhat insecure about his ability to apply these criteria to reports of paranormal phenomena. The layman often does not have ready access to the original publication, and must rely on secondary sources. Can we supply guidelines for this latter situation? While there is no truly adequate substitute for examining the original report, there are some guidelines that can help. At the very least, the following questions can help quickly eliminate from further consideration many of the striking accounts that reach the public through the regular information channels.

1. *How reliable is the source?*

Roughly, there are two sources to consider. The *secondary source* is usually the one from which you first learn of the report. It is a second- or third-hand account given by an acquaintance or reported in the media. The *primary source* is the one in which the scientist involved reported the allegedly paranormal happenings. Crookes's reports on his seances with Florence Cook appeared only in the spiritualistic magazines. He did not attempt to get them published in regular scientific journals. The nature of the primary source here counts against the report because it was not subjected to review by other scientists. But the report on the die-in-box experiment with Uri Geller appeared in *Nature*, one of the oldest and most prestigious journals in science. This in itself counts in favor of the report because it means the report was refereed by three independent scientists.

Presumably the *New York Times*, *Scientific American*, and public broadcasting are more reliable as secondary sources than would be many tabloids, more general circulation magazines, and the commercial broadcasting outlets. And when they report that the primary source was a scientific journal or a paper read at a scientific meeting, the report has passed at least a crude preliminary screening. But if the primary source is not one of those, then little weight should be given to it. If the secondary source is one of the tabloids or commercial broadcasting, no weight need be given to it.

2. *How recent is the research upon which the claim is based?*

The layman has to be especially dubious about reports of paranormal happenings that are based on investigations less than a year old. It is ironic that some scientists, who would insist upon waiting for a year or more before certifying a claim for a new phenomenon within the orthodox boundaries of science, are willing to go on record as endorsing a paranormal claim on the basis of one or two brief sessions and with no time for subsequent digestion of what has been witnessed. (See Panati[30] for several flagrant examples.) If the secondary source is reporting on the result of a long series of investigations that began a few years ago, this is much more compelling. Unfortunately, it is the nature of "news" that the media like to play up "new" and "recent" breakthroughs. It is just these recent and undigested outcomes that the media find worth covering. When, as is most often the case, time has allowed second thoughts and further considerations to demystify what at first seemed like a paranormal happening, the media are no longer interested and, instead, are perusing new "miracles," hot out of the laboratory.

3. Has the original investigator been able to successfully replicate his findings?

Crookes was at least able to report the materialization of Katie King on several different occasions. But many of the reported psychic feats are one-shot affairs. For whatever reason, Targ and Puthoff never repeated the die-in-box experiment. This is unfortunate, because it would have been very simple to do.

4. Have the phenomena been replicated by an independent investigator in another laboratory?

If a scientist announces the discovery of a new element, the remainder of the scientific community will withhold judgment until the finding has been independently verified in one or more separate laboratories. We should require nothing less of a claim for an event that defies all natural laws. In none of the cases reported in this essay was there such independent verification.

5. Does the original report conform to the standards required for observing human performance?

The issues involved in this criterion have already been discussed in detail. This clearly is the most blatantly abused criterion in the complete series of reports that I have examined. The descriptions not only fail to conform to any standards of objectivity, reliability, validity, or specificity, but they invariably fail badly as simple written accounts. To the extent that the descriptions are made under conditions for which no existing observational and recording standards have been developed, they need to be even more detailed and complete than ordinary scientific accounts. Yet the opposite is invariably true.

Again let us look at the die-in-box experiment with Uri Geller. For such a potentially important experiment, the details are so incomplete and sketchy as to be almost worthless. We are told that "a single 3/4-inch die was placed in a 3 × 4 × 5-inch steel box." Nothing else is said about the die, its composition, etcetera. In fact, the statement is ambiguous in that we do not know if the same die was used in all ten trials. In their report of this experiment in their book *Mind-reach*, Targ and Puthoff add that the die and the box were supplied by SRI and the die had a serial number stamped on it.[38] This latter description clearly implies that the same die was used for all ten trials. But Wilhelm, who spent considerable time interviewing all the relevant parties to the experiment, writes that "a number of different dice were used, each one etched with an identifying serial number to guard against surreptitious switching. At times the experimenters also used a transparent die to ensure that Geller did not substitute one with a miniature radio inside that could signal which number faced up."[42] Apparently, then, a number of different dice were employed. Why did not the investigators inform us of this in the first place? The report tells us that Geller would write down his guess before either the experimenters or Geller knew which face was uppermost in the box. But the report says nothing about who opened the box and checked its contents. Here Wilhelm's account is more specific and actually more favorable to the investigators: He tells us that Geller would draw the number of spots he thought was on the upper face and then hold his drawing up to the video camera. Targ and Puthoff mention nothing about videotaping the procedure, either in the *Nature* report or in the account in their book. Possibly this could be because not all trials were taped. The "scientific" report mentions nothing about who were the observers, who was the investigator who shook the box, or how they made sure that Geller could not peek into it (in response to criticisms, they assert in their book that Geller had no opportunity to peek into the box, but they do not tell us how they prevented such opportunities). Nor do they tell us anything about the physical arrangements of the experiment—where it took place, where he sat, etcetera. The reader might readily assume that the experiment was done at one sitting in a laboratory room at SRI. But we are surprised to discover the following in Wilhelm's account:

> On some tests conducted in his motel room, Geller shook the dice himself. Questioned as to whether this might be a breach in test protocol since he might have been able to control the roll of the dice, Puthoff replies that Geller shook the box vigorously enough to ensure an honest shake. "It's very clear," adds Targ. "He's like a kid in that he had something that made a lot of noise and he just shook and shook it. I probably terminated it by saying 'That's enough.' " Why was he allowed to shake the dice part of the time? "We just wanted to see what it was he would do." [42]

We also learn that Geller sometimes placed his hands upon the box when trying to divine the uppermost face.

All of this strongly suggests that not only have the authors failed to provide a scientific account, but that they have provided a grossly inadequate and misleading description.

I suspect that the above simple criteria will suffice to screen out just about all accounts in which scientists endorse psychics. It is a sobering thought to realize that not a single report of this sort over a period of 125 years has managed to stand up to scientific scrutiny. When I have discussed the cases of Hare, Wallace, Crookes, and Zoellner before public audiences, some physicists in the audience tell me that such faulty reports could not occur today because natural sciences have come a long way in that time and we know much more. The sad fact, however, is that the reports on Uri Geller, Ted Serios, and other contemporary psychics by trained scientists show no improvement in scientific sophistication over those of their predecessors of more than a century ago. Indeed, the reports of Crookes on his experiments with Daniel Home, despite all their defects, are far superior as scientific evidence to anything that has been published subsequently in support of the claims of a psychic.

I have no quarrel with any scientist who wants to investigate the claims of an alleged psychic. Indeed, the willingness of such men to risk their reputation and to face ridicule is probably a good thing for the growth of science in the long run. What seems to be lacking is a recognition on the part of such scientists of what it will take to put such an investigation onto a scientific footing. Standardized procedures, instrumentation, variables, controls, concepts, data analyses, and other necessities of scientific inquiry will have to be developed, tested, debugged, and validated from scratch. This will not be easy and probably cannot be done by one or two men working alone. But until such groundwork is laid, scientists who wish to challenge the establishment should not be surprised that their claims are dismissed summarily. To ask their colleagues to take time to consider their reported miracles at the current level of documentation is to ask them to abandon the very thing that has made science into the powerful intellectual tool it is.

9

On Double Standards

BARRY SINGER

In 1962, James V. McConnell and his colleagues announced that worms that ate ground-up portions of their fellow worms thereby acquired their fellow worms' knowledge.[1] McConnell had conditioned planaria, small freshwater flatworms that are the most primitive organisms to possess a brain, to scrunch up when a bright light came on. After enough trials where the light was immediately followed by electric shock, the worms had learned to scrunch up in anticipation of the shock as soon as they perceived the light. These planaria then became a meal for other planaria (the worms are cannibalistic), which within a day of digesting their peers showed that they had picked up the scrunching trick without training of their own.

These dramatic results startled the scientific community, especially those scientists concerned with brain function and the physiological locus of memory in the brain. The results suggested that memory is chemically rather than structurally coded in the brain, but at that time many scientists doubted that specific knowledge could be represented by specific chemical alterations. It was much easier to imagine a specific memory or bit of knowledge as coded in changes in the structure of a few nerve cells among the billions in the brain, or from changes in connections between cells. Even if memory were chemically coded, it did not seem reasonable that a specific memory could be transferred from one organism to another by so crude a procedure as one organism's eating the brains of another. Yet the results, if true, were of enormous significance. Scientists had visions of a college education being acquired by swallowing a pill. Jokes about grinding up older professors and feeding them to younger ones immediately made the rounds. Scientists set out to replicate and extend the experiment.

The story of cannibalism in planaria is entertaining, and it can illuminate the issue of scientific standards. In the brief case history to follow, note the parallels between the worm-cannibalism story and psychic research. In both cases the experiments are highly dramatic, the results potentially revolutionary.

McConnell's seeming breakthrough quickly ran into trouble. Scientists in other laboratories had difficulty repeating the observation. They could not induce the worms to learn in the first place, or, if learning did occur, they could not produce transfer of the learning through cannibalism. But they kept trying. I was a graduate student in psychology at Berkeley at the time, and investigators there sought help from McConnell's colleague Allan Jacobson, who had moved to UCLA and reported positive results there. Jacobson was invited to Berkeley to supervise the investigators who were trying to replicate the experiment. It didn't help. The Berkeley group still could not repeat the observation. Finally, in 1966 twenty-three scientists from seven different laboratories, including Berkeley, wrote a joint letter to the prestigious journal *Science*, announcing that they could not repeat McConnell's results.[2] "A positive result," the letter said, "should have demonstrable replicability and generality. Unfortunately, the data bearing on both generality and replicability appear to be on the negative side." The message being diplomatically conveyed here was, "We don't believe the result." The letter went on to say that such a result, if correct, was so significant that they would nevertheless continue to try to repeat it.

McConnell and his colleagues continued to assert that the results were real and repeatable. In a barbed commentary some years later, McConnell noted that "although several thousand high-school students were able to train planaria with little difficulty—and to perform transfer experiments as well—there were many senior investigators who never got the knack and who complained loudly."[3]

In 1967, Allan Jacobson was again invited to Berkeley, this time to give a colloquium (which I attended) before the assembled psychology faculty and graduate students on planaria memory transfer and on his own work in particular. In his talk Jacobson appeared to be uncertain about some important elements of procedure. Instead of feeding knowledgeable worms wholesale to ignorant ones, Jacobson had concocted an RNA chemical extract from the former which he injected into the latter, which allegedly produced the memory transfer. When asked about the amount of extract injected, Jacobson cited a quantity injected into each worm that was twice the average body weight of the worms. When confronted with the apparent physical difficulty of this procedure, Jacobson appeared uncertain and confused. When asked why other investigators had difficulty replicating his work, Jacobson replied, "They have no feeling for the worms. You've got to have a feeling for the worms." In other words, the vibes between worm and skeptical experimenter were just not right.

This comment did not sit well with the audience. If a result is valid and real, it ought to be repeatable by different investigators in different laboratories. Scientists are very suspicious of any result that can be produced only some of the time and only by some investigators. This sort of phenomenon looks very much like either a fluke, a chance result, or an error in procedure ("artifact," as it is termed) on the part of the investigators reporting the positive result. Scientists will quite sensibly not believe differently until they too can repeat the result.[4] In the case of memory transfer in planaria, even the most careful supervision of procedure in another laboratory by one of the original investigators had failed to achieve a replication. Jacobson's claim that failure to replicate was due to the inability of other investigators to commune with the worms was regarded as bizarre. Chemical memory transfer should occur even when the observer fails to empathize with the worms' sense of themselves in the cosmos. If the actual handling of the animals does make a difference, those handling procedures that produce positive results ought to be observable and specifiable. Otherwise, the phrase "no feeling for the worms" is meaningless and evasive.

At the present time the planaria research is regarded as still inconclusive. It has been recommended that experimenters might obtain clearer results with other species, and research on chemical memory transfer, particularly with other species, has in fact accelerated.[5]

We could easily substitute "ESP" for "memory transfer in planaria" above; the history of the research and the attitude of scientists toward that phenomenon have been quite similar. A number of other examples of controversial phenomena from conventional science could also have been chosen to illustrate the same point. ESP has not been singled out by establishment scientists for prejudicial treatment. If a phenomenon is not consistently repeatable, appears only some of the time and in some laboratories, it may nevertheless be a valid phenomenon. But these same kinds of capricious results would appear even if the phenomenon were not valid—if, for example, some researchers were committing procedural errors or simply measuring random variation. Unless the phenomenon is repeatable, there is no way to tell the difference, and no reason to assume validity—for chemical memory transfer in planaria, or for ESP. Thus, ESP is not the victim of scientific double standards.

There is another sense, however, in which scientists are often said to be prejudiced against ESP. It is sometimes claimed that ESP is not a capricious, uncontrollable, and unreplicable laboratory phenomenon. It is asserted instead that parapsychology has advanced to the point where ESP is in fact a well-established phenomenon, even by usual scientific standards, and that conventional scientists will not even read the relevant studies that establish this fact. Although not all parapsychologists would make such a claim, Charles Tart, for instance, for years a leading parapsychologist, has been aggressive in his accusations of this sort of scientific double standard. Tart has claimed that there are hundreds of watertight scientific studies establishing psychic phenomena. Parapsychologists, he asserts, "have for many years filled three scientific journals with excellent evidence about extrasensory perception, so there is a very large backlog of data. The general situation is that there are now several basic psi phenomena whose existence has been established beyond any reasonable doubt."[6] Establishment science's skeptical attitude is characterized as "not a matter of rational rejection of poor experimentation and insufficient data on the part of an educated scientific community, but a simple case of prejudice. Almost all scientists are simply totally ignorant as to what the data of parapsychology are, and prejudiced against looking at it."[7]

In replying to this claim, it seems appropriate and fair to evaluate one of Tart's own paranormal studies. In 1976 Tart published a fascinating experiment purporting to scientifically demonstrate astral projection.[8] A woman who claimed to have frequent out-of-body experiences was invited into Tart's laboratory. Since the woman, "Miss Z," experienced herself as floating out of her body while asleep and looking down upon herself, Tart constructed a test to determine whether the experience was valid or merely a dream. For four nights Miss Z slept in Tart's laboratory, "on a comfortable bed, just below an observation window where I could peek through and see that she wasn't up to any 'no good' at any time. . . . There were electrodes glued to her head, to measure her brain waves [during astral projection], and then up above her, about seven feet off the floor, was a shelf. . . . After she was wired up for the evening (and couldn't get out of bed because of the delicate connections), I would go off to my office and randomly select a five-digit number from a table of random numbers, write it in big letters on a sheet of paper and come in and slip it flat on the shelf . . . anybody floating up near the ceiling could read the five-digit number right off." Miss Z, if she floated out of her body, was to try to float near the shelf, read the number, and report it to Tart in the morning.

On the first three nights a number of astral-projection experiences were reported, but Miss Z couldn't seem to float near enough to the shelf to read the number. Miss Z was about to move out of the geographic area, and the fourth night in the laboratory was to be her last. On the early morning of the fourth night she awoke, reported on an out-of-body experience, and correctly reported the five-digit number. Tart discusses the possibility that she cheated by use of concealed mirrors, but labels this hypothesis as excessively paranoid. "The main thing I think this particular study demonstrated was that it's possible to take a really exotic phenomena [sic] like what seems to be your soul leaving your body, study it in the laboratory, have it actually happen there . . . and you *may* also take it as proof that out-of-body experiences can be 'real' in the sense that you really can perceive (extrasensorially) from a location different from your physical body." Tart then discusses the implications of these results for the religious concept of soul, suggesting that "soul" is indicated by this study as possibly real: "While out-of-the-body experience is an improbable thing in terms of the rest of our scientific world view, we should look very *seriously* at this then and the idea of soul. Soul is not 'just' a word."

In a word, this study is preposterous. It is preposterous to do just one experiment with just one subject, obtain one positive observation, and then publicly claim that a highly improbable phenomenon like astral projection is real and has been demonstrated, to say nothing of the concept of soul. Normally, before announcing in print anything so highly dramatic and inherently improbable, a scientist would check and recheck his observations many times. Also, even the most scientifically naive reader can imagine elementary controls that were missing from this experiment: First, the woman should have been constantly under observation—the mere presence of an observation window is not a sufficient deterrent; second, an infrared camera should have recorded her every movement; and third, she should have slept confined by a locked glass or metal cage. Anyone who has had EEG electrodes glued to his scalp knows that the electrode connections are not that "delicate." They permit ample freedom of movement. We are not given enough information about the length and nature of the connections to allow us to assess the possibility, but it seems quite conceivable that Miss Z stood up quickly in bed, unobserved, and peeked at the shelf.

I find it strangest of all that the experiment was discontinued at this point because Miss Z "moved from the area where my laboratory was located." If astral projection is real, it is certainly one of the scientific finds of the century. If I truly believed that I had found a subject like Miss Z who could help me demonstrate astral projection, I would follow her to the sands of Zanzibar. I'd mortgage my home to pay her to continue to work with me.

It seems fair to say that this study is not science; it's a caricature of science. Yet I would imagine it is one of those that Tart would cite among the "hundreds" that conclusively demonstrate psychic phenomena. I do not want to claim that all or even most parapsychological research is as flawed as this is. Much of it is methodologically sound, and in fact some of the best research has been done by Charles Tart. Yet I cannot agree that the research on ESP is so obviously positive and conclusive, as Tart and others claim. The research that is methodologically sound generally appears inconclusive to me, and the research that reports dramatic and apparently convincing results often seems as methodologically ridiculous as the above. I cannot agree that these judgments of mine and my colleagues' represent a double standard. Nor can I agree that my lack of thorough familiarity with psychic literature, to which I plead guilty, represents "ignorance and prejudice." On the contrary, I give myself pats on the back for continuing to read the occasional parapsychological literature that looks promising, because so often the promise turns out to be the preposterous. It is not a sound use of my time to read hundreds of studies like the above.

I will begin to believe in the possibility of psychic phenomena when I am told of procedures that will allow me to observe it reliably in my own laboratory, as with any ordinary scientific phenomenon, and when I read parapsychological literature with convincing results which meets normal standards of scientific rigor. These attitudes are representative of usual scientific standards, not "double" ones. I sincerely believe that, in ascribing negative personal qualities to scientists when we are applying only the usual scientific standards, in asking for acceptance of virtually unreplicable phenomena when we do not extend such favors to any other scientific area, and in claiming that the scientific community is ignorant and prejudiced about masses of supposedly conclusive parapsychological research when so much of it is patently ridiculous, some psychic researchers themselves legitimately stand accused of using double standards.

10

The Subtlest Difference

ISAAC ASIMOV

The belief in some sort of survival after death is ages old, and recently case studies of persons who have undergone near-death experiences have been offered as confirming evidence for "life after life." If we are to "survive" in any sense after physical death, however, it must be an immaterial vital essence that survives, since the body decays. The presence or absence of this vital essence, usually termed the "spirit," is what some say constitutes the essential difference between life and death.

In the following essay Isaac Asimov, with customary wit and literary flair, analyzes the concept of spirit historically and scientifically. Asimov offers some plausible speculations about how the notion of spirit originated and discusses to what extent it has scientific backing, on the basis of either human biochemistry or recent clinical interviews of near-death patients. Finally, Asimov elegantly explains the mainstream scientific position on the essential ingredient of life and on our spiritual survival after death.

What is life and what is death and how do we distinguish between the two?

If we're comparing a functioning human being with a rock, there is no problem.

A human being is composed of certain types of chemicals intimately associated with living things—proteins, nucleic acids and so on—while a rock is not.

Then, too, a human being displays a series of chemical changes that make up its "metabolism," changes in which food and oxygen are converted into energy, tissues, and wastes. As a result, the human being grows and reproduces, turning simple substances into complex ones in apparent (but only apparent) defiance of the second law of thermodynamics. A rock does not do this.

But the human/rock contrast offers so simple a distinction between life and death that it is trivial and doesn't help us out. What we should do is take a more difficult case. Let us consider and contrast not a human being and a rock, but a live human being and a dead human being.

In fact, let's make it as difficult as possible and ask what the essential difference is between a human being just a short time before death and a short time after death, say five minutes before and five minutes after.

What are the changes in those ten minutes?

The molecules are still all there, all the proteins, all the nucleic acids. Nevertheless, *something* has stopped being there, for where metabolism and adaptive behavior had been taking place (however feebly) before death, they are no longer taking place afterward.

Some spark of life has vanished. What is it?

One early speculation in this respect involved the blood. It is easy to suppose that there is some particular association between blood and life, one that is closer and more intimate than that between other tissues and life. After all, as you lose blood, you become weaker and weaker, and finally you die. Perhaps, then, it is blood which is the essence of life—and, in fact, life itself.

A remnant of this view will be found in the Bible, which in places explicitly equates life and blood.

Thus, after the Flood, Noah and his family, the only human survivors of that great catastrophe, are instructed by God as to what they might eat and what they might not eat. As part of this exercise in dietetics, God says: "But flesh with the life thereof, which is the blood thereof, shall ye not eat" (Genesis 9:4).

In another passage on nutrition, Moses quotes God as being even more explicit and as saying, "Only be sure that thou eat not the blood: for the blood is the life; and thou mayest not eat the life with the flesh" (Deuteronomy 12:23). Similar statements are to be found in Leviticus 17:11 and 17:14.

Apparently, life is the gift of God and cannot be eaten, but once the blood is removed, what is left is essentially dead and has always been dead and may be eaten. By this view, plants, which lack blood, are not truly alive. They do not live, but merely vegetate, and serve merely as a food supply.

In Genesis 1:29–30, for instance, God is quoted as saying to the human beings he has just created: "Behold, I have given you every herb bearing seed which is upon the face of all the earth, and every tree, in the which is the fruit of a tree yielding seed; to you it shall be for meat. And to every beast of the earth, and to every fowl of the air, and to every thing that creepeth upon the earth, wherein there is life, I have given every green herb for meat."

Plants are described as "bearing seed" and "yielding seed," but in animals "there is life."

Today we would not make the distinction, of course. Plants are as alive as animals, and plant sap performs the functions of animal blood. Even on a purely animal basis, however, the blood theory would not stand up. Although loss of blood in sufficient quantities inevitably leads to loss of life, the reverse is not true. It is quite possible to die without the loss of a single drop of blood; indeed, that often happens.

Since death can take place when, to all appearances, nothing material is lost, the spark of life must be found in something more subtle than blood.

What about the breath then? All human beings, all animals breathe.

If we think of the breath, we see that it is much more appropriate as the essence of life than blood is. We constantly release the breath, then take it in again. The inability to take it in again invariably leads to death. If a person is prevented from taking in the breath by physical pressure on his windpipe, by a bone lodged in his throat, by being immersed in water—that person dies. The loss of breath is as surely fatal as the loss of blood, and the loss of breath is the more quickly fatal, too.

Furthermore, where the reverse is not true for blood—where people can die without loss of blood—the reverse *is* true for air. People cannot die without loss of air. A living human being breathes, however feebly, no matter how close he is to death; but after death, he does not breathe, and that is always true. Furthermore, the breath itself is something that is very subtle. It is invisible, impalpable, and, to early people, it seemed immaterial. It was just the sort of substance that would, and should, represent the essence of life and, therefore, the subtle difference between life and death.

Thus, in Genesis 2:7, the creation of Adam is described thus: "And the Lord God formed man of the dust of the ground, and breathed into his nostrils the breath of life; and man became a living soul."

The word for "breath" would be *ruakh* in Hebrew, and that is usually translated as "spirit."

It seems a great stretch from "breath" to "spirit," but that is not so at all. The two words are literally the same. The Latin *spirare* means "to breathe," and *spiritus* is "a breath." The Greek word *pneuma*, which means "breath," is also used to refer to a "spirit." And the word *ghost* is derived from an old English word meaning "breath." The word *soul* is of uncertain origin, but I am quite confident that if we knew its origin, it, too, would come down to breath.

Because in English we have a tendency to use words of Latin and Greek derivation, and then forget the meaning of the classic terms, we attach grandiosity to concepts that don't belong there.

We talk of the "spirits of the dead." The meaning would be precisely the same, and less impressive, if we spoke of the "breath of the dead." The terms "Holy Ghost" and "Holy Spirit" are perfectly synonymous and mean, essentially, "God's breath."

It might well be argued that the literal meaning of words means nothing, that the most important and esoteric concepts must be expressed in lowly words and that these words gather their meaning from the concept and not vice versa.

Well, perhaps if one believes that knowledge comes full-blown by supernatural revelation, one can accept that. I think, however, that knowledge comes from below, from observation, from simple and unsophisticated thinking that establishes a primitive concept that gradually grows complex and abstract as more and more knowledge is gathered. Etymology, therefore, is a clue to the *original* thought, overlaid now by thousands of years of abstruse philosophy. I think that people noticed the connection of breath and life in a quite plain and direct way and that all the subtle philosophical and theological concepts of spirit and soul came afterward.

Is the human spirit as formless and impersonal as the breath that gave it its name? Do the spirits of all the human beings who have ever died commingle into one mixed and homogenized mass of generalized life?

It is difficult to believe this. After all, each human being is distinct, and different in various subtle and not-so-subtle ways from every other. It would seem natural then to suppose that the essence of his life has, in some ways, to be different from every other. Each spirit, then, would retain that difference and would remain somehow reminiscent of the body it once inhabited and to which it lent the property and individuality of life.

And if each spirit retains the impress that gave the body its characteristic properties, it is tempting to suppose that the spirit possesses, in subtle, airy and ethereal manner, the form and shape of the human body it inhabited. This view may have been encouraged by the fact that it is common to dream of dead people as being still alive. Dreams were often given much significance in earlier times (and in modern times, too, for that matter) as messages from another world, and that would make it seem like strong evidence that the spirits resembled the bodies they had left.

For modesty's sake, if for no other reason, such spirits are usually pictured as clad in formless white garments, made of luminous cloud or glowing light, perhaps, and that, of course, gives rise to the comic strip pictures of ghosts and spirits wearing sheets.

It is further natural to suppose a spirit to be immortal. How can the very essence of life die? A material object can be alive or dead according to whether it contains the essence of life or not, but the essence of life can only be alive.

This is analogous to the statement that a sponge can be wet or dry depending on whether it contains water or not, but the water itself can only be wet; or that a room can be light or dark depending on whether the sun's rays penetrate it or not, but the sun's rays can only be light.*

If you have a variety of spirits or souls, which are eternally alive, and which enter a lump of matter at birth and give it life, and then

---

* You can argue both points and say that water at a temperature low enough to keep it non-melting ice, or water in the form of vapor, is not wet; and that the sun's rays, if ultraviolet or infrared, are not light in appearance. However, I am trying to argue like a philosopher and not like a scientist—at least in this paragraph.

leave it and allow it to die, there must be a vast number of spirits, one for each human being who has ever lived or ever will live.

This number may be increased further if there are also spirits for various other forms of life. It may be decreased if the spirits can be recycled; that is, if a spirit on leaving one dying body can then move into a body being born.

Both these latter views have their adherents, sometimes in combination, so that there are some people who believe in transmigration of souls throughout the animal kingdom. A man who has particularly misbehaved might be born again as a cockroach, whereas conversely, a cockroach can be reborn as a man if it has been a very good and noble cockroach.

However the matter is interpreted, whether spirits are confined to human beings or spread throughout the animal kingdom; or whether there is transmigration of souls or not, there must be a large number of spirits available for the purpose of inducing life and taking it away. Where do they all stay?

In other words, once the spirit is accepted, a whole spirit world must be assumed. This spirit world may be down under the earth, or up somewhere at great heights, on another world, or on another "plane."

The simplest assumption is that the spirits of the dead are just piled up underground, perhaps because the practice of burying the dead is a very ancient one.

The simplest underground dwelling place of the spirits would be one that is viewed as a gray place of forgetfulness, like the Greek Hades or the Hebrew Sheol. There the situation is almost like a perpetual hibernation. Sheol is described as follows in the Bible: "There the wicked cease from troubling; and there the weary be at rest. There the prisoners rest together; they hear not the voice of the oppressor. The small and great are there; and the servant is free from his master" (Job 3:17–19). And Swinburne describes Hades in "The Garden of Proserpine," which begins:

> Here, where the world is quiet,
>   Here, where all trouble seems
> Dead winds' and spent waves' riot
>   In doubtful dreams of dreams . . .

This nothingness seems insufficient to many people, and a rankling feeling of injustice in life tempts them to imagine a place of after-death torture where the people they dislike get theirs—the Greek Tartarus or the Christian Hell.

The principle of symmetry demands the existence of abodes of bliss as well for the people they like—Heaven, the Islands of the Blest, Avalon, the Happy Hunting Grounds, Valhalla.

All of this massive structure of eschatology is built up out of the fact that living people breathe and dead people don't and that living people desperately *want* to believe that they will not truly die.

Nowadays, we know, of course, that the breath has no more to do with the essence of life than blood does; that it, like blood, is merely the servant of life. Nor is breath insubstantial, immaterial and mysterious. It is as material as the rest of the body and is composed of atoms no more mysterious than any other atoms.

Yet despite this, people still believe in life after death, even people who understand about gases and atoms and the role of oxygen. Why?

The most important reason is that, regardless of evidence or the lack of it, people still want to believe. And because they do, there is a strong urge to believe even irrationally.

The Bible speaks of spirits and souls and life after death. In one passage, King Saul even has a witch bring up the spirit of the dead Samuel from Sheol (I Samuel 28:7–20). This is enough for millions of people, but many in our secular and skeptical generation are not really inclined to accept, undiscriminatingly, the statements present in the collection of the ancient legends and poetry of the Jews.

There is, of course, eyewitness evidence. How many people, I wonder, have reported having seen ghosts and spirits? Millions, perhaps. No one can doubt that they have made the reports, but anyone can doubt that they have actually seen what they have reported they have seen. I can't imagine a rational person will accept these stories.

There is the cult of "spiritualism" which proclaims the ability of "mediums" to make contact with the spirit world. This has flourished and has attracted not only the uneducated, ignorant, and the unsophisticated, but, despite the uncovering of countless gross frauds, even such highly intelligent and thoughtful people as A. Conan Doyle and Sir Oliver Lodge. The vast majority of rational people, however, place no credence in spiritualism at all.

Then, too, about twenty years ago, there was a book called *The Search for Bridey Murphy* in which a woman was supposedly possessed by the spirit of a long-dead Irishwoman, with whom one could communicate if her hostess were hypnotized. For a while, this was advanced as evidence of life after death, but it is no longer taken seriously.

But then is there *any* evidence of life after death that can be considered as scientific and rational?

Right now, there are claims that scientific evidence exists.

A physician named Elizabeth Kubler-Ross has been presenting statements she says she has received from people on their deathbeds that seem to indicate the existence of life after death—and a whole rash of books on this subject are being published, each book, of course, being guaranteed large sales among the gullible.

According to these reports now coming out, a number of people who have seemed to be "clinically dead" for a period of time have nevertheless managed to hang on to life, to have recovered, and then to have told of their experiences while they were "dead."

Apparently, they remained conscious, felt at peace and happy, watched their body from above, went through dark tunnels, saw the spirits of dead relatives and friends, and in some cases encountered a warm friendly spirit, glowing with light, who was to conduct them somewhere.

How much credence can be attached to such statements?

In my opinion, none at all!

Nor is it necessary to suppose the "dead" people are lying about their experiences. A person who is near enough to death to be considered "clinically dead" has a mind that is no longer functioning normally. The mind would then be hallucinating in much the same way it would be if it was not functioning normally for any other reason—alcohol, LSD, lack of sleep, and so on. The dying person would then experience what he or she would expect to experience or want to experience. (None of the reports include hell or devils, by the way.)

The life-after-deathers counter this by saying that people from all stations of life, and even from non-Christian India, tell similar stories which lead them to believe there is objective truth to it. I won't accept that for two reasons:

1. Tales of afterlife are widespread all over the world. Almost all religions have an afterlife, and Christian missionaries and Western communications technology have spread our notions on the subject everywhere.

2. Then, too, having experienced hallucinations of whatever sort, the recovered person, still weak perhaps and confused,

must describe them—and how easy it must be to describe them in such a way as to please the questioner, who is usually a life-after-death enthusiast and is anxious to elicit the proper information.

All the experience of innumerable cases of courtroom trials makes it quite plain that a human being, even under oath and under threat of punishment, will, with all possible sincerity, misremember, contradict himself, and testify to nonsense. We also know that a clever lawyer can, by proper questioning, induce almost any testimony from even an honest, truthful and intelligent witness. That is why the rules of evidence and of cross-examination have to be so strict. Naturally, then, it would take a great deal to make me attach any importance to the statements of a very sick person elicited by an eager questioner who is a true believer.

But in that case, what about my own earlier statement that some change must have taken place in the passage from human life to human death, producing a difference that is not a matter of atoms and molecules?

The difference doesn't involve blood, or breath, but it has to involve *something!*

And it does. Something was there in life and is no longer there in death, and that something *is* immaterial and makes for a subtle difference—the subtlest difference of them all.

Living tissue consists not merely of complex molecules, but of those complex molecules *in complex arrangement*. If that arrangement begins to be upset the body sickens; if that arrangement is sufficiently upset, the body dies. Life is then lost even though all the molecules are still there and still intact.

Let me present an analogy. Suppose one builds an intricate structure out of many thousands of small bricks. The structure is built in the form of a medieval castle, with towers and crenellations and portcullises and inner keeps and all the rest. Anyone looking at the finished product might be too far away to see the small individual bricks, but he will see the castle.

Now imagine some giant hand coming down and tumbling all the bricks out of which the castle is built, reducing everything to a formless heap. All the bricks are still there, with not one missing. All the bricks, without exception, are still intact and undamaged.

But where is the castle?

The castle existed only in the arrangement of the bricks and when the arrangement is destroyed the castle is gone. Nor is the castle anywhere else. It has no existence of its own. The castle was created out of nothing as the bricks were arranged and it vanished into nothing when the bricks were disarranged.

The molecules of my body, after my conception, added other molecules and arranged the whole into more and more complex form, and in a unique fashion, not quite like the arrangement in any other living thing that ever lived. In the process, I developed, little by little, into a conscious something I call "I" that exists only as the arrangement. When the arrangement is lost forever, as it will be when I die, the "I" will be lost forever, too.

And that suits me fine. No concept I have ever heard, of either a Hell or of a Heaven, has seemed to me to be suitable for a civilized rational mind to inhabit, and I would rather have the nothingness.

11

Life After Death

RONALD K. SIEGEL

The promise of life after death is central to many religions and is an important part of the personal philosophy of many of us. As such, a belief in an afterlife is really an article of faith, not a scientific theory. There is no necessity for scientific views to conflict with personal faith, and perhaps no good purpose is served by scientists treating the idea of an afterlife as a scientific hypothesis and attempting to support or refute it.

The problem is that the idea of life after death has recently been advanced as just that—a scientific hypothesis—as a real possibility supported by observable evidence. This claim has aroused intense widespread public attention. When such a claim is made, not theologically but in the name of science, then it becomes imperative for the scientific community to evaluate it objectively.

UCLA psychologist Ronald Siegel has carried out extensive research on the subject and is able to evaluate the claim with great thoroughness. In the following essay he describes and closely examines the recently offered evidence for the afterlife based on the commonality of the strikingly ethereal experiences reported by dying persons. An expert on hallucinations, Dr. Siegel shows that the descriptions given by dying persons are virtually identical to descriptions given by persons experiencing hallucinations, drug-induced or otherwise.

We thus have a plausible alternative hypothesis to account for the experiences of dying patients. However, it is not a case of having two competing scientific theories. The hypothesis of hallucinogenic induction of near-death experiences is supported by hard data; the alternate hypothesis, that dying patients are in fact experiencing glimpses of the afterlife, has no compelling evidence to support it.

The time is 1920. Thomas Edison has always been a believer in electrical energy. He once wrote that when a man dies, a swarm of highly charged energies deserts the body and goes out into space, entering another cycle of life. Always the scientist, Edison feels that some experiment demonstrating the immortal nature of these energies is necessary. In an interview in *Scientific American*, he states:

> I have been thinking for some time of a machine or apparatus which could be operated by personalities which have passed onto another existence or sphere. . . . I am inclined to believe that our personality hereafter does affect matter. If we can evolve an instrument so delicate as to be affected by our personality as it survives in the next life, such an instrument ought to record something.

The time is 1973. Based upon pioneering research started at UCLA, Raymond Western has just completed the development of a vast electronic computer nicknamed MEDIUM. Operating on complex electromagnetic principles, MEDIUM has been designed to communicate with unique electromagnetic configurations orbiting in a space–time continuum separate from that which we call reality. These unique configurations are the energies of departed human personalities. Although Western does not like the word *soul*, he agrees with the theologians and scientists who try his device that communication with the dead is possible. Life after death is a reality.

Although the above 1973 scenario was constructed by science-fiction writer Philip José Farmer, the science-fiction genre has always been a barometer of the social times, predicting and even designing future scientific realities. And so it is somewhat less surprising that in

An alleged photograph of "spirits" surrounding a male subject. This trick photograph was made by double exposure with a painting by Sichel. Courtesy Dover Publications, Inc.

1976 author Arthur Koestler wrote a serious essay in which he claimed that evidence of man's life after death could be based on survival of electromagnetic energies that may exist independent of the brain matter.

The time is 1978. The California Museum of Science and Industry opens an exhibit organized around the thesis that energy is indestructible, that consciousness can exist independent of the physical body, and that there is much evidence that consciousness continues after death. Designated *Continuum*, the exhibit stresses the words of great philosophers who have supported the belief in life after death. Displays bombard the visitor with reports of visions of the dead and descriptions of the afterlife, in order to demonstrate that consciousness can exist without the physical body. However, the exhibit avoids the tricky philosophical problem posed by the fact that a conscious physical body is always the one to make such reports!

Epistemological difficulties aside, the belief in life after death thrives. A recent Gallup poll reveals that approximately 70 percent of the people in the United States believe in the hereafter. An earlier survey conducted in the Los Angeles area (Kalish and Reynolds, 1973) indicated that 44 percent of the respondents claimed encounters with others known to be dead. The weekly *National Enquirer* ran a front-page headline (June 20, 1978) declaring "New Evidence of Life After Death" and advertised "science's answer to the afterlife"—for a mere three dollars. The money buys a copy of *The Circular Continuum* (Masterson, 1977), which explains the eternal Einsteinian nature of energy and matter as proof of life after death and provides an illustration depicting a man falling through a long, spiraling tunnel into the afterlife. That version is a poor adaptation of psychologist LeShan's (1975) longer explanation of the phenomenon in terms of the field theory of modern physics.

Hollywood takes notice as Sunn Classic Pictures releases *Beyond and Back* (1977) as a documentary look at this new evidence. The film contains many reports from people who were on "the other side" following near-death accidents or resuscitation from clinical death. They all had similar experiences of passing through that long spiraling tunnel, hearing a strange noise, seeing their own physical bodies from a distance, reviewing memories, meeting with deceased relatives and friends, confronting a blinding white light, and transcending with love and acceptance to a realm of heavenly scenery.

Popular books abound with stories of reincarnation, mediums, spirits, ghosts, parapsychology, and other evidence for man's survival after death (e.g., Rogo, 1973; Bayless, 1976). Even a Nobel laureate's speculations on paranormal phenomena—including life after death—are reprinted for popular audiences (Maeterlinck, 1975). And if you try to escape from it all at your local airport, Hare Krishna cultists may try to sell you a copy of *Beyond Birth and Death* (Prabhupada, 1972), with the reassuring, albeit cryptic, message that there is no death because there is no birth, for the soul is eternal.

Even popular-science books join the growing literature on life after death. Rogo (1977) presents evidence of tape-recorded voices as a breakthrough into the paranormal spirit world. And if some people can't hear such evidence, Weinberger (1977) argues that Venus's-fly-traps can, and he presents "experimental evidence" of those plants' ability to communicate with discarnate persons!

Life-after-death themes become increasingly reflected throughout the science-fiction literature as well. In the 1954 novel *Messiah*, Gore Vidal created the character of John Cave, who became the prophet of a new religion based on the worship of death and the quest for the experience through suicide. Science-fiction writers Nolan and Johnson (1967) envisioned a world where inhabitants voluntarily submit to death in order to be "renewed" and reincarnated. Philip José Farmer wrote an extremely popular novel (1971) based on the theme that everyone who has ever died on earth is resurrected on another planet. And finally, Richard Matheson (1978) captures critical acclaim for his science-fiction novel directly based on the current life-after-death literature, to which reference is made in the novel itself.

Medical journals start publishing reports of patients who have had afterlife visions following near-death experiences (e.g., MacMillan and Brown, 1971). New therapeutic approaches to dying, based on a sympathetic assurance that life continues after bodily death, are developed (e.g., Gordon, 1970; Grof and Halifax, 1977; Huxley, 1968). A major psychiatric periodical, *The Journal of Nervous and Mental Disease*, sets a precedent by publishing a literature review of the reincarnation and life-after-death research (Stevenson, 1977). Aware of the controversial nature of such a publication, the *Journal* invites a commentary on the work. Regrettably, the commentary (written by Stevenson's close friend, admitted "admirer," and colleague of twenty-five years) is not critical, but heavy with superfluous platitudes.

How should we judge such evidence? Should there be a trial by faith, by fact, or perhaps by combat—reminiscent of holy wars of bygone days? Perhaps a modern jury trial could weigh the evidence. Indeed, such a trial was conducted in 1969 (see *The Great Soul Trial*, by John Fuller), with the testimony of numerous expert witnesses supporting the belief in survival of the soul after death. The evidence to be presented in this essay can be considered exhibits in a trial for scientific evidence of life after death. The reader, as trier of fact, must decide the case on the merits of the facts, not on the eloquence of the advocates. The reader must resist influence by the passionate and romantic pleadings of highly credentialed "expert" witnesses, since equally qualified experts of opposing viewpoints can always be found. For example, Sigmund Freud wrote that "we really survive as spectators" in the afterlife, and the German poet and scientist Goethe agreed that "the soul is indestructible . . . its activity will continue through eternity." Conversely, the equally famous philosopher Auguste Comte replied that "to search for the soul and immortality is a product of a childish phase of human development."

Nonetheless, man's concern with life after death has been more than a passing amusement of childhood. Modern writers who are "pro" life after death are not transparently unscientific in method or data. They acknowledge that their "data" arise spontaneously and are not subject to controlled experiments (e.g., Osis and Haraldsson, 1977). They also note that "visits to the other side" can be simulated by ingestion of hallucinogenic substances, but they curiously discount the possibility of controlled studies with these drugs. Rather, they endorse the use of parapsychological approaches. The bulk of the resultant data consists of phenomenological reports from individuals who have "experienced" life after death. There are a few surveys and questionnaire studies, but many of these are conducted on individuals who only observed dying patients and make inferences as to the nature of deathbed visions of the afterlife. Other studies use highly selected data, although the researchers are honest enough to say so (e.g., Osis and Haraldsson, 1977). Such better-documented studies as Moody (1975) and Osis and Haraldsson (1977) admit that the reported phenomena are open to several interpretations. Most researchers do not appear to be "cranks" who rationalize their interpretations with strong religious convictions, unjust attacks upon opposing viewpoints, or complex neologisms. A rare few (e.g., Matson, 1975) compare themselves with Einstein, Columbus, or Galileo in respect to the unconventional investigation of sacred scientific doctrine. But unlike the pseudoscientists, described by Gardner (1952), who manifest strong compulsions to attack the greatest scientists and best-established theories, many current investigators of life after death try to accommodate their interpretations to established scientific thinking. These quasi-scientific orientations are all the more deserving of scrutiny because they give the appearance of valid scientific thought and testing. Neither the evangelism of the true believers, the popularity of their books, nor the crudeness of their phenomenological inquiries should deter us from evaluation of the data on their own merits.

Taken together, the evidence to be discussed here views life after death as a phenomenon involving physical, biological, behavioral, imaginal, experiential, cognitive, and cultural variables. But all nature presents itself to man primarily as phenomena with such attributes. In perceiving natural phenomena, man recognizes groups of events that share many cohesive features, in contrast to other events displaying less stability and persistence of pattern. As Weiss (1969) points out, the "success of science over the ages has validated the abstractions involved in our dealing with such reasonably constant entities as if they had an autonomous existence of their own" (page 32). Life after death is one such abstraction, and its phenomena of behavior, experience, and theory are the subject of this essay. (See Siegel [1980] for a more detailed discussion based on this chapter.)

ORIGINS OF BELIEF IN AN AFTERLIFE

Historian Arnold Toynbee noted in 1976 that all living organisms that are subject to death exert themselves to stay alive, whether or not they have produced progeny. While many species grieve, as humans do, at the loss of mates or members of a social grouping, Toynbee echoes the popular notion that human beings are unique in being *aware* that death comes to all. Death, in terms of its physical sequels, is no mystery. After death the body disintegrates and is reabsorbed into the inanimate component of the environment. The dead human loses both his life and his consciousness. Toynbee asks the age-old question of what happens to consciousness after death, since both life and consciousness are invisible and intangible. The most logical guess is that consciousness shares the same fate as that of the corpse. Surprisingly, this common-sense view is not the prevalent one, and the majority of mankind rejects the hypothesis of annihilation at death. Instead, they continue to exert their basic motivation to stay alive, and formulate a myriad of beliefs concerning man's survival after death. Many of these beliefs revolve around the notion that the intact human personality survives in another dimension—an afterlife. (Toynbee finds that idea suspicious, for although the body disintegrates, ghosts and spirits of the dead always appear in the familiar form of an embodied human: "Moreover, ghosts appear not naked, but clothed, and this sometimes in the dress of an earlier age than the ghost-seer's own. . . . It seems more likely that the apparent visibility of a ghost is an hallucination" [1976, page 4]. Conversely, Holzer, a contemporary researcher of life after death, believes that the apparitions of the dead wish to be recognized and thus, considerately, appear as they did in physical life [1969, page 88].)

Other versions emphasize reincarnation, whereby humans have many successive lives in this world, each life with a different body, interrupted by short stays in another dimension (e.g., Miles, 1907; Gould, 1919; Addison, 1932). This idea of immortality through reincarnation seems to have been suggested to man both by his dreams and by inherited resemblances of the living to the deceased, resemblances in both physical and behavioral traits (cf. Frazer, 1913). Recent LSD research has also suggested that under suitable conditions individuals often have transpersonal experiences in which they experience their own identities but in different times, places, or contexts (Grof and Halifax, 1977, page 55). These experiences also include distinct feelings of reliving memories of a previous incarnation. However, the allied ability of these LSD subjects to identify with various animals or even inanimate objects strongly suggests that the reincarnation stories are little more than vicariously retrieved memories and fantasies. While some writers, like psychologist William James, have termed such experiences mere "dream creations," others have given serious philosophical and theological thought to the topic (see review by Hick, 1976).

Recently these beliefs in life after death have been related to several scientific disciplines, including physics and biology. Author Arthur Koestler has noted (1976) that the elementary particles of modern physics, like photons of light, can behave as both waves and particles. Similarly, he says that "the contents of consciousness that pass through the mind, from the perception of colour to thoughts and images, are un-substantial 'airy nothings,' yet they are somehow linked to the material brain, as the unsubstantial 'waves' and 'fields' of physics are somehow linked to the material aspects of the sub-atomic particles" (Koestler, 1976, page 242). Furthermore, Koestler believes that such waves of consciousness can exist independent of brain matter, but he is unable to describe this association. He argues that perhaps ghosts and spirits are simply the reverberating waves of humans who, like radio transmitters, generate signals somewhere in the universe even after being turned off (dead). This idea is related to the "energy body" which parapsychologists claim leaves the physical body at death (Moss, 1974). Surely we can hear the sounds of distant dead stars through our radio telescopes. Koestler would have us believe that personalities or souls of dead humans persist in a similar way and, like the phantom limbs of amputees, can only be "felt" by those who have been attached to them in the past. With imperialistic zeal he carries speculation one step further and suggests that these dead souls go on to join some "cosmic mind-stuff" which contains the record "of the creative achievements of intelligent life not only on this planet, but on others as well" (1976, page 258).

Charles Darwin wrote a scholarly paper in 1891 stating his belief that ghosts and spirits were *really* visions of the departed. He expressed the traditional assumption among biologists that man is the only living creature that entertains the idea of immortality. The idea was further examined by a German biologist, August Weisman (1892), who mentioned the "continuity of the germplasm" and "the immortality of unicellular beings and of the reproductive cells of multicellular organisms" (page 74). Weisman compared biological immortality to a certain form of perpetual motion, like the cycle of water evaporation and rain, whereby the cycle of life is repeating. While the individual and its body cells will "perish utterly" at death, the germ cells (i.e., genetic material) will maintain a continuity of life through reproduction—a type of immortality. But in the sense that a discrete soul or mind survives death, both Weisman and contemporary biologist Ashley Montagu (1977) reject the immortality principle. Montagu adds that man's belief in survival after death is probably related to some deep biological craving of the organism. The belief is maintained and strengthened because it contributes to the stability of social groups and other human endeavors.

Since nonhuman animals are governed by physical and biological principles similar to those governing man, the analysis of their behavior associated with dying and death may reveal important insights into related human behaviors. It is presently impossible to ask another animal if it believes in life after death, but much of man's belief in the afterlife is manifested by nonverbal, albeit overt, behaviors. These include religious ritual and ceremony, burying behavior, and the superstitious association of events in nature with ongoing behavioral acts.

Anthropologists cite the deliberate interments of the dead by Neanderthal man (c. 100,000 years ago) as the first evidence of man's belief in life after death. Excavations at the famous Shanidar cave in Iraq show evidence of Neanderthal funeral rites, including feasts, burials with flowers and food, and carefully prepared graves with markers. Even the skeletal remains of Cro-Magnon man are found buried in the fetal position, in adherence with the primitive myth that such a position facilitates rebirth (cf. Jonas, 1977). The study of such allied behaviors in nonhuman animals provides an opportunity to understand their nature and function in man. Furthermore, whether animals believe in an afterlife or not, there's as good evidence that they survive as that humans do. For example, when asked if they have dogs in the next world, a famous psychic named Betty, who was already on "the other side" at the time, replied yes (White, 1940). Bayless (1973) reports that the spirits of departed animals, like those of humans, have an ectoplasm that can be shaped and molded into ghosts when triggered by the thoughts of those still alive. And, in the ambitiously titled book *The Evidence for Life After Death*, author Martin Ebon (1977) reports that ghosts of dead animals have been seen and heard almost as often as ghosts of departed humans.

If deliberate burials are signposts of the belief in life after death for man, one cannot ignore the elaborate burying behavior of elephants as a similar sign of ritualistic or even religious behavior in that species (Siegel, 1977a). When encountering dead animals, elephants will often bury them with mud, earth, and leaves. Animals known to have been buried by elephants include rhinos, buffalos, cows, calves, and even humans, in addition to elephants themselves (Douglas-Hamilton and Douglas-Hamilton, 1975, pages 240 ff). Other ethologists have observed elephants burying their dead with large quantities of food, fruit, flowers, and colorful foliage. Not only do these large animals display death rituals, but some of the smallest social insects also display stereotyped patterns of "necrophoric" behavior in regard to corpses. For example, Wilson notes that ants of the genus *Atta* carry their dead into deserted nest chambers and galleries, and that the *Strumigenys lopo-*

tyle ant of New Guinea "piles fragments of corpses of various kinds of insects in a tight ring around the entrance of its nest in the soil of the rain forest floor" (1971, page 279). Other types of funeral rites have been observed among both elephants and chimpanzees in Africa (Jonas, 1976, page 174). Ethologist Eugene Marais describes an equally mysterious and quasi-religious behavior among South African baboons; they ritually huddle together with the setting of the sun, gaze at the western horizon, observe a period of silence, and "then from all sides would come the sound of mourning, a sound never uttered otherwise than on occasions of great sorrow—of death or parting" (1969, page 139). Similar behavior has been observed among the Colobus monkeys of Madagascar at sunrise and again at sunset. Elephants are also aware of natural cycles as they practice "moon worship," behavior consisting of waving branches at the waxing moon and engaging in ritual bathing when the moon is full (Siegel, 1977a).

Given the similarity of human and some nonhuman death behaviors, should we postulate the existence of an animal soul or belief in the afterlife? Human vanity has traditionally denied this position. But the hypothesis of a soul or belief in life after death is also unnecessary to explain the human counterpart behaviors. Rather, it may be speculated that burials and allied religious behaviors came about through a gradual shaping of "instinctive" behaviors. For humans, such behaviors may include copying observed behaviors of other animals. It is well known that many primitive peoples learned the rudiments of medicine by observing what animals did when they were sick and wounded (see Siegel, 1973). For example, Cherokee Indians learned to treat snake bites and fever with cold baths after watching deer stand in cold rivers after being bitten by venomous snakes. Both Old World and New World peoples also learned about the healing properties of mud and clay applied to open wounds after watching wounded animals roll around in the substances. In Africa, elephants will engage in similar mud-rolling behavior in order to regulate temperature, cover wounds, and treat attacks by parasites. When elephants encounter another that is sick or dying, they attempt to apply mud or offer food to the stricken animal. When the animal dies, they will continue this process until the corpse is gradually covered. When encountering dead or decaying corpses, elephants will bury them. Some ethologists speculate this is done in order to remove the smell (and perhaps sight) of the decomposing bodies. Early African man may have copied this behavior or initiated it for similar reasons. A common explanation is found in the basic animal and human motivation to avoid the sick and dying if one cannot help them (cf. Ardrey, 1970). Healthy social animals will isolate themselves from unhealthy ones in response to this helplessness, either by leaving the dying or sick animals behind or by segregating them. Burial behavior can be viewed as a gradual extension of this isolation, particularly useful when death occurs in a habitat where living must go on.

As do other animals, humans have a strong instinct to survive. Unlike other animals, humans are credited with the capability of realizing that death comes to all. And so, as Cavendish (1977) states, "The human solution to this grim dilemma is a life in some different world after death" (page 7). Anthropologists have endorsed this solution (e.g., La Barre, 1972), praising man for his "discovery" of the afterlife. Early man's awareness of his own repeating biological cycles (e.g., regeneration of tissue or replacement of baby teeth with permanent teeth) may have provided a basis for this belief. Cavendish credits the belief in an afterlife to man's cognizance of seasonal cycles, wherein "death" in winter is followed by "rebirth" in spring. And man may have been influenced by his observation of other natural cycles, such as the rising and setting of the sun, day and night, the waxing and waning moon, low and high tide, and so on (cf. MacHovec, 1975). Indeed, many primitive peoples have religious ceremonies celebrating life after death in close association with natural seasonal events. The Hindus made the direct connection by comparing life after death with the flourishing of this year's grass and flowers, their dying, and their replacement by similar yet not identical grass and flowers in the next year. Ancient Egyptians believed in eternal life in association with the sun: "The sun rose each day in renewed strength and vigour, and the renewal of youth in a future life was the aim and object of every Egyptian believer" (Budge, 1967, page lv). The sun was the symbol of the afterlife for the Aztecs, who believed that if you died properly, as in battle or sacrifice, you were reborn as a hummingbird or butterfly. Among many indigenous groups in South America, the mysterious cyclical appearances of mushrooms following rainstorms were considered gifts from the gods, and the hallucinations resulting from subsequent ingestion of certain species confirmed for them the reality of an afterlife.

Early man's inevitable ecological encounters with animal life suggested similar fates for nonhumans as well. The butterfly was an ancient Greek symbol of reincarnation, and St. Theresa of Avila (1515–

1582) used the metamorphosis of a caterpillar from gravelike cocoon to beautiful butterfly to symbolize resurrection. Contemporary psychiatrist Elizabeth Kübler-Ross tells her terminal patients (1968, 1975) that dying is like a butterfly's shedding its cocoon and emerging into a new life. *The Egyptian Book of the Dead* (c. 1500–1400 B.C.) uses as a symbol of reincarnation the snake, which sheds its skin for a new body. And where nature did not provide examples, man invented them. In ancient Babylon, India, Egypt, and Persia, the phoenix was a mythological bird symbolizing reincarnation. According to the legend, when a phoenix dies, another bird wraps the body in myrrh and brings it to a funeral pyre in a temple. There it is burned and rises again from its own ashes to begin another life cycle (cf. Clair, 1967).

Other anthropological origins of belief in an afterlife may have been somewhat accidental. For example, when early Egyptian man buried his dead, he would have observed that the hot, porous sands of Egypt naturally disinfected and preserved the corpses buried in them. This probably gave rise to a belief in an eternal physical hereafter, since the body itself did not disintegrate (cf. Cavendish, 1977, page 17). Similar accidents may have reinforced and strengthened this belief. If the body survives, then it needs assistance, and the contents of graves, tombs, and pyramids testify to the gradual development of this belief in survival after death.

The nature of that survival has been embellished by man's verbal descriptions, examined next as additional evidence for life after death.

DESCRIPTIONS OF THE AFTERLIFE

Man's study of life after death is highly dependent on the words, pictures, and other symbols used in description. Many of these words have sensory qualities and describe such properties as sights, sounds, tastes, and smells. Accident victims who have had near-death experiences often report visions of long, dark tunnels or sounds of ringing and buzzing. Surgical patients who are resuscitated following cardiac or respiratory failure frequently report floating out of their bodies and watching the operation from a distant perspective. Terminal patients often experience unbidden memory images of long-forgotten childhood events and deceased relatives. These images arise with such startling vividness that they often prompt the patient to react by speaking with the image or moving toward it. A British psychiatrist described such images as "mental representation so intense as to become mental presentation" (Maudsley, 1939, page 98).

Man's descriptions of the afterlife have also used words with affective and evaluative qualities. Many see a blinding white light and regard it as a higher being or god. In a similar way, the vivid visions and voices that often accompany epileptic seizures were once thought to be so mysterious that the sufferer believed "he really saw or heard an angel from heaven, or had a visit with the Holy Ghost, or was carried up into heaven or down into hell" (Maudsley, 1939, page 89).

There are numerous commonalities in descriptions from various cultures of death experiences and an afterlife (Eliade, 1951). These descriptions are similar to reports examined below collected in Western cultures from persons or groups involved in dying experiences. It seems plausible that common processes and mechanisms underlie these similar descriptions in various cultures and by various persons. After reviewing this evidence in more detail, we will discuss a hypothesis offered by La Barre (1975) and others that such supernatural psychic phenomena are caused by dissociative or hallucinatory activities of the brain.

Many reports from individuals are generated from communication with the dead via mediums, spiritualists, ghosts, apparitions, automatic writing, clairvoyance, and allied techniques. If such methods appear tenuous to the skeptic, Spraggett typifies the field by responding that "if we are to examine the evidence for an after-life honestly and dispassionately we must free ourselves from the tyranny of common sense" (1974, page 6). Accordingly, he argues that ghosts and apparitions are indeed hallucinations but they are projected telepathically from the minds of dead people to those of the living! Both classic and contemporary literature are replete with these reports (e.g., White, 1937; Harlow, 1968; Ford, 1969, 1971; Wetzl, 1974; Taylor, 1975; Stearn, 1976; Mehta, 1977). In one report a dead man communicated to his living wife that the afterlife had "a lawn that would put any Earth golf club to shame. Flowers I've never seen before. Even new colors. And everywhere, people. Thousands of them. Happy people, doing things they really liked to do" (Loehr, 1976, page 48). Other reports can be humorous when read with the proper set. For example, Ebon describes a seance (where ghosts often ring bells or tap on tables) in which he heard the name *Margery* but "the name *Margery* rang no bell with me" (1977, page 8).

Other reports are less casual and present descriptions in a more serious tone. A classic case that initiated much of the serious research in the field occurred in 1943. George Ritchie (1978) died of pneumonia for nine minutes (although there are no medical records to document this), was revived, and reported a journey to the afterworld where he met Jesus and was shown heaven and hell. Wheeler (1976) provides an interesting collection of reports from the "clinically dead," those in near-death accidents, or who have had out-of-body experiences and deathbed visions. He acknowledges that it may be impossible to separate these reports from hallucinations, but he feels that hallucinations would be much more idiosyncratic and varied than these reports. His collected reports of the afterlife are highly consistent, which he argues is evidence of a singular separate reality in the hereafter.

Physician Raymond Moody (1975, 1977) has also attempted to describe that prototypical vision of life after death. He collected a series of reports and interviews of near-death experiences, which he defines as "an event in which a person could very easily die or be killed (and even may be so close as to be believed or pronounced clinically dead) but nonetheless survives, and continues physical life" (Moody, 1977, page 124). Moody interviewed these people but was admittedly "sympathetic" and even "in a couple of cases I did ask very loaded questions" (1977, page 131). Consequently, he is aware that his investigation is unscientific but does not even attempt to provide statistics or complete patient histories, which would have contributed greatly to the value of his work. Nonetheless, he has compiled an inventory of afterlife descriptions.

According to Moody, the prototypical experience of dying includes the following common elements: ineffability (meaning that the experience is impossible to describe with words); hearing doctors or spectators pronouncing him dead; feelings of peace and quiet; a loud ringing or buzzing noise; a dark tunnel through which the person may feel himself moving; out-of-body experiences; meeting others, including guides, spirits, dead relatives and friends; a glowing light with a human shape; a panoramic review of one's life; a border or limit beyond which there is no return; visions of great knowledge; cities of light; a realm of bewildered spirits; supernatural rescues from real physical death by some spirit; a return or coming back with changed attitudes and beliefs.

A few studies have verified this basic phenomenology of life-after-death experiences. In a questionnaire study, parapsychologist Karlis Osis (1961) obtained information from 640 physicians and nurses who observed the behavior of dying patients. A high frequency of deathbed visions was reported. These included the phenomena described by Moody and "scenes of indescribable beauty and brilliant colors resembling those experienced under the drug influence of mescaline or LSD" (page 104). But Osis argued that the dying patient's otherwise clear sensorium indicated that the experiences were not hallucinations. However, it is important to note that hallucinations can occur in states where consciousness is "clear." Indeed, drug-induced hallucinations are frequently marked by heightened perceptual sensitivity. In addition, Mitchell (1972) has shown that hallucinations of dead relatives and friends can occur in states of clear consciousness when triggered by emotional states surrounding death, such as mourning.

Another study (Osis and Haraldsson, 1977) presents a more detailed examination of deathbed visions. Once again they confirm the typical phenomenology, which they argue only *appears* similar to dreams, hallucinations, or depersonalization experiences (cf. Noyes and Kletti, 1976), but their evidence fails to present any significant differences. These authors remain convinced that there is a real "postmortem survival" out there somewhere, and they suggest that only those individuals sensitive to ESP and telepathy may experience it. But if deathbed visions are similar to other hallucinatory visions, they may have similar explanations that do not require belief in untestable constructs such as an afterlife, soul, or ESP.

All these phenomena bear a strong resemblance to those reported in drug-induced hallucinations and in hallucinations produced by other conditions (cf. Siegel and Jarvik, 1975). For example, ineffability is a characteristic of peak religious and mystical experiences, including those induced by psychedelic drugs. These episodes are marked by suppression of verbal behavior, which has been related to states of central nervous system activity. The hearing of voices or other sounds is reminiscent of surgical patients recovering from anesthesia who often recall auditory stimuli that occurred during surgery. This is particularly common with the dissociative anesthetics nitrous oxide, ether, and ketamine, which allow sensory input to the brain.

The bright light is characteristic of many types of mental imagery; it is due to stimulation of the central nervous system that mimics the effects of light on the retina. It can also occur when the electrical activity in the brain is altered in such a way that the threshold for percep-

Bright light in center of the visual field reported during early stages of a marijuana intoxication. Light is often seen during hallucinogenic experiences and interpreted as God.

tion of phosphenes (electrical activity in the visual system) is lowered and bright lights are seen in otherwise dark surroundings. This point of light creates a tunnel perspective and individuals will report viewing much of their imagery in this regard. Compare the following reports from afterlife and drug hallucinations:

Tunnels in Afterlife Reports

My awareness of the room dimmed, and the world immediately around me became like a tunnel with walls that glowed with a slight orange-red, reflected light (Wheeler, 1976, page 2).

I felt like I was riding on a roller coaster train at an amusement park, going through this tunnel at a tremendous speed (Moody, 1975, page 32).

I found myself in a tunnel—a tunnel of concentric circles
. . . [a] spiralling tunnel (Moody, 1975, page 33).

Tunnels in Drug Hallucinations

I'm moving through some kind of train tunnel. There are
all sorts of lights and colors (Siegel and Jarvik, 1975, page
116).

It's sort of like a tube, like I sort of feel . . . that I'm at the
bottom of a tube looking up (Siegel and Jarvik, 1975, page
117).

I am traveling into a tunnel and out into space (Siegel and
Jarvik, 1975, page 117).

The cities of light and other geometric patterns in afterlife visions
resemble the geometric forms, often seen from aerial perspectives,

*Tunnel of pulsating lights reported during a marijuana intoxication. These
tunnels are conspicuous in both hallucinogenic intoxications and visions of the
afterlife.*

which dominate early hallucinogenic intoxication and other hallucinatory experiences. Like the bright lights and tunnels, these geometric forms are partially produced by entoptic phenomena (structures within the eye) and electrical activity in the visual system. Consider the similarity of these accounts in afterlife reports and drug hallucinations:

Cities and Lights in Afterlife Reports

There were colors—bright colors—not like here on earth, but just indescribable. . . . I could see a city. There were buildings—separate buildings . . . a city of light (Moody, 1977, page 17).

I believe that it was at the very instant when I felt myself die that I started moving at very high speed toward a net of great luminosity and brilliance (Wheeler, 1976, page 11).

Cities and Lights in Drug Hallucinations

There are tall structures all around me . . . it could be buildings, it could be anything . . . and in all colors (Siegel, 1971, page 81).

Like extremely futuristic architecture, something like you would see at Expo '80 or something like that, like spheres and things constructed very differently (Siegel, 1971, page 79).

And it seems like I'm getting closer and closer to the sun, it's very white . . . and there's like a geometric network or lattice in the distance (Siegel, 1971, page 80).

The out-of-body experiences are common in a wide variety of altered states and hallucinations. Moody (1975) cites one respondent who lost part of a leg in a near-death accident: "I could feel my body, and it was whole. I know that. I felt whole, and I felt that all of me was there, though it wasn't" (page 53). On the basis of this single case, Moody hastily concludes that severe damage to the physical body does not adversely affect the spiritual body. It seems more likely that the patient was reporting a "phantom limb" experience, a phenomenon common among recent amputees and associated with persisting neurological activity in sensory cerebral centers. The meeting of others is similar to hallucinatory states wherein guides will appear to lead the individual through novel and potentially anxious experiences. It is also similar to the appearance of "imaginary companions," who guide lonely explorers and shipwrecked sailors, and similar to the "imaginary playmates" who amuse young and lonely children (Siegel, 1977b).

The guides and spirits are often dead relatives or religious figures which Osis and Haraldsson (1977) label "otherworldly messengers" from "a postmortem mode of existence." The fact that such relatives may be dead now or that such religious figures may never have existed does not prove they are alive and well in the hereafter. Rather, the experiences support the argument that these deathbed visions are retrieved memory images (or fantasy images) that were alive and well when originally stored. This could also account for the appearance of memory imagery common in both afterlife and drug visions. The panoramic review or "flash of life" is vivid, spontaneous, colorful, three-dimensional, kinetic, and veridical, all common features of hallucinations produced by states of central nervous system arousal. For example, compare the following descriptions of this imagery in afterlife and drug visions:

Memory Imagery Format in Afterlife Reports

It just flashed before me like a motion picture that goes tremendously fast, yet I was fully able to see it, and able to comprehend it (Moody, 1975, page 70).

The best thing I can think of to compare it to is a series of pictures like slides. It was just like someone was clicking off slides in front of me, very quickly (Moody, 1975, page 71).

Memory Imagery Format in Drug Hallucinations

Everything's changing really fast, like pictures in a film, or television, just right in front of me. I am watching it happen right there (Siegel and Jarvik, 1975, page 116).

People standing in the office, appearing like slides crossing my field of vision (Siegel and Jarvik, 1975, page 116).

Osis and Haraldsson (1977) assume that hallucinations will only portray information stored in the brain and, unlike real perceptions of the afterlife, could not portray what they consider "strange new environments" or novel experiences. But hallucinations (like dreams, images, thoughts, and fantasies) are often elaborate cognitive embellishments of memory images, not just mere pictorial replicas. This constructive aspect of hallucinations can be illustrated by a simple exercise. Recall the last time you went swimming in the ocean. Now ask yourself if this memory includes a picture of yourself running along the beach or moving about in the water. Such a picture is obviously fictitious, since you could not have been looking at yourself, but images in the memory often include fleeting pictures of this kind. Hallucinations also include equally improbable images such as aerial perspectives, feelings of flying, and panoramic vistas of incredible beauty and novelty. As in hallucinations, the visions of the afterlife are suspiciously like this world, according to accounts provided by dying patients themselves.

> . . . beautiful surroundings where green grass and flowers grow. She seemed very pleased, happy that she could see these pleasant things. She said that it was like a garden with green grass and flowers. She was fond of flowers and had a garden at home (Osis and Haraldsson, 1977, page 162).

Osis and Haraldsson argue that the word *like* in this account indicates a glimpse of the beyond and not an actual garden. Here they are confusing similes with veridicality. The phrasing of *like, as if,* and *it is as though* are characteristic of hallucinatory reports when individuals do not perceive a reality to the images or when the images are modified sufficiently so as to prevent convenient description. Even when individuals attribute reality to afterlife or drug visions, the reports possess all the elements of vivid dreams, complete with feelings of flying and "supernatural" rescues. This is why hallucinations are sometimes called "waking dreams." Consider the following similar reports:

Perceived Reality in Afterlife Reports

> I floated down to a grassy field which had horses, cows, lions, and all kinds of wild and tame animals. It was a painting at first, then it became real. I was in that field looking at all those great things when you [indicating the doctors] pulled me back (Wheeler, 1976, page 98).

Perceived Reality in Drug Hallucinations

> In fact, the scenes in my head are very real. . . . I mean if you get right into it it's as though you are there sort of like in a movie or something. . . . That's a mental image, not a real one. I guess it's hard to tell the difference. . . .
> Now it looks like a comic book scene, not at all vivid only I'm not daydreaming, I see these things! (Siegel, 1971, pages 78, 88).

My mind left my body and apparently went to what some describe as the "second state". I felt I was in a huge, well-lit room, in front of a massive throne draped in lush red velvet. I saw nothing else but felt the presence of higher intelligence tapping my mind of every experience and impression I had gathered. I begged to be released, to return to my body. It was terrifying. Finally I blacked out and slowly came to in the recovery room. That's my ketamine experience (Anonymous, *High Times*, 1978, page 8).

The border or limit in afterlife reports is similar to states of "ego loss" or "psychological death" experienced in altered states of consciousness, including drug-induced hallucinations. These experiences can include transcendence of space and time; awe, wonder, and a sense of sacredness; a deeply felt positive mood, often accompanied by intense emotions of peace and tranquility; a feeling of insight or illumination or some universal truth or knowledge (the "noetic" quality); and changed attitudes and beliefs that pass into an afterglow and remain as a vivid memory. Collectively these experiences constitute the ineffable mystical experience induced by both psychedelic drugs and true religious experiences. They are triggered by a variety of stimuli that result in massive cortical disinhibition and autonomic arousal (Siegel, 1977a).

EXPLANATIONS OF THE
AFTERLIFE AS HALLUCINATION

The remarkable similarity of imagery in life-after-death experiences and in hallucinatory experiences invites inquiry about common mechanisms of action. The experiences can be considered as a combination of simple and complex imagery. The simple imagery consists of tunnels, bright lights and colors, and geometric forms. As discussed, they are probably caused by phosphenes, which are visual sensations arising from the discharge of neurons in structures of the eye. They also reflect the electrical excitation of organized groups of cells in the visual cortex of the brain (see Siegel, 1977c).

Most of the investigators undertaking to explain complex imagery of people and places have described the visions as the result of an excitation of the central nervous system. As early as 1845 French psychiatrist Jacques Moreau was maintaining that hallucinations resulted from cerebral excitation that enabled thoughts and memories to become transformed into sensory impressions. Recent electrophysiological research (Winters, 1975) has confirmed that hallucinations are directly related to states of excitation and arousal of the central nervous system, which are coupled with a functional disorganization of the part of the brain that regulates incoming stimuli. Behaviorally the result is an impairment of perceptions normally based on external stimuli and a preoccupation with internal imagery (Fischer, 1975).

These states of excitation can be triggered by a wide variety of stimuli, including psychedelic drugs, surgical anesthetics, fever, exhausting diseases, certain injuries and accidents, as well as by emotional and physiological processes involved in dying. In studies with the fatally ill, Verwoerdt found (1966) that in the transition from health to fatal illness a patient passes through a period in which he is alone with his symptoms. Sensory signals from the body, albeit subliminal at times, trigger a mental awareness of feeling different or peculiar, followed by reactions of flights into fantasy and imagery in order to direct attention away from physical concerns and escape into private comforting thoughts. Visions of the afterlife can be among these reactions. Weinberg (1975) describes a similar experience in the dying based on physiological changes. He notes that as organs degenerate the perception of physical stimuli may not go beyond the point of the sensory receptor, and stimuli become blocked from awareness. Consequently, the individual becomes disengaged from physical concerns and turns attention inward to self-reflection, reminiscence, and thoughts of approaching death. These experiences may be coupled with a fear of death, a fear that is an effective trigger of altered states of consciousness in death and near-death situations (cf. Garfield, 1975). Such physiological and psychological triggers were undoubtedly present in many deathbed visions of afterlife, as Osis and Haraldsson report that 75 percent of their respondents suffered from cancer, heart attacks, or painful postoperative conditions.

A classic example of a chemically triggered death experience can be found in intoxications with phencyclidine (also known as PCP or Angel Dust), a psychoactive drug with mixed excitatory, sedative, cataleptoid-anesthetic, and hallucinatory properties. Domino and Luby (1972) describe a salient feature of phencyclidine intoxication as reduced verbal productivity, the appearance of calm in the subjects, and reported experiences of sheer "nothingness." One subject reported lying in a meadow and that "this meadow was a place that he has often considered he would like to be buried in. The theme of death ran through most of his retrospective account of the episode. Possibly the experience of combined cutoff of interoceptive and exteroceptive cues is close to one's conception of what death must be like" (page 42). Other common deathlike experiences in phencyclidine intoxications include ineffability of the experience and difficulty in verbal behavior; feelings of peace and quiet; disturbances in space and time perception; out-of-body phenomena (including ecstatic feelings of timelessness, weightlessness, peace, serenity, and tranquility); no perception of smells, odors, temperature, or kinesthesia; fear; and confusion. Naturally, this can lead to a concern with death and deathlike thoughts for the phencyclidine-intoxicated individual. This state of preoccupation with death, termed *meditatio mortis*, may develop into a transient psychotic state that can predispose certain individuals to suicidal or homicidal behavior (Siegel, 1978).

The specific content of complex hallucinatory imagery is greatly determined by set (expectations and attitudes) and setting (physical and psychological environments). For many dying and near-death experiences, the sets (fear of approaching death, changes in body and mental functioning, etc.) and settings (hospital wards, accident scenes, etc.) can influence specific eschatological thought and images. Grof and Halifax (1977) suggest that the universal themes of this imagery may be related to stored memories of biological events that are activated in the brain. Accordingly, they suggest that the feelings of peace and quiet may be related to the original state of intrauterine existence when there is complete biological equilibrium with the environment. The experience of moving down a dark tunnel may be associated with the clinical stage of delivery in which the cervix is open and there is gradual propulsion through the birth canal. The border or limit may be associated with the experience of incipient emergence from the mother, which is followed by delivery and feelings of transcendence. In a sense, Grof and Halifax are suggesting that the dying or near-death experience triggers a flashback or retrieval of an equally dramatic and emotional memory of the birth experience. Thus, the state of arousal present at death evokes memories or feelings associated with previous states of such arousal, as may have occurred during birth. Such a process would be similar to that which occurs when a specific song or melody spontaneously evokes an image of a loved one or when a child's behavior causes the remembrance of one's own long-forgotten childhood.

Perhaps the most integrated explanation of life-after-death hallucinations can be based on the perceptual-release theory of hallucinations, formulated by the British neurologist Hughlings Jackson in 1931. As updated by psychiatrist L. J. West (1975), the hypothesis assumes that normal memories are suppressed by a mechanism that acts as a gate to the flow of information from the outside. An input of new information inhibits the emergence and awareness of previous perceptions and processed information. If the input is decreased or impaired while awareness remains (e.g., as in dying or shock), such perceptions are released and may be dynamically organized and experienced as hallucinations, dreams, or fantasies. Or if the storage of perceptions in the brain is sufficiently stimulated (e.g., by drugs, fear, etc.) and persists for a suitable time, these released perceptions can also enter awareness and be experienced as hallucinations.

West offered an analogy to illustrate the process. Picture a man in his living room, standing at a closed window opposite his fireplace and looking out at the sunset. He is absorbed by the view of the outside world and does not visualize the interior of the room. As darkness falls outside, though, the images of the objects in the room behind him can be seen reflected dimly in the window. With the deepening of darkness the fire in the fireplace illuminates the room and the man can now see a vivid reflection of the room, which appears to be outside the window. As the analogy is applied to the perceptual-release hypothesis of life-after-death experiences, the daylight (sensory input) is reduced while the interior illumination (the general level of arousal of the central nervous system) remains bright, so that images originating within the rooms of the brain may be perceived as though they came from outside the windows of the senses.

AN OVERVIEW

From early observations of animals burying their dead, through awareness of the seasonal cycles of nature, to recognition of the inherited resemblances of the living to the dead, man developed the concept of life after death in an effort to explain these behaviors and the feelings underlying them. Anthropological studies of afterlife concepts and of the soul's posthumous journey are strikingly similar for all cultures of man. The state of death may have idiosyncratic meanings for different individuals, but the experience of dying involves common elements and themes that are predictable and definable. These elements and themes arise from common structures in the human brain and nervous system, common biological experiences, and common reactions of the central nervous system to stimulation. The resultant experience, universally accessible, is interpreted by self-referential man as evidence of immortality, but this interpretation is little more than a metaphor to describe a common subjective state of consciousness (cf. Koestenbaum, 1977). That subjective state can be remarkably real and convincing for many individuals. While satisfied that Western science may explain many elements of life-after-death phenomena, believers in the afterlife, like believers in other paranormal experiences, are nevertheless dubious when anyone dismisses the value of the total experience too readily (cf. Slater, 1977).

Even if the experience of life after death doesn't lead to a "real" other world, the belief may very well change behavior in this one. Already the contemporary literature has glorified the afterlife trip. The popular writer A. Matson (1975) titled a chapter "The thrill of dying" and makes the experience seem as harmless as an amusement park ride. Weldon and Levitt (1977) begin a chapter in their book called "The wonderful world of death" by assuring the reader he will be born again.

In the past, dying and death were often accompanied by fear and loneliness, as if the individual were possessed by Pan, the Greek god of lonely places and panic. The belief in life after death provided much comfort and security. Through the research and explanations discussed here we have begun to understand the nature of these life-after-death experiences as hallucinations, based on stored images in the brain. Like a mirage that shows a magnificent city on a desolate expanse of ocean or desert, the images of hallucinations are actually reflected images of real objects located elsewhere. The city is no less intriguing and no less worthy of study or visitation because it is not where we think it is. With such understanding we can counsel the dying to take the voyage, not with Pan at their side but with Athena, the Greek goddess of wisdom. But for the living, may the idea of an objectively supportable life after death rest in peace.

12

Psychic Healing

WILLIAM A. NOLEN

During the 1978 nationally televised finals of World Team Tennis, it was publicly announced that Tony Roche had finally been cured of an incapacitating case of tennis elbow by a psychic healer in the Philippines. Roche's career had been hampered for years by tennis elbow, and conventional medical treatments did not seem to help. Like growing numbers of desperate people, he turned to psychic surgery.

But psychic healers in the Philippines and elsewhere, as William Nolen, a surgeon and best-selling medical author, shows, use amateur sleight of hand in performing their "surgery." Other psychic healers, especially those within a religious tradition, probably act in good faith, but they do not produce healing effects beyond the scope of those that have already been amply demonstrated in medical suggestibility studies and psychosomatic medicine. Nor is there any documented instance of the use of ESP to locate a brain tumor, or of psychic healing to cure muscular dystrophy or any other organic ailment.

William Nolen has taken the hypothesis of psychic healing quite seriously. Between 1972 and 1974 he devoted much of his time to investigating psychic healing. Since that time he has, occasionally, looked *into the work of unorthodox "healers": people whose work can be accurately labeled "paranormal." It is as a result of these investigations— some of which he reported on in depth in his book,* Healing; A Doctor in Search of a Miracle *(Random House, 1974)—that he is well qualified to report on psychic healing. (Most of his time is devoted to the orthodox healing arts; he is a general surgeon, certified by the American Board of Surgery, and has been in the private practice of surgery since August 1960.) His travels around the world to investigate psychic healers, and his systematic efforts to document actual cures by faith healer Katherine Kuhlman and others, have made him a foremost scientific authority on the subject. His failure to find anything other than chicanery and the effects of suggestibility must be regarded as sobering.*

It may be especially tempting to invoke the supernatural in explaining healing by suggestion, because mind–body interactions are so astounding and so little understood. Not only may a strong faith combined with a healer's reassurance sometimes cure ulcers or headaches, but recent scientific discoveries indicate that hypnosis may help to cure warts; people can in part control the dates of their own deaths (more Jews may die immediately after Yom Kippur, the annual day of atonement, than before, for example); yoga masters can willfully control their metabolism in ways not previously thought possible; and, with the aid of biofeedback, apparently even the action of a single muscle or brain cell among billions may be voluntarily controlled.

In most cases we do not even begin to understand how these mind–body effects occur. There is no reason at all, however, to think that they depend on spiritual or paranormal causes. Labeling something we do not understand "supernatural" gets us nowhere. The history of science is filled with discoveries of natural mechanisms that cause puzzling phenomena when we have looked for them long and hard enough.

Psychic healing may be defined as the practice of healing by psychological methods. The best publicized of the healers are those who claim to have supernatural powers that enable them to heal the diseases of patients. These healers often attribute their healing power to God. Frequently they claim that they, themselves, do not heal the patient, but rather that they act as a conduit through which God (or, sometimes, a saint) works to achieve the healing. Many of these healers claim that they enter a trancelike state when they heal patients, and so are not completely aware of what they are doing. I have never met or read about a healer who can or will explain precisely how the healing he (or she) supposedly performs is accomplished.

The act by which the healer accomplishes the healing of a patient varies from healer to healer. Some, especially those associated with Christian churches, use prayers and laying-on of hands. Others have their own special rituals. For example, Norbu Chen (a former convict from Kentucky whose previous name was Mike Alexander) dresses up in the garb of a Buddhist monk and, after howling like a wolf in a dark, chapellike, incense-scented room, simply "shoots" his power into the patient without even bothering to lay on hands. When I last heard of him, in 1974, he charged patients $750 for a treatment and claimed a 70 percent cure rate. Norbu Chen claims to have learned how to heal during some months spent in Lhasa, the capital of Tibet. He resents interrogators who press him for details of his life.

The psychic surgeons of the Philippines, about fifteen men and one woman who live and work in Manila or Asignan province, use what they call psychic surgery to cure the patients who come to them. Psychic surgery is a sleight-of-hand technique in which the "surgeons" palm the viscera of small animals, usually chickens. They then appear to reach into the body cavities or extremities of patients and remove diseased organs. Using this surgery they claim that they, as instruments of saints who take possession of their bodies, can cure any disease—from multiple sclerosis to brain cancer. The psychic surgeons have assistants who slip them plastic vials containing animal blood or dye made from betel nuts; it thus appears to the patient/victim as if real blood is issuing from his own body. The surgeon kneads the soft tissues of the patient's body, the skin and fat, so that to the untrained eye it appears that the surgeon's hand has actually entered the patient's body.

There are, in the United States, many films taken of "psychic surgeons" at work. To a lay person who has never seen a real surgical procedure, these pseudo-operations look authentic; since they are quick, painless procedures and involve no risk of hemorrhage or infection, they are understandably a very attractive alternative to the real operation that may be required to remove a patient's appendix, diseased gall bladder, or malignant tumor.

After seeing dozens of films of psychic surgeons at work, and after talking to many patients who had been "operated" on by them, I flew to the Philippines in 1973 to watch some of the most renowned of the

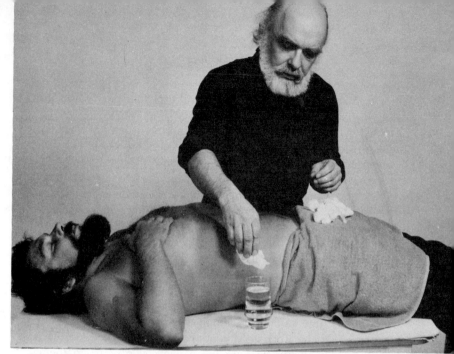

In the following sequence, James Randi simulates a psychic healer removing a supposed tumor. 1. The patient is prepared. The skin is wet with water and massaged about.

2. The "surgeon" places his hands flat on the abdomen.

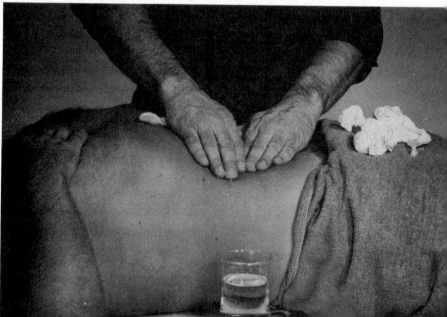

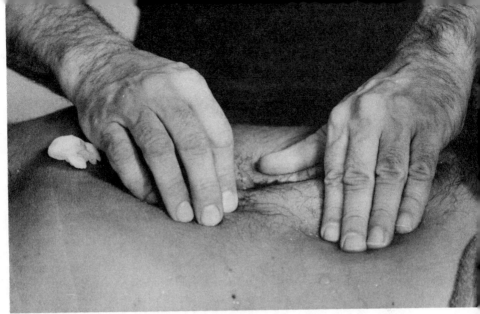

3. *A fold is formed in the skin and blood appears, producing the illusion that an incision has been made. The gimmick used is a plastic false thumb that contains the blood and chicken livers that pass as "tumors." It is worn on the right thumb (not discernible in this photograph) and will be discarded with the cotton swabs. The thumb is only one of many different gimmicks used by "psychic" surgeons.*

4. *The "tumor" is removed from the body.* Photographs courtesy *Gong*, Hamburg.

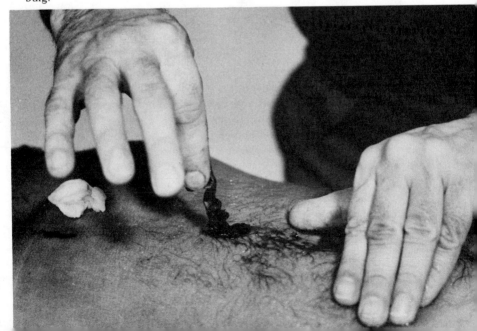

psychic surgeons at work. As an experienced surgeon I immediately recognized what I had previously suspected from viewing the films: These so-called operations were simply feats of legerdemain. I managed to persuade Joe Mercado, one of the best-known psychic surgeons, to operate on me, explaining that I had high blood pressure (true) and that high blood pressure might be caused by kidney disease (also true). He operated on me while I stood by the side of the altar in his church (at six foot one I was too tall to lie down on the altar on which he operated on most of his patients). Looking down on his hands, I could easily see as he began the "operation" that he had palmed the intestines and fat of a small animal. I watched him carefully as he pushed against me and it was apparent, both visually and from the way his hands felt as they pressed on my abdominal musculature, that he had not penetrated my abdominal wall. When he "removed" the fatty tissue, he held it up for all the spectators to see and said, "Evil tissue." He immediately tossed it into a can of flaming alcohol kept behind the altar. Mercado's assistant later told me that the evil tissue was a tumor of my left kidney. Now, I have seen hundreds of kidneys. This tissue was chicken fat, not a kidney. It is customary for psychic surgeons to immediately destroy the tissue they "remove"; that way there will be no chance for a patient to seize the tissue and take it to a pathologist. On the few occasions when patients have managed to acquire tissue ostensibly removed from their bodies it has been proven, by microscopic examination, to be of nonhuman animal origin.

Still, thousands of people from all over the world fly to the Philippines each year, seeking a painless operation for an illness that may or may not be critical. Sham operations are what, in fact, they receive. It is estimated, by a man who knows him well, that Tony Agpoa, one of the most highly publicized and most popular of the psychic surgeons, "operates" on an average of three hundred patients a month. The average donation to Tony's church (of which he is founder and owner) is two hundred dollars a patient. This amounts to over $700,000 a year, not a bad income.

There are certain rules that, I learned, all psychic healers follow. First, they invariably attribute their healing powers to God, saints, or disembodied spirits. Arigo, for example, who was so well publicized by John Fuller's book *Surgeon of the Rusty Knife*, claimed that when he "operated" his body was possessed by the spirit of a surgeon who lived in Germany several centuries ago (no one has ever been able to prove that such a surgeon ever lived). Arigo, a healer in Brazil, used techniques almost identical to those of the psychic surgeons of the Philippines. I never investigated his work, since he had died in an auto accident some years before I began my investigation and I had decided it would not be productive to pursue the reported cures of dead healers, particularly when so many live healers were still at work.

The obvious advantage to a healer of claiming that his power comes from some other source, one over which he has no control, is that when his attempt to heal fails he can put the blame on someone other than himself. He can say, for example, "My saint is not giving me healing powers today"; or—and this is almost as common as an excuse—he can say, "You [the patient] have not got faith. Therefore my healing powers won't work." Unlike the orthodox physician, a psychic healer never has to take the responsibility when his healing fails. I must confess that I would like the option of resorting to such an excuse when I encounter a patient whom I cannot cure.

Second, healers almost invariably claim an average of 70 percent cure rates. Since it is estimated by practitioners of orthodox medicine that about 80 percent of the patients who come to a primary practitioner (family practitioner, internist, or pediatrician) have self-limited diseases—that is, diseases from which they will recover spontaneously, the natural healing powers of the body being what they are—the healer actually allows himself a 10 percent margin of error when claiming that at least 70 percent of his patients will get well. In other words, if any reader chose to go into business as a healer, all that would be necessary would be to acquire some strange costume, develop an impressive ritual, and accept as patients all those who might come knocking at your door. You could safely guarantee that 70 percent of these patients would eventually be cured, provided you did nothing to interfere with the natural healing powers of their bodies.

To be more specific, orthodox medical practitioners estimate that 80 percent of patients who first seek a physician's help have self-limited diseases such as back strains, colds, laryngitis, or headache; 10 percent have diseases that are already so far advanced as to be beyond the help of any practitioner; and 10 percent have diseases where proper diagnosis and treatment by the doctor will cure or at least alleviate the ailment. The trick is to recognize which patients have diseases that fall into this latter category; to do that requires all the education and experience a physician receives in medical school and during his apprenticeship as an intern and resident.

Finally, the successes that healers occasionally achieve are due to the fact that many diseases are, in fact, subject to psychological influences. Physicians usually divide ailments into three categories: purely organic ailments, including broken bones, cuts, traumatic injuries to internal and external organs, infectious diseases such as tuberculosis and measles, and (probably) cancer; purely psychological illnesses, such as hysteria, anxiety, and nervous tics; and, finally, diseases which result from a combination of psychological and organic factors. Many of the most common, persistent, and troublesome diseases fall into the last category. Examples include asthma, duodenal and stomach ulcers, dysmenorrhea, colitis, allergic reactions, and migraine headaches. A complete list of psychological–organic disease would be a very long one.

Healers have no success in treating purely organic diseases. In fact, most healers, if they are clever enough to recognize that a patient is suffering from a purely organic disease, will tell the patient, "Your disease is a simple one. It can be easily treated by regular doctors. I save my powers for the patients who suffer from ailments that regular doctors cannot successfully treat." There are no well-documented cases of hernias, stone-laden gall bladders, inflamed appendixes, ruptured spleens, or cancers that have been successfully treated by healers.

The treatment of purely psychological or psychological–organic ailments is a different matter. Take, for example, the patient with paralysis of her legs. If that paralysis has been caused by a severed spinal cord, then it falls into the category of purely organic diseases. A healer will have no success if he uses his "power" to try to restore that patient's ability to walk.

Assume, however, that the patient is suffering from hysterical paralysis; that the patient, faced with a family problem that he cannot solve, develops an inability to move his legs because that is an easier problem to deal with than the family problem.

A healer may be able to "cure" the patient of this paralysis, if its cause is entirely psychological. The healer may develop such rapport with the patient, so persuade the patient that his laying-on of hands or psychic surgery will restore the patient's ability to walk, that, after the healer's ministrations, the patient will, indeed, begin to walk again. The patient will attribute the cure to the healer, thus adding to the healer's reputation as a miracle worker. In fact, a capable and caring psychologist, psychiatrist, family doctor, or clergyman could achieve the same result.

The psychological–organic ailments will, in many cases, respond equally well to the ministrations of the psychic healer. Duodenal ulcers, for example, often result from hypersecretion of hydrochloric acid by the cells that line the stomach. Emotional stress is one factor that works, through the autonomic nervous system, to cause such hypersecretion. A psychic healer who gains the confidence of a patient with an ulcer, who helps that patient learn to relax and avoid situations which produce stress, may, by so doing, cause the stomach to secrete less acid, allowing the ulcer to heal. The patient considers this miraculous and attributes the "miracle" to the power of the psychic healer.

Ulcerative colitis, migraine headaches, hypertension, asthma, some heart disorders (particularly those which produce irregular beats)—in fact, all psychological–organic ailments—are often caused in whole or in part by malfunctioning of the autonomic nervous system, that part of the nervous system over which we have little or no control. The voluntary nervous system, which includes most of the brain and the spinal cord, is the system we use when we lift a glass, walk, speak—do all the things we do because we will ourselves to do them. The autonomic nervous system regulates such functions as digestion, heart rate, blood pressure, erections in males, and menstrual periods in females. Some people, using biofeedback, yoga, or other techniques, can gain partial control of their autonomic nervous system, but, for the most part, it is self-governing. (This is, of course, to our benefit. If we had to worry about how rapidly to make our heart beat when we ran a mile, how much pancreatic fluid to secrete in order to digest our food, or how much our pupils should contract or dilate to adjust to a given amount of light we would have no time for other endeavors.)

The autonomic nervous system is susceptible to manipulation by suggestion—and that is precisely what psychic healers do when they treat patients with psychological–organic diseases. In psychic surgery, for example, sham operations are used to suggest to the patient that a diseased organ has been removed and therefore will not trouble the patient again. Norbu Chen, when he bays like a wolf and "shoots his power" into a patient, is using these actions to reinforce the suggestion he has already made to the patient: that Chen will use his mysterious skills to cure the patient. When evangelical healers dramatically call on God to transmit His power through them to cure their patients' diseases, they are using the power of suggestion in the hope that it will so affect the patient's malfunctioning autonomic nervous system that the disease or symptoms caused by the derangement of that system will be cured. Sometimes these techniques will work; the patient's symptoms, and perhaps even his disease, will be cured. (Often, unfortunately, the cure is only temporary. When the patient is again put into a stressful situation his autonomic nervous system will, again, respond by malfunctioning, and the migraine, asthma, ulcer, or other disorder will return.)

There is nothing wrong with using these psychological techniques to alleviate symptoms or cure diseases; orthodox physicians also use them. The danger lies in the possibility that a psychic healer may use suggestion successfully to relieve a patient of pain, without in fact curing the underlying disease. This can even prove fatal. For example, the patient whose stomach pain is temporarily alleviated by the psychic healer may not seek orthodox medical diagnosis and treatment. If it turns out that the pain was caused by a stomach cancer rather than stress-related hyperacidity, the patient may not receive proper surgical therapy until the stomach cancer has spread to other organs and become incurable.

The suggestions that psychic healers employ to treat patients are essentially hypnotic techniques, though few psychic healers recognize them as such. There is a principle in the medical profession that says a doctor should not use hypnotic techniques to treat a patient's disease unless he is capable of treating the disease by other medical or surgical methods. Most doctors respect and follow this; to do otherwise can lead to trouble. Psychic healers, since they know little or nothing of more orthodox medical and surgical diagnostic and therapeutic techniques, cannot adhere to this rule. It is this lack of knowledge that occasionally causes disasters for patients who rely on psychic healers.

There is no evidence that psychic healers have supernatural powers, nor that they serve as conduits through which healing powers flow from supernatural sources to ordinary humans. Psychic healers are ordinary people using the power of suggestion, just as each of us, physician or layman, uses the power of suggestion in innumerable transactions every day of every week. The cures that psychic healers achieve are neither miraculous nor manifestations of any extraordinary powers.

Some of those who practice psychic healing are sincere, dedicated people who are suffering from the delusion that they have been granted supernatural powers. Others—and unfortunately there are many such—are charlatans who prey on those patients afflicted with diseases for which medical science has not yet found a cure, and on those patients who are afraid of the medicines and operations that must sometimes be employed to cure disease. Unfortunately, the flight to psychic healers is often precipitated by a patient's encounter with a physician who offers the patient satisfactory scientific medicine, but fails to give him the affection, the sense of genuine caring that should be part of the art of medicine. The psychic healers know little or nothing of the science of medicine; however, most of them are experts at the art of developing a confidence-inspiring patient–healer relationship.

We doctors could well learn something about patient–doctor relationships by studying even the charlatans who practice psychic healing. But if one has an organic disease, or even a disease which is part psychological and part organic, one is much safer in the care of even the most callous of orthodox physicians than in the care of the most compassionate of psychic healers.

Psychic healing is painless, quick, and relatively inexpensive. But if the disease being treated is life-threatening, psychic healing is not only worthless, but potentially fatal.

13

Kirlian Photography*

BARRY SINGER

Almost everyone has seen a Kirlian photograph of a leaf or a fingertip surrounded by a strange glow and light streamers, sometimes in vivid color. Most people are also aware that there are spectacular claims that match the striking aesthetics of this photographic process. It has been claimed, for instance, that the photographs depict the human aura, or the "energy body" of living tissue, and that the process measures the transfer of energy in psychic healing. Kirlian photography as a reliable and easily measurable physical process has, in fact, even been hailed as a rare breakthrough in paranormal research.

In the following essay, Barry Singer reveals that the mechanisms causing the varied and colorful photographs are not completely understood. Enough is understood, however, to warrant the warning that the assumption that extraordinary processes are involved in Kirlian pho-

*I am much indebted to J. O. Pehek, Harry Kyler, William Eidson, and David Faust, upon whose work this chapter is substantially based. They have provided significant clarification and advice. Responsibility for errors of fact or interpretation is of course mine.

tography is not justified. The photographs may seem exotic and mysterious, but that feeling of mystery may simply stem from the lay person's unfamiliarity with the complex but apparently mundane physical processes involved.

Objective investigation of the Kirlian effect requires considerable expertise in the physics of electrical phenomena, and thorough, rigorous experiments to determine why and how the photographs vary. Singer shows that the answers we are beginning to acquire to questions about the Kirlian process, while they may lead in interesting and even important directions, are not the answers offered by paranormal speculations.

Semyon Davidovich Kirlian, a talented and curious Armenian electrician, discovered the "Kirlian aura" in 1937. While repairing an electrotherapeutic device, he experienced a sparking between his hand and a glass-covered electrode attached to the device. His curiosity awakened, he wondered if the sparks surrounding his hand would show up in a photograph. Kirlian's first attempt at such photography led to burns but did in fact produce an image of his hand surrounded by a glow.

Kirlian, in collaboration with his wife, Valentina, continued to investigate this effect, refining his photographic and electrical techniques and experimenting with photography of various animate and inanimate objects. The Kirlians concluded that the process was of value in making early diagnoses of disease in humans, animals, and plants, and in studying electrical and physiological properties of living plant and animal tissue. In the late 1950s, through lectures and papers, the Kirlians' work reached the attention of the Russian academic community. Russian investigators began to visit the Kirlians' laboratory, and various Russian scientists published accounts of the Kirlian effect in their scientific journals. One of the Kirlians' papers, a review of techniques and devices used in the process, was translated by the United States Air Force in 1963 but aroused little interest.

In 1970 two journalists, Sheila Ostrander and Lynn Schroeder, published the best-selling *Psychic Discoveries Behind the Iron Curtain.*[1] In this book the Kirlians' work was reported to be a technique for photographing the "human energy field" or "aura." The "aura," in turn, was said to be sensitive to the emotional and psychic states of the person photographed. Kirlian photography was soon after highlighted by the entertainment and news media, because of both the controversy the above claims inspired and the colorful and intricate appearance of the photographs themselves. Newsmagazines published Kirlian photographs in vivid color, which allegedly portrayed states of love, hate, drug intoxication, disease, and psychic healing[2] (see below). At this point, however, American investigation of the Kirlian effect had barely begun.

In the early 1970s Thelma Moss, teaching a course in parapsychology, sparked an interest in Kirlian photography in Kendall Johnson, one of her students. Since they did not have access to the details of the Russian wiring diagrams, Moss and Johnson experimented by trial and error until they hit upon the proper photographic and electrical techniques. They were then able to produce strikingly beautiful photographs of leaves, coins, fingertips, and even entire animals, outlined in intricate streamers of bluish-white light. There followed a long series of experiments, and published work suggesting that the Kirlian effect was a breakthrough in paranormal research.[3] Not only was the technique said to reveal the human "aura" or "energy body"; it was also hypothesized that the color and shape of the photographed aura indicated the state of consciousness of the person photographed—for instance, revealing meditative and drug states. Emotional arousal was also allegedly depicted by the photographs. The investigators further speculated that we might be able to diagnose cancer

Kirlian photographs of a subject's fingertips reflecting states of meditation (top) *and anger* (bottom). Courtesy R. Wagner.

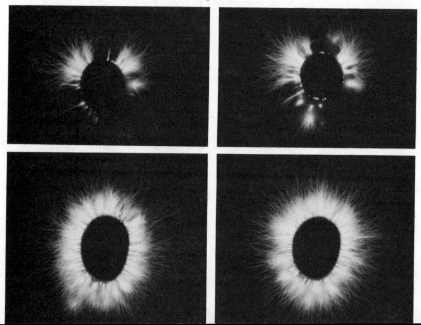

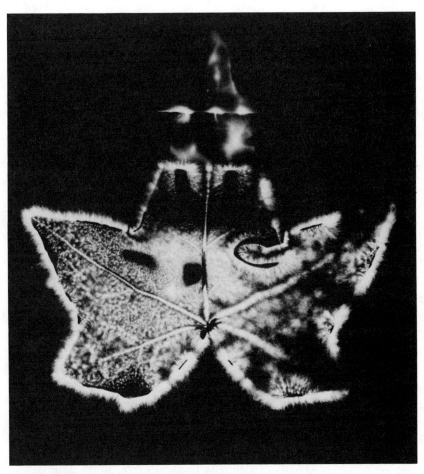

The "phantom leaf." Courtesy R. Wagner.

earlier and better through Kirlian photography than through standard medical techniques. The process was also said to show transfers of energy between a psychic healer and the person healed, the aura of the healer diminishing after healing, while the aura of the person healed brightened and grew. And the "phantom leaf" effect, in which a Kirlian photograph of a leaf with a small piece snipped off has sometimes shown the outline of the whole leaf (see above), has been interpreted as evidence supportive of the existence of an "energy body" in all living things.[4] Writings by Krippner and others in the paranormal community elaborated upon Moss and Johnson's work.[5]

Today almost everyone has seen a Kirlian photograph and heard some of the claims for the effect. Kirlian photography kits are sold by mail order for fifty dollars or less, and many people have tried Kirlian photography themselves. There seems to be a general impression that the Kirlian effect is a dramatic discovery, a technique that displays and documents a form of psychic energy that we all possess. What are the facts about this startling and vivid effect?

It is important to distinguish two kinds of paranormal claims about the Kirlian effect: that Kirlian photography depicts astral bodies, and that it reveals psychic states and processes.

Thelma Moss and Kendall Johnson assert that Kirlian photographs depict the "astral body" or some mysterious new form of energy:

> The Kirlian effect . . . provides us with the possibility of viewing unseen patterns of energies and force fields that may permeate all substance, including life itself. [6]

> All living things have not only a physical body, but also an "energy body" consisting of "bioplasma." [7]

> It is clear to us that radiation field photography [Kirlian effect] reveals a highly complex, perhaps still unknown phenomenon which may be linked to Inyushin's concept of the bioplasma body. [8]

The astral body, otherwise known as energy body, etheric body, or, more recently, bioplasma body, is a longstanding paranormal concept. It is said to be a nonmaterial body, perhaps a new form of energy, that coexists with and permeates the physical body of all living things. When the astral body projects beyond the physical body, it forms an "aura," appearing in various colors, which psychics have often claimed they can see.

However, all those in the paranormal-research community are aware that the Kirlian effect bears more than a passing resemblance to a quite common physical effect known as corona discharge, a sparking in the atmosphere around any object in a strong electric field (discussed below). The rationale some investigators offer for believing that the Kirlian effect is photographing an "energy body" rather than ordinary corona discharge seems to be as follows:

1. The Kirlian effect looks like what an aura or energy body is supposed to look like.

2. There is "not enough known" about corona discharge to say for certain that the Kirlian process is an example of this effect. The Kirlian effect seems quite varied and complex.[9]

3. In a series of experiments, Moss and Johnson found that the Kirlian auras did not correlate well with measured skin resistance, skin temperature, or blood pressure. This is taken as evidence that the shape and colors of the Kirlian effect are determined by nonphysiological means—that is, by psychological and psychic inner states.[10]

Some paranormal investigators simply acknowledge that the physical processes involved in the photographs are probably ordinary, that no occult form of energy is involved in producing the image on the photographic plate. They theorize instead that the Kirlian process is an electrophysiological measurement technique that is somehow sensitive to psychic states of the person photographed. For example: "Of course, the Kirlian photography process itself is *not* a psychic event or psychic photography. The Kirlian technique per se has nothing whatever to do with occultism any more than the electroencephalograph."[11]

The suggestion, rather, is that emotional states such as love and excitement, or altered states of consciousness induced by drugs or meditation, are measured by various features of the photographs. Also, the photographs are said to measure the "transfer of energy" in psychic healing or the effects of an individual's psychic rapport with plants. The physical mechanisms of producing the vivid photographs, while ordinary in themselves, are thus said to index or reflect various psychic events in the object photographed

In order to evaluate the above claims, we need to review briefly the physics of corona discharge and compare this physical process with the Kirlian effect.

Corona discharge is an electrical discharge, a movement of electrons, that may occur over a short physical range when a high-intensity electric field exists in a gaseous atmosphere. This discharge will cause a glow without necessarily producing sparks. The discharge is the result of ionization of some of the atoms and molecules that comprise the gas; that is, the stripping of one or more electrons from atoms or molecules. When ionization takes place, the subsequent flow of free electrons through the gas creates a current, which, in general, will flow in directions determined by the paths of highest conductivity (least resistance). When the free electrons strike individual atoms making up the gas, they impart energy to, or excite, those atoms, which in turn reradiate energy in the form of photons of light, which causes the visible glow.

Examples of such naturally occurring electrical discharges that produce glowing "coronas" (halos) or that can actually produce sparking are ordinary atmospheric lightning, St. Elmo's fire, the eerie glow sometimes seen by mariners surrounding the masts of their ships, the glow sometimes seen around high-potential power-transmission lines, neon lights, and the sparking that can occur from walking across a carpet on a dry winter's day and then touching a doorknob.

As a physical process, corona discharge has been recognized for many years, although of course there remains much we still do not know about it. All investigations to date of the Kirlian effect have employed a technique that is capable of producing a corona discharge. That is, a high voltage difference has been applied between the object to be photographed (the "subject") and an electrode.

As shown below and on the next page, in Kirlian photography the subject (for instance, a fingertip) is connected to one end of an interrupted

A Kirlian apparatus. Courtesy Elsevier-Dutton Publishing Company, Inc.

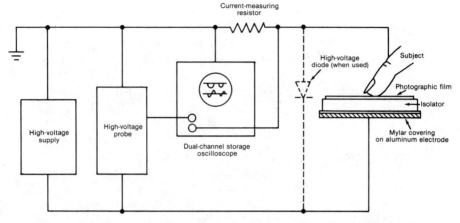

Circuit diagram of a Kirlian apparatus. After J. O. Pehek, H. J. Kyler, and D. L. Faust, "Image Modulation in Corona Discharge Photography," *Science*, 15 October 1976.

circuit and thus constitutes an electrode. A photographic plate is placed beneath the fingertip, which actually rests on the plate. An insulator, usually a piece of glass about one-half-inch thick, is placed between the photographic plate and the second electrode, which is a flat metal plate.

When a brief current (actually a series of pulses lasting somewhat less than a second) is discharged into the circuit, the fingertip, functioning as an electrode, will create an electric field that diminishes rapidly as the distance from the finger increases. This electric field will produce ionization of gases in the area around the fingertip. The Kirlian apparatus is designed so that a full transmission of current, which would produce a spark, is prevented by the insulator. Instead, the electric field produces a corona discharge, a roughly circular glow in both visible and ultraviolet light in the atmosphere above the photographic plate, which the plate, acting as a kind of lensless camera, will register. Kirlian photography is actually done in a darkroom, so that the plate will not register any extraneous light.

It is worth noting in passing that the Kirlian apparatus requires a fair amount of technical expertise to operate. Ordinarily such high voltage differences as are used in Kirlian photography are associated with a high amperage (amount of current), and even minimal amperage can cause physiological havoc in the human body. In order to avoid fried fingertips, the Kirlian process uses insulators and other special devices to create high voltage differences without permitting a large current flow, and it uses high-frequency current, which tends not to interact physiologically with the body at low amperage. Experimentation using Kirlian processes is not recommended for the amateur.

Under such circumstances, then, we would expect a corona discharge to form in the air around the subject, and the film should image the corona. Early work by physicists Cooper and Alt [12] showed that no image resulted when the atmosphere around the subject was removed (by creating a vacuum), and that the image was brightest around points and prominences of the subject. These results are precisely predictable if the phenomenon is an ordinary corona discharge, but not if it is an "energy body." The most reasonable working assumption, then, is that the Kirlian effect is a corona discharge. The facts that the image is quite varied and complex, and that a few preliminary measurements failed to find physiological determinants, do not in the least imply that something mysterious and nonphysical, such as a "psychic state" or an "energy body," is being manifested in the Kirlian process. A large number of physical factors could be influencing the shape and color of the corona, and scientists have barely begun to investigate them. In a Kirlian photograph of a fingertip, for instance, such factors might include position and pressure of the finger on the photographic plate; air temperature; air pressure; air moisture (humidity); skin resistance; moisture extruded from the skin; electrical circuit characteristics: amperage, voltage, frequency, duration; number of pulses, rate of voltage rise; photographic plate characteristics: size, sensitivity, resistance qualities, type of emulsion; electrode characteristics: size, shape, resistance, polarity; and insulator characteristics.

While it is not ruled out that some other, occult phenomenon is being photographed in addition to corona discharge phenomena, indications are otherwise, and the burden of proof is on those making such a claim.

Nor is it really true that Kirlian photography is a new discovery, as Kirlian himself recognized early in his career. The first account of imaging of a corona discharge was by G. C. Lichtenberg in 1777. He noted that a starlike pattern occurred in dust in a resin cake when a large voltage was discharged to it from the point of a needle. At the turn of this century the electrical genius Nikola Tesla, who developed many applications of alternating current, often publicized his inventions by running a low-amperage, high-voltage, high-frequency current through his entire body, enveloping himself in a halo and shooting sparks from his fingertips. Tesla took photographs of himself during this process.

Thus, the Kirlians rediscovered an already known physical and photographic process. In fact, some Czech investigators also published a paper on the process in 1939 almost simultaneously with, but independently of, the Kirlians.[13] Kirlian's contributions and those of later American investigators were to excite interest in the process, greatly refine the photographic techniques, and extend the range of objects that could be photographed.

What affects the shape and color of the photographs? As previously mentioned, Kirlian photographs may in fact vary as a result of the psychological state of the person photographed. The color, size, and brightness of the circular region of glow, or the range and density of the "streamers" (the thin, branched shafts of light emanating from the center), may look different when a person is in a state of anger as compared to sexual arousal, or in meditative states, or after a "healer" has finished the "laying-on of hands." Although not enough systematic research has been done on these effects, they are not in themselves in dispute. What is in dispute is their interpretation. Do the observed variations result from changes in the "energy body" of the subject photographed, or from something more prosaic?

In answering this question we are indebted to a team of physicists and psychologists from Drexel University. William Eidson, Harry Kyler, David Faust, and J. O. Pehek have been carefully investigating the Kirlian effect for several years. Their research is a model of objective, careful, and expert scientific investigation.[14]

Preliminary experimentation indicated that the amount of moisture exuded from the subject being photographed was an important factor. For instance, page 206 shows a piece of wood photographed by the Kirlian process when dry and when wetted with tap water.

Hypothesizing that moisture could therefore account for many of the effects observed with human subjects, the Drexel investigators photographed fingertips under a variety of wet and dry conditions. The results showed that moisture in or on the fingertip functioned to change the size and brightness of the glow region and resulted in fewer streamers. The effect probably occurs because a damp fingertip excretes moisture onto the photographic plate and into the atmosphere above the plate, influencing the path of the current and the consequent propagation of the corona through those regions.

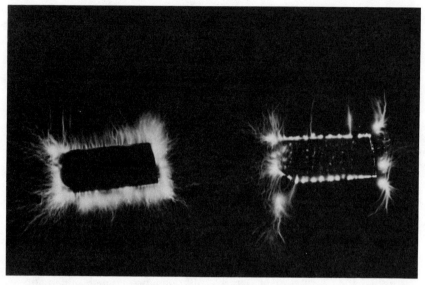

Wood photographed when dry (left) *and wet* (right). Courtesy Pehek, Kyler, and Faust, "Image Modulation in Corona Discharge Photography," *Science,* 15 October 1976.

The research team also found that emotionally arousing stimuli, such as a loud noise or a pinch with forceps, did in fact change the photographic images, and once again these changes were related to changes in the moisture of the subject photographed. These results are not surprising. We have known for some time that the moisture content of the skin changes under even mild emotional stress, and this fact is the basis of the lie detector. The types of moisture changes measured by the Kirlian process are similar to those measured by the lie detector, although the Kirlian process may turn out to be an even more sensitive instrument. It therefore seems plausible that most, if not all, of the changes observed in subjects photographed under differing emotional states or states of consciousness are due to associated moisture differences on the surface of the skin.

The explanation of the color changes in the photographs forms an interesting detective story. The Kirlian images are usually blue to bluish white when color film is used, though the exact colors obtained are also affected by type of film. Sometimes, however, orange and yellow colors appear in the photographs, and these effects have been given dramatic paranormal interpretations. Acting upon earlier suggestions by Boyer and Tiller at Stanford and Poock at the U.S. Naval

Postgraduate School, the Drexel team observed that the oranges and yellows seemed to occur when the *backing* of the photographic plate was transparent, but not when it was opaque, and the colors also tended toward orange when the moisture count of the subject was high.

Further investigation revealed the following:

In color film, there are three layers of pigment or dye—blue, green, and red—arranged from top to bottom. Under normal conditions, light of a particular color is absorbed by the corresponding dye layer. More energetic radiation (blue) is absorbed by the top (blue) layer, leaving only less energetic components to be selectively absorbed in turn by the lower layers. Unless overexposed, the image will thus depict the colors of the object photographed. However, in the Kirlian process the subject to be photographed is placed in contact with the film itself, an unusual photographic condition. The Drexel investigators found that when moisture from the subject was exuded onto the film, corona discharge not only flowed around these moist areas but also *beneath* them. That is, corona discharge was occurring on the back side of the film. If the film had a transparent backing, the red die layers on the bottom of the film would be stimulated by any impinging light, regardless of its true color, and a red-orange image would result. Once again, a finding that had been interpreted vaguely and mystically in the paranormal literature was shown to have simple physical causes.

Research on the Kirlian effect is still in progress. We have found that it is a quite complex phenomenon. Rather than being able to claim immediately that something supernatural is being photographed or measured when a healer's "aura" changes before and after "psychic healing," we now know that there are more than twenty-five physical variables that influence the images. All these physical variables must be understood and controlled before we can begin to understand the Kirlian process. As one more example, the Drexel team repeatedly found that streamer range—the physical extent of the branching shafts of light that emanate from a photographed fingertip—is influenced by film type, unipolar versus bipolar current, voltage, electrical pulse rate, pulse rise time, circuit resistance, thickness and other properties of the insulator, water vapor in the atmosphere, and geometric characteristics of the surface of the photographed subject.

As yet, no mysterious process has been discovered by mainstream scientists investigating the Kirlian process. The paranormal claims about the photographs seem to have resulted from misunderstandings about the physical processes involved, and lack of expertise in conducting rigorous technical measurements. Although not all the paranormal claims have been investigated, it seems a reasonable strategy at present to explain observations regarding the Kirlian effect by means of conventional scientific knowledge already on hand.

The Kirlian process produces beautiful, fascinating photographs. Further scientific work may show that these natural works of art are a sensitive and useful index of the moisture characteristics of plant and animal tissue. We will very probably not find, however, that the Kirlian process is the road to the edge of reality that some paranormal investigators had hoped.

14

Science and the Chimera

JAMES RANDI

Some of the public's confusion about the validity of the paranormal arises because while most establishment scientists do not seem to comment on or notice it at all, some reputable scientists have indeed voiced their convictions supporting the validity of various paranormal phenomena. While the latter's views are sometimes widely publicized, most of their dissenting colleagues are reluctant to debate with them publicly. Does this mean that establishment scientists are simply ignoring valid paranormal phenomena, or that they are tacitly admitting that there lie truths that are hidden from conventional science?

In this essay, magician James Randi, professionally known as The Amazing Randi, assumes the role of privileged observer of the scientific community in its behavior toward the paranormal. As he has demonstrated many times, Randi understands how fraudulent psychics can produce their hoaxes in ways that baffle or impress conventional scientists. He observes that scientists' training and "linear thinking" ill equip them to discover psychic hoaxes, and he shares his observations on the reactions of conventional and parascientists when hoaxes are exposed. The fact that occasionally scientists, usually working outside

209

their own fields of expertise, may lend their support to paranormal claims does not necessarily make those claims correct, or mean that they are supported by the scientific community in general.

Some of Randi's remarks are directed toward conventional scientists, who generally refrain from commenting critically on the wild ideas of a few of their colleagues because it is bad manners, or who refrain from communicating their opinions of the paranormal to the public because it is beneath their dignity. But Randi's experience gives him far more insight into recognizing chicanery than most scientists possess. He has also interacted extensively with scientists and observed them shrewdly. He is thus eminently qualified to offer what we hope is highly constructive criticism.

Since I first discovered the world of the paranormal at the age of thirteen, I have not ceased being amazed at the prodigious powers of rationalization exhibited by those who pursue this highly elusive quarry. Even at that age, I was somehow immune to the imaginative excuses that I found were thrown about freely whenever a failure became evident, or the results were not quite what the miracle mongers could have wished. I was not at all deceived by the sleight-of-mind that I found being peddled at The Assembly of Inspired Thought in my home town of Toronto, yet only recently I found exactly the same brand and quality of quackery being practiced in that very spot. Barnum was being quite conservative in his estimate of the public's gullibility.

I recall very clearly how, in the perfumed and creaking temple of spiritualism that first revealed to me the perfidy of the opportunistic, bad guesses were dismissed as the result of "negative thoughts" or "mischievous entities." Incorrect predictions were the product of "interventions," and healings that did not succeed were proof that "the spirits know better than we." And all this claptrap was accepted easily by the regulars there, who had been carefully coached in acceptance over many months of attendance at the assembly. Sunday after Sunday, disappointments were swallowed, and Pollyannic prognostications and promises were carried away like trophies to be admired until they crumbled away.

The small group who had embarked on this curious pursuit of miracles with me came to recognize most of the maneuvers that I still find in my present investigations of everything from table tippers and dowsers to spoon benders and prophets. Most of the chicanery is accomplished by psychological means; only a fraction involves actual physical manipulation or hardware. And it is this basic fact that has led a few misguided scientists through the looking glass and into the study of things that are far beyond their ability to handle rationally. They look for the hardware and for the logic behind it all, and often there is none to be found.

Let me clear up two prominent misconceptions that defenders of the paranormal constantly throw in the way of intelligent dialogue. The first is the claim that I and fellow investigators, able to duplicate by simple trickery the apparent miracles we examine, also claim that this provides proof that the many miracles of "psychics" are also done this way. It is not proof, but it *is* a strong indication. What it does establish is the fact that, contrary to most preliminary claims, these miracles *can* be duplicated. Second, I hear cries of outrage that we are saying such things as ESP, UFOs, and apparitions *cannot exist*. To make such a claim would be illogical, and besides, one cannot prove a negative. We only say that there is insufficient good-quality proof to accept such matters. Surely these two stances are reasonable.

Scientists, far from being the hardest audience for the professional charlatan, are often the easiest. A scientist thinks logically and in a straight line; his profession requires him to be able to do so. That's the way science works. When the scientist has gathered what he believes to be the facts, he wants to put them into proper form and publish them. This is a form of ceremonial behavior that is found in the species without exception. An organized "paper" is prepared and sent until it falls on the right desk. It is published and is thereby accepted as fact even though the information therein may have been the result of data supplied by a professional deceiver providing the scientist with what *appeared* to be legitimate information obtained by "straight-line" thinking.

We demand repeatability of science: experiments or demonstrations of some claim must be replicable by other workers in the discipline, using essentially the same tools and working under the same conditions. But this requirement has failings that the parapsychologists have flaunted gleefully. Consider such a phenomenon as a meteorite. True, we can produce a stonelike or metallic lump that we claim fell from the open sky. Examination shows it to be unlike the vast majority of other terrestrial minerals, with specific peculiarities. But we obviously cannot demand repeatability of visual observation of meteorites' descent to earth in order to prove the claim that they do indeed come from the sky. It is simply not possible to stand at any one spot at any given time and expect a meteor to flash overhead and descend into a waiting specimen-collector. In psychology, too, there are variations in human behavior that are just not obtainable on demand, and conclusions are often reached from a great number of observations of similar and related situations that bear on the sought-after set of conditions. Thus, in quite legitimate science we can easily find examples where repeatability is not only waived as a requirement but is almost impossible to obtain.

In investigating the claims of the paranormal, we must admit that the "sporadic" occurrence—such as a once-only, startlingly accurate prediction of an unlikely event—cannot be properly looked into, although, even there, careful investigation may well reveal the selective or prejudiced nature of the reconstruction. But by the same standards, we must maintain that since such an event is not examinable as it occurs, we are not required to accept it, either. The parapsychologists have claimed that many of their experiments *can* be replicated, and we must pursue these.

Of course, it is impractical to refuse to recognize any scientific claim until and unless it has been replicated independently by others in that area of science. The word of an authority can safely be accepted on the basis of his prior work and his established reputation. However, failure to achieve replication should bring with it serious doubt about the value of the conclusions previously accepted, and a return to the old drawing board. Mistakes in science should be quite acceptable as part of the learning process; ignoring mistakes to save the feelings and reputations of the persons involved simply cannot be condoned. But it is.

Even now, as the dust settles over the matter of Sir Cyril Burt, whose extensive and well-accepted work on hereditary influences as studied among twins was found to be considerably reinforced by his imagination, there are scientists who blush at a discussion of the exposure. Visiting Kings College in London years ago, I myself heard amused mumblings about the fudged results that were even at that time very strongly suspected, yet no one there took the responsibility of making an issue of it. Here was a highly pertinent study by a now-deceased authority, the basis for many learned studies by hard-working biologists throughout the world, yet no move was contemplated to brand it for what it was. It fell to the lot of a visiting American scientist to blow the lid off the issue, and I am sure that gentleman has been viewed askance by some ever since.

The classic N-rays fiasco is another case in point. When one Blondlot, full of honors and appointments, startled the world of science in 1903 by announcing the discovery of previously unsuspected radiation exhibiting impossible properties, others immediately claimed that they, too, could detect the rays. Reports tumbled in to journals, and while most scientists far away from France, where the marvelous discovery had been made, reported failure after failure in replicating these results, dozens of Europeans confirmed the impossible. Mind you, there was a predisposition to such acceptance, since X rays, which also exhibited unsuspected properties, were by then firmly established. But the N-rays case illustrates one important point: though the matter was shown to be a huge mistake, Blondlot's colleagues around the globe tended to merely let it slip out of history, and learned very little from the example. Visiting Nancy recently and speaking on the subject of parascience, I gently introduced this example of scientific flummery, and though I stood in the very city that gave the name to N rays, not one of my audience had ever heard of them, or of Blondlot. And several there were professors from the University of Nancy.

Should we go about in lynch parties, holding the cadavers of mistaken scientists aloft in flame? Hardly. But the system that we depend upon for our present existence and our future safety should be ready to declare itself in error when the occasion demands, without embarrassment and free of guilt. We learn from errors.

Rationalization, too, is an accomplished art among believers and is particularly well developed among some scientists involved in paranormal research. They have a bigger vocabulary than most of us, and many more obscure ways of explaining things, by which they can process the uncomfortable facts they encounter when pursuing the paranormal chimera. Heisenberg writes that an observed phenomenon is interfered with by the very process of observation; they then alibi that paranormal demonstrations are best performed when not being too closely observed. Professor John Taylor* even named this the "shyness

* John G. Taylor, of Kings College, London, a British mathematician. In a recent issue of the British journal *Nature*, Taylor reversed completely his position of support for parapsychology. (Eds.)

effect," meaning that wonders preferred to happen out of sight.

When the psychic surgeons of the Philippines got suddenly popular by removing deadly tumors from their patients merely by stroking bare fingers across the abdomens and extracting messes of gooey material accompanied by copious blood flows—without making any incision— some brave souls troubled to bring back samples of blood and some of what was removed. Tests showed the blood was bovine or avian, and the "tumors" were pig entrails or chicken livers. Were the parapsychologists dismayed by this evidence? Not at all. They marveled that the mysterious powers possessed by these miracle-workers had not only penetrated the dermis of the unfortunate sufferers, but had converted the deadly growths into innocuous and harmless substances! When the "surgeons" claimed to have removed metal pins from bones that had been implanted by legitimate surgeons with less flamboyant methods, X rays proved the lie to all but those who were desperate or foolish enough to accept the flimflam. Said they, the psychic surgeons had in reality only extracted the "essence" of the metal parts. The mind boggles at such insanity.

How, then, *did* the Philippino charlatans perform their wonders? I myself have demonstrated the "operation" at my lectures, perhaps a hundred or more times—without ever being caught at the trick. It is quite convincing to laymen and to the scientists, no matter how well they are prepared to observe. But it is perfectly transparent to any magician! It involves a simple gimmick* that may be purchased from a magic-supply store for about a dollar, and with a modicum of practice, it becomes simple to perform the trick.

It is interesting to note that the many excellent film documentaries that have been made on the subject of psychic surgery, declaring the process to be fakery, failed to discover the method. True, it was ascribed to "sleight-of-hand," but that hardly satisfied the viewer. But in at least one notable case (the MacLeer–CTV film in Canada) the gimmick showed up on camera and was identifiable in freeze-frame. Yet the producers did not think to call in a conjuror before releasing the work. Only afterward, when I approached them with the solution, did they realize how easy that would have been, and how effective. They even troubled to go back on the air with an addition to the original material.

---

* Containing animal blood or dye; for other tricks practiced by psychic surgeons, see William Nolen's essay (Chapter 12).

In studies of the paranormal, the scientific community has been extremely lax in declaring itself.* Those few scientists who have announced what they believe to be great discoveries in basic science related to what are otherwise known as psychic, supernatural, or occult matters, having in most cases earned respect and authority in other fields, remain, in the public's eye at least, spokesmen for science in general. Their words are hung upon by the press, who nurture their theories from mere repetition. And responsible scientists sit in the background, mildly horrified by what they observe, yet unwilling to protest except among themselves, and even then in hushed tones.

Several exceptions stand out. In 1978, a long-suspect set of observations was carefully examined by a believer and exposed as pure fake. A prominent worker with the British Society for Psychical Research, examining the work of the famous Dr. Soal on what has become known as the Shackleton experiments, suspected that all was not right with this most definitive and positive investigation of ESP abilities in one "gifted" subject. She looked into the raw data and concluded that not only had the learned Dr. Soal changed a lot of data entries to improve the performance after the fact (1s were often doctored into 4s, for instance, to make the numbers correspond with the subject's guesses), but when he selected "at random" his target digits, he inserted a few extra digits from time to time—and these inserts were winners. By two clever and thoroughly dishonest means, he had weighted the otherwise insignificant experiments to make them positive in favor of ESP. I would ask for a round of applause for the researcher who, in spite of her stated belief in such matters, nonetheless did a staggering amount of honest research to disprove Soal's work. I note, in passing, that the Society for Psychical Research for a long time resisted publishing her results, but was finally pressured into it. And the comic note of the affair, which easily proves my contention that rationalization of negative results is an inbred characteristic of parascientists, is that one researcher, named Pratt, told readers of the journal in which this exposé appeared that it was not at all probable that Soal had cheated. Instead, Pratt said he found it easier to postulate that in inserting the extra "winning" digits, Soal had unconsciously exhibited "precognition," knowing by ESP, in advance, what the subject was about to call in response to the target! I wonder if Dr. Pratt is in the market for a bridge? I have the Brooklyn model for sale . . .

---

* Which is one of the reasons for this book. (Eds.)

Professor John Taylor, long a staunch supporter of parascience, wrote extensively on the subject. He was one of Uri Geller's disciples and chided his colleagues for standing by conventional scientific standards when confronted with the miracles of spoon bending and teleportation as exhibited by the young Israeli conjuror. Taylor has recently reversed himself on these matters and once again joined the ranks of conventional scientists. Finding no explanation in electromagnetic theory for the "psychokinetic" wonders he witnessed, Professor Taylor now tells us that there is no place in science for such claims of miracles. But, I assure him, a place can be made, and an explanation given, by the conjurors. To them, it's more of the same old thing.

A word should be said about the courage required for such reversals. It is a brave scientist, indeed, who says either "I was wrong" or "I don't know" after having declared himself to the contrary. Another aspect of bravery in the academic world is exemplified by those who decide to override the established mores of their profession and agitate loudly for rationality in situations where there may be embarrassment for their colleagues who have made rash, untenable claims. It simply isn't done, and the vociferous are frowned into submission or reminded by pointed memos that their first obligation is to uphold the traditions of their craft. Obviously, those who have chosen (or been forced) to recant are given every consideration in being brought back into the academic body, fully restored in stature. In fact, I would personally be more apt to trust one who has made errors and learned by the experience than one who has never erred at all.

When *The Humanist* printed "Objections to Astrology" in 1975, bearing the signatures of 192 leading scientists—nineteen of them Nobel Prize winners—it made literally front-page news around the world. It was a breakthrough in which responsible investigators actually stood up to be counted in defense of rationality and against a demonstrably false pseudoscience that had earned wide public acceptance (largely through lack of authoritative denials). In the text itself, Bart J. Bok, an angry astronomer, complained that he had urged the Council of the American Astronomical Society to issue a statement telling the world that in their opinion there was no scientific basis for a belief in astrology. He was turned down both times he tried to get action from them. The reason echoed down through decades past from other similar requests made before scientific councils: it is beneath the dignity of scientists to recognize that irrational beliefs are prevalent.* The argument did not gain stature from its antiquity; it was musty and tired.

Dignity be damned. Science assumes responsibility for our lives—with our approval. Its authority springs from the public's funding of it and tolerance for it. Science thus owes that public an honest and immediate response to needs. One of those needs is an authoritative and clear opinion on the cults, pseudoscientific notions, and various forms of augury which are presented to us all as accomplished and verified disciplines. But this seems too mundane a pursuit for the learned to trouble with.

Recently I was presented with an excellent example of the rationalization that theologians as well as scientists often employ, to the amusement of the layman and the probable embarrassment of their peers. I had addressed the Utah State University and fallen into conversation with some of the staff about Mormon matters. As a result of that exchange, I was given what turned out to be one of the most remarkable revelations of my life, embodied in an "explanation" given by a professor of religious history, Hugh Nibley of Brigham Young University. This scholar was brought up short by finding that scraps of Egyptian papyrus that one of the founding fathers of the religion had emphatically declared to be actually written by Abraham, and which thus constituted one of that religion's most basic holy books, the Book of Abraham, turned out to be quite mundane extracts from well-known texts of instruction for the departed citizens of the long-dead kingdom of the Nile. Such texts were commonly interred with the dead.

But the founder hadn't stopped there. Using other scraps of papyrus, he had produced an *Egyptian Alphabet and Grammar*, which delighted the believers no end. All this was before hieroglyphic translation had truly begun, and was not readily available. It was quite safe for anyone to produce a "translation" of the strange sign writing of Egypt and have it accepted by the unsophisticated. And it was gladly accepted.

The Metropolitan Museum of Art, in 1967, returned to the church the original writings which the founder had "translated" for his Book of Abraham, and when submitted for a modern translation, the docu-

---

* Another reason is that the council feared that a strong stand opposing astrology might actually arouse sympathy for it. (Eds.)

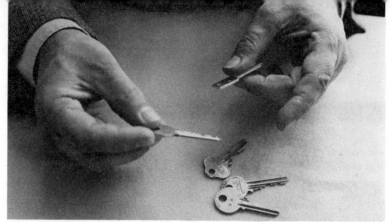

The "psychic key bending" trick. 1. First the performer proffers the keys, casually showing that they are straight.

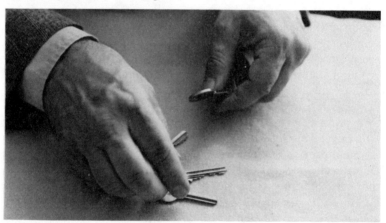

2. One key is placed inside the slot of the other. The observer cannot see it from this angle.

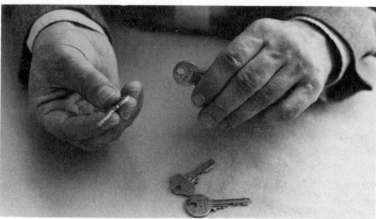

3. As the fingers of the left hand apply pressure on the two keys, the performer misdirects the observer's attention to the other keys.

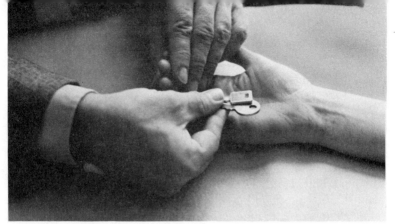

4. *The two keys are separated and the bend is concealed as they are placed into the observer's hand.*

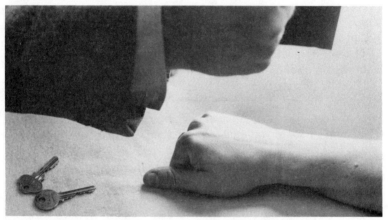

5. *The performer makes the mystic passes to perform the miracle.*

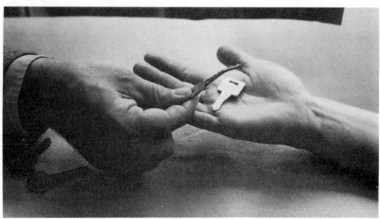

6. *The key is revealed as bent. The miracle is accomplished.* Photographs by Michael Feirtag.

ments proved that not only had the founding father done an extremely free translation, but he had done so with many fragments inserted in place wrongly from other documents, upside down in some cases, and in a mixture of period, style, and content. But such discoveries did not dampen the professor's enthusiasm and determination to keep intact this most important document as a real "revelation." He easily explained away the fraud by telling the faithful that the founder's interpretation was an "inspired" one rather than a literal one, and averred now that his *Egyptian Alphabet and Grammar* (which was certainly in trouble because there *is* no Egyptian alphabet as such) need not be taken literally. The columns of hieroglyphics therein which faced similar columns of English words and sounds were not meant to be taken as corresponding to one another, said the scholar.

The spirit of charity must be invoked to accept such rationalizations, and the mind must be emptied of all logic to do so.

There is no question of it: Joseph Smith was totally incapable of translating the Egyptian language. He needed a mysterious discovery to produce the Book of Abraham, and he invented a totally fanciful translation of some common papyrus scraps to perpetrate his deception. Now that it has been uncovered, scientists who will not *ever* throw out the theory have turned to throwing out the facts. It is rationalization in a very obvious and infantile form. But it is far outdone by modern parapsychologists.

Can the skeptics properly attack religious beliefs, however? Yes, in limited situations. Largely, religious beliefs and claims are matters of faith: no scientific basis can properly be used to judge or evaluate them. Nor do their proponents require scientific proof of any kind. Their preferred belief structure is dictated by need, not reason. There are religions that claim resurrection, others that claim reincarnation. Some aver that chanting magic formulas leads to divinity, others that shades of the departed may be conjured up in dark rooms. One even tells its followers that they may relive former lives, back into antedeluvian periods. And it is not within the parameters of science to investigate these claims—*unless the adherents claim that science may be invoked to support their tenets.*

At least one semireligious group unequivocally lays itself open to investigation when it makes just such claims. The Transcendental Meditators of the Mahareshi publish vast amounts of carefully selected data that they present as *proof* that their discipline will allow followers to soar about the sky like Peter Pans. They also tell inquirers that their people have learned to become invisible and to walk through solid brick walls. These claims are topped off by assertions that an accomplished TMer attains the blessed state of omniscience—that he or she knows *all*, past, present, and future. How astonishing to us skeptics sound these claims. For it would seem we should have become aware, by now, of at least one of these wonderful abilities. But with a claimed forty thousand registrants in the Levitation Course, the Mahareshi has failed to produce one demonstration, though his literature tells us that these miracles have been registered on TV monitors in laboratory tests. May we see any tapes or films of these experiments? Requests to witness such events are ignored.

To look back with 20/20 hindsight, it would have been better if some of the scientific experts, hearing of an obscure San Francisco religious leader who not only performed "psychic surgery," but also literally raised the dead, had troubled to cry "Fake!" rather than sitting by quietly. But they didn't want to interfere with his freedom of religion. The rest of that story was told in Guyana when nearly a thousand unfortunate people who had been duped by the man drank cyanide, convinced that Jimmy Jones had a direct line to the gods. But the constitutional rights of every one of them were protected . . .

Science and the media owe to the inquiring public that supports them an explanation and revelation of pseudoreligious and pseudoscientific claims. Though it suits the majority of scientists to remain silent on these matters, and the newspapers, magazines, radio and TV outlets, and book publishers are well aware of the desire of the public to have Things-That-Go-Bump-In-The-Night as realities rather than hear rational explanations for these phenomena, there is an obligation on both science and the media that is largely unfulfilled at present. The evidence of that failure is all around us.

In one public library, in Vancouver, Canada, I counted 102 titles on the open shelves dealing with positive attitudes toward ESP, witchcraft, UFOs, and allied claptrap. And there was *not one* book there that adopted a counterview—though many such are available. The CBS-TV network has, in spite of information and objections from the Committee for Scientific Investigation of Claims of the Paranormal, continued to feature the "In Search of . . ." series with actor Leonard Nimoy, former Science Officer of "Star Trek." The series misrepresents various subjects ranging from the Curse of King Tut to the Bermuda Triangle, not dealing with the facts. Instead, it plays up the fiction. A disclaimer precedes each program, stating that "This series presents information based in part on theory and conjecture. The producer's purpose is to suggest some possible explanations but not necessarily the only ones to the mysteries we will examine." The series' "Project UFO" told viewers that the shows were based on information from the U.S. Air Force's Project Blue Book, and presented as a clincher at the end of each episode a full-color shot of the official Air Force Seal overlaid with the words "The United States Air Force, after twenty-two years of investigation, concluded that none of the unidentified flying objects reported and evaluated posed a threat to our national security." That statement remained on the screen for precisely *2.4 seconds*. It was impossible to read it in that time, of course, and worse still, this was only a fraction of the *actual* conclusion of Project Blue Book. The USAF also said, in the same concluding document, that there was no evidence that the "UFOs" indicated any superior technology, or even that they were extraterrestrial in nature. CBS chose not to tell us about that. . . .

The reversals by prominent formerly deluded scientists, the increasing availability, if not popularity, of books such as this volume, and the evident dissatisfaction of academics as a whole with the irrationalities of parascience and pseudoscience will, I am confident, result in a demand for the truth. But as I write I am well aware that there are yet unborn rascals who will liven up the annals of science in the future, and hordes of scientists-to-be who will hurry down the Yellow Brick Road to plead for recognition in the streets of the Emerald City. It is an idiocy that will repeat itself so long as human naiveté exists and someone is about to exploit it.

But back to the fray. My wingèd horse awaits. . . .

15

An Analysis of "Worlds in Collision"*

CARL SAGAN

In the 1940s, Immanuel Velikovsky (1895–1979), an immigrant Russian physician, invented a theory to account for certain biblical stories and many ancient legends in terms of catastrophic encounters between the earth and other celestial bodies. Briefly, Velikovsky hypothesized that a comet had been ejected from Jupiter before the middle of the second millennium B.C. *Over a period of several hundred years the comet twice passed near the earth, causing great upheaval and at times raining insects and manna upon the earth, and also passed near Mars, diverting that planet from its orbit so that Mars also passed near the earth, causing additional tidal disruptions. Eventually, about the seventh century* B.C., *the comet transformed itself into the planet Venus, which has occupied its present orbit since.*

In April 1950, Macmillan and Company published this theory in Worlds in Collision. *Favorable reviews appeared in such respected*

* I am very grateful to many of my colleagues who have made helpful suggestions and criticisms—but particularly to Steven Soter, E. E. Salpeter, Thomas Gold, Philip Morrison, David Morrison, and Sidney Coleman.

publications as Harper's *Magazine. But when* Worlds in Collision *came to the attention of scientists and archeologists, reactions were a mixture of amusement at the absurdity of the idea, dismay that the public took it seriously, and outrage that it was released by a respected publisher of science textbooks. Some astronomers, in fact, were outraged enough to announce that they would cease to use Macmillan texts in their classes if the company continued to publish the book. Consequently,* Worlds in Collision *was transferred to Doubleday in June 1950.*

The astronomical community has been accused of suppression, although we think that a case can be made that the boycotting of books of a publisher who produces an irresponsible and misleading work in the name of science is not morally different from boycotting the products of, say, a manufacturer that deals with South Africa, or of a state that has not ratified the Equal Rights Amendment. In any event, Worlds in Collision *sold more than fifty thousand copies in the three months before Doubleday took over, and it subsequently became a best-seller. It and several later books by Velikovsky have now sold several million copies; Velikovsky is one of the most widely read of all authors. Most of us would be grateful for such suppression!*

In the three decades since the appearance of Worlds in Collision, *a faithful cult of Velikovsky supporters has arisen, and its members even include some with scientific training. The 1970s saw a new surge of interest in Velikovsky, and from 1972 to 1974 the Student Academic Freedom Forum published a quality magazine,* Pensée, *devoted exclusively to Velikovsky's theories and their alleged proofs.*

The Velikovsky followers could rightly claim that his theories were not only rejected but ignored by the scientific community at large. To answer the growing popular criticism of scientists for their attitude toward Velikovsky, an eminent group led by astronomer Carl Sagan urged the American Association for the Advancement of Science to sponsor a special symposium on the theories of Velikovsky, where he and his supporters could meet face to face with members of the scientific community. The symposium was held at the San Francisco meeting of the AAAS on February 25, 1974. The proceedings were published by Cornell University Press in Scientists Confront Velikovsky *(1977). Sagan's own contribution to that conference, somewhat revised and condensed by us, follows.*

Scientists, like other human beings, have their hopes and fears, their passions and despondencies—and their strong emotions may sometime interrupt the course of clear thinking and sound practice. But science is also self-correcting. The most fundamental axioms and conclusions may be challenged. The prevailing hypotheses must survive confrontation with observation. Appeals to authority are impermissible. The steps in a reasoned argument must be set out for all to see. Experiments must be reproducible. The history of science is full of cases where previously accepted theories and hypotheses have been entirely overthrown, to be replaced by new ideas which more adequately explain the data.

While there is an understandable psychological inertia—usually lasting about one generation—such revolutions in scientific thought are widely accepted as a necessary and desirable element of scientific progress. Indeed, the reasoned criticism of a prevailing belief is a service to the proponents of that belief; if they are incapable of defending it, they are well-advised to abandon it. This self-questioning and error-correcting aspect of the scientific method is its most striking property and sets it off from many other areas of human endeavor, such as politics and theology.

The idea of science as a method rather than as a body of knowledge is not widely appreciated outside of science, or indeed in some corridors inside of science. Vigorous criticism is constructive in science more than in some other areas of human endeavor because in it there are adequate standards of validity which can be agreed upon by competent practitioners the world over. The objective of such criticism is not to suppress but rather to encourage the advance of new ideas: those which survive a firm skeptical scrutiny have a fighting chance of being right, or at least useful.

Emotions in the scientific community have run very high on the issue of Immanuel Velikovsky's work, especially his first book, *Worlds in Collision*, published in 1950.

My own strongly held view is that no matter how unorthodox the reasoning process or how unpalatable the conclusions, there is no excuse for any attempt to suppress new ideas—least of all by scientists committed to the free exchange of ideas.

In this essay I have tried to analyze critically the thesis of *Worlds in Collision*. I have attempted to approach the problem both on Velikovsky's terms and on mine—that is, to keep firmly in mind the ancient writings that are the focus of his argument, but at the same time to confront his conclusions with both the facts and the logic I have at my command.

Velikovsky's principal thesis is that there have been in the relatively recent history of the earth a set of celestial catastrophes, near-collisions with comets, small planets, and large planets. There is nothing absurd in the possibility of cosmic collisions. Astronomers in the past have not hesitated to invoke collisions to explain natural phenomena.

Collisions and catastrophism are part and parcel of modern astronomy and have been for many centuries. In fact, in the early history of the solar system, when there were probably many more objects about than there are now—including objects on very eccentric orbits—collisions must have been frequent.

What then is all the furor about? It is about the time scale and the adequacy of the purported evidence. In the 4.5-billion-year history of the solar system, many collisions must have occurred. But have there been major collisions in the last thirty-five hundred years, and can the study of ancient writings demonstrate such collisions? That is the nub of the issue.

Velikovsky has called attention to a wide range of stories and legends held by diverse peoples, separated by great distances, which stories show remarkable similarities and concordances. I am not expert in the cultures or languages of any of these peoples, but I find the concatenation of legends which Velikovsky has accumulated stunning. It is true that some experts on these cultures are less impressed. I can remember vividly discussing *Worlds in Collision* with a distinguished professor of Semitics at a leading university. He said something like, "The Assyriology, Egyptology, biblical scholarship, and all of that talmudic and midrashic *pilpul* is of course nonsense; but I was impressed by the astronomy." I had rather the opposite view. But let me not be swayed by the opinions of others. My own position is that even if 20 percent of the legendary concordances which Velikovsky produces are real, there is something important to be explained. Furthermore, there is an impressive array of cases in the history of archeology—from Heinrich Schliemann at Troy to Yigael Yadin at Masada—where the descriptions in ancient writings have subsequently been validated as fact.

Now if a variety of widely separated cultures share what is palpably the same legend, how can this be explained? There seem to be four possibilities: common observation, diffusion, brain wiring, and coincidence. Let's consider these in turn.

One explanation is that the cultures in question all witnessed a common event and interpreted it in the same way. There may, of course, be more than one view of what this common event was.

The legend originated within one culture only, but during the frequent and distant migrations of mankind gradually spread with some changes among many apparently diverse cultures. A trivial example is the Santa Claus legend in America, which evolved from the European Saint Nicholas (*Claus* is short for *Nicholas* in German), the patron saint of children, and which ultimately is derived from pre-Christian tradition.

A hypothesis also sometimes known as racial memory or the collective unconscious. It holds that there are certain ideas, archetypes, legendary figures, and stories that are intrinsic to human beings at birth, perhaps in the same way that a newborn baboon knows to fear a snake, and a bird raised in isolation from other birds knows how to build a nest. It is apparent that if a tale derived from observation or from diffusion resonates with the "brain wiring," it is more likely to be culturally retained.

Purely by chance, two independently derived legends may have similar content. In practice, this hypothesis fades into the brain-wiring hypothesis.

If we are to assess critically such apparent concordances, there are some obvious precautions that first must be taken. Do the stories really say the same thing or have the same essential elements? If they are interpreted as due to common observations, do they date from the same period? Can we exclude the possibility of physical contact between representatives of the cultures in question in or before the epoch under discussion? Velikovsky is clearly opting for the common-observation hypothesis, but he seems to dismiss the diffusion hypothesis far too casually; for example (page 303*), he says, "How could unusual motifs of folklore reach isolated islands, where the aborigines do not have any means of crossing the sea?" But it is apparent that the inhabitants of an island must have gotten there somehow.

Let us take an example of Velikovsky's approach to the question of coincidence. He points to certain concordant stories, directly or vaguely connected with celestial events, that refer to a witch, a mouse, a scorpion, or a dragon (pages 77, 264, 305, 306, 310). His explanation is that divers comets, upon close approach to the earth, were tidally or electrically distorted and gave the form of a witch, a mouse, a scorpion, or a dragon, clearly interpretable as the same animal to

---

* The page numbers refer to the canonical English language edition (I. Velikovsky, *Worlds in Collision*. New York, Doubleday, 1950).

culturally isolated peoples of very different backgrounds. No attempt is made to show that such a clear form—for example, a woman riding a broomstick and topped by a pointed hat—could have been produced in this way, even if we grant the hypothesis of a close approach to the earth by a comet. Our experience with Rorschach and other psychological projective tests is clearly that different people will see the same nonrepresentational image in different ways. Velikovsky even goes so far as to believe that a close approach to Earth by the planet Mars so distorted it that it took on the clear shape (page 264) of lions, jackals, dogs, pigs, and fish; and goes on to say that in his opinion this explains the worship of animals by the Egyptians. This is not very impressive reasoning. We might just as well assume that the whole menagerie was capable of independent flight in the second millennium B.C. and be done with it. A much more likely hypothesis is diffusion. Indeed, I have in a different context spent a fair amount of time studying the dragon legends on the planet Earth, and I am impressed at how different these mythical beasts, all called dragons by Western writers, really are.

Another problem with Velikovsky's method is the reader's suspicion that vaguely similar stories may refer to quite different periods. This question of the synchronism of legends is almost entirely ignored in *Worlds in Collision*, although it is treated in some of Velikovsky's later works. For example (page 31), Velikovsky notes that the idea of four ancient ages terminated by catastrophe is common to Indian as well as to Western sacred writing. However, in the Bhagavad-Gita and in the Vedas, widely divergent numbers of such ages, including an infinity of them, are given; but, more interesting, the duration of the ages between major catastrophes (see, e.g., Campbell, 1974) is billions of years, entrancingly close to the actual age of the solar system. This does not match very well Velikovsky's chronology, which requires hundreds or thousands of years. Here Velikovsky's hypothesis and the data that purport to support it differ by a factor of about a million. Or (page 91) vaguely similar discussions of vulcanism and lava flows in Greek, Mexican, and biblical traditions are quoted. There is no attempt made to show that they refer to even approximately comparable times and, since lava has flowed in historical times in all three areas, no common exogenous event is necessary to interpret such stories.

Despite copious references, there also seem to me to be a large number of critical and undemonstrated assumptions in Velikovsky's argument. Let me just mention a few of them.

There is the very interesting idea that any mythological reference, by any people, to any god who also corresponds to a celestial body, represents in fact a direct observation of that celestial body. It is a daring and interesting hypothesis, although I am not sure what one is to do with Jupiter's appearing as a swan to Leda, and as a shower of gold to Danae. On page 247 the hypothesis that gods and planets are identical is used to date the time of Homer. In any case, when Hesiod and Homer refer to Athena being born full-grown from the head of Zeus, Velikovsky takes Hesiod and Homer at their word and assumes that the celestial body Athena was ejected by the planet Jupiter. But what *is* the celestial body Athena? Repeatedly it is identified with the planet Venus (Part I, Chapter 9, and many other places in the text). One would scarcely guess from reading *Worlds in Collision* that the Greeks characteristically identified Aphrodite with the planet Venus and Athena with no celestial body whatever. What is more, Athena and Aphrodite were "contemporaneous" goddesses, both being born at the time Zeus was king of the gods. On page 251 Velikovsky notes that Lucian "is unaware that Athena is the goddess of the planet Venus." Poor Lucian seems to be under the misconception that Aphrodite is the goddess of the planet Venus. But in the footnote on page 361 there seems to be a slip, and here Velikovsky uses for the first and only time the form "Venus (Aphrodite)." On page 247 we hear of Aphrodite, the goddess of the moon. Who then was Artemis, the sister of Apollo the sun, or, earlier, Selene? For all I know, there may be good justification in identifying Athena with Venus, but it is far from the prevailing wisdom of either now or two thousand years ago, and it is central to Velikovsky's argument. It does not increase our confidence in the presentation of less familiar myths when the celestial identification of Athena is glossed over so lightly.

Other critical statements that are given extremely inadequate justification, and that are central to one or more of Velikovsky's major themes, are as follows: the statement (page 283) that "meteorites, when entering the earth's atmosphere, make a frightful din"—when they are generally observed to be silent; the statement (page 114) that "a thunderbolt, when striking a magnet, reverses the poles of the magnet"; the translation (page 51) of "Barad" as meteorites; and the contention (page 85), "As is known, Pallas was another name for Typhon." On page 179 a principle is implied that when two gods are hyphenated in a joint name, it indicates an attribute of a celestial body—as, for example, Asteroth-Karnaim, a horned Venus, which Velikovsky interprets as a crescent Venus and evidence that Venus was once close enough to Earth to have its phases discernible to the naked eye. But what does this principle imply, for example, for the god Ammon-Ra? Did the Egyptians see the sun (Ra) as a ram (Ammon)?

There is a contention (page 63) that instead of the tenth plague of Exodus killing the "first born" of Egypt, what is intended is the killing of the "chosen." This is a rather serious matter and at least raises the suspicion that where the Bible is inconsistent with Velikovsky's hypothesis, Velikovsky retranslates the Bible. The foregoing queries may all have simple answers, but the answers are not to be found easily in *Worlds in Collision*.

I do not mean to suggest that all of Velikovsky's legendary concordances and ancient scholarship is similarly flawed, but much of it seems to be; and the remainder may well have alternative—for example, diffusionist—origins.

I therefore cannot find the legendary base of Velikovsky's hypothesis at all compelling. If, nevertheless, his hypothesis of planetary collisions and global catastrophism were strongly supported by physical evidence, we might be tempted to give it some credence. If the physical evidence is, however, not very strong, the mythological evidence will surely not stand by itself.

Let me now give a short summary of my understanding of the basic features of Velikovsky's principal hypothesis. I will relate it to the events described in Exodus.

The planet Jupiter disgorged a large comet that made a grazing collision with Earth around 1500 B.C. The various plagues and pharaonic tribulations of the book of Exodus all derive directly or indirectly from this cometary encounter. Material that makes the river Nile turn to blood drops from the comet. The vermin described in Exodus are produced by the comet—flies and perhaps scarabs drop out of the comet, while indigenous terrestrial frogs are induced by the heat of the comet to multiply. Earthquakes produced by the comet level Egyptian but not Hebrew dwellings.

All this evidently falls from the coma (head) of the comet, because at the moment that Moses lifts his rod and stretches out his hand, the Red Sea parts—either due to the gravitational tidal field of the comet or to some unspecified electrical or magnetic interaction between the comet and the Red Sea. Then, when the Hebrews have successfully crossed, the comet has evidently passed sufficiently farther on for the parted waters to flow back and drown the host of Pharaoh. The Children of Israel during their subsequent forty years of wandering in the Wilderness of Sin are nourished by manna from heaven, which turns out to be hydrocarbons (or carbohydrates) from the tail of the comet. Another reading of *Worlds in Collision* makes it appear that the plagues and the Red Sea events represent two different passages of the comet, separated by a month or two. Then after the death of Moses and the passing of the mantle of leadership to Joshua, the same comet comes screeching back for another grazing collision with the earth. At the moment that Joshua says "Sun, stand thou still upon Gibeon; and thou, Moon, in the valley of Agalon," the earth—perhaps because of tidal interaction, again, or perhaps because of an unspecified magnetic induction in its crust—obligingly ceases its rotation, to permit Joshua victory in battle. The comet then makes a near collision with Mars, so violent as to eject it out of its orbit so it makes two near collisions with Earth that destroy the army of Sennacherib, the Assyrian king, as he is making life miserable for some subsequent generation of Israelites. The net result was to eject Mars into its present orbit and the comet into a circular orbit around the Sun, where it becomes the planet Venus. The earth meantime had somehow begun rotating again at almost exactly the same rate as before these encounters. No subsequent aberrant planetary behavior has occurred since about the seventh century B.C., although it might have been common in the second millennium B.C.

That this is a remarkable story no one, proponents and opponents alike, will disagree. Whether it is a likely story is, fortunately, amenable to scientific inquiry. Velikovsky's hypothesis makes certain predictions: that comets are ejected from planets; that comets are likely to make near or grazing collisions with planets; that vermin live in comets and in the atmospheres of Jupiter and Venus; that carbohydrates can be found in the same places; that enough of these carbohydrates fell in the Sinai Peninsula for nourishment during forty years of wandering in the desert; that eccentric cometary or planetary orbits can be circularized in a period of hundreds of years; that volcanic and tectonic events on the earth and impact events on the moon were contemporaneous with these catastrophes; and so on. We will discuss each of these ideas, as well as some others: for example, that the surface of Venus is hot (this is clearly less central to his hypothesis, but it has been widely advertised as powerful post hoc support of it). We will also examine an occasional additional "prediction" of Velikovsky's—for example, that the Martian polar caps are carbon or carbohydrates. My conclusion will be that where Velikovsky is original he is very likely wrong, and that where he is right the idea has been preempted by earlier workers. There are also a large number of cases where he is neither right nor original. The question of originality is important because of circumstances—for example, the high surface temperature of Venus—that are said to have been predicted by Velikovsky at a time when everyone else was imagining an earthlike Venus. As we shall see, this is not quite the case.

In the following discussion we will try to use simple quantitative reasoning as much as possible. Quantitative arguments are obviously a finer mesh with which to sift hypotheses than qualitative arguments. For example, if I say that a large tidal wave engulfed the earth, there is a wide range of catastrophes (from the flooding of littoral regions to global inundation) that might be pointed to as support for my contention. But if I specify a tide one hundred miles high, I can only be talking about the latter, and, moreover, there might be some critical evidence to counterindicate or support a tide of such dimensions. Perhaps I need not mention that such quantitative testing of hypotheses is entirely routine in the physical and biological sciences today. By rejecting the hypotheses that do not meet these standards of analysis, we are able to move swiftly to hypotheses in better accord with the facts.

Now, not all scientific statements have equal weight. Newtonian dynamics and the laws of conservation of energy and angular momentum are on extremely firm footing. On the other hand, questions on the nature of planetary surfaces, atmospheres, and interiors are on much weaker footing, as the substantial debates on these matters by planetary scientists in recent years clearly indicate. The same distinction between well-founded scientific arguments and arguments based on a physics or chemistry that we do not fully understand must be borne in mind in any analysis of *Worlds in Collision*. Arguments based on Newtonian dynamics or the great conservation laws of physics must be given very great weight. Arguments based on planetary surface properties, for example, might have correspondingly lesser weights. We will find that Velikovsky's arguments run into extremely grave difficulties on both these scores, but the one set of difficulties is far more damaging than the other.

PROBLEM 1. THE EJECTION
OF VENUS BY JUPITER

Velikovsky's hypothesis begins with an event that has never been observed by astronomers and that is inconsistent with much that we know about planetary and cometary physics, namely the ejection of an object of planetary dimensions from Jupiter. From the fact that the aphelia (points most distant from the sun) of the orbits of short-period comets have a statistical tendency to lie near Jupiter, LaPlace and other early astronomers hypothesized that Jupiter was the source of such comets. This is an unnecessary hypothesis because we now know that long-period comets may be transferred to short-period trajectories by the perturbations of the planet Jupiter, and LaPlace's view has not been advocated for a century or two, except by the Soviet astronomer V. S. Vsekhsviatsky, who seems to believe that the moons of Jupiter eject comets out of giant volcanoes.

To escape from Jupiter, such a comet must have a kinetic energy of $\frac{1}{2} mv_e^2$, where m is the cometary mass and v_e is the escape velocity from Jupiter, which is about 60 km/sec. Whatever the ejection event—a volcano or a collision—some significant fraction, at least 10 percent, of this kinetic energy will go into heating the comet. The minimum kinetic energy per unit mass ejected is then 2×10^{13} ergs per gram, and the quantity that goes into heating is more than 2×10^{12} ergs/gram. The latent heat of fusion of rock is about 4×10^9 ergs per gram. This is the heat that must be applied to convert hot solid rock near the melting point to a fluid lava. About 10^{11} ergs/gm must be applied to raise rocks at low temperatures to their melting point. Thus, any event that would have ejected a comet or a planet from Jupiter would have brought it to a temperature of at least several thousands of degrees and, whether composed of rocks, ices, or organic compounds, would have completely melted it. The likelihood of a planet, much less an icy comet, surviving ejection seems small.

Another problem is the very critical speed with which the comet would have to be ejected from Jupiter. The speed of escape from the planet itself is 60 kilometers per second, and that from the solar system at Jupiter's distance is about 20 km/s. If the comet were ejected from Jupiter at less than 60 km/s it would fall back to Jupiter; if greater than about $[(20)^2 \times (60)^2]^{\frac{1}{2}} = 63$ km/s, it would escape from the solar system. There is only a narrow and therefore unlikely range of velocities consistent with Velikovsky's hypothesis.

A further problem is that the mass of Venus is very large—more than 5×10^{27} grams, or, according to Velikovsky's hypothesis, possibly originally even larger before it passed close to the sun. The total kinetic energy required to propel Venus to Jovian escape velocity is then easily calculated to be on the order of 10^{41} ergs, which is equivalent to all the energy radiated by the sun into space in an entire year, and 100 million times as powerful as the largest solar flare ever observed. We are asked to believe, without any further evidence or discussion, an ejection event vastly more powerful than anything on the sun, which is a far more energetic object than Jupiter.

Any process that makes large objects makes even more small objects. This is especially true in a situation that is dominated by collisions, as in Velikovsky's hypothesis. Here the comminution physics is well known, and a particle one-tenth as large as our biggest particle should be a hundred or a thousand times more abundant. Indeed, Velikovsky does have stones falling from the skies in the wake of his hypothesized planetary encounters and imagines Venus and Mars trailing swarms of boulders; the Mars swarm, he says, led to the destruction of the armies of Sennacherib. But if this is true, if we had near collisions with objects of planetary mass only thousands of years ago, we should have been bombarded by objects of lunar mass hundreds of years ago, and bombardment by objects that can make craters a mile or so across should be happening every second Tuesday. Yet, there is no sign, either on the earth or the moon, of frequent recent collisions with such lower-mass objects. Instead, the few objects that, as a steady-state population, are moving in orbits that might collide with the moon are just adequate, over geological time, to explain the number of craters observed on the lunar maria. The absence of a great many small objects with orbits crossing the orbit of the earth is another fundamental objection to Velikovsky's basic thesis.

PROBLEM 2. REPEATED COLLISIONS AMONG THE EARTH, VENUS, AND MARS

"That a comet may strike our planet is not very probable, but the idea is not absurd" (page 40). This precisely correct; it remains only to calculate the probabilities, which Velikovsky has unfortunately left undone.

Fortunately, the relevant physics is extremely simple and can be performed to order of magnitude even without any consideration of gravitation. Objects on highly eccentric orbits, traveling from the vicinity of Jupiter to the vicinity of the earth, are traveling at such high speeds that their mutual gravitational attraction to the object with which they are about to have a grazing collision plays a negligible role in determining the trajectory. Elementary calculation (Sagan, 1977) shows that a single "comet" with the aphelion (the farthest point from the sun) near the orbit of Jupiter, and the perihelion (near point to the sun) inside the orbit of Venus, should take at least 30 million years before it strikes the earth. Therefore, the odds against a collision with the earth in any given year are at least 3×10^7 to 1; the odds against it in any given millennium are 30,000 to 1. But Velikovsky has (see, e.g., page 388) not one but *five* or *six* near collisions between the comet (Venus) and either the earth or Mars. If the probabilities are independent, then the joint probability of five such encounters in the same millennium is on the short side of 4.1×10^{-23} (odds of almost a hundred billion trillion to one). For six encounters in the same millennium the odds rise to about a trillion quadrillion to one. Actually, these are lower limits, both for the reason given above and because close encounters with Jupiter are likely to eject the impacting object from the solar system altogether, more or less as Jupiter ejected the Pioneer 10 spacecraft from the solar system. These odds are a proper calibration of the validity of Velikovsky's hypothesis, even were there no other difficulties with it. Hypotheses with such small odds in their favor are usually said to be untenable. With the other problems mentioned both above and below, the probability that the full thesis of *Worlds in Collision* is correct becomes negligible.

PROBLEM 3. THE EARTH'S ROTATION

Much of the indignation directed toward *Worlds in Collision* seems to have arisen from Velikovsky's interpretation of the story of Joshua and related legends as implying that the earth's rotation was once braked to a halt. The image that the most outraged protestors seem to have had in mind is that in the movie version of H. G. Wells's story

"The Man Who Could Work Miracles": the earth is miraculously stopped from rotating but, through an oversight, no provision is made for all objects not nailed down, which then continue moving at their usual rate and therefore fly off the earth at a speed of a thousand miles per hour. But a gradual slowing of the earth's rotation could occur in a period of much less than a day, and then no one would fly off, and even stalactites and other delicate geomorphological forms could survive.

This is, however, not the most serious objection to Velikovsky's exegesis of the story of Joshua. Perhaps the most serious objection is rather at the other end: how does the earth get started up again, rotating at approximately the same rate of spin? The earth cannot do it by itself, because of the conservation of angular momentum.

Nor is there any hint in the book as to why braking the earth to a "halt" by cometary collision is any more likely than any other resulting spin. In fact, the chance of precisely canceling the earth's rotational angular momentum in a cometary encounter is tiny, and the probability that subsequent encounters, were they to occur, would start the earth spinning again even approximately once every twenty-four hours is tiny squared.

Velikovsky is vague about the mechanism that is supposed to have braked the earth's rotation. Perhaps it is tidal gravitational, perhaps magnetic. Both of these fields produce forces that decline very rapidly with distance. Tidal forces decline as the inverse cube of the distance, and the tidal couple as the inverse sixth power. The magnetic dipole field declines as the inverse cube, and any equivalent magnetic tides fall off even more steeply than gravitational tides. Therefore, the braking effect is almost entirely at the distance of closest approach. The characteristic time of this closest approach is about $2R/v$, where R is the radius of the earth and v the relative velocity of the comet and the earth. With v about 25 km/sec, the characteristic time works out to be under ten minutes. This is the full time available for the total effect of the comet on the rotation of the earth. The corresponding acceleration is small enough that armies still do not fly off into space. But the characteristic time for acoustic propagation within the earth (the minimum time for an exterior influence to make itself felt on the earth as a whole) is 85 minutes. Thus, no cometary influence even in grazing collision could make the sun stand still upon Gibeon.

If the earth had been braked to a halt by a strong magnetic field, the field strength required would have to have been enormous (Sagan,

1977, Appendix 3). There is no sign in rock magnetization of terrestrial rocks ever having been subjected to strong field strengths and, what is equally important, we have quite firm evidence from both Soviet and American spacecraft that the magnetic field strength of Venus is negligibly small—far less than the earth's own surface field of 0.5 gauss, which would itself have been far inadequate for Velikovsky's purpose.

PROBLEM 4. TERRESTRIAL GEOLOGY AND LUNAR CRATERS

Reasonably enough, Velikovsky believes that a near collision of another planet with the earth might have had dramatic consequences here—by gravitational tidal, electrical, or magnetic influences (Velikovsky is not very clear on this). He believes (pages 96 and 97) that "in the days of the Exodus, when the world was shaken and rocked . . . *all* volcanoes vomited lava and *all* continents quaked" (my italics).

There seems little doubt that earthquakes would have accompanied such a near collision. Apollo lunar seismometers have found that moonquakes are most common during lunar perigee, when the earth is closest to the moon; and there are possible hints of earthquakes at the same time. But the claim that there were extensive lava flows and volcanism involving "all volcanoes" is quite another story. Volcanic lavas are easily dated and what Velikovsky should produce is a histogram of the number of lava flows on the earth as a function of time. Such a histogram, I believe, would show that not all volcanoes were active between 1500 and 600 B.C., and that there is nothing particularly remarkable about the volcanism of that epoch.

Velikovsky believes (page 115) that reversals of the geomagnetic field are produced by cometary close approaches. Yet the record from rock magnetization is clear: such reversals occur about every million years, and not in the last few thousand, and they recur more or less like clockwork. Is there a clock in Jupiter that aims comets at Earth every million years? The conventional view is that the earth experiences a polarity reversal of the self-sustaining dynamo which produced the earth's magnetic field; it seems to be a more plausible explanation.

Velikovsky's contention that mountain building occurred a few thousand years ago is belied by all the geological evidence, which puts

those times at tens of millions of years ago and earlier. The idea that
mammoths were deep-frozen by a rapid movement of the earth's geographical pole a few thousands of years ago can be tested—for example, by carbon 14 or amino acid recemization dating. I should be
very surprised if a very recent age results from such tests.

Velikovsky believes that the moon, not immune to the catastrophes
that befell the earth, had similar tectonic events occur on its surface a
few thousand years ago, and that many of its craters were formed then
(see Part II, Chapter 9). There are some problems with this idea as
well: Samples returned from the moon in the Apollo missions show no
rocks melted more recently than a few hundred million years ago.

Furthermore, if lunar craters did form abundantly twenty-seven
hundred years ago, there must have been a similar production at the
same time of terrestrial craters larger than a kilometer across. Erosion
on the earth's surface is inadequate to remove any crater of this size in
twenty-seven hundred years. Not only are there not large numbers of
terrestrial craters of this size and age, there is not a single one. On
these questions, Velikovsky seems to have ignored critical evidence.
When the evidence is examined, it strongly counterindicates his hypothesis.

Velikovsky believes that the close passage of Venus or Mars to the
earth would have produced tides at least miles high (pages 70 and 71);
in fact, if these planets were ever tens of thousands of kilometers away,
as he seems to think, the tides, both of water and of the solid body of
our planet, would be hundreds of miles high. To the best of my
knowledge, there is no geological evidence for a global inundation of
all parts of the world in either the eighth or the fifteenth centuries B.C.
If such floods occurred, even if they were brief, they should have left
some clear trace in the geological record.

PROBLEM 5. CHEMISTRY AND BIOLOGY OF THE TERRESTRIAL PLANETS

Jupiter is composed primarily of hydrogen and helium, whereas the
atmosphere of Venus, which Velikovsky supposes to have arisen inside
of Jupiter, is composed almost entirely of carbon dioxide. Moreover,
Velikovsky holds that the manna that fell from the skies in the Sinai
Peninsula was of cometary origin and therefore that there are carbohy-

drates on both Jupiter and Venus. On the other hand, he quotes copious sources for fire and naphtha falling from the skies, which he interprets as celestial petroleum ignited in the earth's oxidizing atmosphere (pages 53–58). Because Velikovsky believes in the reality and identity of both sets of events, his theory requires the existence of both carbohydrates and hydrocarbons in the atmosphere of Venus. At some points it appears that the Israelites may have been eating motor oil rather than divine nutriment during their forty years wandering in the desert.

Velikovsky's text appears to arrive at the conclusion (page 366) that Martian polar caps are made of manna, which are described ambiguously as "probably in the nature of carbon." Carbohydrates have a strong 3.5 micron absorption feature, due to the stretching vibration of the carbon-hydrogen bond. No trace of this feature was observed in infrared spectra of the Martian polar caps taken by the Mariner 6 and 7 spacecraft in 1969. On the other hand, Mariner 6, 7, and 9 have acquired abundant evidence for frozen water and frozen carbon dioxide as the constituents of the polar caps.

Velikovsky's thesis of a celestial origin of petroleum is difficult to understand. Some of the accounts (for example, in Herodotus) provide perfectly natural descriptions of the combustion of petroleum upon seepage to the surface in Mesopotamia and Iran. As Velikovsky himself points out (pages 55–56), the fire-rain and naphtha stories derive from precisely those parts of the earth that have natural petroleum deposits. There is, therefore, a straightforward terrestrial explanation of the stories in question. The amount of downward seepage of petroleum in twenty-seven hundred years would not be very great. The difficulty in extracting petroleum from the earth, which is the cause of certain practical problems today, would be greatly ameliorated if Velikovsky's hypothesis were true. It is also very difficult to understand on this hypothesis how it is, if oil fell from the skies in 1500 B.C., that petroleum deposits are intimately mixed with chemical and biological fossils of tens to hundreds of millions of years ago. But this circumstance is readily explicable if, as most geologists have concluded, petroleum arises from decaying vegetation of the Carboniferous and other early geological epochs, and not from comets.

Even stranger are Velikovsky's views on extraterrestrial life. He believes that much of the "vermin," and particularly the flies referred to in Exodus, really fell from his comet. Shall we expect houseflies or *Drosophila melanogaster* in forthcoming explorations of the clouds of

Venus and Jupiter? Will Velikovsky's hypothesis fall if no flies are found?

The idea that, of all the organisms on the earth, flies alone are of extraterrestrial origin is curiously reminiscent of Martin Luther's exasperated conclusion that, while the rest of life was created by God, the fly must have been created by the Devil because there is no conceivable practical use for it. But flies are perfectly respectable insects, closely related in anatomy, physiology, and biochemistry to the other *insecta*. The possibility that 4.5 billion years of independent evolution on Jupiter—even if it were a physically identical place to Earth— would produce a creature indistinguishable from other terrestrial organisms is to misread the evolutionary process. Flies have the same enzymes, the same nucleic acids, and even the same genetic code (which translates nucleic acid information into protein information) as do all the other organisms on the earth.

Then there is the curious fact that flies metabolize molecular oxygen. There is no oxygen on Jupiter, nor can there be, because oxygen is thermodynamically unstable in an excess of hydrogen. Velikovsky (page 187) alludes to the "ability of many small insects . . . to live in an atmosphere devoid of oxygen," but he misses the point. The question is how an organism evolved on Jupiter could live in and metabolize an atmosphere rich in oxygen.

Another problem is that small flies have just the same mass and dimensions as small meteoroids, which are burned up at an altitude of about 100 kilometers when they enter the earth's atmosphere on cometary trajectories. The light emitted accounts for the visibility of such meteors. Not only would cometary vermin be transformed rapidly into fried flies on entrance into the earth's atmosphere; they would, as cometary meteors today, be vaporized into atoms and never "swarm" over Egypt to the consternation of the Pharaoh. Likewise, the temperatures attendant to ejection of the comet from Jupiter, referred to above, would fry Velikovsky's flies. Impossible to begin with, then doubly fried and atomized, cometary flies do not well survive critical scrutiny.

PROBLEM 6. MANNA

Manna, according to the etymology in Exodus, derives from the Hebrew words *man hu*, which mean "What is it?" Indeed, an excellent question! The idea of food falling from comets is not absolutely straightforward. Optical spectroscopy of comet tails, even before *Worlds in Collision* was published in 1950, showed the presence of simple fragments of hydrocarbons; but no aldehydes (the building blocks of carbohydrates) were known then. They may nevertheless be present in comets. However, from the passage of Comet Kohoutek near the earth, it is now known that comets contain large quantities of simple nitriles—in particular, hydrogen cyanide and methyl cyanide. These are poisons, and it is not immediately obvious that comets are good to eat.

But let us put this objection aside, grant Velikovsky his hypothesis, and calculate the consequences. How much manna is required to feed the hundreds of thousands of children of Israel for forty years (see Exodus 16:35)?

In verse 20 we find that the manna left overnight was infested by bread worms in the morning—an event possible with carbohydrates but extremely unlikely with hydrocarbons. This event also shows that manna was not storable. It fell every day for forty years, according to the biblical account. We will assume that the quantity which fell every day was just sufficient to feed the children of Israel, although Velikovsky assures us (page 138) from midrashic sources that the quantity that fell was adequate for two thousand years rather than a mere forty. Let us assume that each Israelite ate on the order of a third of a kilogram of manna per day, somewhat less than a subsistence diet. Then each will eat 100 kilograms per year and 4,000 kilograms in forty years. Hundreds of thousands of Israelites, the number explicitly mentioned in Exodus, will then consume something over a hundred million kilograms of manna during the forty years wandering in the desert.* But we cannot imagine the debris from the cometary tail falling each day preferentially on the portion of the Wilderness of Sin in which the Israelites happened to have wandered. This would be no less miraculous than the biblical account taken at face value. The area occupied by a few hundred thousand itinerant tribesmen, wandering

* Actually, Exodus states that manna fell each day except on the Sabbath. A double ration, uninfected by bread worms, fell instead on Friday. This seems awkward for Velikovsky's hypothesis. How could the comet know? Indeed, this raises a general problem about Velikovsky's historical method. Some quotations from his religious and historical sources are to be taken literally; others are to be dismissed as "local embellishments." But what is the standard by which this decision is made? Surely such a standard must involve a criterion independent of our predispositions to Velikovsky's contentions.

under a common leadership, is, very roughly, several times 10^{-7} the area of the earth. Therefore, during the forty years of wandering, the whole earth must have accumulated several times 10^{18} grams of manna, or enough to cover the entire surface of the planet with manna to a depth of about an inch. If this indeed happened, it would certainly be a memorable event and may even account for the ginger-bread house in "Hansel and Gretel." But now there is no reason for the manna to have fallen only on the earth. In forty years, the tail of the comet, if restricted to the inner solar system, would have traversed some 10^{10} km. Making only a modest allowance for the ratio of the volume of the earth to the volume of the tail, we find that the mass of manna distributed to the inner solar system by the event is larger than 10^{28} grams. This is not only more massive by many orders of magni-tude than the most massive comet known; it is already more massive than the planet Venus. But comets cannot be composed only of manna. (Indeed, no manna at all has been detected so far in comets.) Comets are known to be composed primarily of ices, and a conserva-tive estimate of the ratio of the mass of the comet to the mass of the manna is much larger than 10^3. Therefore, the mass of the comet must be much larger than 10^{31} grams. This is the mass of Jupiter. If we were to accept Velikovsky's midrashic source above, we would deduce that the comet had a mass comparable to that of the sun. In-terplanetary space in the inner solar system should even today be filled with manna. I leave it to the reader to make his own judgment on the validity of Velikovsky's hypothesis in the light of such calculations.

PROBLEM 7. THE CLOUDS OF VENUS

Velikovsky's prognostication that the clouds of Venus were made of carbohydrates has many times been hailed as an example of a success-ful scientific prediction. From Velikovsky's general thesis and the cal-culations just described, it is clear that Venus should be saturated with manna. Indeed, Velikovsky says (page x) that "the presence of hydro-carbon gases and dust in the cloud envelope of Venus would consti-tute a crucial test" for his ideas. We see here another example of his confusion between hydrocarbons and carbohydrates. It is also not clear whether "dust" in the foregoing quotation refers to hydrocarbon dust or just ordinary silicate dust. On the same page, Velikovsky quotes himself as saying "On the basis of this research, I assume that Venus must be rich in petroleum gases," which seems to be an unambiguous reference to the components of natural gas, such as methane, ethane, ethylene, and acetylene.

As I pointed out many years ago (Sagan, 1961), the vapor pressure of simple hydrocarbons in the vicinity of the clouds of Venus should make them detectable if they comprise the clouds. They were not detectable then, and in the intervening years, despite a wide range of analytic techniques used, neither hydrocarbons nor carbohydrates have been detected in significant amounts. These molecules have been searched for by high-resolution ground-based optical spectroscopy, including Fourier transform techniques; by ultraviolet spectroscopy from the Wisconsin Experimental Package of the Orbiting Astronomical Observatory OAO-2; by ground-based infrared observations; and by direct entry probes of the Soviet Union and the United States. Typical abundance upper limits on the simplest hydrocarbons and on the aldehydes that are essential to carbohydrates are a few parts per million (Connes *et al.*, 1967; Owen and Sagan, 1972). (The corresponding upper limits for Mars are also a few parts per million [Owen and Sagan, 1972].) All observations are consistent in showing that the bulk of the Venus atmosphere is composed of carbon dioxide. Indeed, because the carbon is present in such an oxidized form, at best trace constituents of the simple reduced hydrocarbons could be expected. Observations on the wings of the critical 3.5 μ region show not the slightest trace of the C-H absorption feature common to both hydrocarbons and carbohydrates (Pollack *et al.*, 1974). All other absorption bands in the Venus spectrum, from the ultraviolet through the infrared, are now understood; none of them is due to hydrocarbons or carbohydrates. No specific organic molecule has ever been suggested that can explain with precision the infrared spectrum of Venus as it is now known.

Moreoever, the question of the composition of the Venus clouds—a major enigma for centuries—has now been solved (Young and Young, 1973; Sill, 1972; Young, 1973; Pollack *et al.*, 1974). The clouds of Venus are composed of an approximately 75 percent solution of sulfuric acid. This identification is consistent with the chemistry of the Venus atmosphere, in which hydrofluoric and hydrochloric acid have also been found; with the real part of the refractive index, deduced from polarimetry, which is known to three significant figures

(1.44); with the 11.2 μ and 3 μ (and, now, far infrared) absorption features; and with the discontinuity in the abundance of water vapor above and below the clouds. These observed features are inconsistent with the hypothesis of hydrocarbon or carbohydrate clouds.

With such organic clouds now so thoroughly discredited, why do we hear about space-vehicle research having corroborated Velikovsky's thesis? This requires explanation. On December 14, 1962, the first successful American interplanetary spacecraft, Mariner 2, flew by Venus. Built by the Jet Propulsion Laboratory, it carried, among other, more important instruments, an infrared radiometer for which I happened to be one of four experimenters. This was at a time before even the first successful lunar Ranger spacecraft, and NASA was comparatively inexperienced in releasing the scientific findings. A press conference was held in Washington to announce the results, and Dr. L. D. Kaplan, one of the experimenters on our team, was delegated to describe the results to the assembled reporters. After describing the technical results of the experiment, Kaplan, in response to reporters, described his view that the greenhouse effect, needed to keep the surface of Venus hot, might not work because the atmospheric constituents seemed to be transparent at a wavelength in the vicinity of 3.5 μ. If some absorber at this wavelength existed in the Venus atmosphere, the window could be plugged, the greenhouse effect retained, and the high surface temperature accounted for. He proposed that hydrocarbons would be splendid greenhouse molecules.

Kaplan's remarks were misinterpreted by the press, and the next day headlines could be found in many American newspapers saying, "Hydrocarbon Clouds Found on Venus by Mariner 2." Unfortunately, this account found its way into the Jet Propulsion Laboratory's report on the mission, prepared by a group of laboratory publicists, and since called "Mariner: Mission to Venus." Subsequently, this incorrect interpretation was repeated in government reports, and even in some textbooks.

The true situation is very different, as we have seen. Neither Mariner 2 nor any subsequent investigation of the Venus atmosphere has found evidence for hydrocarbons or carbohydrates, in gas, liquid, or solid phase. It is now known (Pollack, 1969) that carbon dioxide and water vapor adequately fill the 3.5 micron window. It is ironic that the Mariner 2 "argument" for hydrocarbon clouds on Venus in fact derives from an attempt to rescue the greenhouse explanation of the high surface temperature, which Velikovsky does not support. It is also ironic that Professor Kaplan was later a co-author of a paper which set a very sensitive upper limit on the abundance of methane, a "petroleum gas," in a spectroscopic examination of the Venus atmosphere (Connes *et al.*, 1967).

In summary, Velikovsky's idea that the clouds of Venus are composed of hydrocarbons or carbohydrates is incorrect. The "crucial test" fails.

PROBLEM 8. THE TEMPERATURE OF VENUS

Another curious circumstance concerns the surface temperature of Venus. While the high temperature of Venus is often quoted as a successful prediction and a support of Velikovsky's hypothesis, the reasoning behind his conclusion and the consequences of his arguments do not seem to be widely known or discussed.

Let us begin by considering Velikovsky's views on the temperature of Mars (pages 367–68). He believes that Mars, being a relatively small planet, was more severely affected in its encounters with the more massive Venus and Earth, and therefore that Mars should have a high temperature.

Velikovsky states, "Mars emits more heat than it receives from the Sun," in apparent consistency with his collision hypothesis. This statement is, however, dead wrong. The temperature of Mars has been measured repeatedly by Soviet and American spacecraft and by ground-based observers, and the temperatures of all parts of Mars are just what is calculated from the amount of sunlight absorbed by the surface. Had Mars proved to be unexpectedly hot, perhaps we would have heard of this as a further confirmation of Velikovsky's views. But when Mars turns out to have exactly the temperature everyone expected it to have, we do not hear of this as a refutation of Velikovsky's views. There is a planetary double standard at work.

When we now move on to Venus, we find rather similar arguments brought into play. We are told that, because of its close encounters with Earth and Mars, Venus must have been heated; but also (page 77) "the head of the comet . . . had passed close to the Sun and was in a state of candescence." Then, when the comet became the planet Venus, it must still have been "very hot" and have "given off heat" (page ix).

What I think Velikovsky is trying to say here is that his Venus, like his Mars, is giving off more heat than it receives from the sun. But this is a serious error. The bolometric albedo of Venus is about 0.73, entirely consistent with the observed infrared temperature of the clouds of Venus of about 240°K; that is to say, the clouds of Venus are precisely at the temperature expected on the basis of the amount of sunlight that is absorbed there.

Velikovsky proposed that Venus is hot because of its encounters with Mars and Earth, and its close passage to the sun. Since Mars is *not* anomalously hot, the high surface temperature of Venus must then be attributed primarily to the passage of Venus near the sun during its cometary incarnation. But it is easy to calculate the maximum amount of energy Venus could have received during its close passage to the sun and how long it would take for this energy to be radiated away into space. When this calculation is performed, we find that all this energy is lost in a period of months to years after the close passage to the sun, and that there is no chance of any of that heat being retained at the present time in Velikovsky's chronology.

Velikovsky nowhere states the temperature he believed Venus to be at in 1950, so what precisely he meant by saying that Venus is "hot" is to some degree obscure. Velikovsky writes in his 1965 preface that his claim of a high surface temperature was "in total disagreement with what was known in 1946." This turns out to be not quite the case. In a paper in the *Astrophysical Journal*, Rupert Wildt (1940) argued that the surface of Venus was much hotter than conventional astronomical opinion had held, because of a carbon dioxide greenhouse effect. Carbon dioxide had recently been discovered spectroscopically in the atmosphere of Venus, and Wildt correctly pointed out that the observed large quantity of CO_2 would trap infrared radiation given off by the surface of the planet, until the surface temperature rose to a higher value, so that the incoming visible sunlight just balanced the outgoing infrared planetary emission. Wildt calculated that the temperature would be almost 400 K, or around the normal boiling point of water (373 K = 212° F = 100° C).

We now know from ground-based radio observations and from the remarkably successful direct entry and landing probes of the Soviet Union that the surface temperature of Venus is within a few degrees of 750 K (Marov, 1972). The surface atmospheric pressure is about ninety times that at the surface of the earth and is comprised primarily of carbon dioxide. This large abundance of carbon dioxide, plus the smaller quantities of water vapor that have been detected on Venus, is adequate to heat the surface to the observed temperature via the greenhouse effect (Sagan, 1961; Pollack, 1969; Marov *et al.*, 1973).

A repeated claim by Velikovsky is that Venus is cooling off with time. In many publications he compares published temperature measurements of Venus made at different times and tries to show the desired cooling. An unbiased presentation of the microwave brightness temperatures of Venus—the only nonspacecraft data that apply to the surface temperature of the planet—is exhibited below. The error bars represent the uncertainties in the measurement processes as estimated by the radio observers themselves. We see that there is not the

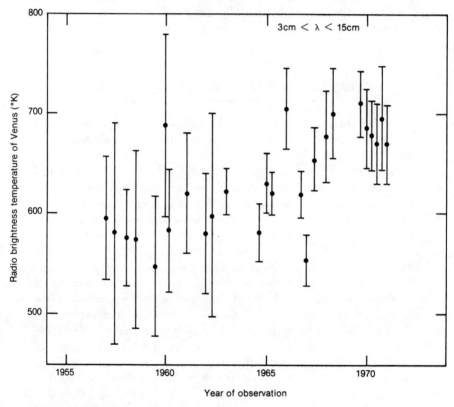

Microwave brightness temperatures of Venus as a function of time. The vertical lines indicate the uncertainty of the observations. The wavelength of the observation is denoted by λ. *After a compilation by D. Morrison.*

faintest hint of a decline in temperature with time. (If anything, there is a suggestion of an increase with time, but the error bars are sufficiently large that such a conclusion is also unsupported by the data.) Similar results apply to measurements, in the infrared part of the spectrum, of cloud temperatures: they are lower in magnitude and do not decline with time.

The high surface temperature of Venus is another of the so-called proofs of the Velikovsky hypothesis. We find (1) that the temperature in question was never specified; (2) that the mechanism proposed for providing this temperature is grossly inadequate; (3) that the surface of the planet does not cool off with time as advertised; and (4) that the idea of a high surface temperature on Venus was published in the dominant astronomical journal of its time and with an essentially correct argument ten years before the publication of *Worlds in Collision*.

PROBLEM 9. THE CRATERS OF VENUS

In 1973 an important aspect of the surface of Venus was discovered by Dr. Richard Goldstein and associates, using the Goldstone radar observatory of the Jet Propulsion Laboratory. Goldstein *et al.* found, from radar that penetrates Venus's clouds and is reflected off its surface, that the planet is cratered, and, perhaps, like parts of the moon, saturation cratered—that is, so packed with craters that one crater overlaps the other. These craters, like the craters in the lunar maria, on Mercury, and in the cratered regions of Mars, are produced almost exclusively by impact of interplanetary debris. Large crater-forming objects will not be dissipated as they enter the Venus atmosphere, despite its high density. Now the colliding objects cannot have arrived at Venus in the last ten thousand years, or the earth would be as plentifully cratered. One source of these collisions is minor planets and small comets, but for them to produce as many craters as Venus possesses, the cratering process on Venus must have taken billions of years. Alternatively, the cratering may have occurred more rapidly in the very earliest history of the solar system. But there is no way for it to have happened recently. On the other hand, if Venus was, thirty-five hundred years ago, in the deep interior of Jupiter, there is no way it could have accumulated such impacts there. The clear conclusion from the craters of Venus is, therefore, that Venus has been for billions of years an object exposed to interplanetary collisions—in direct contradiction to the fundamental premise of Velikovsky's hypothesis.

PROBLEM 10. THE CIRCULARIZATION OF THE ORBIT OF VENUS AND NONGRAVITATIONAL FORCES IN THE SOLAR SYSTEM

The idea that Venus could have been converted, in a few thousand years, from an object in a highly eccentric orbit to its present orbit, which is—except for Neptune's—the most nearly perfect circular orbit of all the planets, is at odds with what we know about the three-body problem in celestial mechanics. However, it must be admitted that this is not a completely solved problem, and that, while the odds are large, they are not absolutely overwhelming against Velikovsky's hypothesis on this score. Furthermore, when Velikovsky invokes electrical or magnetic forces, with no effort to calculate their magnitude or describe in detail their effects, we are hard pressed to assess his ideas. However, simple arguments from the magnetic energy density required to circularize a comet show that the field strengths implied are unreasonably high and are counterindicated by studies of rock magnetization.

We can also approach the problem empirically. Straightforward Newtonian mechanics is able to predict with remarkable accuracy the trajectories of spacecraft—so that, for example, Mariner 9 was placed within 100 kilometers of its designated orbit; Venera 8 was placed precisely on the sunlit side of the equatorial terminator of Venus; and Pioneer 10 was placed in exactly the correct entry corridor in the vicinity of Jupiter to be expelled from the solar system. No mysterious electrical or magnetic influences were encountered. Newtonian mechanics is adequate to predict, with great precision, for example, the exact moment when the Galilean satellites of Jupiter will be eclipsed in the planet's shadow.

Comets, it is true, have somewhat less predictable orbits, but this is due to the fact that there is a boiling off of frozen ices as these objects approach the sun, and a small rocket effect. The cometary incarnation of Venus, if it existed, might also have had such icy vaporization, but there is no way in which the rocket effect would have preferentially brought that comet into close passages with Earth or Mars. Halley's Comet, which has been observed probably for two thousand years, almost as long as the age of Velikovsky's "comet," remains on a highly eccentric orbit and has not been observed to show the slightest tendency toward circularization. It is extraordinarily unlikely that Velikovsky's comet, had it ever existed, became the planet Venus.

Worlds in Collision is an attempt to validate biblical and other folklore as history if not theology. I have tried to approach the book with no prejudgments. I find the mythological concordances fascinating and worth further investigation, but they are probably explicable on diffusionist or other grounds. The scientific part of the text, despite all the claims of "proofs," runs into the ten distinct and very grave difficulties that I have just discussed, but there are other problems as well (Sagan, 1977).

Of the ten tests of Velikovsky's work described above, there is not one case where his ideas are simultaneously original and consistent with simple physical theory and observation. Moreover, many of the objections—especially Problems 1, 2, 3, and 10—are objections of high weight, based on the motion and conservation laws of physics. In science, an acceptable argument must have a clearly set forth chain of evidence. If a single link in the chain is broken, the argument fails. In the case of *Worlds in Collision*, we have the opposite case: virtually every link in the chain is broken. To rescue the hypothesis requires special pleading, the vague invention of a new physics, and selective inattention to a plethora of conflicting evidence. Accordingly, Velikovsky's basic thesis seems to me clearly untenable on physical grounds.

Moreover, there is a dangerous potential problem with the mythological material. The supposed events are reconstructed from legends and folktales. But these global catastrophes are not clearly presented in the historical records of many peoples. Where concordances exist, Velikovsky is prepared to draw the most sweeping conclusions from them. Where concordances do not exist, the difficulty is dismissed by invoking "collective amnesia." With so lax a standard of evidence, *anything* can be "proved."

There are many strange inconsistencies in *Worlds in Collision*, some of which I have already mentioned. But on the next-to-last page of the book, a breathtaking departure from the fundamental thesis is casually introduced. Here we read of a hoary and erroneous analogy between the structures of solar systems and of atoms. Suddenly, we are presented with the hypothesis that the supposed errant motions of the planets, rather than being the result of collisions, are instead due to changes in the quantum energy levels of planets attendant to the absorption of a photon—or perhaps several. Solar systems are held together by gravitational forces, atoms by electrical forces. While both forces depend on the inverse square of distance, they have totally different characters and magnitudes: as one of many differences, there are positive and negative electrical charges, but only one sign of gravitational mass. We understand both solar systems and atoms well enough to see that Velikovsky's proposed "quantum jumps" of planets are based on a misunderstanding of both theories and evidence.

To the best of my knowledge, there is not a single astronomical prediction correctly made in *Worlds in Collision* with sufficient precision for it to be more than a vague lucky guess—and there are, as I have tried to point out, a host of claims made which are demonstrably false. The existence of strong radio emission from Jupiter is sometimes pointed to as the most striking example of a correct prediction by Velikovsky, but all objects give off radio waves if they are at temperatures above absolute zero. The essential character of the Jovian radio emission—that it is nonthermal, polarized, intermittent radiation, connected with the vast belts of charged particles that surround Jupiter, trapped by its strong magnetic field—is nowhere predicted by Velikovsky. Indeed, his "prediction" is clearly not linked in its essentials to the fundamental Velikovskian theses.

With these enormous liabilities, how is it that *Worlds in Collision* became so popular? Here I can only guess. For one thing, it is an attempted validation of religion. The old biblical stories are literally true, Velikovsky tells us, if only we interpret them in the right way. The Jewish people, for example, saved from Egyptian pharaohs, Assyrian kings, and innumerable other disasters by obliging cometary interventions, had every right to believe themselves chosen. Velikovsky attempts to rescue not only religion, but also astrology: the outcomes of wars, the fates of whole peoples are determined by the positions of the planets. In some sense, his work holds out a promise of the cosmic connectedness of mankind—a sentiment with which I sympathize, but in a somewhat different context (see Sagan, 1973)—and the reassurance that ancient peoples and other cultures were not so very dumb after all.

The outrage that seems to have seized many otherwise placid scientists upon colliding with *Worlds in Collision* has produced a chain of consequences. Some people are quite properly put off by the occasional pomposity of scientists, or they are concerned by what they apprehend as the dangers of science and technology, or perhaps they merely have difficulty understanding science. They may take some comfort in seeing scientists get their lumps.

To the extent that scientists have not given Velikovsky the reasoned response his work calls for, we have ourselves been responsible for the propagation of Velikovskian confusion. But scientists cannot attempt to deal with all areas of borderline science (of which the number is legion in America today). The thinking, calculation, and preparation of this chapter, for example, took badly needed time away from my own research. But it was certainly not boring, and at the very least I had a brush with many an enjoyable legend. I hope that in the future the views of other popular proponents of borderline science will receive a reasoned, if hopefully briefer, scientific response.

The attempt to rescue old-time religion, in an age that seems desperately to be seeking some religious roots, some cosmic significance for mankind, may or may not be creditable. I think there is much good and much evil in the old-time religions. But I do not understand the need for half measures. If we are forced to choose—and we decidedly are *not*—is the evidence not better for the God of Moses, Jesus, and Mohammed than for the comet of Velikovsky?

16

Recasting the Past: Powerful Pyramids, Lost Continents, and Ancient Astronauts

E. C. KRUPP

Paranormal mysteries and legends from the past have paradoxical qualities, as illustrated in the following essay by Dr. E. C. Krupp, Director of the Griffith Observatory. On the one hand, pyramid power, ancient astronauts, and Atlantis are among the silliest notions being bandied about today in the paranormal marketplace. They are based on highly selected, contorted, or just plain fabricated evidence. On the other hand, these particular pseudosciences are also among the all-time best-sellers; for example, von Däniken's books alone have sold more than 50 million copies!

The past does contain mysteries. Since we cannot go back thousands of years to make observations and check our hypotheses, it is not surprising that this should be so. We will never attain certain knowledge about long-past human history as definitive as our knowledge about the present. But the mysteries of the past are not that mysterious or inexplicable; there are reasonable hypotheses to account for them, and there are no knowledge gaps or puzzles that compel us to paranormal explanations. When ancient people planted seed corn and saw a plant spring up, the mechanisms of growth seemed miraculous, and they de-

scribed them in terms of the goddess Ceres, who lived underneath the earth and pushed the corn up every spring. The reverential invocation of ancient astronauts, Atlantis, and other ancient miracles to account for our uncertainties about the past ignores the intellectual advances man has made since the time of our ancestors millennia ago.

The wildness of absurd speculation about ancient mysteries can be disguised by elaborate numerical calculations and generous use of supporting circumstantial evidence. It is not difficult to play such pseudoscience games, and there are many popular writers who have played these games very well. Krupp, a well-known expert on the subject, provides detailed examples of how authors have fabricated and distorted evidence, or have thrown together numbers and facts in quite arbitrary ways to support unsupportable claims. It is exciting to imagine ancient visitors from other solar systems, or exotic cultures that are now forever lost, but one cannot credibly support such theories with twisted and manufactured evidence.

THE PAST IS WHERE YOU FIND IT

Myths, legends, relics, and ruins are the souvenirs we have collected on our journey from the past. Despite these mementoes, the record of our origins and development is incomplete. Although we have some understanding of our ancestors, mysteries remain in the traditions, tales, and antiquities by which we interpret the past. We are like amnesiacs who grasp at the random and fragmented memories that emerge now and then from the unconscious. They tantalize us with intimations of our own forgotten identities.

The past will probably always elude us. Each archeological discovery prompts at least as many new puzzles as the questions it answers. Whether our data are discouragingly sparse or more abundant than we can ever absorb, we impose our own concerns and viewpoints upon antiquity. It is possible, then, for us to misread whatever elusive record we have. The archeologist tries, however, to avoid subjectivity and misinterpretation through systematic, scientific acquisition of information. And the archeologist has an obligation to extend hypotheses no further than the data permit. The reward for this kind of discipline is confidence in the conclusions that may be drawn. The penalty is a picture of the past riddled with blank spots and unanswered questions.

Where the archeologist has the discipline not to tread, many others feel free to wander. Speculation is the logical response to mystery. The human imagination has no trouble repopulating the ancient monuments and reconstructing the motives of their builders. Stonehenge, the pyramids of Egypt, the lines and drawings of the Nazcas in Peru, and numerous other ancient and prehistoric sites have all been explained with a daring and romance that owe little to orthodox reasoning and scientific method. The rich variety of the unconventional accounts is itself appealing to an unbridled imagination. We may leap from one notion to the next—from lost civilizations to sunken continents, from supercivilizations to ancient astronauts, from secret symbolic knowledge to unknown energy sources right under our noses—without inhibition or common sense. Both are overwhelmed by the power of a mystery seemingly revealed.

We encounter those who think every dimension of the Great Pyramid of Giza reflects detailed information about the size and shape and motion of the earth. Others propose that many of the myths and legends of the ancient world are but an imperfect account of the history of Atlantis, a continent which catastrophically sank and carried the first civilization—the mother of human culture—with it. Partisans of Atlantis find evidence of the influence of this great lost race in the monuments, language, and legends of numerous peoples on both sides of the Atlantic.

In yet another approach, the modern myth concerning UFOs and the modern reality of space travel are combined with the mysteries of the past to conjure up the image of space travelers from other worlds who long ago visited the earth and were instrumental in setting humanity off on the road to civilization and, ultimately, to the stars. Despite the obvious differences between all these ideas, they share a common theme: the lost knowledge of the past.

When scientists generalize about the development of civilization, they tend to emphasize the continuity of culture and society. But the proponents of lost continents and ancient astronauts react instead to the holes in scientists' reconstruction of the past, and they fill those cavities with ancient peoples who knew much that was subsequently lost. All these notions represent a nostalgia for a golden age. This is where all the new myths of the human past ultimately reside. Our modern myths are framed in contemporary images. They are decorated with scientific language and rely upon scientifically obtained information. But they bear the trappings of fancy as well. The image of our ancestors recovered from oblivion and restored to their former exalted state is a reflection of our time-honored yearning for paradise.

Of course, our ancestors very likely could have been more clever, more complex, more resourceful, and perhaps even more like us than we've previously surmised. Even should scientific investigation demonstrate this, however, we shall be under no obligation to reassess the arguments of pyramidologists and apologists for ancient astronauts. Their claims can be evaluated now in terms of the evidence cited in their defense. We can ask if the evidence is factual and if the rules of handling evidence have been followed. We can ask if the arguments are consistent with the evidence and whether logic is obeyed. We can determine if the hypotheses extend beyond what the data can tell us. We can explore these evergreen notions—with an open mind and a hard nose—for what grains of truth, if any, they may contain, and determine where scientific interpretation ends and belief begins.

PYRAMIDS, POWER, AND PI

It is hard to imagine a more fitting symbol of the mysteries of the past than the pyramids of Egypt. These huge geometric intrusions upon the natural desert landscape suggest, by their silence and antiquity, the ancient and the unknown.

The pyramids at Giza, just a twenty-minute drive from the modern hotels of Cairo, are particularly famous. They have fascinated travelers for millennia. In the fifth century B.C., Herodotus told his Greek countrymen fabulous tales about what was considered (even in antiquity) one of the Seven Wonders of the World: the Great Pyramid (see page 257).

To see for oneself the celebrated pyramids is a desire that continues to draw tourists to Egypt. One's first visit to them quickly confirms that they are everything they are reputed to be. Despite the interruptions of bead vendors, tour guides, and camel drivers soliciting passengers, the pyramids mystify the eye and mind. The more contemplative environment of the sound-and-light show provides a sunset and twilight penetrated by pyramidal silhouettes, and at night, in moonlight, the pyramids become huge dark phantoms, deliciously indistinct.

Even though the Great Pyramid is now thirty-one feet shorter than its builder (the pharaoh Khufu) intended, it is still the largest of the

The Great Pyramid of Khufu at Giza is regarded by some as a repository of ancient knowledge, as a model of the earth's northern hemisphere, and as a device that can exploit "pyramid energy." Photograph by Robin Rector Krupp.

eighty or so known pyramids in Egypt. Its summit once reached 481.4 feet above the rocky plateau of Giza, but the top twelve courses of stone are now missing. With each side of the base once 756 feet long, the Great Pyramid covered 13.1 acres.

Khufu reigned in the Fourth Dynasty, during the period known as the Old Kingdom. His father, Sneferu, had already built the now-collapsed pyramid at Meidum, fifty-six miles south of Cairo. The Bent Pyramid and the Northern Stone Pyramid, both at Dahshur, thirty miles back to the north from Meidum, were also built by Sneferu, who extended a tradition of pyramid building that had been inaugurated in the Third Dynasty by the pharaoh Zoser. Zoser built the Step Pyramid at Saqqara, about twenty miles south of Cairo and near the ruins of Memphis, the capital of the Old Kingdom.

Zoser's pyramid dates from about 2780 B.C. A century later, Khufu's pyramid was well under construction. When completed, its outer faces, covered with fine, smooth limestone casing blocks, gleamed in the sunlight.

Today the Great Pyramid is in ruins. Nearly all of the outer Tura limestone facing is gone, quarried for the convenience of later builders. Much of it is probably to be found in the thirteenth-century buildings and walls of old Cairo.

Most of the Great Pyramid's 2,300,000 blocks of stone were cut from nearby limestone quarries, at Giza, although the fine casing stone came from the Tura quarries, located a few miles upriver on the east side of the Nile. Some granite was used as well, particularly in the Great Pyramid's interior chambers. Granite was highly valued by the Egyptians for its hardness and strength, but it is difficult to quarry and dress, and the nearest granite quarries were located at Aswan, more than five hundred miles south. Understandably, relatively little granite was used in the pyramids.

On the average, the Great Pyramid's blocks of stone weigh 2.5 tons each, with some as heavy as fifteen tons and none less than 1.5 tons. Even in ruins the monument is prodigious.

Most of the Great Pyramid's mysteries involve details of its construction. Why was it built in the way that it was? How was it erected? What was its purpose? Pyramidology, the esoteric and unorthodox interpretation of the Great Pyramid, evolved as pyramid enthusiasts attempted to read symbolic meaning into each detail of the Great Pyramid's dimensions and design. Often these efforts involved a tradition of biblical prophecy, and it is easy to see why this was so.

Egypt figures prominently in the Bible, particularly through the Old Testament accounts of the bondage of the Hebrews and their subsequent exodus. These events took place long after the time of the Great Pyramid, probably in the reign of the pharaoh Ramses II, fourteen centuries after Khufu built his pyramid—but Hebrews have been depicted slaving upon the pyramids time and again, despite the fact that the archeological evidence suggests that no slaves were used to build them.

At times Egypt's pyramids were identified as the granaries in which Joseph stored the surplus from the seven good years for the seven difficult years to follow. Other biblical associations with the pyramids had been made, but the tradition took an elaborate new turn in the second half of the nineteenth century.

In 1859, John Taylor, a London publisher and editor, revealed in his book *The Great Pyramid: Why Was It Built? and Who Built It?* that the architect responsible for the Great Pyramid was not an Egyptian at all, but an Israelite—in fact, Noah! Under divine guidance,

Noah incorporated important geographical and mathematical truths into the very measurements of the Great Pyramid.

Taylor discovered, for example, that the height of the Great Pyramid, if multiplied by 270,000, equaled the circumference of the earth. "How," asked Taylor, "could the Egyptians have known the size of the earth?" He further argued that multiplying the height by itself and comparing the result with the area of one face of the pyramid resulted in the same proportion dictated by the Golden Section, the proportion obtained when a line segment is divided into two lengths so that the smaller is to the larger as the larger is to the whole. The discovery of this principle of harmonious design is attributed to the Greeks, and some Greek architecture was based upon it. But if this is so, how could the Egyptians have embodied it in the Great Pyramid?

Pi, the number that relates the circumference of a circle to its diameter, was known at least approximately to the ancient Egyptians. The Rhind papyrus, a copy of a mathematical text attributed to the Middle Kingdom and Twelfth Dynasty, implies that the Egyptians used the value 3.16 for pi. Actually, a good approximation of pi is 3.14159. Taylor calculated, however, that dividing the perimeter of the Great Pyramid's base by twice its height gives 3.14, apparently a close approximation to pi. He was convinced that the pyramid builders knew pi well and designed the pyramid with this number in mind.

In Taylor's mind, the Great Pyramid could be thought of as a symbolic representation of the earth. The perimeter of the Great Pyramid's base corresponded to the earth's equator, its height to the earth's polar radius.

Taylor also claimed that key features of the Great Pyramid were set out in units of the "sacred cubit." Allegedly, the Temple of Solomon, the Tabernacle of Abraham, and Noah's Ark were all built in terms of the same unit. The sacred cubit is about 25 inches long, but more importantly, 20 million of them equal the length of the earth's polar diameter. Taylor was convinced that the Great Pyramid's dimensions were tied to a profound geodetic system.

Some of Taylor's conclusions are quite arbitrary. There is no reason to think that there is anything particularly significant about the number 270,000 or 20 million. We also know that Taylor, who never visited the Great Pyramid, overestimated its height.

Numerous imaginative and extravagant books have been written on the lost Egyptian science revealed by the Great Pyramid. Even Sir Isaac Newton got caught up in the search for the sacred cubit. The high-water mark for such pyramid studies occurred in 1864, with the publication of *Our Inheritance in the Great Pyramid* by Charles Piazzi Smyth.

Smyth's name has become synonymous with pyramidology. He was the Astronomer Royal of Scotland and as such commanded attention. After coming across a copy of Taylor's book, Smyth thought deeply about the Great Pyramid, made numerous calculations, and concluded that there was far more to the Great Pyramid than anyone had surmised. Eventually, Smyth went to Egypt and made measurements, which confirmed (at least for him) his hypotheses.

Builders of the Great Pyramid were again credited with accurate knowledge of pi. Smyth reiterated the claim that the perimeter of the Great Pyramid's base bore the same relation to twice its height as the circumference of a circle bears to its diameter. Additionally, Smyth reported that the distance between the earth and the sun is exactly one thousand million times the Great Pyramid's height.

Smyth, like others before him, believed that the Great Pyramid was built in terms of a fundamental unit of measurement, which he tried to discover. He concluded that the width of the outer casing stones was the key to finding this unit, for his results indicated that the distance all around the pyramid's base divided by the width of a casing stone (of which only few remained) gave 365.2422, a symbolic numerological record in stone of the number of days in the year. The width of the casing stone could, in turn, be divided by 25, and this length, which was one one-thousandth of an inch less than the standard British inch, Smyth called the Pyramid inch.

Other claims about the geographical placement of the Great Pyramid were made by Smyth, and, in fact, he also mentioned that the volume of the monument, in cubic Pyramid inches, equaled the total number of people who have lived since the time of the Creation!

Once Smyth made his findings known, general confidence in the state of Scottish astronomy waned, but other pyramid enthusiasts were stimulated to develop even more elaborate interpretations.

While Smyth was at Giza in 1865, he became acquainted, through correspondence, with Robert Menzies, a young Scottish shipbuilder. Menzies' interest in the Great Pyramid was wedded to his belief that biblical scripture was reflected in the monument's complex arrangement of internal passages and chambers. Inspired by Menzies, Smyth applied the Pyramid inch to the floors and walls of various corridors and decoded a chronological record of the past in marks and scratches found at seemingly significant locations. This symbolic history verified the Bible and extended, in fact, into the future.

Piazzi Smyth imagined the Great Pyramid to be the oldest man-made structure in the world. Not only did it record, on a scale of one year to the Pyramid inch, the entire history of the world, according to the Bible, prior to the pyramid's construction, but it also predicted the future as well. Of course, Egyptologists of Smyth's day were skeptical. They knew that the Great Pyramid was not the oldest structure in the world, but was actually one of the later pyramids. Even John Greaves, two centuries before, had concluded that the Great Pyramid was the tomb of Khufu and that it contained no esoteric meaning. Smyth's scientific colleagues cringed at the component of religious prophecy in his work. Although Smyth's ideas were rejected by scholars, it was difficult to dismiss his work entirely. Piles of debris covered the base of the Great Pyramid and prevented direct measurement of its perimeter. No one, not even Smyth, had determined accurately the Great Pyramid's dimensions.

Late in 1880, William Flinders Petrie, the father of modern archeology, arrived in Egypt and began a comprehensive survey of the Great Pyramid that eventually disproved Smyth's claims. Petrie demonstrated that the Great Pyramid was indeed based upon an ancient Egyptian unit of measurement, but it was the royal cubit (approximately 20.63 inches long) and not the Pyramid inch.

Neither the accurate measurement of the length of a side of the pyramid's base nor the pieces of casing stone (found to have various widths) could permit belief in the Pyramid inch. Smyth's estimate of the length of a side was shown to have been in error by approximately 0.8 percent. This may not seem much, but Smyth's notion that the base symbolized the 365 days of the year was demolished by Petrie's accurate measurements.

The presence of the number pi in the Great Pyramid's dimensions may also be understandable in terms of the Egyptians' unit of measurement, the royal cubit, and in. terms of the way in which they measured angles. The Egyptians, unlike ourselves, did not specify angles in degrees. Instead they indicated what angle they wanted by specifying two numbers: a vertical length, and a horizontal displacement from its upper end. The vertical length was understood to be a royal cubit. A royal cubit, in turn, equaled 7 "palms." Any desired slope could be indicated simply by stating, in palms, the horizontal displacement. This technique involved known units of measurement

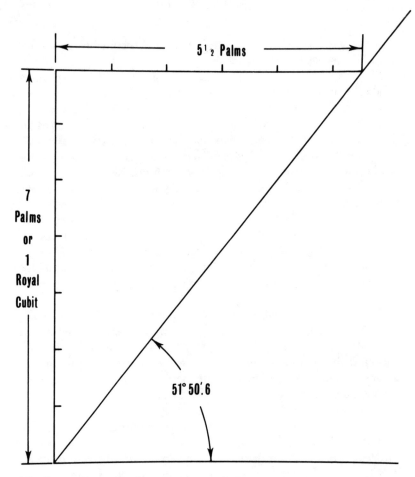

The Egyptians measured out angles in terms of "palms" up and "palms" over, not in terms of degrees. A horizontal displacement of 5½ palms from the standard 7 palm (or 1 "Royal Cubit") vertical gives an angle that agrees exceptionally well with the actual slope on the remaining facing stones of the Great Pyramid. Courtesy Griffith Observatory.

and a simple right triangle. The hypotenuse represented the slope. Normally, the Egyptians specified the horizontal displacement in whole units or in simple fractions. The slope produced by a triangle with a vertical leg equal to 7 palms and a horizontal leg equal to 5½ palms is 50°50′.6 (see above). If instead the Egyptians intended to have the perimeter of the base and the height of the Great Pyramid related through pi, the slope angle would have been 51°51′.2. These two results are barely distinguishable from each other, and Willy Ley showed as well that building the pyramid on the principle of the Golden Section gives a slope of 51°49'.6. The true slope of the Great Pyramid, 51°50'40" ± 1'05", is consistent, within the errors of measurement, with all three possible principles of construction. The choice of a 5½-palm angle is the simplest and perhaps the most likely explanation.

We know from the Rhind papyrus that, seven centuries or so after the Great Pyramid was built, Egyptians were using a value for pi equal to 3.16. If the Old Kingdom pyramid builders intended to incorporate pi into the Great Pyramid, its dimensions should give this value, not 3.14. Partisans of the pyramid pi would argue, however, that by the Middle Kingdom the old knowledge was lost.

A British physicist, Kurt Mendelssohn, has discussed the various pyramids and interpreted their differing slopes ingeniously. In *The Riddle of the Pyramids* Mendelssohn concludes that the pyramid at Meidum collapsed during construction. Subsequently, the Egyptians built pyramids at "safer" angles and with sounder internal engineering. The peculiar change to a less-steep slope partway up the Bent Pyramid and the conservatively low slope of the Northern Stone (or Red) Pyramid, both at Dashshur, were, he thinks, responses to the catastrophe at Meidum.

Although Petrie's survey disproved some of the more flamboyant claims about the Great Pyramid, his work, particularly as refined by J. H. Cole in 1925, demonstrated that the sides of the Great Pyramid were aligned with the cardinal directions with remarkable accuracy. In worst agreement is the east side, only 5½ arc minutes west of north. This error is only about one-sixth the apparent size of the full moon, and you can cover up the moon with your thumb held at arm's length. The other sides agree even better. This accuracy is consistent, however, with Egyptian surveying techniques. What is marvelous is that the Great Pyramid maintained this accuracy of alignment on such a monumental scale and, of course, that the Egyptians thought this important enough to devote their energies to it.

Cardinal orientation of the sides of the Great Pyramid reflect the Egyptians' awareness of fundamental astronomical phenomena. Charles Piazzi Smyth also thought the Great Pyramid had astronomical significance. Following a suggestion by astronomer John Herschel, Smyth proposed that the Descending Corridor, with a slope of 27°17', had been aligned with the lowest swing of the star Thuban, in Draco the Dragon, as the star circled around the north pole of the sky. This alignment, Smyth thought, was established in the era when Thuban was 3°42' from the pole. Precession, the 26,000-year cycle of wobbling of the earth's axis, would have permitted this alignment in 3440 B.C. or 2170 B.C., were the Great Pyramid located at a latitude of 29°40' north, as Smyth claimed. Actually, the Great Pyramid's latitude is 29°58'51" north, and its known date of construction agrees with neither date above.

It has been argued that the Great Pyramid was used as an observatory. Richard Proctor, the celebrated British popularizer of astronomy, in the late nineteenth century developed an elaborate system involving alignments of the pyramid's passages.

Proctor also thought the Descending Corridor had been aligned intentionally with Thuban, probably to help maintain alignment of the cardinal orientation during construction. Furthermore, Proctor thought that the Great Pyramid had been used in a truncated form as an observation platform built to the height of the upper level of the Grand Gallery. Proctor imagined the Grand Gallery was itself used as a kind of meridian transit by the ancient astronomers to map in detail the stars of the Egyptian sky. As clever as Proctor's ideas are, they are most certainly wrong. The Descending Corridor did not align with Thuban, and there is no evidence that the Egyptians used or needed the Grand Gallery to measure the positions of the stars. There is astronomical significance to the Great Pyramid, however.

Two shafts extend from the King's Chamber, deep within the Great Pyramid—one to the north face and the other to the south. These narrow features traditionally have been called air shafts, but Egyptologist Alexander Badawy and astronomer Virginia Trimble have shown that the angles of ascent, 31° for the north shaft and 44°5' for the south, permit good alignment with the uppermost arc of Thuban, in the north, and with the transit of the stars of the belt of Orion, in the south (see page 265). Astronomical observation was not intended, however. From the King's Chamber both shafts extend horizontally for a short distance before turning upward. The sky cannot be seen.

It is equally unlikely that the shafts were intended to allow air into the chamber. The ancient Egyptians, it is known, ventilated their homes more effectively than these shafts ventilate the burial room. Had this been the intention it would have been far easier to run a horizontal shaft through a single course of blocks. Badawy invokes written material from the *Pyramid Texts* and argues effectively that the two

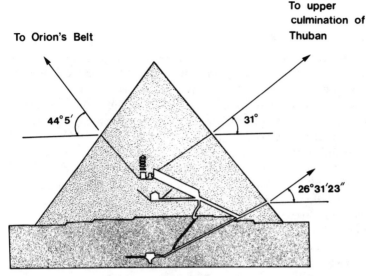

To upper
culmination of
Thuban

To Orion's Belt

44° 5′

31°

26°31′23″

The two so-called "air shafts" of the Great Pyramid are astronomically aligned, one to Thuban and the realm of the circumpolar, imperishable stars, the other to the belt of Orion, who represented the resurrected god Osiris. The significance of these alignments, verified in the Pyramid Texts, *allow us to conclude that the Great Pyramid indeed was a tomb.* Courtesy Griffith Observatory.

shafts are symbolic means of ascent to the "undying" (circumpolar) stars and to the stars of Osiris (Orion). They represent the stellar destiny of the pharaoh.

Although the real flowering of pyramidology took place in the nineteenth century, unorthodox interpretation of the Great Pyramid's placement, orientation, dimensions, and design is by no means dead. The most serious student of these matters today is Professor Livio Stecchini. His complex analysis was most fully described in a three-hundred-page appendix to Peter Tompkins's uneven book *Secrets of the Great Pyramid.*

Stecchini is quite knowledgeable about ancient metrology—that is, the systems and units of weights and measures in antiquity. He does not indulge in any fancies about fictional units of length, like the Pyramid inch, but recognizes (quite rightly) that an understanding of ancient units of measurement can tell us something important about the cultures that used them and about the transmission of information from one civilization to another.

Some of Stecchini's ideas, though highly speculative, are not altogether implausible. He imagines, for instance, that even the Old

Kingdom Egyptians had an abstract, idealized conception of the geography of their land, which was manifested in a geodetic system of placement of cities, temples, and sanctuaries. The political and religious influence of these sites was, in part, authenticated by their geographical locations. And according to Stecchini the units of measurement of length, area, volume, weight, and time were all interrelated and derived from the geodetic representation of Egypt.

Stecchini's work looks formidable. It is abstruse and filled with intricate detail. Its quantitative, mathematical arguments and its circuitious, difficult style make it inaccessible to the average reader. As a result, his efforts have received little attention. This cuts two ways, however, for Stecchini has also escaped critical evaluation.

There is no direct or textual evidence to prove that the ancient Egyptians did devise such a geodetic system, but something of the sort could have been within the range of fundamental astronomical and geographical knowledge accessible to them. Stecchini's clever arguments, for example, about Akhenaten, the heretical and unique pharaoh of the Eighteenth Dynasty, and his transfer of the capital from Thebes to a barren site downriver, now known as Tel el-Amarna, provide circumstantial support for some of his notions. Stecchini extends his claim quite far, however, and suggests that the geodetic system he proposes implies a detailed, accurate knowledge of the shape and size of the earth. The Great Pyramid enters the picture as Stecchini attempts to show that this unprecedented knowledge is built into that by-now-much-exploited monument.

Although Stecchini makes a number of unprecedented claims about the Great Pyramid, his treatment of its height will serve as an adequate example of his approach. According to Stecchini, the intended height of the Great Pyramid, 280 cubits, symbolized not only the radius of the earth but its polar flattening as well.

The earth is not perfectly round but is flattened at the poles. This fact was anticipated by Newton, and by the late nineteenth century a reasonable estimate of the flattening was available. This was improved in the early twentieth century, and our knowledge of the earth's exact shape continues to be refined even today. According to Stecchini, Egyptians estimated the polar flattening more than four thousand, six hundred years ago.

There is no demonstrative evidence that the Egyptians knew the earth to be round, let alone flattened at the poles, yet Stecchini finds support for his claim in the 280-cubit height. The flattening is actually one part in 298.3. Stecchini argues that the Egyptians found it convenient to assess it to be one part in 280, hence the symbolic 280-cubit height. Obviously, there is no direct, logical connection between the height of the pyramid in cubits and the ratio of flattening. And even if there were, Stecchini explains away the fact that the two numbers really don't agree (280 *vs.* 298.3).

Actually, Stecchini believes that the Egyptians did know the correct value of the polar flattening and he cites a passage from the Book of the Dead to prove it. In Chapter 64 there is a passage which numbers the spirits of the netherworld at 4,601,200. Each spirit is said to be 12 cubits high. Stecchini multiplies these two numbers together to obtain a sort of total length of spirits in cubits of 55,214,400, which he equates, in turn, with 138,036 geographic stadia. This number, Stecchini claims, represents two diameters of the earth. An equatorial diameter equals 69,076 geographic stadia, and two times this value gives 138,152 geographic stadia. This is not the same, of course, as 138,036. It is 116 geographic stadia larger than what Stecchini feels he extracts from the Book of the Dead. Stecchini explains that is what you get if you add an equatorial diameter to a diameter shortened by polar flattening: 138,036. He is obliged, however, to conclude that the second, polar diameter (68,968 geographic stadia) is itself the sum of a normal, equatorial radius and a shorter, polar radius (see page 268). A true polar diameter would equal 68,844 geographic stadia. The short polar radius corresponds to a polar flattening of one part in 298, which is correct, but Stecchini is forced to conclude that the Egyptians thought only the northern hemisphere was flattened. He builds one ad hoc assumption onto another, combines his result with his arbitrary interpretation of the height of the Great Pyramid, and concludes that the Egyptians knew the real value of the earth's flattening but chose to approximate it incorrectly in the height of the Great Pyramid for geodetic reasons.

An argument as thin as this hardly seems to require such detailed commentary, but it is difficult to tell what is at its heart without taking it apart piece by piece. It may be as empty as the sarcophagus of Khufu, but that fact can't be seen without examining the details, as we have done here.

A new dimension to pyramidology was added when the Frenchman Antoine Bovis decided there was something special about the shape of a pyramid after visiting Giza in the early 1930s.

Bovis was an enthusiast of a form of dowsing known as radiesthesia. This technique emphasizes the notion that substances radiate certain energies. These energies are not the sort described by modern physics,

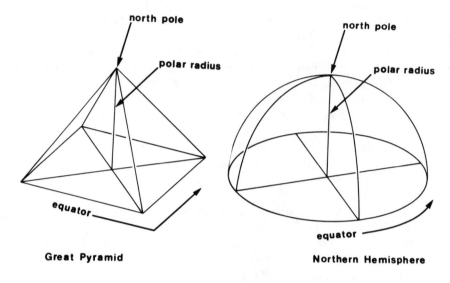

north pole

polar radius

equator

Great Pyramid

north pole

polar radius

equator

Northern Hemisphere

Pyramidologists from John Taylor to Livio Stecchini have argued that the Great Pyramid's dimensions make it an analogue of the earth's northern hemisphere. Courtesy Griffith Observatory.

however. Bovis concluded that the pyramid shape somehow focused an energy that facilitated mummification through quick dehydration. As such it could also be used to preserve food. This unique energy eventually became known as pyramid energy or pyramid power.

A Czechoslovakian radio technician, Karl Drbal, learned about Bovis's experiments with miniature pyramids and in the 1940s started mummifying food, flowers, and dead animals himself. Drbal also experimented with razor blades, in the expectation that the pyramid's energy would blunt the blades. Instead, Drbal's pyramid-treated razor blades seemed to maintain their ability to provide smooth shaves for longer than ordinary blades. Drbal applied for a patent for his Cheops Pyramid Razor Blade Sharpener, or "Pharaoh's Shaving Device," in 1949, and ten years later the Czechoslovak government granted it.

Pyramid power has been publicized greatly in the United States, at first largely through *Psychic Discoveries Behind the Iron Curtain,* by Sheila Ostrander and Lynn Schroeder. Now over a dozen books have been published on the subject, and the marketing of pyramid paraphernalia is a multimillion-dollar industry. According to one newspaper advertisement,

> PYRAMID POWER has fascinated Pharaohs and Kings, scholars and scientists for over 3000 years. Mystical powers have been attributed to it . . . which confer significant and rewarding benefits to its users. Even the way the pyramids were constructed suggests some unexplainable source of energy or power. . . . The pyramid is said to improve one's way of life and power over others . . . to bring health and energy . . . even fame and fortune.

Certainly the pitch is appealing, and many home pyramid experimenters test their commercially made equipment on apples, cheap wine, and razor blades. Pyramid proprietors meditate under their pyramids, sleep under their pyramids, and grow plants under their pyramids. Their activity symbolizes, in a sense, the democratization of science. Anyone may purchase a pyramid, and, like Mr. Wizard with his Science Secrets, conduct experiments. Better yet, pyramid power is a realm where conventional science has yet to tread.

The main fallacy with these pyramid-power investigations is the absence of experimental controls. Most home experimenters have not had experience in setting up a rigorous test. When results are positive, the pyramid is judged a success. Negative results are attributed to the elusive quality of the energy. In either case, the test is usually highly subjective. With food preservation, for example, the experimenter's sense of taste is the deciding factor.

Most pyramid-power experts follow the principles advanced by Bovis and Drbal. The small pyramid must be built to the same proportion as the Great Pyramid. The substance to be tested should be located in the center, at a height one-third the distance from base to peak. This is the height of the King's Chamber in the Great Pyramid. Also, the pyramid should be aligned with magnetic north, and often a small compass is provided with the pyramid to facilitate proper alignment.

Pyramid energy is not the same as magnetism, but it is imagined to be related to the earth's magnetic field as a kind of earth, or "telluric," energy. A similar concept involving prehistoric sites in Britain is also now in vogue. Long-distance alignments of antiquities are postulated to have formed a network of energy centers and conduits throughout the landscape.

The partisans of pyramid power provide us with an answer to the mystery of the pyramids. The ancients were aware of the subtle energy of the pyramid shape, a knowledge lost until the present age. It is odd, then, that the miniature pyramids must be aligned with magnetic north. The ancient Egyptians worked very hard to align the Great Pyramid with cardinal, or true, north. Apparently we still haven't discovered all the secrets of antiquity.

Whatever secrets the Egyptians did possess, we have seen men like Taylor and Smyth obsessed by the problem of the source of these secrets. They concluded that the Great Pyramid was a product of divine inspiration, perhaps executed by an Israelite. Others have attributed it instead to the inhabitants of the lost continent of Atlantis.

CONTINENTS: LOST AND FOUND

The story of Atlantis begins with Plato, in the fourth century B.C. There is no earlier account. In two of his dialogues, the *Timaeus* and the *Critias*, Plato allows the tale of Atlantis to emerge from the mouths of his characters. Critias describes an ancient empire that ruled from an island "beyond the pillars of Hercules." Plato implies that this land once existed out in the Atlantic Ocean. It was larger than "Libya" (North Africa) and "Asia" (Asia Minor) combined. The influence of the Atlanteans reached into the Mediterranean, as far as Egypt and western Italy, but the empire collapsed in a day and a night, in a great natural cataclysm that brought earthquake and flood. Just as quickly, the entire island continent was lost as it slipped beneath the waves.

Critias, who described the fate of Atlantis in the *Timaeus*, was Plato's uncle, and Critias said he heard the story from his own grandfather, Critias the Elder. Critias the Elder heard it, in turn, from Dropides, a relative of Solon, the great Athenian statesman. It was Solon, then, who brought the narrative from Saïs, in Egypt, where he heard it from the priests. Already this story is five times removed from Plato. Furthermore, we have no guarantee that the entire issue wasn't created by Plato as a fictional device for his dialogue.

According to Plato's fable, whether it is true or not, the Egyptian priests explained to Solon that the Athenians' knowledge of even their own history was fragmented, distorted, and incomplete. The Athenians, it turns out, even defeated the Atlanteans in the distant past and stemmed Atlantean advancement eastward. Both Athens and Atlantis were of far greater antiquity than Solon knew. They flourished, in fact, nine thousand years before the time of Solon.

An important theme in the myth of lost knowledge of the past shows up in Plato's dialogue. If the knowledge becomes lost, something must cause that to happen. The Saïtic priests chide Solon for speaking of only one great flood in antiquity, and they point out that many natural catastrophes have occurred to bring about the near destruction of the world. The catastrophes themselves are the agents of destruction of the record of the past. Not only are continents lost but the memory of them as well.

Plato continues the story of Atlantis through the words of Critias in the dialogue that bears his name. Inconsistencies appear, particularly with respect to chronology, but Atlantis is described in more detail.

Like most origins, the beginning of Atlantis is presented in mythological terms. When the earth was divided amongst the gods, Atlantis fell to the lot of Poseidon, the god of the sea and earthquakes as well. Atlantis was already inhabited, and Poseidon lost his heart to one of the local women, named Cleito. She had just turned a marriageable age when she and Poseidon started living together. Poseidon's concern for the safety of his mortal roommate was translated into a set of concentric rings, two barriers of land and three moats of water, which he built around the hill on which they had set up house. Together Poseidon and Cleito had five sets of twins, all sons, who eventually became the ten kings of Atlantis. Poseidon divided the land among them and they ruled as a confederacy. Atlas, the eldest, was the chief of the ten, and Atlantis derives its name from him.

Many specific aspects of Atlantean culture and society are mentioned in the *Critias*. There were distinct social classes and specialization of labor. As a rival of Egypt and the proto-Athenians, Atlantis was a strong military power. Its agriculture was highly organized; irrigation and felicitous soil permitted the harvest of two crops each year. Plato's reference to "inscribed records" implies that the Atlanteans had a system of writing. The use of precious metals (gold, silver, copper, and tin) and alloys (bronze and orichalcum) was known. Furthermore, the Atlanteans worked in monumental architecture. Its megalithic construction, in white, black, and red stone, was at least comparable to what the Mycenaeans built. Surplus, leisure, and civility—this was Atlantis, a perfect example of a Bronze Age civilization.

Plato's Atlantis was actually an archipelago. Although the largest island dominated his account, his geography implied that several islands were bound and ruled by the confederacy. The hill of Cleito and Poseidon was located at the very center of what Plato called the Ancient Metropolis. There the Atlanteans had built a palace and temple to Cleito and Poseidon. The three rings of water were bridged, and a channel for ships was cut through the two inner rings of land and the land of the outer city. This reached to the outer sea, six miles from the center of the palace. By this description we may conclude that the Ancient Metropolis was a roughly circular island approximately twelve miles in diameter.

After describing the Ancient Metropolis of Atlantis, Plato's mouthpiece, Critias, informs us about the "rest of the country." It rose, he says, sheer out of the sea to a great height, and much of it was a great rectangular plain. This in turn was surrounded by mountains. The plain measured 340 miles by 227 miles, about the size of Iowa. Inconsistencies and ambiguities in the text allow us to conclude that this kingdom of Atlantis was distinct from the Ancient Metropolis already described. Because there were ten such kingdoms, we can estimate that Atlantis was roughly ten times this size, or about eight hundred thousand square miles.

In the twentieth century, extravagant claims have been made about the high level of science and technology of lost Atlantis, but from Plato's account we can conclude that Atlantis, if it existed at all, was a high Bronze Age civilization. It flourished until 9600 B.C., when it sank in a day and a night. Traditionally, Atlantis has been described as a vast continent in the Atlantic, but Plato's description allows us to regard Atlantis as a system of at least two neighboring islands.

Modern archeology tells us there were no Bronze Age civilizations twelve thousand years ago. There is no geologic evidence at all for the existence of a vast submerged continent in the Atlantic. Any theory of Atlantis must rationalize these two discrepancies. The ancient Greeks were not burdened by these insights, but many, including Aristotle, were skeptical of Plato's Atlantis.

Enthusiasm for Atlantis declined still further through the Middle Ages, but the myth was revived in the sixteenth century, after discovery of the New World. Atlantis became a convenient explanation of the puzzling existence of the rich and complex Indian civilizations in Mexico and Peru. Europeans were troubled by the presence of these culturally developed peoples and could not understand how they had managed to advance so far without benefit of European influence. The answer was, of course, Atlantis. The true source of civilization was the Atlantic island continent. Its emissaries carried art, science, and language west to the benighted Indians and east to the receptive (but not so benighted) Mediterranean peoples.

The New World was an Atlantiphile's delight. Here was an entire hemisphere filled with mysterious ruins, unfamiliar myths, and strange peoples. A resourceful interpreter could easily find at this stage, before many facts were in, ample evidence for nearly any unorthodox claim one might care to make. In 1864 Abbé Charles-Étienne Brasseur de Bourbourg even unearthed a written Mayan account of the destruction of Atlantis.

Bourbourg, a French scholar, spent a considerable part of his life in the United States. He devoted himself to study of the native Indian culture, and during the last decade of his life he departed from the conventional view. What to him were uncanny similarities between ancient Egypt and ancient Mexico could be explained by an Atlantis connection. He became convinced Atlantis was the source of both New World and Old World culture. With a list of alphabetic equivalents for the Maya glyphs, Bourbourg proceeded to translate one of the few surviving Maya codices, or illustrated manuscripts. This document, the so-called Troano Codex, was kept in Madrid. It revealed an admittedly confused chronicle of earthquake, volcanic eruption, and flood. A recurring pair of glyphs equated by Bourbourg with the letters M and U led him to read this document as a literal report of the destruction and drowning of Atlantis, which he called MU (pronounced "moo").

Actually, the Troano Codex and the Cortesianus Codex (another Maya manuscript, transported to Spain) are two halves of the same 112-page "book." Together they are now called the Tro-Cortesianus Codex. The Maya "alphabet" Bourbourg devised to translate part of this codex was based upon material reported by Fra Diego de Landa in his *Relación de las cosas de Yucatán*.

Landa began his ethnographic study of the Maya by torturing thousands of Indians; destroying idols, vases, and altars; and burning all the hieroglyphic manuscripts within his inquisitional reach. Recalled to Spain and censured for his brutal and high-handed action, Landa wrote his *Relación* as a kind of defense. Eventually he was exonerated and returned to Yucatán as bishop.

Today, Mayanists still wince at Landa's wholesale destruction of Maya writings and, ironically, depend upon his account for firsthand information of the Maya of Yucatán. We can forgive Landa in part, for his intentions were good. Human sacrifice, particularly of children, was still practiced by the Maya, and Landa was determined to obliterate the custom. He succeeded, of course, in obliterating many other customs and records as well, and we are the poorer for it.

After consigning as many Maya books to the flames as he could, Landa decided to reconstruct the writing system by interviewing native informants. The destruction of the codices didn't make his job any easier, and Landa's own erroneous preconceptions led him to believe the Maya had a phonetic alphabet.

There was no Maya alphabet, phonetic or otherwise, but Landa's assumption to the contrary prompted him to ask the wrong questions, to which he thus received the wrong answers. The ultimate product of these futile exchanges was the completely fictitious Maya "alphabet" upon which Bourbourg based his Troano translation of the scuttling of a continent. Since the time of Abbé Bourbourg we have learned to read many of the Maya glyphs, and we now know that the Tro-Cortesianus Codex is an astrological text and has nothing to do with a historical record of natural catastrophe.

Partisans of Velikovsky's close encounters of the worst kind between the earth and Venus are very taken with the intriguing myths and legends he cited in defense of his unorthodox history of the solar system's last three thousand, five hundred years. Despite Velikovsky's erratic astronomy, his supporters and curious bystanders are quick to remark that there must be some truth to the Velikovskian scenario. How else can we explain cataclysm myths from around the world? Part of the problem here is the validity of the original source material. A quick check of the "scholarly" note on page 64 of the first edition of *Worlds in Collision* reveals that Velikovsky's Maya record of cosmic catastrophe is Brasseur de Bourbourg's completely unreliable version of the Troano Codex.

The real classic of Atlantology is *Atlantis: the Antediluvian World*, published in 1882 by Ignatius Donnelly. It is hard to classify Donnelly. He was an entrepreneur, a land speculator, but the seamier side of his business activities is balanced by what seems to have been a sincerely visionary desire to create a great Midwestern metropolis in what was then the undeveloped state of Minnesota. He was active politically and at the tender age of twenty-eight was elected lieutenant governor of the state. He served in the state legislature as well, and as a U.S. Congressman for eight years. At times he practiced politics as cynically and unscrupulously as he conducted business, but his politics also reflected genuine idealism. He helped found the Populist Party and supported hopeless splinter movements. He seems to have been a genuine "amateur," one who does what he does for the sheer love of it. His enthusiasms and eccentricities are understandable in these terms. He was a peculiar combination of common sense and fancy, and these both found remarkable expression through his reconstruction of lost Atlantis.

Donnelly's views on Atlantis cannot be dismissed simply as nonsense. He approached his subject systematically, and he based his ideas upon the best data available in his day. We may have doubted Donnelly in his own day, for he oversimplified our vision of the past and answered all unanswered questions in terms of Atlantis. We can tell today, now that our knowledge of geology, archeology, and anthropology has increased, that Donnelly's answers were both unnecessary and wrong. But we cannot say that Donnelly's concept of Atlantis was trivial. On the contrary, it was grandiose and complex.

Donnelly assumed without question that Plato's tale was genuine history. Atlantis once existed—an island continent in the Atlantic, beyond the Pillars of Hercules. Donnelly's Atlantis was the mother of culture and the mother of empires. It was the site of the world's first civilization, and civilization spread from it to Europe, the Americas, and Africa. Our legacy of myths and legends is really just a garbled memory of the history of Atlantis. The ancient civilizations of Egypt and Peru were among the many colonies established by Atlantis, and Egyptian culture is the most reliable indicator of what Atlantean civilization was like. Donnelly was convinced that Atlantis sank in a tremendous natural cataclysm. The few who escaped carried the news to the Americas and to Europe, where the tradition of the submergence of Atlantis was preserved in the myths of the Deluge.

In the 1870s the H.M.S. *Challenger* discovered evidence for a vast, submerged mid-Atlantic ridge. Soundings by the U.S.S. *Dolphin* and other ships also led Donnelly to conclude that sunken Atlantis had been found. The submarine mountain range associated with the Azores was geological confirmation of the Atlantis legend (see page 276).

Donnelly bolstered his arguments for Atlantis with numerous comparisons between the Old World and the New. Fossil remains of camels, cave bears, mammoths, and musk oxen from both sides of the Atlantic were cited. Domesticated plants, including the tomato, the guava, and the banana were found in the Americas and Asia. Don-

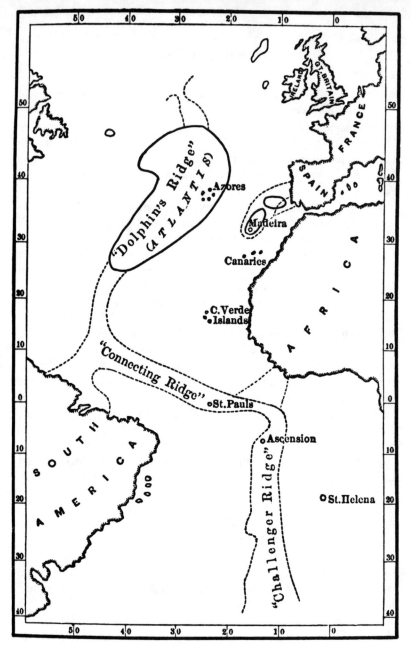

Ignatius Donnelly's Atlantis coincided with the mid-Atlantic ridge. Soundings of the sea floor topography convinced Donnelly that there was physical evidence of a sunken Atlantic continent. From Atlantis: the Antediluvian World *by Ignatius Donnelly, published by Steinerbooks, a division of Multimedia Publishing Corp.*

nelly pointed out pyramids in Mexico and Egypt. Legends and languages from both sides of the Atlantic were compared and their similarities cataloged. Only Atlantis, he explained, could account for these parallels (see below).

We now know that submarine ridges are not restricted to the mid-Atlantic, nor are they formed by sinking continents. Although some shorelands can rise and fall with relative rapidity, no known geologic cataclysm can deep-six a continent in a weekend.

Actually, the mid-Atlantic is the last place we might expect to find a sunken continent, for the land there is rising, not sinking. The ridge is a fracture line between continental plates. As the crustal plates drift upon the mantle, molten rock emerges from the fracture and builds gradually into a midoceanic ridge. Through this process the sea floor spreads and rises. Other boundaries of the plates form trenches, and there one crustal plate is forced under another and into the mantle.

We now know much more about the individual species of flora and fauna, and the comparisons that Donnelly drew, which even in his day were weak, are still less acceptable today. The few genera shared on either side of an ocean can probably be explained in terms of

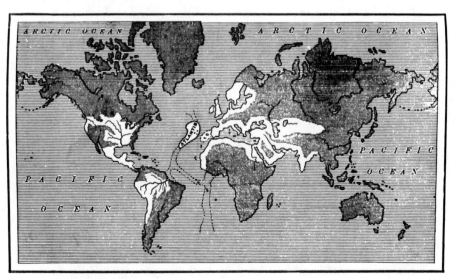

Donnelly's map of Atlantis and its empire is shown here in white. From *Atlantis: the Antediluvian World* by Ignatius Donnelly, published by Steinerbooks, a division of Multimedia Publishing Corp.

chance voyages via ocean currents. We would expect, in fact, far more similarities between Old and New worlds had there been a physical and cultural bridge between them. When considered in detail, Donnelly's arguments about cultural parallels in the calendar, religion, language, writing, and technology are also without merit. They sink like the legendary continent they were invoked to support.

Donnelly's inventory of resemblances between peoples on both sides of the Atlantic is impressive in its own way and beguiling, too. But to play this game fairly, you have to catalog the differences as you would the similarities. Transoceanic contact still emerges these days to explain some of the remaining odd parallels, but cultural diffusion from the motherland of Atlantis creates more problems than it solves. Donnelly worked hard on his vision of Atlantis. Some of the "evidence" he gathered together is interesting for its sake . . . even though his conclusions are now demonstrably wrong.

But however debatable Donnelly's ideas and evidence may have been, he tried to at least approach the problem of Atlantis scientifically. Donnelly's book was comprehensive, and it reignited interest in Atlantis. This interest is still alive today. It has taken many odd turns since Donnelly's time, however. An entire body of Atlantean lore is based upon occult tradition and intuitive knowledge. This was largely created by Madame Blavatsky, the founder of the Theosophical movement. She exploited the notions of a lost Pacific continent, Lemuria, which had already acquired some currency as an explanation of certain parallels between the New World civilizations and those in the Far East.

In *The Secret Doctrine* (1888–1938), Blavatsky fabricated an incredibly long-winded, convoluted pseudohistory of the physical and spiritual development of the human race through an elaborate sequence of sinking continents and seven Root Races, each of which had seven Subraces, which we encounter in the manner of the man who was going to St. Ives.

Although there is no evidence for a sunken land mass in the Atlantic, tenuous evidence for a long-gone Pacific land mass may exist. Most recently, Dr. David L. Jones of the U.S. Geological Survey and his collaborators attributed a forty-thousand-square-mile piece of the Pacific Northwest coast to a Pacific continent that fragmented more than 100 million years ago.

Another treatment of a lost Pacific continent has enjoyed steady public interest since 1926, when it was published by James Churchward in *The Lost Continent of Mu,* his first of five books on the subject. Churchward had been in the British army in India. He was an adventurer and had traveled widely. His books on Mu are presented as the result of archeological research, but, in fact, the sources of his information range from nonexistent tablets in India to fictitious records from discreet, unnamed monasteries of Tibet; as-yet-untranslated Easter Island inscriptions; and the ever-green Troano Codex. Churchward's "translations" of these and numerous other obscure artifacts from the past are actually arbitrary interpretations of their pictorial or symbolic content. From these he contrived a panorama of civilization on a vast Pacific continent stretching from Hawaii to the Fijis and from Easter Island to the Marianas. As early as fifty thousand years ago the civilization of Mu was superior to our own. This golden age collapsed twelve thousand years ago, however, when "rumblings from the bowels of the earth, followed by earthquakes and volcanic outbursts began to unsettle the placid land. Eventually the whole continent heaved and rolled like the ocean's waves. . . . Temples and palaces came crashing to the ground. . . . With thunderous roarings the doomed land sank. Down, down, down, she went into the mouth of hell."

Churchward had a ready explanation for the doom that came to Mu. The earth, he contended, was honeycombed with vast cavities filled with highly explosive volcanic gases. As the subterranean bubbles gradually lost their contents, the crust of the earth was weakened and Mu collapsed, a victim of geological flatulence. It is amusing, in this regard, that astrophysicist Thomas Gold of Cornell University has recently theorized that tsunamis, luminous displays associated with earthquakes, and the mysterious East Coast offshore booms may all be explained in terms of vast methane reservoirs embedded in the earth's crust at the time of the earth's formation.

A reasonably satisfying explanation of the Atlantis legend was proposed in 1947 by two Greek archeologists, professors J. Koumaris and S. Marinatos. Koumaris suggested that the Atlantis legend had originated in some local Mediterranean catastrophe. At the same meeting of the Hellenic Anthropological Society, Marinatos equated the catastrophe with the volcanic explosion of what is now the Santorini group of islands, located approximately one hundred miles north of Crete. The largest of the group is called Thera, and together all five islands are the remains of a collapsed volcanic caldera. In 1909, K. T. Frost, a British professor of classical history, had suggested that the Atlantis tale may have evolved from the relatively sudden collapse of Minoan civilization in 1500 B.C. Thirty years later, Marinatos added archeological evidence for the volcanic destruction of Crete by the explosion of Thera. Further evidence from Thera, obtained by Marinatos, by seismologist A. G. Galanopoulos, and others, lent further support to the Atlantis-as-Thera-and-Crete idea, and eventually Galanopoulos was able to demonstrate a startling conformity, in detail, between Minoan civilization and Plato's description of Atlantis and its fate. Of course, the destruction of Thera occurs about ten times too recently, and Crete and Thera are too small by about a factor of ten in comparison with Plato's description. A number of authors, from Willy Ley to Immanuel Velikovsky, have rationalized this discrepancy as a mistranslation of the ancient Egyptian symbol for 10 as that for 100.

The golden age of Atlantis, or at least of speculation about it, must still be with us. Despite the implausibility of the Thera theory, new hypotheses continue to appear.

Sometimes critics of Velikovsky's notion of worlds in collision have allowed that the myths, legends, and anecdotes he wove together may indicate some ancient catastrophe—perhaps the explosion of Thera—if not the detailed celestial scenario to which Velikovsky himself subscribes. The German engineer and pyramidologist Otto Muck twisted the idea back again and explained the destruction of a real—not legendary—Atlantis in terms of a collision between the earth and a minor planet, one of a group whose orbits cross the earth's. According to Muck, this cataclysm produced the Caroline crater field near Charleston, and the Puerto Rico Trench. Every volcano in the mid-Atlantic ridge was ignited, and Atlantis, a huge island in the vicinity of the Azores, sank in a day and a night. Muck's book, *The Secret of Atlantis*, was published posthumously and anonymously updated, and for the most part it simply resurrects the shopworn arguments Atlantiphiles have voiced since Donnelly.

Muck was willing, however, to outdo the claims of all of his predecessors by pinpointing the moment of the destruction of Atlantis to 8:00 P.M., Atlantean Standard Time, June 5, 8498 B.C. (obviously prior to enactment of Daylight Savings Time legislation). This remarkable claim is based upon the alleged starting date of the Maya calendar cycles. Muck's arithmetic and mastery of Maya calendrics leave something to be desired. The mythical starting point of the so-called Long Count is not at all a date in early June in the middle of the ninth millennium B.C. but actually in 3113 B.C., according to the Goodman-

Martinez-Thompson correlation. How Muck actually arrived at his date is not at all clear from his text.

The best-known New Atlantis now seems to be located in the Bahamas and has been associated with submerged features in the shallows off Bimini. The most famous of these underwater curiosities is the so-called Bimini Wall or Road, described as a megalithic construction that extends nineteen hundred feet in a line parallel with the shore. These large blocks were first described by Dr. J. Manson Valentine of Miami in 1969, and since that time Valentine and others have identified more examples of what they regard as ancient Bahamian ruins.

Charles Berlitz has gotten a lot of mileage out of the Bimini mysteries in a string of books on the lost continent of Atlantis, the lost knowledge of the past, and the lost travelers in the Bermuda Triangle. He has equated the discovery of the Bimini Road and other Bahamian wonders with the 1933 prediction by the American clairvoyant Edgar Cayce that ruins of an Atlantean temple might be discovered near Bimini. Berlitz maintains that sunken Atlantis and its advanced technology may account, in some way, for the alleged disappearances of planes, ships, and people in the perilous Bermuda Triangle.

The claims of Valentine and Berlitz were challenged by W. Harrison, R. J. Byrne, and M. P. Lynch, who argued that close inspection of the Bimini Road reveals it to be a natural limestone feature whose blocklike construction is a deceptive result of erosion and fracture. They further deduced that two fluted marble columns and several cylinders found underwater off Entrance Point of South Bimini are the remains of building materials transported to Bimini in the nineteenth century and lost or discarded offshore. The barrel-shaped cement cylinders probably hardened in wooden casks. Presumably these original containers for the once-dry cement rotted away.

More recently, E. A. Shinn has underscored the similarity between the Bimini Road and other "beach rock" formations. The placement of the stones of Bimini is best explained geologically. They bear no signs of human workmanship.

Finally, the rectangular structure photographed off Andros Island by Trigg Adams and Robert Brush and proclaimed to be the first rediscovered Atlantean temple of Cayce's predictions has been called a holding pen for sponges by a Nassau man who claims he helped build it over forty years ago.

Dr. David Zink, a professor of English literature, describes the Bimini Road and other alleged structures in *The Stones of Atlantis*.

Not content to regard the ruins simply as evidence of Atlantis, Zink appeals to the earth-mystery and ley-line lore associated with British prehistoric sites to demonstrate similar meaning in the Bimini stones. He has recently reported finding artifacts in the vicinity of the Road, too.

With the help of psychic archeology and some misleading (and not particularly relevant) archeoastronomy, Zink concludes that there may be a Bahamian-Atlantean spiritual link to galactic missionaries from the Pleiades. Atlantis has been shifted to the stars.

TWILIGHT OF THE GODS

Surely the great days of pseudoscience must be past; today we do not often see the likes of Charles Piazzi Smyth and his numerological mysteries of the Great Pyramid. And few in this era devote as much energy as Ignatius Donnelly did in manufacture of the lost civilization of Atlantis. These gentlemen of the old school of dubious pursuit still command a respect for the immensity of their efforts. The faint-hearted critic is routed by the sheer mass of data and verbiage. Erich von Däniken, author of *Chariots of the Gods?* and several other books on the ancient-astronaut theme, runs, by contrast, a poor second to the eccentric parascholars of the past.

It ill befits the heir apparent to be unworthy of the crown, but Erich von Däniken, in defense of the notion that earth was visited in ancient times by astronauts from another world, is superficial at best.

Von Däniken obscures the real knowledge we have of ancient people at a time when archeology is coming of age and applying sophisticated, quantitative techniques from the physical sciences. There *are* mysteries and anomalies in our past. We marvel at ancient monuments of stone and earth and find ourselves unable to sense precisely the motivations and methods of the people who built them. But evidence is accumulating that ancient and prehistoric people were more clever than we have normally assumed. Von Däniken chooses instead to invoke visits by ancient astronauts to explain a host of enigmatic artifacts and odd traditions.

The idea that the earth was visited some time in the past by space travelers from another world is not necessarily a bad one. It was discussed by others before von Däniken so successfully popularized the notion. I. S. Shklovskii, the Soviet astrophysicist, and Carl Sagan, the celebrated American astronomer, considered the idea in *Intelligent Life in the Universe* (1966). The hypothesis is very difficult to prove. The "evidence" is equivocal and can be interpreted in many ways.

What makes von Däniken's treatment distinctive is his filtration of the facts. The residue is designed to convince the reader that only von Däniken's interpretation will work. His books are comprehensive examples of spurious reasoning. Most of the classic fallacies are invoked.

Despite the fact that other authors have shown most of von Däniken's interpretations to be sheer nonsense based upon incomplete understanding of the archeological material in question, von Däniken still brandishes some of the same mysterious artifacts six books later. In *Von Däniken's Proof*, his most recent effort, the "astronaut" at Palenque, a Mayan site in Mexico, is paraded as incontrovertible evidence of space visitors among the Maya in the seventh century A.D.

Conventional interpretation of what is depicted on the sarcophagus cover in Palenque's Temple of the Inscriptions (see page 284) has evolved considerably in the last few years. Von Däniken seems to take a mischievous delight in the fact that archeologists have been changing their minds about this spectacular relief. This does not, however, mean that archeologists are any closer to accepting the idea that the carving shows a man dressed for space travel and piloting a rocket; on the contrary, the funereal and religious content of the design is understood better than ever.

We should not be at all surprised that we now know much more about the meaning of the carving at Palenque. During the last two decades considerable progress has been made in the decipherment of Mayan glyphs, and we now realize through the work of Tatiana Proskouriakoff, David Kelley, Peter Mathews, John Graham, and others that the glyphs on stelae and walls contain a considerable amount of historical information. It is becoming possible to reconstruct the succession of rulers at Palenque, and now we even know the name of the so-called astronaut: Pacal.

Pacal's name means "shield." He was king at Palenque from A.D. 615 until he died in A.D. 683. The twelve-foot-long sarcophagus cover symbolically shows the death of Pacal.

The Temple of the Inscriptions sits atop a pyramidal platform seventy-five feet high. The pyramid consists of eight steps, or terraces, and Pacal, like a pharaoh of Egypt's Old Kingdom, was buried in a crypt deep within.

Von Däniken's "astronaut" is actually the dead Pacal (see page 285). Linda Schele, a Mayanist who has played an important role in the

The celebrated Palenque "astronaut" is located in a burial chamber deep within the Temple of the Inscriptions (right, foreground). Photograph by Linda Mac-Safan.

decipherment of hieroglyphic inscriptions at Palenque, has noted that Pacal is shown falling. Just below him is the face of a monster, and Pacal and the monster are together entering the stylized reptilian jaws of the underworld, the realm of the dead.

There is little room for von Däniken's ancient-astronaut hypothesis here, for we can identify the monster that accompanies Pacal. At the Temple of the Inscriptions, as well as at the Temple of the Cross, this face is accompanied by the same symbolic elements. Among these is the *kin* glyph, which means "sun," "time," and "day." At both temples the monster's upper face is fleshed, while the lower face is skeletal, implying that the monster is passing from life to death—falling, like Pacal, into the underworld. In fact, at the Temple of the Cross, emblems for the night appear on one side of the monster and symbols for the day on the other. Schele concludes on the basis of this and evi-

The relief on the sarcophagus at Palenque depicts not an astronaut but a Maya king, Pacal, as he falls from life into the realm of the dead. Drawing by Agustín Villagra, from *The Civilization of the Ancient Maya,* by Alberto Ruz Lhuillier, 1970. Courtesy Instituto Nacional de Antropologia e Historia, Cordoba, Mexico.

dence from other sites that the monster is the sun and that it is shown at Palenque at its moments of death: sunset and the winter solstice, when the sun follows its lowest arc through the sky.

Schele also reports that the winter solstice sun appears to sink behind a ridge—that is, enters the earth—when viewed from the Palenque tower. The setting sun actually appears above the Temple of the Inscriptions, and its path follows the angle of the stone stairway that leads into Pacal's tomb. On the same day a spot of sunlight strikes the Temple of the Cross, and the last of this light falls at the feet of the god of the underworld carved at the sanctuary entrance.

There is a celestial content in the symbolism of the temples at Palenque, but it does not involve a portrayal of a literal voyage in outer space. We see instead the funerary monument of a strong king and the temples that commemorated his son's accession to the throne. The cycle of life and death and the succession of kings were linked allegorically to the sun. The sun even "entered" the underworld through Pacal's tomb. Several lines of evidence converge to indicate the same interpretation, and von Däniken's astronaut is squeezed out.

Von Däniken obviously regards the Palenque sarcophagus as one of his best pieces of evidence. It is one of the few antiquities he actually includes in *Von Däniken's Proof* (which contrasts markedly with his earlier books). In *Chariots of the Gods?*, *Gods from Outer Space*, *The Gold of the Gods*, and *In Search of Ancient Gods*, the reader is propelled past numerous prehistoric puzzles and ancient mysteries. There is little respite from the barrage of paragraphs and pictures. Von Däniken's fifth book, *Miracles of the Gods*, is not really about ancient astronauts at all but about religious visions, and it too is packed with examples and case histories. *Von Däniken's Proof*, however, spends little time on archeological anomalies.

Von Däniken's Proof is intended to be its author's answer to his critics. Because the critics have challenged von Däniken's faulty logic so well and have taken him so explicitly to task for factual errors, it is just as well for von Däniken that his latest book avoids the kind of material that gets him into so much trouble. Without this component, however, the ancient-astronaut hypothesis loses much of its romance. As a result, *Von Däniken's Proof* is rather colorless and thin in comparison with its predecessors.

Von Däniken constructs his most recent book around the literary device of a trial in a court of law. He portrays himself as the defendant and his readers, of course, as the jury. Neither von Däniken nor his critics would deny that there are unsolved mysteries of the past. The problem here is interpretation. Von Däniken's basic premise—that the earth was visited in ancient and prehistoric times by astronauts from outer space—cannot be disproved. Proving a negative hypothesis like this is simply impossible. How could one demonstrate that ancient astronauts have never been here? Experts and skeptical bystanders, however, are under no obligation to provide such proof. It is von Däniken, after all, who has advanced the idea that astronauts came to earth, created intelligent human beings in their image through genetic manipulation, and left evidence of their presence in religion, myth, legend, and artifact. It is up to him to prove this happened.

Circumstantial evidence may be admissible in a court of law, and von Däniken argues that he is permitted to summon circumstantial evidence in support of his notions. Science, however, is not conducted in a court of law. It requires more rigorous demonstration of the truth of a theory. Even if von Däniken's circumstantial evidence were favorable, it would show only that ancient astronauts *could* have come to earth, not that they did. The possibility of prehistoric space travelers is not the issue here. We are looking for evidence instead that they did actually come. In this regard von Däniken's arguments are singularly disappointing.

Von Däniken's Proof includes a lengthy and somewhat pedestrian evaluation of the plausibility of interstellar travel. Von Däniken sets up his critics as figures of straw. They are, he says, unable to realize that interstellar communication and transportation are possible, and he then proceeds to parrot the words of experts in these areas to prove this is so. Ironically, some of the authorities he cites are among the critics he is challenging. He knocks down the straw men with ease and emerges as the victor. The victory, however, is insignificant. Astronomers and space scientists do not say that interstellar travel is impossible. On the contrary, they are well aware of the accelerated technology that already has shown us, in a few short years, more details about our planetary neighbors than we could have imagined just a few decades ago. Contrary to von Däniken's claims, the skeptics are not silenced by his defense of the possibility of interstellar travel; they simply do not see any proof that interstellar travelers actually came, nor do they see any point in echoing von Däniken's echo of their own studies.

Another lengthy chapter of *Von Däniken's Proof* disputes Darwinian evolution and argues that life on earth is a result of direct intervention by "astronaut-gods." This chapter is a bit of a puzzle, however, for much of it is devoted to the very origin of life, in the Precambrian era more than 3.5 billion years ago. Admittedly, it is very difficult to reconstruct exactly how life did first appear, and even scientists sometimes indulge in what paleobiologist and expert on the Precambrian period Dr. J. William Schopf calls "bio-geopoetry." It is still possible, however, to find clues in the fossil evidence, and just such painstaking search is under way.

Why von Däniken spends so much time on the controversies surrounding the origin of life is not clear at first. In the past he has claimed that astronaut intervention came late, long after hominids evolved. The early apes were the beneficiaries of selective breeding and genetic mutation, and human beings with human intelligence were the result. This notion is at odds with evolution, however, and von Däniken is eager to strike a creationist blow at any point on the evolutionary tree, whether the implications are at odds with his original hypothesis or not. For example, he is perfectly happy to introduce the so-called fossil human footprints into the conversation simply for the sake of confounding his opposition. These footprints are allegedly found in a variety of geological strata, corresponding to Cretaceous times (140 million years ago), Permian times (250 million years ago), and Cambrian times (400 million years ago).

One set of these "human footprints" is preserved in the ancient bed of the Paluxy River near Glen Rose, Texas, allegedly in association with dinosaur tracks. This is curious, to be sure, but is hardly relevant to ancient astronauts. A reliable scientific report is not yet available for the Paluxy footprints, and the possibility of forgery or misinterpretation is still very real. One famous set of "human" footprints found in Pliocene sandstone near Carson, Nevada, at the end of the last century was subsequently shown to be tracks left by a giant ground sloth.

There have been by now at least seventy books on the ancient-astronaut theme published in English. In addition, about a half-dozen novels have been based on the same premise. A magazine, *Ancient Astronauts*, appears on the newsstand nine times a year, and several motion pictures and television programs have exploited the public's interest in von Däniken's "chariots of the gods." As mentioned earlier, von Däniken wasn't the first to propose the idea of ancient astronauts. In addition to Shklovskii, George Hunt Williamson and Brinsley LePoer Trench anticipated von Däniken by nearly a decade. But most of the other commentators have followed in von Däniken's wake, and few have had his audacity and flair. Some of the second-generation chariotmongers have made such imaginative contributions to the legend that von Däniken quotes them in *Von Däniken's Proof.*

Karl Brugger is a German journalist living in Brazil and the author of *The Chronicle of Akakor.* The *Chronicle* is well known to von Däniken—he wrote the brief preface to it—and *The Chronicle of Akakor* dovetails nicely with von Däniken's own speculations about the astronaut-gods.

According to Brugger, his book is actually a transcription of twelve tapes he made in his air-conditioned hotel room in Manaus, Brazil, of the narrative of a white Indian chieftain, Tatunca Nara. Nara is said to be the last legitimate prince of an Amazonian tribe known as the Ugha Mongulala. Their epic, as recited by Nara, begins in 13,000 B.C. with the appearance of several shining, golden ships in the sky accompanied by blasts of fire and thunder. It transpires that these celestial visitors come from a distant world known as Schwerta, and their mission is to bring culture and knowledge to the people of other planets.

Certain families were chosen by the strangers from the stars. These became the Ugha Mongulala, the "Allied Chosen Tribes." Their history is a pageant of empire and catastrophe. Their capital, Akakor (hence the "chronicle of Akakor"), is alleged to exist still in the upper Amazon, on the east flank of the Andes, between Machu Picchu and Tiahuanaco.

Much of Akakor is underground, and its inhabitants live in its subterranean dwellings. Aboveground, Akakor lies in ruins, but it was destroyed only as recently as 1969, and Nara claims that he, with the support of the supreme council and the priests, ordered the city destroyed lest it betray its inhabitants' presence to outsiders.

In *The Gold of the Gods,* von Däniken claimed to have visited a vast network of Ecuadorian tunnels and caves, and he links them, in his preface to Brugger's book, with the subterranean chambers of Akakor. Juan Moricz, the discoverer of von Däniken's Ecuadorian caves, denied von Däniken's claim that he had taken von Däniken through the caves. In an interview, von Däniken subsequently admitted that he had contrived his account of the caves and what he allegedly saw in them for "theatrical effect," yet two years later in Brugger's book he unblushingly refers to his caves.

But if von Däniken cannot stand in the company of Charles Piazzi Smyth and Ignatius Donnelly, certainly Robert K. G. Temple, author of *The Sirius Mystery,* can. His book bears all the trappings of scholarship: footnotes, obscure references, highly convoluted arguments, and impenetrable detail. Temple must mean business. His book revolves around, but is not limited to, a genuine and interesting mystery: the Dogon tradition of the star Sirius. Von Däniken had the sense to realize the potential impact of Temple's report; in fact, he says he was "electrified" by it. A lengthy segment of *Von Däniken's Proof* is allotted to it.

The Dogon live in the mountainous country south of Timbuctu in what was once the French Sudan and is known now as the Republic of Mali. Over the centuries this African tribe has felt the influence of both Christianity and Islam, but its preservation of its own unique traditions and its elaborate mythology, which differ from most other African beliefs, has made these people well known to ethnographers.

Two French anthropologists, Marcel Griaule and Germaine Dieterlen, collected Dogon beliefs from native informants in the 1940s. Some of this material is astronomical in content. In particular the star Sirius, in Dogon tradition, has a dark, dense, unseen companion.

After the sun, Sirius is the brightest-appearing star in the sky. Although it is about 8.7 light-years (or nearly 52 trillion miles) away, it is a fairly nearby star . . . as stars go. We know quite a bit about Sirius through modern astronomical analysis. It is considerably hotter and brighter than our own sun and twice as massive. Careful measurements of its position over many decades permitted astronomers to detect a gradual shift in the star's location. This movement is due to the difference in velocity between Sirius and our own solar system. The motion would normally show up, if plotted on a map of the sky, as continuous displacement in some direction. Sirius, however, wiggles as it moves. This oscillation to either side of the expected line of motion led Friedrich Bessel, a German astronomer, to conclude, in 1844, that Sirius shares its movement with an unseen companion. Each orbits about the other and completes a cycle in 49.9 years. The slight wiggle in the motion of Sirius is due, then, to the gravitational attraction of another star. In 1862, Alvan Clark, an American telescope maker, was the first actually to see the faint companion. Sirius B, as the companion is called, turns out to be a white dwarf. It is quite small, about the diameter of the earth, yet it contains about as much material as the sun. The star is therefore extremely dense. A cupful would weigh twelve tons (twelve tons in a teacup is a notion that would certainly qualify for the Mad Hatter's Tea Party).

As Temple reports it, the Dogon knowledge of Sirius is quite detailed and accurate. As we have seen, they, as we do, associate an unseen companion with Sirius. This companion the Dogon call *po tolo* (*tolo* = "star"; *po* = the Dogon name for the cereal grain of *Digitaria exilis*, or fonio, an indigenous African food crop). The smallest grain known to the Dogon is the po grain, and presumably the star is given the same name because it is so small as to be invisible. Po tolo is said to be made of the heaviest metal known, heavier even than iron. To Temple this implies Dogon knowledge of the highly dense state of Sirius B.

The Dogon draw many ceremonial pictures of the system of Sirius, and these, Temple claims, indicate an understanding that the orbit of Sirius B around Sirius A is elliptical, with Sirius A located at one focus. The period of this orbit, according to the Dogon, is fifty years. Temple even constructs a diagram of the wiggling paths of Sirius and po tolo and notes a striking similarity with the same sort of diagram obtained by modern astronomers for Sirius A and B.

Dogon astronomical traditions are by no means restricted to Sirius. They say that Jupiter has four moons and that Saturn has a halo (or ring), and their drawings of these two planets show these features unambiguously.

Of course, taken at face value the Dogon beliefs are quite amazing, and Temple loses no time in his search for the origin of Dogon belief. He traces these traditions back across the Sahara to Libya and ultimately the Mediterranean world of Greece and Egypt. The Egyptian preoccupation with the star Sirius is well documented.

It is not at all clear, however, that Egyptian mythology includes the same ideas about Sirius as are found among the Dogon. A large part of *The Sirius Mystery* is therefore devoted to construction of a tenuous bridge of interpretation of myth. Much of this involves the epic of the Argonauts, the representations of legendary figures among the stars as constellations, and the possible existence of ancient systems of geodetic placement of oracle centers based upon celestial mapping. A parallel is drawn as well to the Babylonian legend of Oannes, a fish–human hybrid credited with bringing culture and civilization to Mesopotamia.

Oannes is identified with the Sumerian god Ea and so is part of a very old tradition. The Dogon claim that the arts and sciences were brought to humanity by amphibious, fishlike creatures they associated with Sirius. Temple believes these two traditions are reflections of the same event: a landing of amphibious extraterrestrial astronauts in ancient times from a planet in the Sirius system.

All of this is fascinating, and there is much in Temple's discussions of mythology and "secret" lore that is probably worth pursuing, but the myth interpretation game can be played several different ways. What Temple seems to have going for his version is the unsettling astronomical knowledge of the Dogon. His case is not as straightforward as it might seem, however.

We need not necessarily believe that Dogon astronomical traditions are very ancient and uncontaminated by outside influence. The Dogon have, in fact, long been a relatively cosmopolitan, adaptive people. They live in the general vicinity of Timbuctu, which for centuries has been a major market city and a center for schools and scholars in west Africa. The Dogon have enjoyed regular communication with other cultures because they live so near a major trade route linking North Africa and Egypt with the sub-Sahara. In fact, French schools existed in the Dogon territory as early as 1907 and well before the 1920s, when there was considerable European interest in Sirius and research on its companion.

We cannot be certain that recent outside influence is what injected such curious detail into the Dogon ideas about Sirius, but these ideas themselves are not as unambiguous as Temple claims. The Dogon do not really say Sirius B has an orbital period of fifty years. This is inferred from a less direct statement, and adding to the complication is the fact that one Dogon calendar cycle, allegedly based upon the movement of Sirius B, lasts sixty years, not fifty.

Peter and Roland Pesch have argued that the concept of twinness is so important in Dogon religion that any ritually important star would be said to have a companion. They point out, in fact, that Polaris, which, like Sirius, is important to the Dogon, is said to have a companion.

The alleged elliptical orbit of Sirius B is regarded by the Pesches as a boundary rather than a path of motion, for numerous other Dogon diagrams of the Sirius system include so many additional elements that it is impossible to think of the picture as a drawing of the orbit of a binary star (see page 293).

The Dogon also say that Sirius has a second companion, which they call *emme ya*. The information they supposedly provide on the orbit of emme ya is inconsistent with itself as well as with Kepler's laws. Furthermore, there is no observational evidence for a third

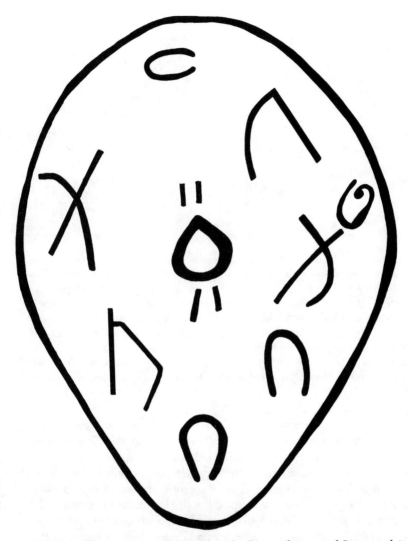

Although it is tempting to believe that the Dogon diagram of Sirius and its "companion" accurately reflects the basic orbital data of the system, Dogon tradition is far more complex than we might first guess. The Dogon draw other pictures of Sirius, like this one, and we must contend with the ambiguities of style and content in them. Here a variety of symbols of creation and birth are mixed in with the alleged stellar components. Courtesy Griffith Observatory, drawing after Marcel Griaule and Germaine Dieterlen, A *Sudanese Sirius System.*

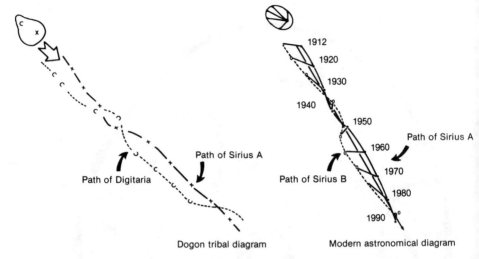

In The Sirius Mystery, *Robert Temple compares the Dogon tradition of Sirius with modern astronomical information by constructing a so-called Dogon Tribal Diagram. The obvious resemblance to a modern plot of the wiggling proper motions of Sirius and its companion is striking. This redrawing of Temple's diagram (with slight modification) should not be taken at face value, however. The Dogon draw nothing like the picture on the left, and its construction is highly subjective. A casual reader might conclude, however, that there must be something to the Sirius mystery because the two drawings agree so well.* Courtesy Griffith Observatory, drawing after Robert K. G. Temple, The Sirius Mystery.

member of the Sirius system. For that matter, Jupiter has at least fourteen, perhaps fifteen, satellites, and not four, as the Dogon draw. And Saturn is the outermost planet of which they speak. Surely extraterrestrials would have briefed them on Uranus, Neptune, and Pluto.

Temple's diagram (Figure 10) of the proper motion of the Sirius-po system is very misleading. Despite the disclaimer in his caption, he labels this design, which looks so much like what contemporary astronomers have actually observed, as a "Dogon Tribal Diagram." It is nothing of the sort. The Dogon draw nothing like it.

Temple's enthusiasm led him to ask Isaac Asimov to read his manuscript in advance of publication. Presumably it was Temple's hope to elicit some favorable comment that could be used to promote the book. Asimov was not impressed, and he declined comment. On the telephone, Temple continued to press Asimov for some comment and finally asked him if he had detected any errors. Asimov replied, "No, I did not detect any errors." Later, Asimov explained that he knew next to nothing about the Dogon and wouldn't have recognized an error had there been any. Press releases and advertisements for *The Sirius Mystery* carried the following endorsement:

> "I couldn't find any mistakes in this book. That in itself is extraordinary."
>
> —Isaac Asimov

Asimov objected, however, and the endorsement was removed from further use.

It is fair to argue that Dogon contact with modern European astronomy probably cannot account entirely for the Sirius mystery. W. H. McCrea, a renowned British astronomer, has proposed a clever alternative that may resolve some of the difficulties, however. McCrea agrees that Dogon interest in Sirius is probably traceable to ancient Egypt. The Egyptians calibrated their calendar with the heliacal, or first predawn, rising of Sirius, after its annual seventy-day disappearance from the night sky.

Later in the year, Sirius set heliacally, just before its seventy-day banishment, and McCrea supposes that a mirage of Sirius could have been produced at heliacal setting, after sunset. This second image of Sirius would appear below the actual star and might suggest to observers, who would have seen it only occasionally, that it was an elusive, dark, and heavy companion.

It is hard to tell how seriously we need take the Dogon mystery. Certainly they tell an interesting tale. Ancient astronauts need not be the answer, however. In any case, *Von Däniken's Proof* takes full advantage of the "Sirius mystery." But of course nothing in the Dogon legend suggests that they had contact with Brugger's Akakorian founders. Similarly, other pieces of evidence von Däniken cites are mutually exclusive.

However we may fault von Däniken or Donnelly or Piazzi Smyth, we cannot fault the urge that prompts us all to marvel at the mysteries they bring to our attention. These memories of our missing past evoke wonder and nostalgia. We love to encounter riddles, and we enjoy best those answers that only prompt more conundrums. The mystery of the past is a mirror. We look upon it and see only our own blank stare, and we are entranced by the lack of self-recognition.

17

The Bermuda Triangle

LARRY KUSCHE

A *theme threading its way through many of these essays is the faulty and sensationalistic coverage of paranormal subjects in the media. It doesn't occur to most of us to doubt alleged statements of fact in print in newspapers or in books, or presented in television news or documentaries. We are too trusting. Even prestigious newspapers or news commentators typically sensationalize their coverage of the paranormal, and in numerous instances we can document deliberate, outright false reporting. For some paranormal topics the only "explanation" necessary is, "We've been lied to."*

The "Bermuda Triangle" is an excellent example. When examined carefully, it is reducible to a media hoax. Could it really be true that all those mysterious incidents, so elaborately described on film and in books, never really happened, or happened much differently from the ways we've been told? Could it really be true that all those magazine articles, movies, publishing houses, and book authors have deliberately built upon each other's fictions to create a story where nothing unusual really ever happened? It could be and is true.

Larry Kusche's 1975 book on the Triangle is the best source for descriptions of the episodes as they really happened—or didn't happen.

In this essay, Kusche tells how the Triangle hoax was originally created and follows an example of an alleged Bermuda Triangle mystery through several sources in a process of increasing distortion and fabrication.

Just as von Däniken's thesis of extraterrestrial intervention is an insult to the intelligence and ingenuity of early mankind, so too is the frequent reliance upon "paranormal" explanations an insult to man's finely developed abilities to use his "normal" senses. Nowhere is the reliance upon the paranormal or on "forces beyond science as we now know it" more atrocious than in the case of the Bermuda Triangle. The Triangle is the ultimate example of the paranormal, pseudoscience, fictional science, and the media run amok. It is the epitome of false reporting; deletion of pertinent information; twisted values among writers, publishers, and the media; mangling of scientific principles; and the often deliberate deception of a trusting public. Strong words, and possibly offensive, but true nevertheless.

The most common misconception about the Bermuda Triangle is that the losses reported in support of its supposed mysteries are descriptions of occurrences that are taking place "out there," and that while the interpretation of the causes may vary, while it may be debatable whether paranormal explanations are required, we *do know* that something unusual definitely is happening out there; the only question is the explanation for it all. That complete line of reasoning is false. The Bermuda Triangle as a place where strange disappearances occur exists only on paper and film. It is "documented" and supported solely by poorly researched information, hearsay, errors, and illogic. The Triangle is supposedly a mental exercise for people who claim to want to "stretch their minds" by delving into the paranormal. The true explanation is much more of a mind stretcher than any of the paranormal, pseudoscientific explanations.

The best way to see how the Triangle illusion was created is to look closely at two of the mysteries I investigated while working on my book *The Bermuda Triangle Mystery—Solved* (1975), which has been acknowledged as the most authoritative work on the subject by Lloyd's of London, the U.S. Coast Guard, and many other reputable organizations and scientists. Any of some sixty-five or so other cases in the book might just as well have been looked at.

When I began writing about the Triangle in 1972 I had already collected the many magazine and newspaper articles and book chapters that had made the Triangle something of an underground topic at the time. According to all these articles, sailors had been talking about the Triangle since the days of Columbus, about how ships sailed away into perfectly calm weather and simply vanished without a trace. The writers said it might all be explained away by coincidence, but there were too many strange cases that were documented. It was asserted that all the usual explanations—storms, mechanical failure, and human error—fell short of solving the mystery. The navy, the Coast Guard, Lloyd's of London, and top scientists who had investigated the losses were also said to be baffled.

The evidence supporting a phenomenon that was "beyond being solved by science as we now know it" consisted mainly of a long list of supposedly mysterious disappearances of ships, planes, and crews. When I began my book I had no idea what I might find, or where my research might lead. I had no thoughts of trying to solve the mystery, but only to report everything I could find about it.

The sources of Triangle information most referred to in 1972 were two pieces by freelance writer Vincent Gaddis. His article "The Deadly Bermuda Triangle" had appeared in the February 1964 issue of *Argosy*, the men's adventure magazine. The next year the article, slightly revised and expanded, became Chapter 13, "The Triangle of Death," in his book *Invisible Horizons*. It was obvious from the similarity of wording and incidents covered that many, if not most, of the later writers lifted their information from Gaddis. The incidents he discussed became the core of the mystery.

One of the first incidents I researched was the case of the *Suduffco*, a freighter that in 1926, according to Gaddis, had "sailed south from Port Newark [New Jersey] into the limbo of the lost with her crew of twenty-nine men." That was it. The entire mystery was a one-liner. Its brevity made me wonder how much investigating Gaddis had actually done. I wondered if the incident was really mysterious or if there was merely a lack of information—some people confuse the two. I noticed that the same brief information was given by several other writers who apparently had used Gaddis as their source and had not bothered to check further. The level of investigative curiosity already seemed to be appallingly low.

Information on the ship came quite easily. The *New York Times*, which has excellent coverage of shipping disasters, had five relevant articles. The first one revealed that company officials had failed to ask the navy to search for the *Suduffco* until it had not been heard from for three and one-half weeks. The last line of the article was, "The *Suduffco* was proceeding down the coast at a time when the coast was swept by storms." But neither Gaddis nor the other writers had mentioned a storm. The remaining articles reported the lack of progress of the search and that the ship had finally been given up for lost early in May. I also found an article about the ocean liner *Aquitania*, which had been approaching New York as the *Suduffco* was leaving. The captain reported that the voyage had been made in the worst seas he had ever seen and that "gales like tropical cyclones" had held the ship back.

My conclusion was that the *Suduffco*, as an inexplicable mystery of the Bermuda Triangle, was the product of sloppy research.

Early in my research I discovered a then little-known 1969 paperback, *Limbo of the Lost*, by John Wallace Spencer. As I examined the book it seemed to me that in case after case much of it consisted of reworded, condensed articles from the *New York Times*. (In one part of Spencer's account of the *Suduffco* a sentence of twenty-two words was exactly the same except for a change of verb tense.) Yet the most crucial sentence from the *Times* was not in Spencer's book: "The *Suduffco* was proceeding down the coast at a time when the coast was swept by storms." The same kind of omission occurred with several other incidents he reported as mysterious.

In the fall of 1974, six months after I finished my manuscript but six months before the book was published (the longest year of my life), two other books on the subject appeared. Both Richard Winer's *The Devil's Triangle* and Charles Berlitz's *The Bermuda Triangle* mentioned the *Suduffco* as an unsolved mystery. From the wording it appears that Winer got his information from the *New York Times* and that Berlitz used Gaddis. Neither one mentioned the storm. The omission of this crucial information by Gaddis, Spencer, Winer, Berlitz, and other writers had to be the result of negligent research at best. In my research into other incidents I found this same pattern of poor research followed by *all* the authors who had written about the subject as a mystery.

Perhaps the best example of what various writers can do with a given "original" piece of information that is not even known to be credible in the first place is demonstrated by the case of the *Ellen Austin*, one of the staple stories of the Triangle. The origin of the story for most of the writers, whether they know it or not, is a 1914 book called *The Stargazer Talks*, by Rupert Gould. His *complete* account is:

> Last, and queerest of all, comes the case of the abandoned derelict, in seaworthy condition, which the British ship *Ellen Austin* encountered, in mid-Atlantic, in the year 1881. She put a small prize-crew on board the stranger, with instructions to make for St. John's, Newfoundland, where she was bound herself. The two ships parted company in foggy weather but a few days later they met again. And the strange derelict was once more deserted. Like their predecessors, the prize-crew had vanished forever.

Gould, unfortunately, did not let his readers know where he got his information. For the sake of comparisons with later articles, the basic information in Gould's article is:

Word count: 86.
Location: Mid-Atlantic.
Date: 1881.
Condition of derelict: Seaworthy.
Parting of ships caused by: Foggy weather.
Second discovery: The ships met again a few days later and the strange derelict was again deserted.
Ultimate fate of the derelict: Not mentioned.

The story next appeared in the article and book by Vincent Gaddis, who gave Gould as his source of information (in the book). The synopsis of Gaddis's 1964 article is:

Word count: 115.
Location: West of the Azores.
Date: 1881.
Condition of derelict: Everything in order, and there was evidence of a struggle.
Parting of ships caused by: A squall.
Second discovery: Schooner was deserted. The new crew had vanished.
Ultimate fate: After a second salvage crew was persuaded to go on the derelict, another squall separated the ships. The schooner and its crew were never seen again.

The account in Gaddis's book, published a year later, differs from his article, and from Gould, his supposed source of information.

Word count: 188.
Location: Mid-Atlantic.
Date: 1881.
Condition of derelict: Seaworthy, everything in order, nothing missing, no sign of a struggle.
Parting of ships caused by: Foggy weather.
Second discovery: The captain, sighting the derelict two days later, after the fog had cleared, astonished to see it sailing an erratic course, ordered the helmsman to approach it. Following a lack of a response to signals, a boarding party searched every foot of the strange ship but found no clue to the fate of the missing men.
Ultimate fate: None of the remaining sailors of the *Ellen Austin* could be persuaded to board the derelict again. It was left behind and was last seen sinking below the horizon as the *Austin* sailed away.

Gaddis's two versions of the story differ considerably. His book version is more than twice as long as the Gould account, his reported source, mostly because of descriptive embellishments. We are told of the captain's astonishment, the derelict pursuing an erratic course, the captain ordering the helmsman, signaling the ship, and searching every foot of it. All this is certainly logical and may well have happened (if the incident did happen at all), but it is unfair for any writer to supply such descriptive details that do not exist in the work he cites as his source.

There are several important differences between Gaddis's two accounts, including the location, although in the book he reverts back to Gould and calls it the mid-Atlantic. The article had "evidence of a struggle," while the book has "no sign of a struggle." This may have been caused by a printer's leaving the word *no* out of the article, so the contradiction is not necessarily Gaddis's fault. However, Gould's only reference to the condition of the schooner was that it was seaworthy. Gaddis had no basis whatsoever to make *any* statement about the sign or the lack of signs of a struggle. He had no evidence for either case. Any statement about a struggle leads the reader to believe that Gaddis possessed more information than he really did.

The contradictions between the two versions about the condition of the ships' parting and the number of salvage crews are indications of poor, hasty research, and low credibility, but I also object to the fictionalization, such as the description of the captain's astonishment and other details that were not in Gould. If that seems picky, let's examine the next account of the incident.

In 1970's *Invisible Residents*, Ivan Sanderson specified having used the Gaddis and Gould books as his sources of information for the *Ellen Austin*. Again, I summarize:

Word count: Description of incident, 242. Analysis, 187. Total, 429.

Location: In the North Atlantic.

Date: 1881.

Condition of derelict: No one was aboard, everything else was in perfect order. The ship was well found, with ample food and water and no sign of violence or accident. The rudder was lashed, the ship had gotten below the wind, and it was pursuing an erratic course in light winds. The shrouds were loosened. The captain bespoke the schooner, received no answer, sent a boarding party over, and decided to attempt salvage with a prize crew.

Parting of ships caused by: A dense fog as they headed for Newfoundland.

Second discovery: Nearly two full days later, when the fog cleared, the schooner was seen performing erratically. Again, it was deserted, everything in perfect order. The rig had been repaired and the sails were set.

Ultimate fate: The remaining crewmen refused to go aboard the schooner and it was left behind.

In his analysis of the incident, Sanderson reported that piracy, barratry (fraudulent ship loss, usually for insurance), or the men of the *Ellen Austin* were probably not involved; that the ship's papers were not found after the first discovery and that a temporary log begun by the salvage crew was either lost or not picked up, and was not *further* mentioned. (The word *further* implies that it once was mentioned. He does not say where.) Sanderson suggested that the incident might be a myth or that the prize crew never existed, or were murdered, but then writes that *their names are on record* (he doesn't say where), and it was unlikely that the remaining men could have carried off a crime and not had someone crack under cross-examination. (He does not give the details of their supposed questioning or where the record of it is supposedly available.) At this point please read again Gould's version, recalling that it is the direct source, and indirect one through Gaddis, of Sanderson's information. Then ask yourself where all the other "information" that Sanderson gave his readers could have come from.

The story of the *Ellen Austin* also appeared in Charles Berlitz's 1974 book *The Bermuda Triangle*. He lists the Gaddis and Sanderson books in his general bibliography but does not say specifically where he took his information for the *Ellen Austin*, although it is obviously the Gaddis article, which he did not list. He also did not list the Gould book, which, apparently unknown to him, is actually the "first" source of information.

Word count: 172.

Location: West of the Azores.

Date: 1881.

Condition of derelict: Abandoned, shipshape, sails furled, rigging intact.

Parting of ships caused by: A sudden squall.

Second discovery: Two days later it was sighted again and boarded, the prize crew had vanished, with no indication why or where they had gone. Berlitz further tells us that the captain was persistent, the crew reticent, but that he finally convinced a second prize crew to go aboard.

Ultimate fate: Another squall hit, contact was lost, and neither the schooner nor the second crew were ever seen again. Berlitz never did tell his readers the destination of the ship.

Thus can be seen a vivid example of how stories grow, of pseudoscience being created by writers. Details such as Sanderson's account of the captain's actions, the loosened shrouds and the repaired rigging, the imaginary fuss over the log book make it look as if the author must really have done in-depth research. How many of the readers, after hearing all the fine detail, would ask the ultimate questions: Did any of this *really* happen at all? How much does the author really *know*, and how much is fiction?

There is a prevalent myth that writers who explore "the fringes of science," speculating on the paranormal, delving where establishment scientists supposedly fear to tread, are the pace setters, the pioneers who boldly blaze the trails that the stodgy establishment will someday reluctantly follow. I heartily disagree. I find that writers of this sort, contrary to popular opinion and their own self-imagery, *retard* the advance of science, or at least the public's knowledge of the advance of science, by cluttering the field with illogic, erroneous information, and public bad will. I see no curiosity or thorough inquiry among them, only rampant gullibility and carelessness. They are the purveyors of hard-core pseudoscience at its very worst.

Where, I wondered, is the writer who is curious enough about the *Ellen Austin* and the other incidents to do some *good* research, to attempt to find contemporary accounts of what actually happened? Where is the writer who has enough respect for the public's intelligence to tell them the truth? I wanted to know the "real truth," and set out to find it myself.

Before beginning my research I analyzed Gould's version of the story, from which the others had descended. I suspected that either his source or his reporting was not good, or the reported date would have been more precise. A crucial factor that no one else had paid any attention to was the reported location of the incident—the mid-Atlantic. That is at least one thousand miles east of Bermuda. Anyone who would write that the incident had occurred in or even near the Triangle was either very careless or had assumed that his readers were careless and would not take the trouble to find the location on a map. After investigating other incidents, however, I saw that the "boundaries" of the Triangle are extremely flexible; its "edges" are very wide. The writers who describe it as "a little patch of ocean just off the Florida coast" have included "mysteries on the edge of the triangle" that actually had occurred as far away as Newfoundland, the Azores, the Canary Islands, and, incredibly, in the Pacific Ocean (Berlitz's version of the *Freya*)! To appreciate the magnitude of this error, please refer to a globe if you have one available, or to an atlas. Locate the Bermuda-Florida-Puerto Rico triangle, then see where those other locations are. And ask yourself how and why the other writers made such enormous errors.

My first step in the research was to contact Lloyd's of London, which keeps records of such happenings at sea. (I would have contacted Gould to ask about this, except that he had been dead for some thirty years.) This incident was unusually complicated, however, because the schooner's name was unknown, and Lloyd's was unable to find any information on it. I checked many standard, reputable books on shipping disasters and could find nothing. I checked the indexes to the *New York Times* and London *Times*, both of which are valuable for researching shipping accidents. The incident was not listed in either. Since the ship was reportedly headed for St. John's, Newfoundland, I contacted the public library there to see if they could help. They found nothing in their files nor in the *Evening Telegram* newspapers for 1881. I borrowed a microfilm copy of another St. John's newspaper, *The Newfoundlander*, and, having no specific date, examined it column by column, page by page, day after day, from January 1, 1881, to July 1, 1882. It was an extremely tedious job—examining small, dim print of often headlineless articles—that took several hours an evening for almost a month. St. John's was not exactly the center of world excitement in 1881. *Anything* of local interest was worthy of being on the front page, perhaps even rating the headline. Yet there was not one mention of the *Ellen Austin*, or of any similar incident involving a ship of any name, in that year and a half. A story that exciting, had it occurred, would have been in the paper for days. There were far less interesting stories of other shipping incidents that were prominently featured.

Although I had found nothing on the incident, the results of my research were not fruitless. I had shown that the incident, *as described by the other writers*, had not happened. *Their mystery could not be verified.* Until the writers who report such incidents provide substantial documentary evidence, preferably reputable contemporaneous accounts, there is no reason for anyone to believe much of what they say, especially when many of the other stories they have written are easily demonstrated to be false when the facts can be found. There is no evidence to show that they got their information other than from each other.

Just as I finished my research on the *Ellen Austin* incident, a new version of it appeared—in Richard Winer's *The Devil's Triangle*, which was published late in 1974. The date he gave was August 20, 1881, the location midway between the Bahamas and Bermuda, the destination Boston. On page 198 Winer wrote that "many writers will twist facts somewhat for the sake of better and more interesting reading. But to completely distort the facts is no more than sensationalism." A sample of this "twisting facts" for the sake of "more interesting reading," which Winer apparently condoned in that statement, was well illustrated in his discussion of the *Ellen Austin*, most of which read like a novel and was clearly beyond his actual knowledge. He told how the "rigging straining against the deadeyes creaked a doleful tempo in rhythm with the sluggish roll of the schooner as she lay dead in the long Atlantic swell." He wrote of the recent holystoning of the teak decks, the smartly furled sails, the luffing mainsail, the coiled lines, and the open galley door banging in time with the ship's movement. He told how a Captain Baker "looked back over his right shoulder" to be certain his four crewmen were still with him, and how he smashed a thumb-sized cockroach under foot as he motioned the men forward with his Colt revolver. Winer even "informed" his readers that the captain was *thinking* about the *Mary Celeste* as he stepped aboard the derelict. So went nearly five pages of descriptive fiction. (The book's spine does say "nonfiction.") According to Winer, after a prize crew was put aboard the derelict, a storm separated the ships. Several days later it was found sailing erratically. Upon boarding the derelict the men found the prize crew's food untouched, the bunks unused, the new log book nowhere to be found, and the schooner looking just as it had upon first being discovered. Winer described at length the precautions taken to ensure the safety of a second prize crew, and how the schooner was slowly engulfed in a watery haze of an afternoon rain, never to be seen or heard from again.

I questioned the lengthy decorative fiction in the account but renewed my investigation anyway on the chance that the new, specific date and destination might lead to some report issued at the time. Much of the research I had done still applied, unaffected by the change of date and destination. Lloyd's of London still had nothing, nor was there any information in the *New York Times* or London *Times*. But now I had to check the Boston newspapers as I previously had checked those of St. John's. The *Boston Globe* had no clippings in their file, nor could they find anything on microfilm. The *Boston Herald-American* was unable to find anything. I searched a microfilm copy of the *Boston Evening Transcript* through October 15 but did not find any articles, nor any mention of the ship in the shipping section, which included information on ships spoken, arrivals and departures, and the record of accidents. I did, however, learn from the Boston Public Library that a ship named the *Ellen Austin* actually had existed. Still, I was not able to verify that the purported incident with the derelict actually occurred. There seemed to be nothing written at the time, at least that I had found, *after at least one hundred hours of research*, to verify it. There were, however, many accounts in books with titles such as *Strange Happenings* and *Invisible Horizons*, in children's magazines such as *St. Nicholas*, and in other collections of supposedly strange occurrences (most of which were apparently copied from one another).

Finally, I felt that I could no longer spend most of my time on that one incident, but had to continue investigating others. It is impossible to "prove a negative" and show that a false story did not really occur, but that does not mean that I had failed to show that the incident did not really happen as described. If the incident had actually occurred, it would have been extremely newsworthy—but not one of the newspapers that would have carried the story so much as mentions it. The results of my lengthy research showed that the writers who told about the purported *Ellen Austin* incident are on shaky ground, that they had relied upon fanciful fictionalized versions and had not troubled themselves to locate reputable sources of information. They had failed to *prove* that the incident actually occurred. In most cases they had not provided their readers with references to their sources of information, as any reputable writer should. They were, in effect, telling their readers to trust them without question. Having investigated other incidents by these writers and having found them often to be inaccurate, I could not take their word for it. They failed to prove that the incident was a mystery. They failed to *prove* that anything like it had ever happened. They even failed to show that if in fact one of the various versions is correct, the incident happened in the Bermuda Triangle.

The case of the *Ellen Austin* is a good example of "paranormal" reporting. The public, rather than accepting such stories, should require that the writers supply proof for what they say. The writers should spell out precisely where they got their information, so their readers and critics can look at these sources if they wish. A reader should be doubly skeptical of any writer who is not precise about his sources of information. Yet the pro-mystery writers cannot spell out their sources of information. If they did so they would reveal the shoddy nature of their research.

I have several other recently written versions of the *Ellen Austin* story, one of which has it en route from Liverpool to New York. I will continue to search for a primary report of the incident, spending another hundred or so hours if necessary. Perhaps someday I will find the *real* story of the *Ellen Austin* incident, if it occurred at all. Yet, even if I should someday verify that the Gould version is correct, it will not require some fantastic paranormal solution, since it is nothing more than an unusual, but certainly not a beyond-the-realm-of-earthly-explanations, incident at sea. In the meantime, the incident does not confirm the "mystery of the Bermuda Triangle" but rather is a perfect example of its questionable nature.

During my research into the Triangle I investigated approximately seventy "inexplicable mysteries" that supposedly gave evidence of strange forces in that area. The results, as given case by case in my book *The Bermuda Triangle Mystery—Solved,* are too extensive to even attempt to summarize here. There is room, however, for the conclusions.

- There is no overall single "theory" to explain all the losses in one nice, neat, bumper-sticker-length phrase. The incidents are unrelated to each other.
- There is no evidence that the percentages of aircraft and shipping losses is higher in the Bermuda Triangle than anywhere else on the oceans. It is certain, however, that the number of vessels that are *falsely reported* as being mysteriously missing is much higher for the Triangle than elsewhere.
- Logical, down-to-earth explanations were found for every incident for which contemporary information was found.
- The only mishaps that remain "unsolved" are those for which no information could be found. In these cases, because of the lack of documentation, no one has yet *proved* that the incidents actually occurred as described. The only evidence is the word of writers whose accounts of other incidents, for which information is available, has been found to be consistently unreliable. A lack of information should not be confused with a mystery.
- Many of the losses that are credited to the Triangle actually occurred as far away as Ireland, Newfoundland, Africa, and in the Pacific Ocean.
- Some of the vessels may have passed through the Triangle, but it has not been established that they "disappeared" there.
- Because of a time lapse, or a lack of communications, the location where some vessels "disappeared" was almost completely unknown, requiring that searchers spread themselves thinly over vast areas, sometimes months after the loss, if they searched at all.
- Most of the losses are "retroactive mysteries." They did not become "mysterious" until many years after they occurred, when writers were seeking new incidents to add to the Triangle lore. In virtually all these cases the circumstances were altered to make them seem mysterious.
- Contrary to the usual story, the weather was bad when many of the incidents occurred. Writers frequently do not mention this—either deliberately, or because of poor research.

· Most of the research into the "mystery" of the Triangle has been extremely poor. Writers and filmmakers have relied upon poorly researched secondary accounts rather than spending the time needed to find reliable primary sources (which often contradict the mystery).

· In many cases, writers withhold information that provides an obvious solution to the disappearances.

· Technical details of the mechanics of flying, shipping, sailing, ditching, searching, and radio have been simplified to the point of becoming inaccurate.

The Bermuda Triangle is what I politely call a "manufactured mystery." Other writers have more bluntly called it an outright fraud or a rip-off. The story has been perpetuated by writers and filmmakers who have made advantageous use of careless research, misconceptions, faulty reasoning, technical errors, and sensationalism.

There are positive lessons to be learned from the solution to the mystery of the Bermuda Triangle. We must remain extremely wary of what we read and see. "Freedom of speech" means that writers have the constitutional right to tell their readers *anything* they want to, whether it is true or not. It also gives others the right to point out these lapses of truth and logic.

We must, however, take care not to become so skeptical of what we read that we disbelieve it all. Extreme skepticism is merely another form of gullibility. Being aware that "manufactured mysteries" of this sort are constantly being perpetrated is the best defense against being taken in by them.

18

UFOs

PHILIP J. KLASS

Just for the sake of argument, consider the following hypothetical situation: Imagine for a moment that UFOs are not "real"—that our planet has not been visited by strange spacecraft of extraterrestrial origin. Imagine also that there has nevertheless been extensive media coverage of the possibility of UFOs on this planet, so that large numbers of people have come to believe in, or at least hope for, the actual existence of extraterrestrial space vehicles. Finally, imagine that the human perceptual system is such that it can play wild tricks on us under conditions of darkness, isolation, fatigue, or unusual stimulation. How many false UFO "sightings" would we expect under such a hypothetical set of circumstances?

A resonable answer is that we would expect a very large number of false sightings, perhaps equal to the number of reports we are currently experiencing.

Now simply change the first assumption above, leaving the others intact, and assume that we have in fact occasionally been visited by extraterrestrial spacecraft, which have deliberately been highly elusive. How would the totality of UFO sightings, which now would include

some few genuine eyewitness accounts, differ under this latter set of as-
sumptions from the sightings under the first set? This is the essential
problem that Philip J. Klass addresses. His argument is that it would
be nearly impossible to tell the difference. Given the human propensity
for perceptual error, the present media encouragement of UFO specula-
tion, and the often demonstrably careless and biased methods of inves-
tigation by UFO proponents, Klass concludes, we do not at present
have any reasonable basis for distinguishing a genuine extraterrestrial-
UFO presence among all the ringers.

We cannot go back in time to thoroughly investigate a UFO sight-
ing; we cannot re-create the exact circumstances. We may never know
for certain whether a sighting was accurately reported, or whether the
account contains perceptual errors, misinterpreted phenomena, biased
reporting, or biased investigation. Since we can reasonably assume that
many false sightings do occur, and since, as Klass has shown here and
elsewhere, careful investigation generally seems to result in plausible al-
ternative explanations, a belief in UFOs as intelligent visitors from
space has to be on very tenuous grounds—not totally denied, but at
least not supported by hard evidence.

The popular idea that some Unidentified Flying Object sightings involve extraterrestrial spaceships reconnoitering Earth is what psychologist Joseph Jastrow has called a "congenial conclusion." In his book
Error and Eccentricity in Human Belief (Dover, 1962), Jastrow defines
congenial conclusions as "beliefs which would make life more interesting if true, and have an engaging air of plausibility."

After all, there are billions of stars in our own galaxy and billions of
such galaxies in the universe. Simple probability suggests that there
must be many stars with inhabitable planets and intelligent life forms.
And at least some of these must be far more mature than Earth, with a
technology so much more advanced than our own that to earthlings it
would appear "indistinguishable from magic," according to author Arthur C. Clarke.

Viewing the progress of our own technology during the relatively
brief span of the past century, it is difficult for us to imagine the technological capabilities of a civilization that is many thousands of years
ahead of us in its development. For example, a mere three hundred
years ago Sir Isaac Newton might well have rejected as wild fantasy the
idea of television, of hand-held electronic calculators, of aircraft and
manned space flight.

All of the foregoing is scientifically sound judgment and speculation. Thus it seems to follow that if thousands of seemingly honest, intelligent persons around the globe, including scientists and experienced flight crews, report seeing unconventional objects in the skies,
reportedly flying at speeds and performing maneuvers that defy our
present technology, then these must be extraterrestrial spacecraft from
very advanced civilizations. Presumably these very advanced civilizations long ago learned how to eliminate the pressing problems, such as
disease, poverty, war, and energy shortages, that plague our primitive
society.

Clearly, belief in UFOs as extraterrestrial visitors is a congenial
conclusion, for it has "an engaging air of plausibility" and "would
make life more interesting if true." But the crucial question of whether
there are indeed strange craft flying in our skies rests entirely on eyewitness reports and on the rigor with which such reports are investigated.

Consider a UFO sighting made during the early evening of October
5, 1973, near Tucson, Arizona, by a very experienced astronomer, a
scientist with many thousands of hours experience in observing the
night sky. According to him it was so "striking and unusual" that he
was motivated to write down his observations while they were still
fresh, and also to search for an explanation.[1]

This astronomer's investigation subsequently revealed that his UFO
sighting was the rocket-engine plume from a large air-force Titan 2 in-
tercontinental ballistic missile being launched from Vandenberg Air
Force Base, California, *more than five hundred miles away*. A USAF
spokesman told the astronomer that ICBM launches shortly after sunset often produce UFO reports from as far away as Oregon and New
Mexico, but this was the first that the Tucson scientist had chanced to
see.

After this puzzling UFO had been transformed into an IFO (Identified Flying Object), the astronomer had the good sense to reexamine
the report he had written immediately after the incident, to check his
own powers of observation of a brief and unfamiliar event. Not surprisingly, he reported finding "several inaccuracies and inconsistencies," which he correctly attributed to "the usual difficulties of perceiving   and   remembering   an   unusual,   rapidly   changing
phenomenon." He also added an especially sage observation: "This
report . . . *is perhaps typical of the reliability of a UFO observation
by a trained observer*" (emphasis added).

But the Tucson astronomer's UFOlogical education was not yet complete. Shortly after the original sighting, he had reported the incident to a large UFO organization with headquarters in Tucson, known as APRO (Aerial Phenomena Research Organization), whose founders, and many of whose members, believe that UFOs are extraterrestrial craft. APRO had assigned the case to a local scientist-member, a graduate student in astronomy at the University of Arizona.

When the senior astronomer's own investigation disclosed that the UFO had been the Titan 2 missile, and he so informed the APRO investigator, the latter declined to accept this prosaic explanation. He "was more prepared to believe that my report and others of the same evening [of the same event by other witnesses], were of a genuine extraterrestrial visitation rather than the more realistic Titan missile launch," according to the senior astronomer.

At approximately 8:45 P.M. CST on the night of March 3, 1968, three well-educated adults, standing outside near Nashville, Tennessee, saw what they later described as a giant, saucer-shaped, metallic craft with many square-shaped windows illuminated from inside the craft, headed out of the southwest toward the northeast.[2] It passed overhead silently, at an altitude estimated at only one thousand feet.

The U.S Air Force also received a UFO sighting report from six persons living near Shoals, Indiana, some two hundred miles north of Nashville, who said they had seen the same object, which was described as being cigar shaped, with numerous square windows illuminated from inside, and with a rocketlike exhaust emitted from the rear of the craft.

Still another report on the same March 3, 1968, incident came from a science teacher in Columbus, Ohio, a mature woman with four academic degrees (including a Ph.D.) Her description was slightly different. She reported seeing three small UFOs, each shaped like an inverted saucer, flying in tight formation—suggesting that they were "under intelligent control," a familiar term in the field of UFOlogy.

The presence of the UFOs seemed to affect the woman's dog. The animal lay on the ground "like she was frightened to death," the science teacher reported. But the effect on the woman herself was equally strange. Upon returning home, she said she suddenly felt an overpowering urge to sleep, despite the fact that she had had ten hours of sleep the night before and had taken a nap that afternoon. The woman said she tried to stay awake by opening the windows to let in the cold night air, because she was expecting a telephone call from a friend. But she could not stay awake. Later, when awakened by the friend's call, the woman said she was now wide awake.

What these persons, and dozens of others, had seen on the night of March 3, 1968, was the reentry of a Russian rocket that had been used to launch the Soviet Zond 4 spacecraft on a translunar-type trajectory. The rocket booster reentered on a southwest-to-northeast trajectory that took it across Tennessee, Ohio, Pennsylvania, and southwestern New York State. As the rocket reentered, it broke up into many luminous fragments as it traversed the atmosphere at very high speed.

The minds of the observers near Nashville and Shoals hurriedly searched for a possible explanation of what they were seeing. The first thing that came to mind was a large airliner flying at night with light from its cabin spilling out through the windows. But the object could not possibly be an airliner, because it seemed so close, yet there was no engine noise. If not an airliner, then the object could only be a "flying saucer," because UFOs usually are reported to fly without any noise. Then the mind, drawing on information it had acquired through the years from news-media accounts, *supplied specific details that the eyes had never seen!* For example, that the object was saucer shaped and that its "fuselage was constructed of many pieces of flat sheets of metal-like material with a riveted-together look."

The science teacher was more accurate in her description of the incident as involving several smaller objects, perhaps because she viewed the luminous fragments through binoculars. She told the USAF that she always carried binoculars when walking her dog because she had earlier had a UFO sighting, became very much interested in the subject, and hoped she might get another UFO sighting opportunity. Despite the use of the binoculars, the woman described the objects as being shaped like "an inverted saucer," a shape that is often used in UFO literature. Thus her well-intentioned account had been unwittingly influenced by what she had read about UFOs.

The woman's overwhelming urge to sleep following the incident can easily be explained as the result of exhilaration at her good fortune of seeing *three* spaceships from a distant world. There is an equally prosaic explanation for the UFOs' seeming effect on the dog as it was presented in the woman's letter to the USAF. At one point she mentioned that the temperature was eight degrees below freezing, and at another she said that her dog hated cold weather. The most likely reason that the dog was whimpering as the woman took time to view the UFOs (and to try to signal them with her flashlight) was simply that the animal wanted to get back to a warm house!

In the late afternoon of June 5, 1969, two jet airliners near St. Louis, headed east, and an Air National Guard fighter plane west of the two airliners, also headed east, had a frightening encounter with a "squadron of UFOs" coming out of the east. As later described by a Federal Aviation Administration traffic controller, who was riding as an observer in the cockpit of the first airliner involved, flying at an altitude of thirty-nine thousand feet, it appeared as if the squadron of UFOs was about to collide with the airliner and *seemed to come within several hundred feet of the aircraft!* The UFOs were described as being the color of "burnished aluminum" and shaped like a "hydroplane."[3]

As soon as the threat of collision had passed, the copilot of the airliner called the St. Louis airport tower to report the encounter and to ask if the tower's radar showed any "unidentified targets" to the west of the airliner, then passing over St. Louis. The tower radioed back that it did have "two unidentified targets" to the west of the airliner— seemingly providing independent confirmation of the UFOs. A few moments later, the crew of a second airliner, some eight miles west of the first, which had heard the radio report on the incident, called the tower to report that the "squadron of UFOs" had just passed by, still headed west. And a few moments later, the Air National Guard pilot, flying at forty-one thousand feet, radioed that the UFOs had nearly collided with his aircraft. At the last moment the UFOs seemed to take evasive action, suggesting that they were "under intelligent control."

The identity of this "squadron of UFOs" not only is now known beyond all doubt, but they were photographed by an alert newspaper photographer in Peoria, Illinois, named Alan Harkrader, Jr. His photo shows a meteor fireball, with a long, luminous tail of electrified air, followed by a smaller flaming fragment, also with a long tail, flying in trail behind. Harkrader told me that he saw another fragment break off but was unable to get a photo of it.

Despite the reports from three experienced flight crews flying near St. Louis that the flaming objects nearly collided with their aircraft, the Harkrader photograph, plus numerous eyewitness reports from ground observers in central Illinois and Iowa, prove beyond all doubt that the fireball and its fragments were at least 125 *miles north* of the aircraft, and not a few hundred feet away, as the experienced flight crews thought. Two general-aviation pilots at the Cedar Rapids, Iowa, airport, who also saw the fireball, promptly reported the incident to FAA officials there. These pilots estimated that the flaming objects had passed directly over the east–west runway, at an altitude of less than fifteen hundred feet. Yet the fireball trajectory was *one hundred miles to the south* and many tens of thousands of feet in altitude.

The explanation for the "radar confirmation" by the St. Louis tower is equally prosaic. At the time of the incident, tower radars were able to determine and display only the azimuth position and range of aircraft—not their identities or altitudes. Since that time, all major airport radars have been modernized so that the altitude and identity of each radar blip is automatically determined and displayed. But in June 1969, when this UFO incident occurred, the St. Louis tower would have been concerned only with the identity of aircraft planning to land at that airport. These would earlier have radioed in and their radar blips would be identified by small plastic markers that would be manually positioned by an assistant controller.

Since none of the three aircraft involved in the incident were coming in to land at St. Louis, their radar blips would be "unidentified" on the tower radar display. Thus, when the first airliner crew called in to report the encounter and said it was then passing over St. Louis, advising that the UFOs now were to its rear, the tower controller hurriedly looked at his radar scope and found two unidentified targets to the west of the airliner. Almost certainly these two blips were the second airliner and the Air National Guard aircraft.

A professional musician from Bridgeport, Connecticut, who is a member of Mensa (an organization whose membership is limited to persons of very high I.Q.), after having seen a strange-looking lighted craft in the night skies with a friend, decided to carry his home movie camera, loaded with high-speed color film, in his car in the hope of again seeing, and photographing, the curious object. Some months later, he and his young son spotted the same object with its blinking lights in the night sky. He jumped out of the car and managed to take a few feet of film before the camera jammed. The next evening, at about the same time, the musician spotted the UFO again and managed to obtain about twenty seconds of movies before the object disappeared. "I could hardly contain my emotions," the musician later wrote me.

Later that evening, when he called the friend who had been with him during the initial sighting to report his good fortune, she told him that she too had seen the UFO and had decided to chase after it in her car. When she managed to get underneath the UFO and got out of the car to look up at it, she saw: "ANTHONY'S AUTO BODY—FREE ESTIMATES." The UFO was an advertising plane, a small aircraft equipped with strings of electric lights that spell out advertising messages. When such advertising aircraft are viewed at an oblique angle, they frequently generate UFO reports. The operators of such aircraft are not unhappy at the UFO reports they generate, because it prompts many more people to search the skies on subsequent nights, providing a larger potential audience for their message.

The important lesson to be drawn from the preceding incidents is summarized in "UFOlogical Principle #1," one of ten that have energed from my more than fourteen years experience in investigating famous UFO incidents. (For the complete list, see my book *UFOs Explained*, published by Random House/Vintage.)

> *Basically honest and intelligent persons who are suddenly exposed to a brief, unexpected event, especially one that involves an unfamiliar object, may be grossly inaccurate in trying to describe precisely what they have seen.*

This poses serious problems for any person who subsequently attempts to investigate the incident and to search for a possible, prosaic explanation—a situation summarized in UFOlogical Principle #2:

> *Despite the intrinsic limitations of human perception when exposed to brief unexpected and unusual events, some details recalled by the observer may be reasonably accurate. The problem facing the UFO investigator is to try to distinguish between those details that are accurate and those that are grossly inaccurate. This may be impossible until the true identity of the UFO can be determined, so that in some cases this poses an insoluble problem.*

UFOlogical Principle #2 is of crucial importance because of the claim of those who argue that *any* "unexplainable" UFO incidents necessarily prove that there is an extraordinary phenomenon at the root of the issue. "UFO proponents" (they strenuously object to being called "UFO believers") admit that most UFO reports turn out to have prosaic explanations, thus proving to be Identifiable Flying Objects.

But UFO proponents offer conflicting figures as to what percentage of the UFO reports are really IFOs and what percentage "genuine UFOs." For example, consider the wide range of figures quoted by Dr. J. Allen Hynek, an astronomer who for many years headed Northwestern University's astronomy department. Hynek was for twenty years a consultant to the U.S. Air Force in its UFO investigations and then was considered a skeptic, but he later switched to become an internationally recognized leader of the UFO movement when the USAF decided to close down its Project Blue Book UFO investigations office and get out of the business.

In a paper presented in January 1975 at a UFO symposium sponsored by the American Institute of Aeronautics and Astronautics, in Pasadena, California,[4] Hynek stated that the "study of some 12,600 cases in Air Force files showed that the great majority of initial reports—about 80 percent of them—proved merely to be misidentifications of common objects or phenomena, other types of mistakes, and a few hoaxes. This finding is fully substantiated by my own many years of experience. . . . The ratio of 4:1 seems to be a sort of invariant." (That is, 80 percent become IFOs and 20 percent remain true UFOs.)

But during 1976, Hynek's own Center for UFO Studies (CUFOS) reexamined the 12,600 UFO cases in the USAF files and concluded that 94 percent of the reports had prosaic explanations and thus were really IFOs, leaving only 6 percent as "genuine UFOs." When CUFOS analyzed the 903 UFO incidents that were reported directly to the center during 1977, it concluded that 91 percent of the incidents really were IFOs and only 9 percent were true UFOs. During the first nine months of 1978 for which CUFOS has released data, more than 94 percent of the UFO reports submitted were, after investigation, characterized as IFOs.

In evaluating the IFO/UFO ratio from CUFOS, and from less responsible sources, it cannot be too strongly emphasized that most UFO incident investigations are carried out by persons who themselves are strong UFO proponents and thus are eager to believe that there is an extraordinary phenomenon at the root of the "UFO mystery."

Because more than thirty years of UFO incidents, involving many tens of thousands of reports, have yet to yield a single physical artifact or photograph that can withstand rigorous scrutiny, UFO proponents are obliged to lean entirely on seemingly inexplicable reports of incidents to support their views. The larger the number of unexplainable UFO cases, the stronger the evidence that UFOs exist, they argue.

It therefore should not be surprising that many UFO investigators would much rather spend their time collecting stories of seemingly mysterious UFO incidents than devoting their energies to trying to seek possible prosaic, earthly explanations. If others conduct a more rigorous investigation and turn up a prosaic explanation, it is usually rejected out of hand and the investigator is bitterly attacked, as I have learned from long, firsthand experience.

Consider, for example, what has become a classic case. It occurred on the night of October 18, 1973, near Mansfield, Ohio, shortly after 11 P.M. EDT. The incident involved a four-man Army Reserve helicopter crew en route to Cleveland, under the command of Capt. Lawrence Coyne. The incident was investigated personally by Dr. Hynek and later by investigators connected with his center. In the spring of 1974, a "blue-ribbon panel" of scientists (all of them UFO proponents) selected the case as the most impressive incident of many that had occurred during a major "UFO flap" in the fall of 1973. As a result, the crew of four members received a five-thousand-dollar award offered each year by the tabloid newspaper *National Enquirer.*

The following account of the incident is based on Captain Coyne's verbal report to a Federal Aviation Administration representative at the Cleveland airport, made less than an hour after the incident occurred; the official written report that Coyne and the other three crew members submitted to their commanding officer on November 23, 1973; Coyne's description of the incident when he appeared on an American Broadcasting Company television network interview show on November 2, 1973, barely two weeks after the incident; and my own discussions with Coyne several months later.

The helicopter, a Bell Helicopter UH-1H, was cruising at a 2,500-foot altitude (above sea level), at approximately 100 knots, on a heading of 30°, en route from Columbus to the Cleveland airport where the crew was based. The time was 11:05 P.M. EDT, and the helicopter was approaching a nondirectional beacon, a radio navigation aid, southeast of the Mansfield, Ohio, airport, where the pilot had planned to land to refuel.

The crew chief, sitting at the right in the rear of the UH-1H cockpit, observed a red light to the east and called it to the attention of the pilot, also sitting on the right-hand side of the aircraft. If the red light was a warning light atop one of several radio/TV antenna towers a few miles to the east, or the "port" wing light on an aircraft flying a parallel course on an airway east of the helicopter, it posed no threat. But Coyne told the crew chief to keep his eye on the light.

A short time later, the crew chief concluded that the red light was converging at high speed on the helicopter and he alerted the pilot. Coyne promptly took over the controls from the copilot and pushed first the collective pitch control (which controls rotor thrust) and then the cyclic pitch stick (the equivalent of the elevator control on a fixed-wing aircraft) all the way forward for maximum possible vertical descent.

Despite the helicopter's rapid descent, which Coyne later estimated to be 2,000 ft/min, the fiery red object continued on what seemed to be a collision course with the helicopter. When Coyne last looked at the altimeter, he later recalled, it was reading only 1,700 feet (above sea level). Despite what appeared to be the onrushing threat of a midair collision, Coyne had glanced at his altimeter because he knew that the hilly terrain below was at an altitude of 1,200 to 1,300 feet above sea level, and his helicopter was perilously close to crashing into the ground—if it managed to escape a midair collision!

Suddenly the approaching object was overhead and, according to the words of the crew's formal report on the incident, "the object was observed to hesitate momentarily over the helicopter." The interior of the helicopter cabin was "flooded with a green light . . . for about a couple seconds," Coyne said during his television interview. Then the glowing object continued on its high-speed trajectory over Mansfield and disappeared to the west or northwest.

When Coyne next remembers looking at the altimeter, he was shocked to discover that the helicopter was at an altitude of 3,500 feet and climbing at 1,000 ft/min (where previously it was at only 1,700 feet and descending at 2,000 ft/min) "with the collective [pitch control] in the full down position," according to the official crew report.

In other words, although the helicopter's cockpit controls still were set for a maximum, auto-rotation, vertical descent position, according to Coyne's recollection, the helicopter was climbing! Seemingly, some mysterious "suction force" exerted by the object, even after it had flown on to the west and disappeared, continued to overpower the helicopter's control functions. During my third interview with Coyne, on January 23, 1974, I asked him what he had done on discovering that the helicopter was climbing. Coyne hesitated before responding, as if this were the first time that question had been posed. Then he replied: "I pulled the collective [pitch control] up. The collective was in the bottom position [calling for maximum, auto-rotational descent]." When I pointed out that pulling back on the collective was an incorrect reaction because it would cause the helicopter to increase its rate of climb rather than halt it, Coyne explained that he had no choice inasmuch as the collective control already was calling for maximum descent and could not be pushed down any further.

In any event, once Coyne discovered that the helicopter was at 3,500 feet and climbing, and he reacted, the helicopter behaved quite normally and he returned it to its original 2,500-foot cruise altitude. He told the copilot to contact the Cleveland airport, to report the incident and to request expeditious/special flight handling because the helicopter was running low on fuel.

When the copilot tuned the helicopter radio to the Cleveland tower's frequency and called in, there was no reply. The pilot told him to try to reach the Akron–Canton airport. The copilot retuned the radio and called the Akron–Canton tower, but there was no reply. Then he tuned to the Columbus tower and placed a call, but there was no reply. He next tuned to the nearby Mansfield airport and made a call, but there was no reply from them, either. He tried the Cleveland frequency again, with the same results. Then he quickly cycled through the other tower frequencies, without receiving a reply from any of them.

The helicopter radio sounded as if it was functioning properly, Coyne explained on the ABC-TV interview, but it was "about six or seven minutes" before radio contact finally was made with the Akron–Canton tower. When Coyne was asked whether he could offer any possible explanation for the seemingly mysterious blackout of helicopter radio communications immediately following the UFO encounter, he replied, "No, no explanation."

The remainder of the flight to Cleveland was uneventful. The next day, Coyne later told me, the helicopter was thoroughly inspected to determine if it had undergone any structural damage. The mechanics used ultrasonic instruments, designed to detect even hidden damage not visible to the eye. But they found none.

This incident is one of the most mysterious and credible in the three decades of UFO reports. It is a multiple-witness incident and one in which the possibility of a hoax can be quickly dismissed. If all of the seemingly mysterious aftereffects reported by the crew were *directly* related to the flaming object that passed overhead, even I would be forced to admit that the incident defies prosaic explanation. But my long experience in the field has shown that in the excitement, or terror, of a UFO encounter, the observer may later deduce a cause-and-effect relationship where none really exists.

The mysterious "blackout" of radio communications immediately following the UFO incident proved the easiest to explain. Air–ground radio communications operate in the VHF and UHF bands. These, like home television signals, are limited to relatively short (line-of-sight) distances. When an aircraft is flying at an altitude of twenty thousand feet, for example, it can communicate with ground stations more than two hundred miles away. But at the relatively low altitude of the Coyne helicopter immediately following the incident, line-of-sight communications range would be limited to roughly forty miles— and at that time the helicopter was approximately sixty miles away from the Cleveland, Akron–Canton, and Columbus airports. During my second interview with Coyne, on January 15, 1974, I asked him to conduct an experiment the next time he was flying near Mansfield: to descend to an altitude of around 2,500 feet (above sea level) and attempt to make radio contact with the Cleveland, Columbus, and Akron–Canton airport towers. Soon afterward he ran the test, and during our third interview he admitted that he had *not* been able to establish radio contact with those airports on a normal day!

Finding an explanation for Coyne's inability to make radio contact with the nearby Mansfield airport was only slightly more difficult. After determining the type of radio equipment used in the UH-1H (Model 807A) and the name of its manufacturer (Wilcox Electric), I arranged to interview the engineer who had designed it. He explained that Model 807A was an old design that could require up to five seconds to retune to a new frequency. Coyne had reported that the copilot had been changing frequencies rapidly in his desperate effort to make radio contact after the frightening UFO encounter. In his haste, the copilot might have called the Mansfield tower before the radio was properly tuned.

Another possible explanation emerged when I talked with the chief of the Mansfield tower, who explained to me that at the time of the UFO incident, there was only a single controller on duty. If he was talking to another aircraft at the time the helicopter called in—assuming that the copilot had waited long enough for the radio to retune— the lone tower operator would not interrupt a conversation with another flight crew. Standard procedure calls for him to continue and for the other flight crew to call in again. But meanwhile, the copilot was busily tuning to other airports, then too distant to reach.

The seemingly mysterious change in the helicopter's flight profile, from an auto-rotational steep descent to a 1,000 ft/min climb, has an equally prosaic explanation.

Just before the glowing UFO passed overhead, Coyne recalls glancing at his altimeter, which read 1,700 feet. This meant that at that moment the helicopter was no more than 400 to 500 feet above the ground. Using Coyne's figure of a 2,000 ft/min descent rate, it was less than 15 seconds away from crashing into the ground and killing the crew. (When I later checked with engineers at the Bell Helicopter Company, who designed the UH-1H, I was told that under the conditions described by Coyne, the helicopter's descent rate would be much higher, perhaps as high as 4,000 ft/min. If this figure is used, then a few moments before the UFO passed overhead the helicopter was less than eight seconds away from crashing into the ground.)

If the helicopter escaped a collision with the UFO, unless the pilot or copilot immediately pulled back on the collective and cyclic pitch controls, the helicopter would have crashed into the ground within a few seconds!

I have discussed this incident with a number of experienced pilots, including several with thousands of hours of flight time in the same UH-1H helicopter. Every pilot agrees that the first thing he would have done, after the collision threat had passed, was "haul back on the collective control stick, and damned fast," as one pilot phrased it.

Yet as Coyne recalled the sequence of events during the frightening encounter, he and the copilot had completely forgotten about pulling the helicopter out of its dive into the ground, even though under the good visibility conditions that existed they would have seen the ground looming up fast before their eyes. If Coyne's recollection of the sequence of events is correct, he and the copilot did not even think to take corrective action or look at the altimeter until nearly two minutes after the UFO collision threat had passed. (This nearly two-minute interval is based on the fact that when Coyne did look at his instruments, he found the helicopter was climbing at 1,000 ft/min, and had climbed 1,800 feet from the earlier 1,700 feet, which would have required approximately 1.8 minutes.)

If Coyne's recollections are correct, he and the copilot were derelict in their duties. It is much easier to believe that Coyne, or his copilot, behaved exactly as any experienced pilot would have done, and that one of them, instinctively, pulled back on the pitch controls to avoid crashing into the ground. If this was the case, they can be faulted only for later having difficulty in accurately recalling what had occurred, and in what sequence, during the terrifying moments of the encounter.

This hypothesis raises the issue of the reliability of even an experienced pilot's recollection of events that occur during a brief period of terror. An indication can be found in a similar midair threat situation that occurred on the night of November 26, 1975, involving an American Airlines airliner and a TWA jetliner. Just in the nick of time, a Federal Aviation Administration controller discovered that the two airliners were on a collision course under adverse weather conditions in which neither crew could see the other. The controller radioed a cryptic message to Capt. Guy Ely, the American Airlines pilot, saying "Descend immediately." The terror of the American Airlines flight crew during the next thirty seconds must have been similar to that of the crew in the Coyne helicopter on October 18, 1973.

The airline incident was investigated by the National Transportation Safety Board, whose report stated that "Captain [Ely] cannot remember the exact sequence of his observations and actions during the short time space in which the traffic conflict materialized and was avoided." Captain Ely, at the time, had more than 21,600 hours of flight time, accumulated over more than a quarter of a century.

If this veteran senior airline pilot admits that he "cannot remember the exact sequence of his observations and actions" during the frightening moments in which he faced a midair-collision threat, it follows that Coyne and his crew would encounter similar difficulties.

Further evidence to support this prosaic explanation for the helicopter's change in flight profile from descent to climb can be found in the fact that once Coyne thought to look at the altimeter and took steps to return to his original cruise altitude of 2,500 feet, the helicopter behaved normally, indicating there were no unusual external forces acting on the craft. Further confirmation comes from the result of the careful inspection of the helicopter the next day. Had some mysterious force been "sucking" the helicopter upward, while its engine, gear train, and rotor blades were trying to descend, there certainly would have been structural damage to at least the blades.

None of the foregoing by itself sheds any light on what the glowing UFO headed out of the east at approximately 11:05 P.M. might have been. But it does open the door to considering more prosaic possibilities, such as a meteor fireball from the Orionids meteor shower, which was at near peak intensity at the time of the helicopter incident.

In investigating this possibility, I talked with Dr. David D. Meisel, a meteor specialist who was director of the American Meteor Society. From Meisel I learned that the Orionids shower "is especially noted for its fireball activity." Further, the Orionids meteors come out of the east—the same direction from which the UFO had come. And the shower *typically* begins around 11 P.M., closely matching the time of the UFO encounter.

If the Mansfield/Coyne UFO was a fireball, as it passed over the helicopter the bright illumination from its long, luminous tail would pass through two green-tinted plastic windows over the pilot and copilot, bathing the interior of the cockpit in green light, exactly as Coyne reported. And the cabin interior would be so illuminated for perhaps a second or two, because the long, luminous tail extends for many hundreds of yards. Later, in trying to explain this extended but brief period of green illumination, the crew could readily *deduce* that the object seemed to "hesitate momentarily" over the helicopter.

During my first interview with Coyne, I raised the possibility that the object might have been a fireball from the Orionids shower, and he responded, "Well, that would sound like a logical explanation." But a few months later, Coyne and his crew were awarded the $5,000 prize by the *National Enquirer* for the best UFO case of 1973, making Coyne and the crew international celebrities in the world of UFOlogy. Later that year, my book *UFOs Explained* was published, reporting the results of my investigation that suggested that the UFO was a fireball from the Orionids shower.

An investigator associated with Dr. Hynek's Center for UFO Studies has sharply denounced my investigation and its conclusions in several articles published in UFO magazines in the United States and Britain. But more recently this investigator has acknowledged that "there is no physical evidence to indicate that the 1,800 foot–1,000 feet-per-minute climb or the apparent radio malfunctions were in any way a product of the object's [UFO's] proximity."[5]

However, the fireball hypothesis still is rejected by this investigator, based on such considerations as the helicopter crew chief's recent statement that the UFO stopped and hovered for some time over the helicopter: "I mean *stopped*, for maybe ten to twelve seconds."[6] Yet the same member of the crew signed the official report to Coyne's commanding officer, only a few weeks after the incident, attesting to the accuracy of the report, which said that the object appeared to "hesitate momentarily."

And an entirely new "mysterious aftereffect" has emerged. According to the CUFOS investigator, during the UFO encounter the helicopter's "magnetic compass was spinning: 90, 180, 270, zero, 90 [degrees]. Coyne said it was still spinning the next day as Triple-Four [the helicopter] sat on the flight line. The instrument had to be replaced." [7]

The curious aspect of this new aftereffect is that Coyne did not mention a permanently disabled compass in the official report to his commanding officer, or in any of our three lengthy interviews, or on the ABC-TV program, or to the FAA, or in any of the many interviews given immediately following the incident. Not until several years later did this remarkable aftereffect emerge.

If the magnetic compass had been affected by the UFO so that it continued to spin many hours after the object had disappeared and the helicopter had landed, this would have been the most mysterious and impressive aftermath of the entire incident—and many other people should have been aware of it, including the FAA mechanics called in the following day to inspect the helicopter. Yet it only emerged several years later, to challenge the hypothesis that the UFO was a fireball.

And so the Center for UFO Studies, one of the most respected organizations in the UFO movement, continues to insist that the Coyne/Mansfield UFO incident cannot be explained in prosaic terms. Thus, the object must have been an extraterrestrial spacecraft, or some other even more exotic phenomenon that defies present knowledge. Dr. Hynek has been quoted as saying that the UFO could not possibly have been a fireball because the Orionids meteor shower "does not produce fireballs at all." [8]

But exactly four years to the day after the Mansfield/Coyne UFO incident, on October 18, 1977, a large fireball came out of the east at around 9:15 P.M. EDT, on a trajectory several hundred miles south of Mansfield. While this "anniversary incident" does not prove that the Coyne UFO was a similar fireball, it does demonstrate the fallacy of the claim that the Orionids shower "does not produce fireballs at all."

The "scientific establishment" has been sharply criticized by UFO proponents for failing to take a more active interest in what is claimed to be "the greatest scientific mystery of all time." But in recent years, UFO proponents have boasted of growing numbers of scientists who, it is claimed, are becoming active in the field of UFOlogy.

If there is any one scientific discipline whose members should be expected to show a keen interest in UFOs if there is even a slight possibility that UFOs might be extraterrestrial spacecraft, it is the field of astronomy. Thus it is interesting to examine the results of a survey, conducted in the mid-1970s, of the 2,611 members of the American Astronomical Society, whose members include both professional and dedicated amateur astronomers. The survey was conducted by Dr. Peter A. Sturrock of Stanford University, himself an AAS member with a keen interest in UFOs. The survey assured respondents of complete anonymity in order to overcome any reluctance by AAS members to describe their own UFO sightings or acknowledge an interest in the subject.

The Sturrock survey revealed that only 7 out of the 2,611 AAS members, or roughly 0.25 percent of the membership, were sufficiently interested in the subject and impressed by the data to devote any personal time to UFOlogy. Presumably two of the seven were Sturrock himself and Hynek.

In an article written by Hynek, published in the December 1967 issue of *Playboy* magazine (which characterized him as "America's leading UFOlogist,"), Hynek had offered his recommendations for quickly resolving the UFO mystery. He urged the formation of a central UFO investigations center, with teams of investigators who could be dispatched quickly to the scene of a UFO sighting. The center would maintain a telephone exchange "UFO-1000," operated twenty-four hours a day to receive UFO reports from around the country.

"If UFOs as previously defined actually exist," Hynek wrote, "we would have photographs, movies, spectrograms, plaster casts of indentations (if a landing occurs) and detailed measurements and quantitative estimates of brightnesses, speeds, and so on *within a year of the initiation of such a no-nonsense program*" (emphasis added).

"*But if the UFO-1000 program is sincerely and intensively carried out for a full year and yields nothing, this, in itself, would be of great negative significance,*" Hynek added. (My italics.)

In the fall of 1973, Hynek created the Center for UFO Studies, an operation similar to the one he had proposed in 1967. CUFOS has a toll-free (800) number that has been made available to law-enforcement agencies around the country, and an operator is on duty around the clock to accept UFO sighting reports. Although CUFOS has not been able to afford to dispatch its own headquarters teams of investigators to the scene of each UFO sighting, it does have a nationwide network of regional UFO investigators who can reach the scene quickly.

As of this time, CUFOS has been in operation for seven years, which is more than seven times the period that Hynek predicted would be needed to obtain such scientifically useful data as "photographs, movies, spectrograms, plaster casts of indentations . . ."

Instead, all the years of CUFOS operations, like those of other groups of UFO proponents that preceded CUFOS, have yielded no scientifically useful data or artifacts that can withstand rigorous scrutiny—only more of what are usually called "incredible tales from seemingly credible people."

It must be recalled that Hynek himself wrote that if such an effort is "intensively carried out for a full year and yields nothing, this, in itself, would be of great negative significance" in assessing whether UFOs "actually exist."

19

Intelligent Life in the Universe

FRANK D. DRAKE

It has been clear for many decades that we would not find technological civilizations on the other planets of our own solar system, but it has also been widely speculated that other stars in our galaxy may well have planets with intelligent life. Since the 1950s there has been serious consideration of the possibilities of life elsewhere in the Galaxy, and one of the pioneering investigators in this serious study is astronomer Frank Drake, now director of the National Astronomy and Ionosphere Center, which operates the Arecibo Observatory in Puerto Rico. Dr. Drake, in fact, conducted the first serious program—Project Ozma, in 1960—actually to search for other civilizations.

Nobody, Drake included, seriously expected that Project Ozma would actually discover radio signals from another planet—the program was far too modest to have much chance of success, even under the most optimistic estimates of the number of planets with intelligent technological societies. But Project Ozma did dramatically call to the attention of the scientific community the real possibility of extraterrestrial communication by radio. Since then many astronomers and other scientists—including such outstanding men as Philip Morrison, I. S.

Shklovskii, and Carl Sagan, and more recently the National Aeronautics and Space Administration—have turned serious attention to SETI, the Search for Extraterrestrial Intelligence.

Not all astronomers share Drake's feeling of certainty that other civilizations exist. While it seems inevitable that the organic building blocks of life will form wherever conditions like those that existed on the primordial earth are found, the step from those prebiological organic molecules to DNA and self-replicating organisms is not yet understood. Is that too a certainty, or was it a long shot on Earth? And some of us are pessimistic about the longevity of a communicating civilization for other reasons than Drake's—for example, our own destruction by our pollution, our waste of natural resources, and overpopulation. Yet most scientists who have examined the problem think that other civilizations are at least highly probable. We know of no astronomer who does not share Drake's belief that if signals from another civilization are detected, it will be the most exciting discovery in the history of science.

Interstellar communication would not be two-way—at least not for us. Distances between stars are so great that hundreds or even thousands of years would elapse between the sending of a speed-of-light message and the receiving of a reply. Our own civilization might well be extinguished in a far shorter time. But what if there are thousands of communicating societies in the Galaxy, each receiving messages from perhaps extinct civilizations and sending out new signals—passing the word along, as it were, to future cultures? It is what Stanford University's Ronald Bracewell has called the Galactic Club. If the club exists, would our own membership in it not be far more sensational to us than all of the combined monsters and psychic mysteries that purveyors of myth would have us believe in?

Be not depressed, dear reader! Yes, you have read chapter after chapter in which one fantasy after another has been relegated to the dustbins of myth or fraud. By now you have known that special depression which befalls us who delve into those exciting reports of the paranormal, to find nothing exciting after all, only the everyday misconceived, or the work of the charlatan.

Happily, one of our most entrancing dreams survives, indeed blossoms, when studied in the light of true science. The existence of other intelligent civilizations in space, perhaps exciting worlds beyond our wildest dreams, is a firm prediction of quite normal science. There should be such worlds, with those shining cities of which many dream, with qualities of life far better than ours, and with knowledge and abilities we would find incredible. If there is a problem, it is not whether such civilizations exist: it is how we find them and communicate with them. Here and there in the vast wilderness of the universe are scattered those diamonds of civilizations. As we shall see, the search is a difficult one, but clearly within the realm of real science.

Of all the exciting subjects discussed in this book, one of the most tantalizing is communication with extraterrestrial intelligent life. Contact with another civilization would undoubtedly provide us with technological information, scientific information, information about social systems, governmental systems, and possibly even art forms and recreational forms that would greatly enrich our own civilization. We could be given excellent guidance as to what the eventual social structure of civilizations becomes, allowing us to reach an optimum civilization much more quickly, bypassing many of the trial-and-error experiments we are presently conducting. But until very recently, contact with another civilization seemed far beyond our capabilities. No reasonable manifestation of life was detectable by the instruments we possessed. But that was yesterday. Within the last decades, the situation has changed, and today we have several forms of instruments that could detect reasonable manifestations of intelligent life— manifestations no greater than those we ourselves release into the universe—over the huge distances that separate the stars. But how many stars must we search before we have a good chance of success, and what is the best way to conduct our search? We believe we have arrived at preliminary, yet good enough, answers to these questions.

We presently estimate that there are, very roughly, ten thousand civilizations in our galaxy, a number based on our rapidly growing knowledge of the structure and evolution of our galaxy and of biochemistry. How did we arrive at that number? We have perceived our galaxy to be a continuously evolving system in which the interstellar dust-and-gas clouds collapse to become stars, perhaps accompanied by planetary systems. In the stars, nuclear reactions take place that create the elements, such as carbon, nitrogen, and oxygen, that are necessary for the development of life. These materials are then spewed back into the Galaxy during the various processes of stellar death: supernova explosions, planetary nebulae, and the red-giant stage. This material enriches the interstellar gas and dust so that future generations of stars and planets will have more of the materials necessary for the development of planets and living things. On some planets of the systems so formed, life develops. Given sufficient time, evolution proceeds to the development of an intelligent species and, in turn, a technological species. The end result is a civilization that through its technology manifests itself to space in several ways: radio transmissions, light emissions, and perhaps massive technological projects such as space colonies and the construction of stellar and planetary systems to provide living room for its increasing population.

This grand picture can be developed in considerable detail. The overall number of technical civilizations in the picture will be proportional to the rate of star formation. This rate is something we now know very well from our census of the numbers of stars of various kinds and our knowledge of how long such stars can survive before consuming their nuclear energy resources. These facts lead to a required rate of replacement of stars, which leads to the conclusion that the rate of star formation in our galaxy has been (and is at present) very nearly one star per year.

How many of these newly born stars will possess planetary systems? A lot. We have learned that stars are produced from rotating gas-and-dust clouds within our galaxy, and thus from clouds that possess an enormous amount of angular momentum, or spin. It is easy to calculate that as a fledgling star collapses it must lose most of its spin or it would fly apart long before it became the size of a star. But there is only one way for a star to divest itself of spin, and that is by transferring it to the orbital motion of another object or objects. We have observed considerable evidence of this: more than half the stars are double stars, indicating that in most cases the spin is transferred to a second single object. In our solar system, the distance from the sun to the bulk of the mass in the planetary system, which is in the planets Jupiter and Saturn, is about equal to the mean distance between members of double-star systems. This indicates that our system was born in a manner very similar to that of the double stars, except that our system happened to make a number of small objects rather than a single large secondary object. In our solar system, 98 percent of the spin is in the orbital motion of the planetary system and only 2 percent in the spin of the sun. All this suggests that virtually every star that appears to be alone in the sky is in fact accompanied by a planetary system.

In each of these planetary systems there will be a few planets on which conditions are suitable for life. We are not clear about the variety of chemistries that can lead to living things, but if we use as a basis for judgment the chemistry of life on Earth, then a planet will be suitable for life if temperatures on that planet lie somewhere between the freezing and boiling points of water. This is probably a very conservative criterion. If we use our own system as a guide, along with theoretical models of the distribution of planets and forming planetary systems, we conclude that in each system there are probably two or more planets that are suitable abodes for life. In our own system there is at least one: Earth. In addition, perhaps Mars and even Jupiter and Saturn are satisfactory potential abodes of life. Taking all of these astronomical facts together, they lead to the conclusion that in our galaxy, about one new planet capable of supporting life is born each year.

But will life arise on such a planet? Here our biochemical experiments in terrestrial laboratories have led to a strongly affirmative answer. They have shown that wherever chemistry was anything like that on the primitive planet Earth, the development of life was not only simple but inevitable. In these experiments, chemical mixtures simulating the atmosphere of the primitive Earth are exposed to the kinds of sources of energy that existed there, each time with the same results: large, organic molecules, common to terrestrial life, are created. A typical experiment of this nature might involve a mixture of hydrogen, water, ammonia, methane, and carbon dioxide, into which is injected ultraviolet light (simulating sunlight), nuclear particles (simulating cosmic rays) or an electrical discharge (simulating lightning). The chemical products from such experiments have included every one of the basic building blocks of life: the biologically relevant amino acids essential to the production of protein, and the sugars and bases essential to the construction of the most central molecule of terrestrial life, DNA. And not in small quantities either; the yields in such experiments may be not simply trace yields but more than 10 percent of the chemical products. There seems no doubt that life will develop wherever conditions are suitable and the chemistry is like that of the primitive Earth, a chemistry which simply reflects the cosmic abundance of elements and thus should be similar all through the universe.

Now each new system of living things will have developed on a planet which has at least one thing in common with all other planets: it is nearly round. As trivial as that may seem, there is an important implication—namely, that there is a finite surface area and therefore finite resources available to the biota of the planet. Inevitably there will be competition for those limited resources, the consequence of which is evolution. We can be confident that evolution will eventually produce high intelligence. Indeed, in the fossil records of the earth there is only one thing that has always improved and always increased: that is the complexity of the brain. At various times we have had larger land creatures than we have today, larger flying creatures, much heavier creatures, and even creatures that can run faster. All these evidently important talents of living things have been tried, altered, discarded, and evolved again. None has been that essential. The fossil records show that only one thing has always increased, and that is intelligence. Intelligence must arise on all suitable planets after a sufficient time, although that time may be measured in billions of years.

We think that most of the intelligent creatures will in time develop technology. On our own planet this has occurred independently at least three times: in China, in the Middle East, and in Mesoamerica. In each case the development of technology was a response to the pressures of an increasing population. As populations grew and the need for more food became apparent, agriculture developed, with its own demands for special tools and artisans to construct and distribute these tools. Soon there were cities, primitive to be sure, but yet the centers of that technological expertise which was to lead us eventually to jet aircraft and nuclear energy. Perhaps not all intelligent creatures will develop technology, for maybe in some places the population pressure never develops. Nevertheless, the odds are that most life-bearing planets will in time produce a technological society.

All these facts add up to the rather startling conclusion that our galaxy probably produces about one new technological civilization per year. Once a year, somewhere in the Milky Way, a new civilization turns on for the first time, transmitting into space light and radio waves, the primary signs of its existence. Our existing radio telescopes could detect these radio waves if we but knew in which direction to turn our instruments and on which frequency to listen.

However, when we scan the sky with our instruments we do not sense that the universe teems with technological activity. The night sky is still, and so far only the quiet rustling of the stars, gas clouds, and galaxies is heard. We have the feeling that although in the march of history billions of civilizations have come into existence, only a few of them are today announcing their presence. It seems that technological civilizations do not release great amounts of energy to space forever, but perhaps do so for a limited time. We hypothesize that new civilizations, like ours, light up, illuminate the universe for a relatively short period, and then disappear from view for reasons which we do not know but are surely very interesting. Why do they leave the scene? Perhaps they've destroyed themselves through nuclear warfare—the ability to do so comes to them at about the same time as they manifest themselves to the universe. Perhaps they are destroyed by cosmic accidents, such as the collision of an asteroid with their planet; but that is very unlikely. Most likely, we believe, the eventual disappearance of a civilization from the cosmic scene is a result of increased technical sophistication. We can detect them only by detecting what they waste—energy thrown off into space. But surely they learn, as we are learning, that the conservation of energy is one of the most important tenets of an advanced civilization. They will, as we are doing, construct a technology that preserves energy, an act beneficial to them but one that may cause them largely to disappear—not because they have vanished, but because they have become even more technologically sophisticated. Right now we see many signs of this happening in our own civilization. One example is the spread of cable television, and the use of fiber optics for the transmission of telephone and television signals on earth. Were cable television to sweep the earth, the main manifestation of intelligent life on Earth would disappear from the cosmos. The second strongest indication of our presence is the air-defense radar systems of the major powers. If peace on Earth were to be achieved, to the degree that the military radar systems could be dismantled, the other most detectable sign of our existence would disappear. In a real sense our civilization would become a very difficult one to detect—though a far better one than we have today.

Thus, we believe that civilizations continuously appear, radiating to the universe. Then, after a while, they become undetectable, like twinkling lights on a Christmas tree. Many older and more advanced civilizations are still there, but they are more difficult to find. The result is a population of brightly shining civilizations whose overall number is roughly constant, but whose exact membership is changing with time.

The number of detectable civilizations in our galaxy at a given moment is nothing more than the numerical product of the rate of production of those civilizations and the average length of the time during which they transmit large quantities of energy into space. We have calculated the rate of production to be about one per year, but how long are such civilizations detectable? We will only know that when we have detected some other civilizations and found out what longevities are typical in our galaxy. Some people feel that the period of detectability is not much longer than our own has been, some thirty years or more, while others feel that some activity such as space exploration will cause civilizations to be visible and detectable for very long periods, perhaps millions of years. If we take a middle ground and assume on the average that civilizations are visible for, say, ten thousand years, then we reach a very important conclusion: the number of detectable civilizations in our galaxy is something like ten thousand, a considerable number. On the other hand, it also implies that only one star in 10 million has such a civilization, and that we will have to search a huge number of stars before we come to the first that does have a detectable civilization. More than that, the distances between the stars are such that the average distance between civilizations will be something like one thousand light-years. Thus, any search for any civilization must use a method that can detect reasonable manifestations of intelligent life over distances of one thousand light-years or more.

What is the most promising method to test some 10 million stars for signs of intelligent activity? As we shall see shortly, we cannot expect "Them" to send spacecraft to us and thus make our task easier. We believe it is up to us to reach out by whatever means we have to detect the existence of other civilizations. How should we do this? We cannot be anthropomorphic and use our own technology as a guide as to what may be brightest in other civilizations. After all, we are a primitive civilization; who knows what levels various technologies have achieved elsewhere? Indeed, in considering technologies both at their end and ours we must be inhibited only by the laws of physics and the arrangement of the universe. It turns out that that doesn't help very much, of course—it leaves virtually every possible pathway open, although making some better than others, as we shall see. We should also recognize that almost certainly there is no one form of technology that is always the best to search for. Various civilizations will use different technologies at different levels, and thus with one civilization one type of search may work, while with another civilization other types may be better. All we can search for is that technology which, in most cases, will be the easiest to detect.

The method that comes most quickly to mind is rockets. Hardly a day goes by without our being told through fiction or fact that rockets are a truly fine way to fly around in space. Thanks to television and movies, a large fraction of the world's population believes that interstellar rockets are just over the horizon and will be little more expensive to build and operate than, say, a modern jet plane. But the problem with all this is that one thousand light-years—the average distances we calculated between civilizations—is a long way. In fact, with the rockets we use these days it would take something like 30 million years to go that far. Present rockets may be fine for flying around the solar system, but for traveling over interstellar distances we need something much faster than we have today: to move from one star to another in a usefully short time would require spacecraft that can travel at nearly the speed of light.

And there's the rub! We come face to face with the unavoidable consequences of the special theory of relativity, which states that as an object approaches the speed of light it becomes heavier. Of course, if it is a rocket, as it becomes heavier it needs more fuel to accelerate it; but the fuel itself becomes heavier, so that more fuel is needed just to accelerate the fuel, and so on and so on. One can work out this vicious cycle mathematically; the result is that a rocket that approaches the speed of light cannot be powered by existing rocket engines; we must envision propulsion systems based on nuclear energy—far beyond anything we have developed in our technology. In fact, to arrive at a spacecraft system that seems at all reasonable, we must assume the use of the most efficient source of energy in physics, a system in which the energy is produced by the mutual annihilation of matter and antimatter. When matter and antimatter are combined there is a complete conversion of the mass into energy in the form of gamma radiation. The gamma-ray flash caused by this combination can become the exhaust of the rocket. Just how you manufacture enough antimatter to fuel even a small rocket, and what material you use to manufacture a rocket that can simultaneously hold matter and antimatter are problems far beyond our present technologies.

Even if these problems could be solved, the demands of such a system are still formidable. A leading scientist, Dr. Bernard M. Oliver, has calculated the requirements of a multistage rocket of this sort designed to travel at only seven-tenths the speed of light, land at a far-off planet, take off from it, and return to Earth again at seven-tenths the speed of light. He has assumed that it would carry a payload of about 1,000 tons, including the physical structure of the spacecraft, which eventually returns to Earth. It turns out that the total weight of the rocket is not that outlandish, about 34,000 tons. Of this, some 16,500 tons is matter, which is easy to come by: Even water from the nearest river will do. But then there is the requirement for 16,500 tons of antimatter, and that is stunning. There are no antimatter mines. We must manufacture the antimatter by some process we have not yet developed. But no matter how it is done, we can calculate how much energy will be required at the minimum in the manufacturing process, and this is simply 16,500 tons times the velocity of light squared, in accordance with Einstein's famous formula. That turns out to be about one half million years of the present annual power production of the United States—all to fuel one rocket for one flight. Of course, to detect other civilizations we will probably have to launch 10 million of these rockets. Obviously, their energy requirements make the rockets prohibitively expensive: this seems certain no matter how advanced and sophisticated the civilization that wants to launch them may be. There is an additional bad side effect of these rockets, by the way, if they are not handled properly: As they take off, they can incinerate one hemisphere of the earth.

These calculations clearly show that we should not expect any widespread use of rockets for interstellar communication. Only where transit times of perhaps hundreds or thousands or even millions of years are acceptable do rockets make any sense at all. And this is certainly not to us; it could only make sense to creatures whose life spans are measured in similar time scales.

This brings us to several important realizations. First, it is never worthwhile to send an actual object across space. It is always better to send the information detailing how to build an object than to send the object itself. Second, it would never be cost-effective to launch an attack on a very distant civilization or to exploit it economically. The vast distances that separate the stars form an effective quarantine, preventing one civilization from preying on another. Thus those who, remembering the history of Earth, fear a possible hostile contact with extraterrestrials simply have not understood how different the distances and speeds are in the universe from those that permit international conflicts on the surface of Earth. Finally, since any advanced civilization must use its resources in economical ways and cope with the above problems, it makes no sense for UFOs to be spacecraft from other civilizations—an additional reason to those that have been given elsewhere in this book.

But should we give up in discouragement? Are the barriers of space and time so great that civilizations are doomed to float across the Galaxy in eternal isolation? No. Those same laws of physics that militate against interstellar spacecraft have provided us with a means of interstellar communication which is fast, efficient, and extremely economical in its consumption of energy: electromagnetic radiation—light waves, radio waves, gamma rays, and so on. This radiation travels at the speed of light and is very inexpensive. For example, with our existing radio telescopes we can send a sixty-word telegram a distance of ten light-years successfully to a similar telescope, using only ten cents worth of energy in the process. This fact alone shows why the search for electromagnetic radiation is far more promising than a search for rockets when it comes to finding other worlds in space. Other civilizations will have reached these same conclusions. We can expect civilizations to detect one another and, indeed, communicate with one another primarily through the transmission of information on electromagnetic waves and only very rarely, if ever, through the actual transportation of objects across interstellar space.

Can our arguments lead us to even more precise choices as to the best means of interstellar contact or communication? In particular, of the many electromagnetic frequencies, are there some that should be universally preferred? The answer is yes; the universe clearly comes to our aid in causing certain electromagnetic frequencies to be very much more economical for interstellar communication than others. Two effects in particular bring this about. One is the quantum nature of electromagnetic radiation. Radiation comes in the form of packets of photons, each of which has an amount of energy directly proportional to its frequency. For example, the energy in a light photon is about one million times greater than that of a typical radio photon. Yet the amount of information that each can carry is about the same, meaning that a radio-frequency photon carries about the same information as a light photon, but at about one millionth the cost in energy.

If this were all that mattered, it would argue strongly for the use of the very lowest radio frequencies for interstellar communication. But there is another phenomenon that complicates matters: radio noise from the Galaxy itself. This noise enters all radio telescopes no matter how they are constructed and, in accordance with the laws of physics, cannot be eliminated. This particular noise is stronger at the lower frequencies. As it enters the telescope it acts to jam our radio receivers, thus interfering with the reliable reception of any signal photons that might be received. The upshot of this is that it takes more than one photon to communicate reliably. Since it takes more than one photon, the cost and energy per bit of information go up. The increase in the galactic radio noise at the lowest radio frequencies causes the cost of communicating each bit of information to rise again. There is a second source of noise that is inevitably present— radio noise, which is the present-day form of the radiation from the primordial fireball from which the universe was formed. This radiation appears as a dull glow over the entire sky. We, along with any other civilization, can use our knowledge of the three phenomena involved to determine at which frequency we can communicate across the Galaxy at least cost. The answer is the same for all civilizations. It turns out to be a radio frequency close to 3,000 MHz, a typical frequency for terrestrial radar systems. In fact, there is a rather broad band over which the cost of transmission is roughly constant, extending from about 1,000 MHz to 40,000 MHz. Within this band there are fundamental special frequencies that are radiated by the hydrogen atom (at 1,420 MHz), the OH molecule (near 1,667 MHz), and the water molecule (near 22,000 MHz). Hydrogen is the most abundant element in the universe, hydrogen and OH when together form water, and water seems to be the material most basic to life as we know it. For these reasons people have suggested that not only should we expect messages or interstellar contact at all of the frequencies within this preferred band, but especially at these three specific frequencies associated with things very special to life on Earth. Because of these coincidences, this region of the radio spectrum has been called the "water hole" and is considered the prime region for the search for extraterrestrial intelligent life. It has been commonly concluded that intelligent creatures like us may meet in space at the "water hole," which is not any geographic place on this planet or anywhere in the universe, but rather a special place in the radio spectrum.

Now, fortunately, we have superb telescopes for the detection of signals in this range of the radio spectrum. There are large radio telescopes in England, Germany, the Soviet Union, and many places in the United States with superb radio receiving equipment for the optimum frequencies. The most sensitive telescope now in existence is the one-thousand-foot-diameter radio telescope of the Arecibo Observatory near Arecibo, Puerto Rico (see page 341). It has a total energy-collecting area of about twenty acres, more than the combined collecting area of all the other telescopes in the world. It also has an extremely powerful radio transmitter, which transmits near the optimum frequencies for interstellar communication. In fact, the radio

The Arecibo Observatory. This observatory with its 1,000-foot radio telescope is located about ten miles from the city of Arecibo, Puerto Rico. Funded by the National Science Foundation, it is operated by the National Astronomy and Ionosphere Center and is open to use by all scientists. Its reflector collecting area of almost twenty acres is the largest in the world, and its radio transmissions the strongest leaving Earth. It has been used extensively in the search for intelligent extraterrestrial radio signals. The Arecibo Observatory is part of the National Astronomy and Ionosphere Center which is operated by Cornell University under contract with the National Science Foundation. Courtesy NAIC.

beam created by this transmitter would be detectable by a twin to the Arecibo telescope pointed in the right direction, if such existed anywhere in the Milky Way Galaxy. The effective power one would have to radiate to create the same radiation level if the radio energy were not focused by the telescope is 20 million million watts, about twenty times the present rate of total electric power production of the entire Earth. In fact, at the frequency at which this beam is radiated, and in the direction it travels, this signal from Earth is many millions of times brighter than the radio emission of the sun, proof that intelligent radio signals can be genuinely bright on the cosmic scale, in contrast to most of our other manifestations of intelligent activity. In 1978, the Arecibo telescope was used to search for intelligent radio signals from two hundred nearby stars. As an indication of how sensitive it is, that search could have detected an intelligent radio signal if that signal delivered to the entire surface of the earth a total power of only one millionth of a millionth of a watt.

There are about ten radio telescopes in existence that can detect radio signals from distances of a thousand light-years or more. Many have now been used in searches for extraterrestrial intelligent signals, most at frequencies near that of the hydrogen atom. Particularly powerful searches have been carried out with the telescopes at the National Radio Astronomy Observatory near Green Bank, West Virginia; at the Ohio State University near Delaware, Ohio; at the Hat Creek Observatory of the University of California; at several observatories in the Soviet Union; and at the Arecibo Observatory. At the Algonquin Radio Observatory of the National Research Council of Canada a sensitive search has been carried out at frequencies near that of the water molecule's spectral line. In most cases the telescopes have been aimed at nearby stars that are similar to the sun.

The first search for extraterrestrial radio signals took place at the National Radio Astronomy Observatory in 1960. At that time an eighty-five-foot radio telescope with a single-channel radio receiver was used to search for signals near the frequency of the hydrogen line, 1,420 megacycles per second. This project, called Project Ozma, searched for signals for about two hundred hours in the nearest two sunlike stars, Tau Ceti and Epsilon Eridani. Today that entire search could be duplicated in a fraction of a second with a telescope like the one at Arecibo.

In recent searches, electronic instrumentation has been used that monitors as many different frequency channels as possible. For example, at Arecibo in a typical radio search as many as 3,024 channels are monitored at the same time. In the 1978 search carried out at Arecibo, a special arrangement of the computer facility was used so that 65,536 frequency channels could be examined simultaneously.

It is important to observe the maximum possible number of channels, because a radio signal can be strengthened and therefore made more detectable by confining its transmission to a very narrow portion of the radio spectrum. However, to detect and receive such a narrow signal, a radio receiver must be tuned to a frequency that is very close to that of the transmitted signal. If indeed very narrow frequency bands are being used in interstellar signaling, then a given search in a few channels monitors only a very small portion of the radio spectrum. If we wish to examine the very broad expanse of the "water hole" within a reasonable observing time, we must monitor a very large number of channels simultaneously. At present there are proposals to build a special radio receiver capable of monitoring one million channels simultaneously, specifically for use in searches for extraterrestrial intelligent radio signals. The ultimate goal is a radio receiver system that can monitor a billion channels at once. Such a receiver is within the realm of present-day technology, although the expense will be many millions of dollars.

In the searches of recent years, the number of combinations of direction in the sky and radio frequency that have been tested for intelligent radio signals has added up to nearly one million. This is a very significant first step in the search of the cosmic haystack for those precious diamonds that are surely out there, but no evidence for signals has yet been detected.

Shouldn't one million tests of our galaxy produce success? No, we have hardly begun. To understand how small "hardly" is, one has to face realistically the dimensions of the cosmic haystack. At any given time, we search in one direction in the sky and at as many frequencies as our radio receiver permits. We must search for signals at certain bandwidths: if our equipment is set up on the wrong one, we lose sensitivity for the detection of a signal. Similarly, we must search for signals with various on/off times. Too short a time or too long a time will again decrease our ability to detect a signal. And then electromagnetic radiation can be *polarized,* and to be sure that we do not miss a signal we must search on both polarizations. Lastly, there is the problem that we call the "duty cycle." We must assume that not all signals are radiated at all times. Certainly any signal from Earth is not detectable at all times. Transmitters are turned on and off, and in any case the earth itself rotates so that many sources of terrestrial radio emission are at times invisible because they are on the opposite side of the earth. Overall, then, there are six different factors influencing the search: place, frequency, bandwidth, signal modulation time, polarization, and duty cycle. Now if we are using pretty large telescopes, then there are about 40 million different places in the sky we can point the telescope without looking at the same place twice. With regard to radio frequencies just in the "water hole," if we search with the minimum bandwidth there are some 100,000 million frequencies to be searched. We estimate that it will be necessary to search five different frequency bandwidths to cover all the reasonable possibilities with good sensitivity, and there are about five different modulation times that must be used for each in order to cover all reasonable possibilities. There are two polarizations to be searched. And lastly, if the most powerful transmitters, the ones we are most likely to detect, are anything like our own, it is possible that only one one-millionth of the time would such a transmitter be aimed in our direction sufficiently well that its signal could be picked up. If we multiply all these figures together to determine the total number of combinations of direction, frequency, bandwidth, modulation time, polarization, and duty cycle which must be searched, the result is the enormous number of 10^{26}. That is the size of our cosmic haystack. It is, once again, a result of the arrangement of our Galaxy. There is no evading it. In contemplating the search for extraterrestrial intelligent life and planning the technology to conduct that search, our main obstacle is that one enormous number, 10^{26}.

Now perhaps ten thousand of those 10^{26} combinations have detectable signals in them (just how many depends on how powerful our telescopes are). That is why the search of one million of these combinations, although a formidable piece of work, is still probably only a tiny step along the path to eventual success. The search for extraterrestrial intelligence is subsumed within what we know and understand in normal science, but in no way does that make it easy. It is surely the most painstaking scientific task ever taken on by humanity. We would certainly never attempt it were it not that we expect the eventual payoff from success to easily justify the effort required. The deepest concern of those searching for extraterrestrial life is not questions as to its nature or existence, but one of terrestrial technology. How can we search that enormous haystack sufficiently thoroughly at an affordable cost?

I have mentioned the steps now being taken to build multichannel radio receivers of enormous capability. Another important step, a much more expensive one, would be to build very large radio telescopes that can be dedicated primarily to the search for extraterrestrial signals. At present we can hope to obtain only a small percentage of the observing time of the major telescopes required for searches. The availability of dedicated telescopes would greatly increase our search time and at the same time lead to much more efficient searches, since with such telescopes the equipment and computer installations could be specialized for signal-searching activities. Designs for such telescopes have been created. Page 346 shows an example of what one of these might look like. This instrument, known as Project Cyclops, is aimed at producing the largest possible telescope collecting area at minimum cost. In this case the telescope, which may cost as much as $10 billion, consists of more than a thousand telescopes like the one already in existence near Bonn, Germany. This system of telescopes, when operating as a single unit, would be capable of detecting television signals (like those we transmit) from distances of hundreds of light-years.

Systems like this will be needed whether we detect life or not. If we do not succeed with lesser telescopes, it will mean that we need ones with a larger collecting area to detect extraterrestrial signals. On the other hand, even if we succeed with lesser telescopes we will undoubtedly want to learn more and to search out even more civilizations; thus there will be a tremendous motivation to build larger instruments. One way or another, there is a Cyclops in our future.

Lastly, what about language? Can we communicate with alien creatures far different from us? It is just possible that we will receive messages in an alien language with so few clues that we cannot interpret them. On the other hand, in our own past we have deciphered very bizarre coding systems from ancient civilizations on Earth. And more important, we have already constructed coding systems or languages that can allow us to communicate rather sophisticated concepts to other creatures without prior contact. Most of these systems make use of pictures with messages consisting of a number of characters of the order of one thousand. It is possible with them to send pictorial sketches that contain basic but very significant information about our civilization. For example, Figure 3 is the decoding of a message sent from the Arecibo telescope. It was sent at a frequency of 2,380 MHz into the "water hole," at a rate of ten characters per second. There is a

One artist's conception of Project Cyclops. This ground-based version would consist of about 1,500 300-meter steerable radio telescopes, connected electrically to produce an instrument whose effective energy-collecting area is roughly 100 times greater than that of the Arecibo reflector. Other designs for Project Cyclops call for the construction of a large radio telescope in space. Courtesy National Aeronautics and Space Administration Ames Research Center, Moffett Field, California.

total of 1,679 characters, so the message takes only about three minutes to send. The message consisted of a series of transmissions at one or two frequencies. One frequency represented characters shown as white on page 347, while the other frequency denoted characters shown as black. Thus even with this small number of characters it is possible to establish a number system that describes some quite com-

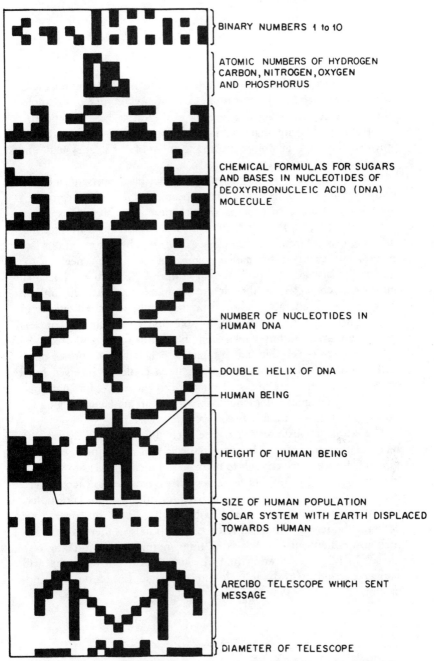

BINARY NUMBERS 1 to 10

ATOMIC NUMBERS OF HYDROGEN
CARBON, NITROGEN, OXYGEN
AND PHOSPHORUS

CHEMICAL FORMULAS FOR SUGARS
AND BASES IN NUCLEOTIDES OF
DEOXYRIBONUCLEIC ACID (DNA)
MOLECULE

NUMBER OF NUCLEOTIDES IN
HUMAN DNA

DOUBLE HELIX OF DNA

HUMAN BEING

HEIGHT OF HUMAN BEING

SIZE OF HUMAN POPULATION
SOLAR SYSTEM WITH EARTH DISPLACED
TOWARDS HUMAN

ARECIBO TELESCOPE WHICH SENT
MESSAGE

DIAMETER OF TELESCOPE

The decryption of the message sent from the Arecibo telescope in November 1974, in the direction of the globular star cluster in Hercules, Messier 13. The message will arrive at the 300,000 stars of the cluster in about 25,000 years. The Arecibo Observatory is part of the National Astronomy and Ionosphere Center which is operated by Cornell University under contract with the National Science Foundation. Courtesy NAIC.

plex chemistry, including the structure of the most important molecule of terrestrial life. It is possible to show how complex this molecule is, thereby implying our level of evolution and even something
about our level of intelligence. Finally, some sketchy information is
provided about our anatomy, the arrangement of our solar system, and
the level of our technology.

At this time the most lengthy message that has been sent out from
Earth is the picture sequence that appears on the records carried by
the Voyager 1 and 2 spacecraft. Each of these records contains a large
assortment of terrestrial music, many typical sounds of Earth, greetings
in human voices from a large number of human beings in various languages, and finally 116 detailed pictures of important aspects of the
earth, the solar system, and human culture in particular. The total
number of characters in the picture sequence is about 100 million.
This number of characters allows one to describe terrestrial culture in
very great detail. It is interesting to note that 100 million characters
can be sent on an ordinary television channel in roughly ten seconds.
It is therefore conceivable that completely detailed depictions of other
civilizations which can be easily deciphered could be received from
other civilizations over interstellar radio links in very short transmission times. Language does not seem to be an obstacle to complex
exchanges of information between galactic civilizations.

The search for extraterrestrial intelligent life is entirely within the
range of normal science. In some respects that makes our task more
difficult, for we know enough to make sound predictions as to what effort and what expenditure of resources will be required to succeed. We
do not call on magic elixirs, crystal balls, or hot tips from an extraterrestrial astronaut to make us rich with results effortlessly. Instead we
embrace the reality of normal science, which tells us there is a monumentally difficult and at the same time monumentally exciting task
ahead. In this case we know that we can succeed, but when that will
happen depends not on a miracle, nor on magic, but on our own motivation.

20

On the Causes of
Wonderful Things: A Perspective

PHILIP MORRISON

*Professor Philip Morrison of the Massachusetts Institute of Technology
is a well-known physicist. Because of his broad knowledge, keen insight,
and eloquent gift of expression, he is frequently invited to provide a
summary review at the conclusion of scientific conferences and symposia. We thought he would be the ideal person to write a perspective of
this book.*

A century before the Royal Society, even before Galileo's Academy of
the Lynxes, there met in Naples a group of amateurs gathered by the
learned and ingenious Giambattista della Porta, among whose inventions was a low-power two-lensed instrument, forerunner of the telescope, probably made while Galileo was yet a child. Those *otiosi* (men
of leisure) in Naples made it a condition of membership that "each
man must have contributed a new discovery of fact in natural
science." Theirs was the first scientific society in modern times, although its main legacy was its founder's publications, books hugely
popular over all Europe for a century or two. For della Porta the practice of Natural Magick (so the first English edition of his book of the

same title called it in 1658) was nothing at all like "Sorcery; an art which all learned and good men detest; neither is it able to yield any truth of Reason or Nature." Rather, it was "the practical part of natural philosophy, which produces her effects by the mutual and fit application of one natural thing unto another."

First among twenty rather specialized chapters of *Natural Magick* ("Of Beautifying Women," "Of Distillation," and "Of Strange Glasses" are three of them) is a theoretical introduction, "Of the Causes of Wonderful Things." The structure of the world, it argues, lies in the internal elements and forms of things, their powers drawn and ruled by the stars. The importance of time and place is obvious, and the richness of combinations can open many valuable new paths. *Sympathy* and *antipathy* are general relationships and can be widely applied. Thus: "A Dog is most friendly to a man; and if you lay him to any diseased part of your body, he takes away the disease to himself, as Pliny reported." On the other hand, in one rare but terrible crisis, "A Dog and a Wolfe are at great enmity; and therefore a Wolves skin put upon any one that is bitten of a mad Dog, asswageth the swelling of the humor."

For nearly a century now we have treated rabies worldwide with excellent results. The modern therapy is on the face of it less plausible than della Porta's, though it shares with his scheme certain unexpected qualities. We prepare our magical inoculum, the spinal cord extracted from a sacrificed rabbit, itself dying of rabies. That tissue is treated according to a precise ritual of times and dilutions with a solution of formaldehyde. Samples of the substance so obtained are placed day after day within the bloodstream of the patient. If treatment is in time, during the few weeks between the infecting bite and the appearance of the first symptoms of the disease, nearly every patient will recover. There is profound antipathy at work here, all right; but we know it as the generation of antibodies by the immune system of the patient.

That repeated inoculation with tissue from a rabid animal treated with a stinking poison like formaldehyde can indeed stave off death from rabies is surely wonderful. Della Porta could have hailed Pasteur's technique as a development out of his own crude ideas. In the bizarre nature of its procedures our practically applied science does not differ from magick. "Nothing is too wonderful to be true": this remark, ascribed to the meticulous experimenter Michael Faraday, appears carved on the physics building at UCLA. He was surely right. The "mutual and fit application of one natural thing unto another," often strangely specific, can work wonders, effects really unmatched within the ordinary noisy experiences that inform what we call common sense.

Della Porta placed his therapy within a generally causal theory of matter, as do we. Della Porta relied upon earlier reports of experience, as do we. Della Porta employed only the objective properties of "natural things"—not, for example, their names in Italian, or their relationships to the life of some saint, or other properties that we could reject out of hand as failing common-sense tests of invariance or causality. It is not easy to point to any broad methodological distinction between his natural magick and modern applied science. In fact, if someone could show, say, that certain stable antigens in most wolf pelts might be involved in some subtle induction of the immune reaction, the della Porta "remedy" could even be assimilated to our theories. Indeed, a placebo effect of the magickal therapy might be invoked, so that the patient internally turns on the healing flow of antibodies.

No, the weakness of wolfskin therapy, like our success with a carefully inactivated virus, does not rest in generalities of method. It certainly cannot lie in the unexpectedness and incongruity of the procedures; the preparation of rabies vaccine seems closer to eye of newt and toe of frog than does plausible and cozy wolfskin. It does not lie either in the power of results achieved by quiet means. We often speak of rapid and internal cures as magical, "working like a charm," whenever they seem to go beyond common-sense experiences, yet the replacement of a single loose wire or the use of the right antibiotic or hormone can induce such results, quite causally, whether in man or in machine, by "mutual and fit application." The truth is instead deep within the hard-worn detail. How many cases did old Pliny see? Had della Porta any better sample, or was he generalizing on an old citation without skeptical questioning? (Even for us, the bite of a rabid dog does not always inject live virus, and so assessment of the value of treatment cannot flow from a single happy case. A big sample itself is not probative under such circumstances, while the demand for a series of untreated control cases that logical inference requires is too stoically heroic to be met, except by chance. Here is one reason, of course, why tragic conditions tend to induce bad theories.)

Next is the question of texture, of the robustness of a theory under diverse tests of its inferences, tests that vary experience under the guidance of theory. Does it matter if the wolf is male or female? Might a cat's skin or a coyote's be used if necessary? Of course, the old scholars made no such tests, nor could we in fact expect them to. But the Pasteur method is by now robust. Nowadays one can use virus from a sheep, or horse, or even from a tissue culture alive in a glass vessel. The formalin inactivation can be replaced by ultraviolet light. The virus particles can be seen in the neurons under the electron microscope, and the antibodies titrated. Practical success leads to refinement of techniques; we expect the statistics to become themselves impeccable one day, unmarred by even a single inexplicable failure in a long series of cases. Step by step down a long causal chain we chase the virus and the antibody; even if here and there logical gaps still remain, we have found a detailed procedure, specific but not capricious, robust to theoretically admissible changes of detail, improving in practice sometimes even under statistical control. By now rabies vaccine is embedded within a much wider view of disease and host, a structure so wonderful as to include the role of the silent thymus gland, the ancient evolutionary sequence of the higher organisms, and a strong molecular dose of protein structure.

The sixteenth-century pioneers fixed one beacon we still steer by. Della Porta sought to explicate, to reveal the secrets, to be open about the use of wolfskin, even to tell why. His style is in strong contrast to that of today's miracle men, such as the psychic surgeons of the Manila countryside, who plainly carry on a successful practice which elevates secrecy and sleight of hand to a major role. When a psychic surgeon takes out the offending tissue through the uncut skin, in a gesture which mocks so reassuringly the deftness of the real knife surgeon's frightening incision, the bloody chicken parts he throws into the fire are calculated to have an effect on patient and spectators. That effect would change if he were to show beforehand how the stuff is palmed or held in some magician's gimmick. If any fraction of such cures is placebo-related, their hidden procedure may well be of practical value. The very same attitude, if less deceptively applied, is still found in medicine, either as a relict of the old ways, like the Latin of the prescription, or as behavior held to fit the social role of a healer with respect to a patient, or as a conscious decision of the doctor to meet his view of the patient's personal need. Trade secrets, military-industrial secrecy, and craft processes of many sorts are more or less distantly related to the healer's covert actions. Here the aim is rather a competitive advantage; some grasp of the natural world is being guarded as a piece of property. Often the hidden procedure is itself not understood; one particular source of a well-known ingredient functions better than any other, say, though just why is not known. The famous discovery that gelatin derived from cows that had grazed on fields golden with mustard made more sensitive photographic emulsion could have been a trade secret—for all I know, it was—before it became clear that its sulfhydryl impurities formed many electron traps in the silver halide crystal grains.

There is a whole spectrum of such occult matters in every complex fabrication. Often the expert himself is not even conscious of his hidden maneuver, for it lies in the black boxes of a system he has not fully understood. That phenomenon is familiar in the homeliest of contexts, too; there is often just the right way to start an old car or to turn a worn-out switch. Empirical results are not in themselves a road to understanding, only to success.

It follows therefore that we must ask more of any procedure than just that it works, if we are to learn *how* it works. High fees, glowing testimonials, accounts of visitors and friends are not firm demonstrations of why something works—whether it is the topic of a TV commercial or an operation by a psychic surgeon. Either there is step-by-step openness, subject to change and deductive questions at each point, or there must enter the machinery of rigorous induction, with careful statistical control and well-designed experiments and double-blind clinical trials. For error in the conclusion can be not only that of the patient who is being denied the truth of his operation by the deliberate stage skills of the psychic surgeon, but even that of an unwitting, sincere experimenter or clinician.

That much is evident; nothing new. There is more. It must be admitted that there are circumstances in which deception, either of others or of the self, can in fact improve the claimed results. The logic is clear; it is even conventional, offered in support of the withholding of the diagnosis of a terminal disease in many cases. The argument is very old; the doctors of the Skidi Pawnee invariably preceded their big seasonal ceremonies with displays of sleight of hand, taking a quartz crystal out of the nose of this or that awed spectator, turning a mud duck into a living one by dropping it into a vessel of water, or swallowing a deer's head, antlers and all. They freely employed the techniques of the carnival and the stage, with accomplices planted in the crowd, prearranged tending of the fire to darken the scene at the crucial moment, and so on. All this was unabashedly known to the inner circle. But these men maintained that their little show was exactly the right way to prepare their audiences for the serious religious ceremonies of the group. They had done so for a millennium or more.

In a parallel if trivial context, the classroom experiments of Craig the magician in "To Believe or Not to Believe" touch the same facet of human nature. The students preferred their mystery; Craig as an amateur sleight-of-hand artist was an example of rational, practiced, and dextrous craftsmanship, not especially remarkable. But Craig as a partaker of hidden and mysterious powers, powers which might—who knows?—descend magically upon anyone, was quite another kind of wonder. The practical outcome here gained from the deception was that the occult thrilled more than those undisclosed but all-too-human skills of planned misdirection and sleight of the hand that are such hard work to perfect. Once the conjuror used to please his audience by faultless and apparently effortless mastery over cards or coins; now he is more likely to claim the need for the warm sympathy of the audience for a trick that will fail once or twice—until the "vibes are right." Most of the time he in fact does exactly the same thing, but he attends closely to the social and psychological climate of the day, a climate which varies from year to year, place to place, and group to group within our complex society.

For science, for natural magick even, there can be no more admirable style than one of openness, bright lights, sleeves rolled up, all really fair. Every departure from it must be seen as reducing the strength of evidence. When the departure is taken in the service of some end other than understanding, as may indeed be necessary in many human contexts, the strength of the evidence declines. This remains true even when the ends are better served by some degree of concealment. What in fact happens overall when one cannot follow an open path from start to completion must be judged finally by that statistical skepticism of elaborate controls. We cannot expect ever to understand procedure that remains intrinsically less than open. We might eventually prove that it works or fails to work, though even that proof is by no means cheap and easy.

These arguments of course are in the sunny spirit of the extended Enlightenment, an ambience very congenial to science. But we do not live in the day of Diderot. One wants to recognize that fact and to admit widespread interest even in what old della Porta did not care for: sorcery. They are, above all, *hidden* powers that sorcery invokes. No arguments are likely to shake theorists who impute such occult layers to the world. Even as a matter of logic it is not easy to demonstrate the error of those who explained away the fact that the stainless-steel pins that held some healed fracture within remained visible in X rays, even after the "surgeon" had assertedly removed them, spilling only chicken blood. The defenders of the procedure observed that the painful "essence" of the implants had indeed been removed, leaving only their physical shadow. A radiologist can hardly dispute such a theory. And if one wishes to argue against such postulates (except by the razor of old Ockham) he had better be able to show that the relief rates do not support extraordinary claims. Enter controls and statistics again, that slow and costly logic of skepticism.

The urgency of healing has always made it a source of bad theory. This is all the more true because it is a safe bet that most healing procedures, whether in the most scientific practice or in a frankly magical one, are unneeded. For what patients present are usually self-limiting conditions (in 80 percent of a random practice, says Dr. Nolen; see Chapter 12). Most medicine has other purposes than a cure, which in time comes naturally. Perhaps the most important is just the assurance that the condition is not something worse, with a poor prognosis. But it is to be kept in mind that a patient is a very complex system indeed, which science by no means understands in detail. When the manifold therapeutic effects of cortisone became known a generation ago, some scientific meetings took on the air of revivals. Witnesses testified all over the hall as to the rapid and disparate cures the drug effected; sudden freedom came to the halt and the lame. We learned then that endocrine systems can work powerful changes in many organs and tissues. The autonomic nervous system as well is capable of much control over normally involuntary bodily functions; the brash positivist denial that an adept can pass into a self-induced passive state of minimal metabolism has been refuted right on BBC-TV. That oversimple model of the complex human body had not taken sufficiently into account the powers of our inbuilt electronics. But there is no mystery here, only wonder. Plenty of hard-wired circuits cross from brain to brainstem to transmit commands to the heart and to the breathing reflexes. So little do we know yet about the details of the relationships between mental and bodily states that we can afford to be tolerant of many claims involving them, secure in the hope that in the end they will be explained by mechanisms as yet unknown to us. But that is not necessarily to admit their existence without powerful proofs. These are even more strongly required, since the system is complicated and its initial state little controlled. We need not expect any forces to be at work save those that flow along the bewildering network of electrochemical pathways, conforming to, but surely extending year after year beyond, what we already know.

The human organism possesses a set of very sensitive amplifying systems. Some of these are chemical, capable of mediating gross physiological changes under stimuli as small as the entry of an invisibly small sample of antigen. Even a mere symbolic signal, properly impressed by light or sound on eye or ear, can work—provided that earlier learning has allowed the form to take on a powerful internally stored meaning. It is of course this fact that forces an ambiguous interpretation on many unorthodox procedures of healing by no means absent from often-used techniques in what we think of as scientific medicine. Placebo is powerful; the will to benefit offers much relief.

Many of the paranormal topics treated in this book are not so much applied science (medicine is of course an important example of that domain) as they are purported accounts of the world as it is, what one might call science without regard to applications. The question of UFOs is a clear case in point. Here the key figure is not a patient, but a close relative of that variable human being: a witness. Witnesses are also remarkably complex systems. What they say is connected to the sensory input that gives rise to their testimony by a very complex and unpredictable set of links, links that certainly can join today's statement to events even as long ago and far away as the infancy of the witness. For language is the usual form of testimony (allowing a few gestures and drawings), and its categories have long been held in every witness's mind. But a lawyer could tell us much more about witnesses and their value than any physicist can.

The first issue is one of competence. Granting veracity, could the witness have learned enough from the experience to draw convincingly the conclusions he offers in testimony? The air crew sees the fireball as a mile or two away, even though it proves to be two hundred miles distant. They were not dishonest, nor even confused, but simply had no way to judge the distance of a light in the sky at night, unless they assume something of its physical size, speed, brightness, or the like. When a fireball is viewed as though it were an aircraft ablaze, its distance cannot be rightly gauged. In such cases perceptual physics is invaluable.

In more social matters, where the degree of disinterest of the witness, the requirements of corroboration by others, and more subtle questions come into play, no natural scientist is very fit by experience to judge. Here the more worldly are at home. One magician as knowing as James Randi is worth a dozen eager nuclear theorists. Once, a London group of academics was testing out the claim that a certain wonder worker could cause a Geiger counter to fire by occult means. The task was accomplished, to everyone's amazement, and the chart recorder that had duly marked the mysterious counts was examined later with care. The paper chart showed strong counts; indeed, the pen had been so strongly deflected that the experts could be sure that the amplifier used did not deliver enough power to move the pen so fast and so far. Energy had probably flowed in from another source. Choose your own occult pathway! The sober view is that the deflection was made by hand, by a spectator friend of the adept who firmly pushed the pen over at the right time. Nobody was steadily watching the recorder; it had been (naively) assumed that all the action was at the counter end. Such an attitude is totally that of the physicist; no magician and few lawyers or detectives would take such a trusting stance. A similar lesson comes clearly through several of the essays in this volume.

Much testimony is written and published. A model of the internal and external examination of printed sources was offered us by Larry Kusche in his account of the "media hoax" called the Bermuda Triangle. A book is of course simply a limited form of witness, whose testimony is fixed in time. Cross-examination cannot be used, but the evidence is open to detailed study. It becomes even easier to ask how the witness came to know what is placed on the page.

In either case, whether it is evidence offered by witnesses who were there, or by those who have mainly documents for their own sources, one method of testing is generally applicable. A step-by-step survey of how the statement came to be made on the basis of the experience recounted is the deepest form of analysis. Questions of motive and judgment remain secondary. The whole topic is a rich one, extending so far that it includes the methods of science themselves. The scientific paper is the written testimony of experimenter and theorist. We know how much we question every novel conclusion, and with what good reason—for most of them turn out somehow to be wrong. New territory is usually opened to science step by confused step. It is ingenuous to demand less from new claimants of grand domains of experience, long sought for and long and unconvincingly claimed, than we ask of authors who offer only a single new proposition within a well-explored discipline.

These pages say very little about that quality of the internal state we call *motive*. Certainly fraud, hoax, and cupidity are real phenomena often found in human affairs, especially when substantial gain (of fame or fortune) is foreseen. That gain is enhanced in our times by the very existence of widespread means of communication and publication. Popular books can sell tens of millions of copies, offering genuine wealth to the few really successful authors. It is certainly relevant to question motives, and to draw inferences about their influence on truth telling and completeness. But they ought not to be held decisive. A true statement can be made by a generally deceptive witness or compiler, and a false one by a person of indubitable integrity. The touchstone for truth is not the honesty of the speaker, but the evidence presented. Sometimes it can take the form of independent repetition, the replication dear to the experimental scientist. But this is not always a possible form of verification. What is essential is a sufficiency of objective evidence, although the criteria for that sufficiency are not simple or clear.

It is certain that unsupported statements by people with an interest in their outcome are not enough. Even in ordinary science, the person who puts forward a new result is by no means disinterested. The tale of Alfred Russel Wallace and his spirits is a perfect example, though drawn from the paranormal. The dry remark made about his stance applies more widely: "Personal conviction is a very fallible guide." The creator of any idea or result is almost surely a partisan of it. Truth is hard to win, and the sense of success is rewarding for any researcher. How can he or she be indifferent to the future of this infant brain child?

In normal science that bias is assumed; another worker must be free to examine the evidence critically and in new ways. Sooner or later the matter will either be dropped as error or become widely accepted. But only a long history of testing and success offers really firm support, while certainty is hard to gain outside of mathematics. We hold every idea with some degree of firmness; the more carefully tested, fruitful, and richly textured the idea, the more firm.

This spectrum of conviction is perhaps the chief difference between the parascientific enthusiasts and the scientists. The latter are willing to doubt, if only a little bit, even the conservation of energy. But in parascience the criteria are far too lax. Every claim of success is seized upon. The burden of proof is freely shirked by those who would put the evidence of a few witnesses, or of a compiler with a livelihood at stake, ahead of manifest contradiction of precisely verified regularities from dozens of contexts. The whole structure is thus weak.

Consider the marvels of the pyramid form. Assertion or even less—a mere suggestion—is the main basis for large claims. The matter is governed rather by a will to believe than a will to *doubt*. It is the fragility of evidence, not the fact of self-interest, which lies behind my pervasive doubt of most of the conclusions in most of the books that are referred to in this volume.

Purity of motive is not a necessity for progress in science. Openness of method, skeptical reception, full publication, and much-tested data are more nearly requisites. An overall judgment can be made only when the overall view is clear. Nor is it right always to expect large discoveries; truth enters more modestly, a little at a time. By and by the fuller meaning becomes clear. In the account of the astral journeys of one subject ("On Double Standards") we learned that the unique adept moved away, so the experimenter was forced to give up on the tests. It would have been quite reasonable to expect a different behavior, more partisan and less detached, from the experimenter. If one had found a person whose perceptions could leave the body, as we are led to believe, for a distance of several feet (to read a paper lying on a shelf above the sleeper) it is unreasonable not to have put him to more tests. To do that an engaged researcher would certainly follow the subject "to Zanzibar or beyond." It is hard here to turn aside the suspicion that the experimenter himself was not passionately convinced; suspecting some defect, he let the discovery rest at the modest test he describes. His result, if true, was enough to shake all of physics—but not enough to demand of him a difficult rearrangement of his time.

I feel a similar sense of guardedness in the millions of readers of all those elaborated books of unlikely marvels. The believers do not truly believe; they entertain the possibility as a diversion from the hard facts of daily life. Somehow the paranormal has a large audience that remains suspended between conviction and tolerance. Science knows such a feeling very well at the frontiers; but the history of its growth has been to watch the seep of certainty across the plains of doubt. Atoms were first speculation, then hypothesis, then convenience, and now hardware. So far, the paranormal has had no such growth. The oldest books we know are just as good a digest of the occult as the latest volumes of the specialists; indeed, skeptical critics in the past argued about as well as we do today on many of these topics.

In the end, belief is social. One who holds unique data cannot convince others in science; the data on the I.Q. of separated identical twins by Sir Cyril Burt were all his own, and most proved to be fictional. But the belief system that still supports hereditary intelligence does not much attend to any empirical data; its strength arises quite elsewhere. So it seems to be with most of parascience. It is not the self-interest of the authors that most vitiates their theories; it is the overall weakness of the inferences, and the ready acceptance by a public whose purposes in reading are broader than the test for truth, topic by topic. In science, too, the experimenter's natural self-bias is of no great consequence; the community will test claims to the point of satisfaction, over the long run at least, or simply neglect the claims until some process of confirmation can go forward.

Purity of motive is more a question of biography than of science. The rise of belief should not follow from mere admiration, as the depth of doubt ought not to come only from the judgment of ulterior motive. Larger stakes are on the table.

It is no surprise, though it is a kind of tribute to science, that the "miracles" of our day are for the most part a sort of modish natural magic. This is surely the recognition of the richness of modern science and the power of its partner, technology. Sorcery, with its appeal to personified powers, survives, to be sure. But most of the widely known claims analyzed in this volume closely follow the model of science. They shadow the subtle interactions and the invisible structures—even the statistical tests—that science and long experience have teased out of this world. Quantum mechanics, with its subtle and surprising limits on the analysis of atomic events, is made to serve as rationalization for poorly demonstrated claims of telepathy and power over remote matter. The implied mathematization of this fuzzy world is seen as no barrier, but a way to prestige. The wonders of the EEG and EKG are made the basis for a doubtful theory of biorhythms. A firm belief in the veridical nature of one scholar's version of very old and often obscure texts is made the vehicle for a wild extrapolation of the possibilities latent in Newtonian celestial mechanics. The original treatise of Velikovsky was so little concerned with the details of science that the molecular combinations of hydrocarbons and carbohydrates were conflated, even though therein lies the enormous common-sense difference between butter and bread, or gasoline and wood. For such scholars in the beginning was the Word, not the category it named.

The careful grids and trowels of the archeologists are condescendingly subsumed, and all is given a fantastic and hyperbolic gloss, tending to suggest, perhaps without saying so, that the old folk, those lesser peoples far from blond Northern Europe, could not lay masonry or carve monumental statues without celestial aid. On the other side, the same painstakingly detailed science is loaded with a charge of unexamined wonders, like the Atlantean columns off Bimini, which appear to be old cement barrels when looked at closely without rosy diving goggles.

That real science and its real wonders acquire such an airy comet's-tail of lesser matter is not without its warnings for science. We have let the wonder become too deeply buried in the mechanisms and concealed in an economical style of publication, too austere for its own good. A serious and responsible popularization is needed that sets a style closer to the best human experiences of science than to the letters in *Nature.* The critiques in this volume are necessary but do not meet the whole need—or even most of it. The positive comment will in the end outgrow the negative; amateur science, playful engineering, and first-rate fascinating exposition are necessities for the health of science as much as the sobriety of clear thought these pages try to offer.

Perhaps Frank Drake's wonderful prospects for finding thinking and erring beings elsewhere, not by magic saucer but by real radio dishes, offer a glimpse of science and exploration to come. The giant squid, perfectly real in the depths, a few specimens modeled in incredible full size in our museums; the basking shark, which in death and decay looks like the sea serpent; the hint of a truly giant octopus not yet fully known; all these offer more in the way of real monsters than the dubious Yeti or Nessie or Sasquatch or sea serpent. And delvers in the Rift have found hard bony evidence of the true "wild men" who were our forebears a million years ago, not monsters but our antique selves. The cetaceans intrigue us with their faint hint of kinship. All these offer evidence that reality can still combat fiction as well as it ever did.

But it takes more than dry briefs to do the full job. Science and technology require their artful exhibitors, too. As travelers leave Orlando Airport, a cautionary pair of road signs confronts them: one points to the fantasy theater of Disneyworld; the other offers the Space Center at Cape Kennedy. "This way," says the latter, "to reality." And you can see Saturn stages lying there, huge cylinders near the vast Vehicle Assembly Building, a giant's country all real.

Of course, our science has its deficiencies and its defects. First is the troubled state of the modern world. The problem is imputed to technology, though surely the responsibility is shared by the structures of social power. The faults of character in science are evident: arrogance, pomposity, insensitivity, the natural faults of preoccupation and highly specialized intellectuality. Complacency is not easy to maintain in the current precarious fiscal state of science, and it must not rule our judgment anymore than our hopes. We can be sure, for example, that some valuable part of the fabric of science we now accept will be held naive and erroneous by those scientists who come after us.

Just which part we are not given to know. To me it does not seem likely that it will come in one of the "paranormal" fields that are discussed in this book. But it is no betrayal of science to admit the certainty that somewhere we are wrong. The challenge is to show where, not to turn the wish for immortality or omniscience into a pseudoscience. If I am asked to make one guess, it is that we will come more to appreciate the steps toward science made long ago, perhaps even by our cave-dwelling forebears. They might turn out to have known a great deal more than we now credit them with, perhaps something like writing, calculation, and certainly naked-eye astronomy. But they will have learned it all, as we do, without extraterrestrials as guides, by hard thinking and sharp seeing. Human beings painted the caves, no one else.

Those cave paintings are wonderful, but like everything we know they are not too wonderful to be true. It is their reality that gives them wonder, and while there will never come a time when some of us will not wish for more than we can have, the happiest of us will wait confidently for other tangible finds. We treasure the cave at Altamira where a century ago a little girl first saw the great painted bison. New caves will be found, year after year, in lab or clinic or sky or ocean depth, or even in ancient markings. That is the promise of real science, which cannot allow wish to rule mind, but nonetheless finds unendingly wonderful things.

Notes and Bibliographies

To Believe or Not to Believe

1. BENASSI, V.; SINGER, B.; and REYNOLDS, C. "Occult Belief: Seeing Is Believing." *Journal of the Scientific Study of Religion*, 1980, in press; *The Skeptical Enquirer*, 1980, in press.

2. EINHORN, H. J., and HOGARTH, R. M. "Confidence in Judgment: Persistence of the Illusion of Validity." *Psychological Review*, 1978, pp. 85, 395–417.

3. FOWLES, JOHN. "The Enigma," in Fowles, J., *The Ebony Tower*. Boston: Little, Brown, 1974.

4. LANGER, E. J. "The Illusion of Control." *Journal of Personality and Social Psychology*, 1975, 32 (2), 311–18.

5. SKINNER, B. F. "The Force of Coincidence." *The Humanist*, 1977, 37 (3), 10–12.

6. TVERSKY, A., and KAHNEMAN, D. "Judgement Under Uncertainty: Heuristics and Biases." *Science*, 27 (September 1974), pp. 1124–31.

Monsters

1. COHEN, DANIEL. *A Modern Look at Monsters.* New York: Dodd, Mead, 1970.

2. ———. *Monsters, Giants and Little Men from Mars.* New York: Doubleday, 1975.

3. COSTELLO, PETER. *In Search of Lake Monsters.* New York: Coward, McCann & Geoghegan, 1974.

4. FORT, CHARLES. *The Books of Charles Fort.* New York: Holt, 1941.

5. GREEN, JOHN. *On the Track of the Sasquatch.* Agassiz, British Columbia: Cheam Publishing Co., 1968.

6. HEUVELMANS, BERNARD. *In the Wake of the Sea Serpents.* New York: Hill and Wang, 1968.

7. ———. *On the Track of Unknown Animals.* New York: Hill and Wang, 1959.

8. MACKAL, ROY. *The Monsters of Loch Ness.* Chicago: Swallow Press, 1976.

9. NAPIER, JOHN. *Bigfoot.* New York: Dutton, 1973.

10. PATTERSON, ROGER. *Do Abominable Snowmen of America Really Exist?* Yakima, Washington: Trailblazer Research, 1968.

11. SANDERSON, IVAN T. *Abominable Snowmen, Legend Come to Life.* Philadelphia: Chilton, 1961.

12. WITCHELL, NICHOLAS. *The Loch Ness Story.* London: Penguin, 1975.

Plant Sensitivity and Sensation

1. TOMPKINS, PETER, and BIRD, CHRISTOPHER. *The Secret Life of Plants.* New York: Harper and Row, 1973.

2. ANDUS, L. T. "Roots of Absurdity." *New Scientist* 17 (October 1974), p. 207; GALSTON, A. W. "The Unscientific Method." *Natural History* 83 (1974), pp. 18–24; HECHT, A. "Emotional Responses by Plants." *Plant Science Bulletin* (December 1974), pp. 46–47.

3. BACKSTER, C. "Evidence of a Primary Perception in Plant Life." *International Journal of Parapsychology* 10 (1968), pp. 329–48.

4. HOROWITZ, K. A.; LEWIS, D. C.; and GASTEIGER, E. L. "Plant 'Primary Perception': Electrophysiological Unresponsiveness to Brine Shrimp Killing." *Science* 189 (1975), pp. 478–80.

5. GALVANI, L. *De Viribus Electricitatis in Motu Musculari Commentarius.* (1791.)

6. BOSE, J. C. *The Physiology of Photosynthesis.* London: Longmans, Green and Company, 1924.

7. BURDON-SANDERSON, J. "Note on the Electrical Phenomena Which Accompany Stimulation of the Leaf of *Dionaea muscipula.*" *Proceedings of the Royal Society* 21 (1873), pp. 495–96.

8. PICKARD, B. G. "Action Potentials in Higher Plants." *Botanical Review* 39 (1973), pp. 172–201; OSTERHOUT, W. J. V. "Some Aspects of Permeability and Bioelectrical Phenomena." *Bulletin of the National Research Council* 69 (1929), pp. 170–228.

9. BOSE, J. C., *op. cit.*; and SIBAOKA, T. "Action Potentials in Plant Organs." *Symposium of the Society for Experimental Biology* 20 (1966), pp. 49–74.

10. SLAYMAN, C. L.; LONG, W. S.; and GRADMANN, D. " 'Action Potentials' in *Neurospora crassa*, a Mycelial Fungus." *Biochim. Biophys. Acta* 426 (1976), pp. 732–44.

11. OSTERHOUT, W. J. V., *op. cit.*

12. ———. "Permeability in Large Plant Cells and in Models." *Ergeb. Physiol. u. Exp. Pharm.* 35 (1933), pp. 967–1021.

13. LUND, E. J. *Bioelectric Fields and Growth.* Austin: University of Texas Press, 1947.

14. LUNDEGAARDH, H. "Anion Respiration: The Experimental Basis of a Theory of Absorption, Transport, and Exudation of Electrolytes by Living Cells and Tissues." *Symposium of the Society for Experimental Biology* 8 (1954), pp. 262–96.

15. MITCHELL, P. "Molecule, Group, and Electron Translocation Through Natural Membranes." *Biochem. Soc. Symp.* 22 (1963), pp. 142–68.

16. LUND, E. J., *op. cit.*

17. BRIGGS, G. E., and HOPE, A. B. "Electrical Potential Differences and the Donnan Equilibrium in Plant Tissues." *Journal of Experimental Botany* 9 (1958), pp. 365–71.

18. LUND, E. J., *op. cit.*; and MCAULAY, A. L.; FORD, J. M.; and HOPE, A. B. "The Distribution of Electromotive Forces in the Neighborhood of Apical Meristems." *Journal of Experimental Biology* 28 (1951), pp. 320–31.

19. SCHRANK, A. R. "Bioelectrical Implications in Plant Tropisms." *Symposium of the Society for Experimental Biology* 11 (1957), pp. 95–117.

20. JAFFE, L. F. "Electrical Currents Through the Developing *Fusuc* Egg." *Proceedings of the National Academy of Sciences* 56 (1966), pp. 1102–9.

21. JAFFE, L. F.; ROBINSON, K. R.; and NUCCITELLI, R. "Local Cation Entry and Self-electrophoresis as an Intracellular Localization Mechanism." *Annals of the New York Academy of Sciences* 238 (1974), pp. 372–89.

22. RACUSEN, R. H., and SATTER, R. L. "Rhythmic and Phytochrome-regulated Changes in Transmembrane Potential in *Samanea* Pulvini." *Nature* 255 (1975), pp. 408–10.

23. SATTER, R. L.; SCHREMPF, M.; CHAUDHRI, J.; and GALSTON, A. W. "Phytochrome and Circadian Clocks in *Samanea*. Rhythmic Redistribution of Potassium and Chloride Within the Pulvinis During Long Dark Periods." *Plant Physiology* 59 (1977), pp. 231–35; and GALSTON, A. W., and SATTER, R. L. "Light, Clocks and Ion Flux: An Analysis of Leaf Movement." In *Light and Plant Development*, H. Smith, ed. (London: Butterworths, 1976).

24. BACKSTER, C. L., *op. cit.*

25. HOROWITZ, LEWIS, and GASTEIGER, *op. cit.*

26. KMETZ, J. M. "A Study of Primary Perception in Plant and Animal Life." Lecture presented at the symposium on "Electrical Responses of Plants to External Stimuli," annual meeting of American Association for the Advancement of Science, January 1975, New York City.

27. *Ibid.*

28. BACKSTER, C. L. *Christian Science Monitor*, December 11, 1973, 2nd section, p. 9.

29. Quoted in TOMPKINS and BIRD, *op. cit.*, p. 27.

Parapsychology and Quantum Mechanics

1. See "The Physical Roots of Consciousness" by Jack Sarfatti in *Roots of Consciousness: Psychic Liberation through History, Science and Experience*, by Jeffrey Mishlove (New York: Random House, 1975), pages 279–93; *Space-Time and Beyond*, by Bob Toben "in conversation with physicists Jack Sarfatti and Fred Wolf" (New York: Dutton, 1975).

2. See "Possible Connections Between Psychic Phenomena and Quantum Mechanics," by Brian Josephson (*New Horizons*, January 1975, pages 224–26).

3. See "Quantum Paradoxes and Aristotle's Two-fold Information Concept," by O. Costa de Beauregard in the Oteri book cited in note

9, and his comments in the book's discussion sections.

4. See *Mind-Reach: Scientists Look at Psychic Ability*, by Russell Targ and Harold Puthoff (New York: Delacorte Press/Elinor Friede, 1977), page 170.

5. The EPR paradox was first set forth by Einstein, Podolsky, and Rosen in "Can Quantum-Mechanical Description of Physical Reality Be Considered Complete?" in *Physical Review*, vol. 47 (1935), pages 777–80. Niels Bohr's reply, which Einstein claimed he could never understand, appeared in the same journal, vol. 48 (1935), pages 696 ff. For a discussion between Bohr and Einstein about the paradox, see *Albert Einstein: Philosopher-Scientist*, edited by Paul Arthur Schilpp (Library of Living Philosophers, 1949), pages 231–41, 681–83. For discussions by Einstein and Max Born of the paradox, see *The Born-Einstein Letters*, edited by Born (New York: Walker, 1971), pages 164–65, 168–76, 178, 188–89, 214–15. A letter from Einstein to Karl Popper, in which he outlines his paradox, appears in Popper's *The Logic of Scientific Discovery* (New York: Basic Books, 1959), pages 457–64; see also pages 244–45, 444–48.

Einstein's objection is in no way met merely by restating the QM formalism that describes the paradox. This is the kind of "resolution" one finds in almost any standard textbook on QM theory. On this point see "Concerning Einstein's, Podolsky's, and Rosen's Objection to Quantum Theory," by Clifford A. Hooker (*American Journal of Physics*, vol. 38 [July 1970], pages 851–57) and Hooker's lengthy paper "The Nature of Quantum Mechanical Reality: Einstein Versus Bohr" in *Paradigms and Paradoxes*, edited by Robert G. Colodny (Pittsburgh: University of Pittsburgh Press, 1972).

6. In 1965, J. S. Bell showed that any theory of hidden variables designed to explain the correlation of two particles, that was both realistic and local, would lead to predictions that differ from those of QM and therefore can be tested. "Realistic" here means that the variables have a space–time structure independent of the observer, and "local" means that the particles, after becoming widely separated, are not in any kind of interaction with each other.

Stronger versions of Bell's proof were later found by others. All are known collectively as Bell's theorem. In 1969, J. F. Clauser, M. A. Horne, Abner Shimony, and R. A. Holt showed how actual tests could be made. Since 1972 there have been seven such tests, most of which clearly confirm QM. The experiments involved particles that remain correlated only for a distance of a few meters. No one can yet say whether the correlation will persist or grow weaker at greater distances.

For a detailed and excellent summary of these momentous results see "Bell's Theorem: Experimental Tests and Implications," by Clauser and Shimony, in *Reports on Progress in Physics*, vol. 41 (1978), pages 1881–1927. "Because of the evidence in favour of quantum mechanics from the experiments based upon Bell's theorem," they conclude, "we are forced either to abandon . . . a realistic view of the physical world (perhaps an unheard tree falling in the forest makes no sound after all)—or else to accept some kind of action-at-a-distance. Either option is radical, and a comprehensive study of their philosophical consequences remains to be made."

7. See H. P. Stapp, "Are Superluminal Connections Necessary?" in *Il Nuovo Cimento*, vol. 40B (July 11, 1977), pages 191–205. To avoid superluminal connection, Costa de Beauregard (in the book cited in note 9) maintains that quantum information travels back in time from the measured particle to the event that produced the two particles, then forward in time to the other particle. The path is a "Feynman zigzag" that brings the information to the second particle at precisely the same moment it left the first one.

8. I am aware that some eminent physicists, notably Eugene Wigner, contend that every "measurement" of a quantum system creates a new state that is in turn subject to measurement, and that this regress does not finally end until it reaches a mind. But this is a point of view held by an extreme minority of physicists. It rests partly on metaphysical suppositions and partly on desperation over the lack of any good theory of wave-packet reduction.

One objection to Wigner's view is that there seems to be no good reason to stop the process with the human observer—not to mention the difficulties that arise in asking whether the process can be said to terminate if the observer is, say, a cow. The observer, too, is an ongoing quantum system with its own wave function that can acquire precise values for its variables only if someone observes the observer, and so into an infinite regress. This is sometimes called the "von Neumann catastrophe" (because it is suggested by John von Neumann's classic formalization of QM), and sometimes the "paradox of Wigner's friend." It is closely tied to the famous earlier paradox of "Schrodinger's cat." The issues are complex and technical, and loaded with semantic pitfalls, but they are largely irrelevant to our topic. Even if one believes that a falling tree has no "reality" until a "mind" observes it, it does not follow that a human mind can alter the way the tree falls.

In a paper on "Wave-Packet Reduction as a Medium of Communication," by Joseph Hall, Christopher Kim, Brien McElroy, and Abner Shimony (*Foundations of Physics*, vol. 7 [October 1977], pages 759–767), the authors report on an ingenious experiment designed to test the ability of observers to reduce wave packets. The results were negative. "Doubt is thereby thrown," the authors conclude with understatement, "upon the hypothesis that the reduction of the wave packet is due to the interaction of the physical apparatus with the psyche of an observer."

9. This paper, Walker's major statement of his theory, appears in *Quantum Mechanics and Parapsychology*, edited by Laura Oteri, published by the Parapsychology Foundation, New York, in 1975. The book contains eleven papers given at the 23rd Annual International Conference of the Parapsychology Foundation, held at Geneva in 1974. The topic had been proposed by Arthur Koestler, who attended as an observer.

10. "Psychokinetic Placement: II. A Factorial Study of Successful and Unsuccessful Series," by R. A. McConnell and Haakon Forwald, in *The Journal of Parapsychology*, vol. 31 (September 1967), pages 198–213.

11. For a listing of Forwald's principal papers and a critical survey, see "A Review of Psychokinesis (PK)" by Edward Girden, in the *Psychological Bulletin*, vol. 59 (September 1962), pages 374–77, 385. Forwald became convinced that the PK placement effect he thought he was getting is gravitational. In his monograph *Mind, Matter and Gravitation* (New York: Parapsychology Foundation, 1969) he argues that his "findings suggest that PK-forces are of a gravitational kind, and that they originate from a mental influence on atomic nuclei in the material which is used in the moveable bodies in the experiments." He believes this theory is tentatively confirmed by his later experiments with an oak ball rolling sideways on an inclined plane.

12. Published in *Psychic Explorations: A Challenge for Science*, edited by astronaut Edgar D. Mitchell and occult writer John White (New York: Putnam's, 1974).

13. Gamow reproduces Pauli's letter in facsimile in his *Thirty Years That Shook Physics: The Story of Quantum Theory* (Garden City, N.Y.: Doubleday, 1966), page 162.

14. Hyperspace theories of the paranormal were popular

during spiritualism's heyday. A classic crank work along such lines is *Transcendental Physics*, by Johann C. F. Zöllner, published in Germany in 1879 and later translated into English. Zöllner was typical of many of today's paraphysicists, learned in science but so gullible that he was easily bamboozled by a famous mountebank of the time, the slatewriting medium Henry Slade. Zöllner's book should be required reading for every executive of Stanford Research Institute.

Hyperspace theories of psi are still with us. See William A. Tiller, "The Positive and Negative Space/Time Frames as Conjugate Systems," and Charles Muses, "Paraphysics: A New View of Ourselves and the Cosmos." Both papers are in *Future Science*, edited by John White and Stanley Krippner (New York: Anchor Press, 1977). Muses, a panpsychist who believes that all basic particles are primitive life forms, explores hyperspaces with his "hypernumbers"—operators that describe how you can do such things as swing an object into hyperspace and back. They account for the Geller effect, the levitations of the British medium D. D. Home, and other wonders.

15. See *Quantum Mechanics and Parapsychology*, pp. 51–52, 124–26, 171, 230, 261, and 274.

Astrology

Among the hundreds (if not thousands) of pro-astrology books that explain its workings, an excellent and representative example is *The Compleat Astrologer*, by Derek and Julia Parker (New York: McGraw-Hill, 1971; also Bantam Books, 1975).

Some books treating the place of astrology in history are:

1. COHEN, D. *The Magic Art of Foreseeing the Future*. New York: Dodd, Mead, 1973.

2. GRAUBARD, M. *Astrology and Alchemy, Two Fossil Sciences*. New York: Philosophical Library, 1953.

3. SHUMAKER, W. *The Occult Sciences in the Renaissance; A Study in Intellectual Patterns*. Berkeley: The University of California Press, 1972.

Some books critical of astrology include:

1. COUDERC, P. *L'Astrologie* (in French). Paris: Presses Universitaires de France, 1974.

2. CULVER, R. B., and IANNA, P. A. *Gemini Syndrome: Star Wars of the Oldest Kind*. Tucson: Pachart Press, 1979.

3. GALLANT, R. A. *Astrology, Sense or Nonsense?* Garden City, New York: Doubleday and Co., 1974.

4. JEROME, LAWRENCE. *Astrology, Disproved.* Buffalo, New York: Prometheus Books, 1978.

5. GAUQUELIN, MICHEL. *Dreams and Illusions in Astrology.* Buffalo, New York: Prometheus Books, 1979.

6. STANDEN, ANTHONY. *Forget Your Sun Sign.* Legacy Publishing Co., 5615 Corporate Boulevard, Baton Rouge, Louisiana 70808, 1977.

Moon Madness

1. See ABEL, L. E. *Moon Madness.* Greenwich, Conn.: Fawcett, 1976, for a sensationalistic account of this.

2. LIEBER, ARNOLD L. *The Lunar Effect.* Garden City, New York: Anchor Press/Doubleday, 1978.

3. The tidal force produced by a body of distance r and mass M on another body of diameter D is proportional to MD/r^3. For an elementary discussion, see GEORGE O. ABELL, *Exploration of the Universe*, 3rd ed. New York: Holt, Rinehart and Winston, 1975, pp. 94–104.

4. LIEBER, ARNOLD L., and SHERIN, CAROLYN R. "Homicides and the Lunar Cycle: Toward a Theory of Lunar Influence on Human Emotional Disturbance." *American Journal of Psychiatry* 129 (1972), pp. 69–74.

5. *The Lunar Effect*, pp. 41–42.

6. POKORNY, A. D. "Moon Phases, Suicide, and Homicide." *American Journal of Psychiatry* 121 (1964), pp. 66–67.

7. ———, and JACHIMCZYK, JOSEPH. "The Questionable Relationship Between Homicides and the Lunar Cycle." *American Journal of Psychiatry* 131 (1974), pp. 827–829.

8. LESTER, D.; BROCKOPP, G. W.; and PRIEBE, K. "Association Between a Full Moon and Completed Suicide." *Psychological Reports* 25 (1969), p. 598.

9. OSBORN, R. D. "The Moon and the Mental Hospital; An Investigation of One Area of Folklore." *Journal of Psychiatric Nursing* 6 (1968), pp. 88–93.

10. POKORNY, A. D. "Moon Phases and Mental Hospital Admissions." *Journal of Psychiatric Nursing* 6 (1968), pp. 325–27.

11. BLACKMAN, S., and CATALINA, D. "The Moon and the Emergency Room." *Perceptual and Motor Skills* 37 (1973), pp.

624–26; and WALTERS, E.; MARKLEY, R. P.; and TIFFANY, D. W. "Lunacy: A Type I Error?" *Journal of Abnormal Psychology* 84 (1975), pp. 715–17.

12. WEISKOTT, G. N., and TIPTON, G. B. "Moon Phases and State Hospital Admissions." *Psychological Reports* 37 (1975), p. 486.

13. BAUER, S. F., and HORNICK, E. J. "Lunar Effect on Mental Illness: The Relationship of Moon Phase to Psychiatric Emergencies." *American Journal of Psychiatry* 125 (1968), pp. 148–49; LILIENFELD, D. M. "Lunar Effect on Mental Illness." *American Journal of Psychiatry* 125 (1969), p. 1454; WEISKOTT, G. N. "Moon Phases and Telephone Counseling Calls." *Psychological Reports* 35 (1974), pp. 752–54; and SHAPIRO, J. L.; STREINER, D. L.; GARY, A. L.; WILLIAMS, N. L.; and SOBLE, C. "The Moon and Mental Illness: A Failure to Confirm the Transylvania Effect." *Perceptual and Motor Skills* 30 (1970), pp. 827–30.

14. CAMPBELL, D. E., and BEETS, J. L. "Lunacy and the Moon." *Psychological Bulletin* 86 (1978), pp. 1123–29.

15. ANDREWS, EDSON J. "Moon Talk: The Cyclic Periodicity of Postoperative Hemorrhage." *Journal of the Florida Medical Association* 45 (1960), pp. 1362–66.

16. *Los Angeles Times*, July 16, 1978, Part XI, p. 4.

17. See note 15.

18. MENAKER, W., and MENAKER, A. "Lunar Periodicity in Human Reproduction: A Likely Unit of Biological Time." *American Journal of Obstetrics and Gynecology* 77 (1959), 905–14.

19. MENAKER, W. D. "Lunar Periodicity with Reference to Live Births." *American Journal of Obstetrics and Gynecology* 98 (1967), pp. 1001–4.

20. OSLEY, M.; SUMMERVILLE, D.; and BORST, L. B. "Natality and the Moon." *American Journal of Obstetrics and Gynecology* 117 (1973), pp. 413–15.

21. RIPPMANN, E. T. "The Moon and the Birth Rate." *American Journal of Obstetrics and Gynecology* 74 (1957), pp. 148–50.

22. ABELL, GEORGE O., and GREENSPAN, BENNETT. "Human Births and the Phase of the Moon." *The New England Journal of Medicine* 300 (1979), p. 96.

Biorhythms

1. ALLUISI, E. S., and CHILES, W. D. "Sustained Performance, Work-rest, Scheduling and Diurnal Rhythms 'in man'." *Acta Psychologica*, vol. 27, 1967.

2. ASCHOFF, J., ed. *Circadia Clocks.* Amsterdam: North-Holland Publishing Co., 1965.

3. BLAKE, M. J. F. "Temperament and Time of Day," in *Biological Rhythms and Human Performance*, edited by W. P. Colquhoun. New York: Academic Press, 1971, pp. 109–48.

4. BROWNLEY, M. W., and SANDLER, C. E. "Biorhythm—An Accident Prevention Aid?" *Proceedings of the Human Factors Society*, 21st Annual Meeting, 1977.

5. BÜNNING, E. *The Physiological Clock.* New York: Academic Press, Inc., 1964.

6. COMELLA, T. M. "Biorhythm—Personal science or Parlor game?" *Machine Design*, Oct. 1976.

7. COLQUHOUN, W. P., ed. *Biological Rhythms and Human Performance.* London: Academic Press.

8. CONROY, R. T., and MILLS, W. L. *Human Circadian Rhythms.* Baltimore: Williams and Wilkins Co., 1970.

9. HARKER, J. E. *The Physiology of Diurnal Rhythms.* London: Cambridge University Press, 1964.

10. HIRSH, T. "Biorhythm, or, is it a Critical Day?" *National Safety News* 113 (1976).

11. KHALIL, T. M., and KURUCZ, C. N. "The Influence of 'Biorhythm' on Accident Occurrence and Performance." *Economics*, vol. 20 (1977).

12. KURUCZ, C. N., and KHALIL, T. M. "Probability Models for Analyzing the Effects of Biorhythms on Accident Occurrence." *Journal of Safety Research*, vol. 9: 4 (1977).

13. LATMAN, N. "Human Sensitivity, Intelligence and Physical Cycles and Motor Vehicle Accidents." *Accident Analysis and Prevention*, vol. 9 (1977).

14. LOUIS, A. M. "Should You Buy Biorhythms?" *Psychology Today*, April 1978, p. 93.

15. LUCE, G. G. *Biological Rhythms in Human and Animal Physiology.* New York: Dover Publications, 1971.

16. MENAKER, M., ed. *Biochronometry.* Washington, D.C.: National Academy of Science, 1971.

17. NAUNTON, E. "Biorhythm May Let You Have a Happy Day." *The Miami Herald*, Sunday, June 2, 1974.

18. NEIL, D. E., and SINK, F. L. "A Laboratory Investigation of 'Biorhythms.'" Man-machines Systems Design Laboratory, Naval Postgraduate School, Monterey, Calif., 1975.

19. NEIL, D. E., and PARSONS, S. O. "Biorhythms—Possible Ap-

plication to Flight Safety." *Papers of the International Air Transport Association*, Twentieth Technical Conference on Safety in Flight Operations. Istanbul: Nov. 1975.

20. NEWCOMB, B. L. "Talk on Biorhythm." National Lead Industries, Titanium Pigment Division, South Ebony, N.J., 1971.

21. OGINSKI, A. "Comparative Research into the Work on Three Shifts: Morning, Afternoon and Night." *Proceedings of the 15th International Congress on Occupational Health*, Vienna, vol. 6, 1966, pp. 384–85.

22. ÖSTBERG, O. "Circadian Rhythms of Food Intake and Oral Temperature in 'Morning' and 'Evening' Groups of Individuals." *Ergonomics* 16 (1973), 203–9.

23. ———. "Interindividual Differences in Circadian Fatigue Patterns of Shift Workers." *British Journal of Industrial Medicine* 30 (1973), 341–51.

24. PALMER, J. D. *An Introduction to Biological Rhythms.* New York: Academic Press, 1976.

25. PARLEE, M. B. "The Rhythm In Men's Lives." *Psychology Today*, April 1978.

26. PATKAI, P. "The Diurnal Rhythm of Adrenal Secretion in Subjects with Different Working Habits." *Acta Physiological Schandinavica* 81 (1971), 30–34.

27. PITTNER, E. D., and OWENS, P. "Chance or Destiny?" *Professional Safety*, vol. 20 (1975).

28. SACHER, D. "The Influence of Biorhythmic Criticability on Aircraft Mishaps." Master's thesis, Naval Postgraduate School, Monterey, Calif., 1974.

29. SANHEIN, J. M. "Biorhythm Analysis as Applicable to Safety." *Papers of the National Safety Congress and Exposition.* Chicago: September 1975.

30. SOLLBERGER, A. *Biological Rhythm Research.* New York: Elsevier Publishing Co., 1965.

31. ———. "Biological Rhythms and Their Control in Neurobehavioural Perspective," in *Neurosciences Research*, vol. 4, edited by Ehrenpreis, S., and Solnitsky, O. New York: Academic Press, 1971.

32. THOMMEN, GEORGE. *Is This Your Day?* New York: Crown Publishers, Inc., 1964.

33. WEAVER, C. A. "The Question of Ups and Downs." *U.S. Army Aviation Digest*, vol. 20 (1974).

34. WEDDERBURN, AL. "General Discussion: Future Research Needs," in *Aspects of Human Efficiency: Diurnal Rhythm and Loss of Sleep*, edited by W. P. Colquhoun. London: English Universities Press, 1972, p. 335.

35. WILLIS, H. R. "Biorhythm and Its Relationship to Human Error." *Proceedings of the 16th Annual Meeting of the Human Factors Society*, Beverly Hills, California, 1972, pp. 274–82.

36. ———. "The Effect of Biorhythm Cycles—Implications for Industry." *American Industrial Hygiene Conference*, Miami Beach, May 12–17, 1974.

37. WOJTCZAK-JAROSZOWA, J. "Physiological and Psychological Aspects of Night and Shift Work." DHEW (NIOSH) Publication No. 78–113, Dec. 1977.

38. WOLCOTT, J. H.; MCMEEKIN, R. R.; BURGIN, R. E.; and YONOWITCH, R. E. "Biorhythms: Are They a Waste of Time?" *TAC Attack*, vol. 15 (1975).

39. WRIGHT, L. W. "Biorhythms: Fact and Fancy." *Proceedings of the Human Factors Society*, 21st Annual Meeting, 1977.

Scientists and Psychics

1. ASIMOV, I. *Asimov's Biographical Encyclopedia of Science and Technology*. New York: Equinox, 1976.

2. BEAUREGARD, L. "Skepticism, Science, and the Paranormal." *Zetetic Scholar*, 1 (1978), 3–10.

3. BICKMAN, L. "Data Collection I: Observational Methods," in C. Selltiz, L. S. Wrightsman, and S. W. Cook. 3rd ed. *Research Methods in Social Relations*. New York: Holt, Rinehart and Winston, 1976.

4. CARRINGTON, H. *The Physical Phenomena of Spiritualism: Fraudulent and Genuine*. Boston: H. B. Turner & Co., 1907.

5. COOVER, J. E. *Experiments in Psychical Research*. Stanford: Stanford University, 1917.

6. DAVEY, S. J. "The Possibilities of Mal-observation and Lapse of Memory from a Practical Point of View: Experimental Investigation." *Proceedings of the Society for Psychical Research* (1887), 405–95.

7. DINGWALL, E. J. *Very Peculiar People: Portrait Studies in the Queer, the Abnormal, and the Uncanny*. New Hyde Park, New York: University Books, 1962.

8. EDMUNDS, S. "Cooking the evidence?" *Tomorrow*, 10 (Autumn 1962), 35–44.

9. ———. *ESP: Extrasensory Perception*. No. Hollywood, Calif.: Wilshire Book Co., 1972.

10. FEDOR, N. *An Encyclopedia of Psychic Science*. Secaucus, New Jersey: The Citadel Press, 1974.

11. FOURNIER D'ALBE, E. E. *The Life of Sir William Crookes*. New York: D. Appleton & Co., 1924.

12. GARDNER, M. GELLER. "Gulls and Nitinol." *The Humanist*, 37 (May/June 1977), 25–32.

13. GAULD, A. *The Founders of Psychical Research*. New York: Schocken, 1968.

14. GEORGE, W. *Biologist Philosopher: A Study of the Life and Writings of Alfred Russel Wallace*. London: Abelard-Schuman, 1964.

15. HALL, T. H. *The Spiritualists: The Story of Florence Cook and William Crookes*. New York: Garrett Publications, 1963.

16. ———. "Florence Cook & William Crookes: A Footnote to an Enquiry." *Tomorrow*, 11 (Autumn 1963), 341–59.

17. ———. *The Strange Case of Edmund Guerney*. London: Duckworth, 1964.

18. ———. *Sherlock Holmes and His Creator*. New York: St. Martin's Press, 1977.

19. HANLON, J. "Uri Geller and Science." *New Scientist*, 64 (October 17, 1974), 170–85.

20. HARE, R. *Experimental Investigation of the Spirit Manifestations, Demonstrating the Existence of Spirits and Their Communion with Mortals: Doctrine of the Spirit World Respecting Heaven, Hell, Morality, and God. Also, the Influence of Scripture on the Morals of Christians*. New York: Partridge & Brittan, 1855.

21. HODGSON, R. "The Possibilities of Mal-observation and Lapse of Memory from a Practical Point of View." Introduction, *Proceedings of the Society for Psychical Research*, 4 (1887), 381–404.

22. ———. "Mr. Davey's Imitation by Conjuring of Phenomena Sometimes Attributed to Spirit Agency." *Proceedings of the Society for Psychical Research*, 8 (1892), 253–310.

23. HYMAN, R. "Review of *The Geller Papers*." *The Zetetic*, 1 (Fall/Winter 1976), 73–80.

24. ———. "Psychics and Scientists: 'Mind-reach' and Remote Viewing." *The Humanist*, 37 (May/June 1977), 16–20.

25. JOEL, Y. "Uri Through the Lens Cap." *Popular Photography*, 77 (June 1974), 135–8, 174.

26. KOTTIER, M. J. "Alfred Russel Wallace: The Origin of Man, and Spiritualism." *Isis*, 65 (1974), 145–92.

27. LUDWIG, J., ed. *Philosophy and Parapsychology*. Buffalo, N.Y.: Prometheus Books, 1978.

28. MARKS, D., and KAMMANN, R. "The Nonpsychic Powers of Uri Geller." *The Zetetic*, 1 (Spring/Summer 1977), 9–17.

29. MEDHURST, R. G., ed. *Crookes and the Spirit World: A Collection of Writings by or Concerning the Work of Sir William Crookes, O.M., F.R.S., in the Field of Psychical Research*. New York: Taplinger, 1972.

30. PANATI, C., ed. *The Geller Papers: Scientific Observations on the Paranormal Powers of Uri Geller*. Boston: Houghton-Mifflin, 1976.

31. PLAYFAIR, G. L. "Letter." *Journal of the Society for Psychical Research*, 48 (1975), 121–3.

32. PODMORE, F. *Mediums of the 19th Century*. New Hyde Park, New York: University Books, 1963.

33. PUTHOFF, H. E., and TARG, R. "Information Transmission under Conditions of Sensory Shielding." *Nature*, 252 (Oct. 18, 1974), 602–7.

34. PALFREMAN, J. "William Crookes: Spiritualism and Science." *Ethics in Science and Medicine*, 3 (1976), 211–27.

35. RANDI, J. *The Magic of Uri Geller*. New York: Ballantine, 1975.

36. ———. "New Evidence in the Uri Geller Matter." *The Skeptical Inquirer*, 2 (Spring/Summer 1978), 27–30.

37. SIDGWICK, MRS. H. "Results of a Personal Investigation into the Physical Phenomena of Spiritualism with Some Critical Remarks on the Evidence for Genuineness of Such Phenomena." *Proceedings of the Society for Psychical Research*, 4 (1886–87), 45–74.

38. TARG, R., and PUTHOFF, H. *Mind-Reach: Scientists Look at Psychic Ability*. New York: Delacorte, 1977.

39. TART, C. "Review of *The Magic of Uri Geller*, by the Amazing Randi; *The Geller Papers*, edited by Charles Panati; and *My Story*, by Uri Geller." *Psychology Today*, 10 (July 1976), 93–4.

40. *Time* magazine. "The Magician and the Think Tank." March 12, 1973. Pp. 110, 112.

41. WALLACE, A. R. *My Life: A Record of Events and Opinions*. Vol. 2. New York: Dodd, Mead, 1906.

42. WILHELM, J. L. *The Search for Superman.* New York: Pocket Books, 1976.

43. ZOELLNER, J. C. F. *Transcendental Physics.* New York: Arno Press, 1976.

On Double Standards

1. McCONNELL, J. V. "Memory Transfer Through Cannibalism in Planarians." *Journal of Neuropsychiatry,* 3 (Supplement 1, 1962), pp. 542–48.

2. BYRNE, W. L., *et al.* "Memory Transfer." *Science,* 153 (1966), p. 658.

3. McCONNELL, J. V. "Psychotechnology and Personal Change." In *Psychological Research: The Inside Story,* by M. H. Siegel and H. P. Zeigler. New York: Harper and Row, 1976, pp. 327–55.

4. GARDNER, R. A. "On Box Score Methodology as Illustrated by Three Reviews of Overtraining Reversal Effects." *Psychological Bulletin,* 66 (1967), pp. 416–9.

5. CHAPOUTHIER, G. "Behavioral Studies of the Molecular Basis of Memory," in *The Physiological Basis of Memory,* by J. A. Deutsch. New York: Academic Press, 1973, pp. 1–27.

6. TART, C. T. *Transpersonal Psychologies.* New York: Harper and Row, 1975, p. 120.

7. *Ibid.,* p. 119.

8. ———. "Out-of-the-Body Experiences," in *Advances in Altered States of Consciousness and Human Potentialities,* vol. 1. New York: Psychological Dimensions, Inc., 1976, pp. 579–87.

Life After Death

1. ADDISON, J. T. *Life Beyond Death in the Beliefs of Mankind.* Boston: Houghton-Mifflin, 1932.

2. ANONYMOUS. "Ketamine and Back." *High Times,* 36 (August 1978), p. 8.

3. ARDREY, R. *The Social Contract.* New York: Dell, 1970.

4. BAYLESS, R. *Apparitions and Survival of Death.* New Hyde Park, N.Y.: University Books, 1973.

5. ———. *Voices from Beyond.* Secaucus: University Books, 1976.

6. *Beyond and Back.* Sunn Classic Pictures, 1977. Directed by James L. Conway. Screenplay by Stephen Lord.

7. BUDGE, E. A. W. (translation). *The Egyptian Book of the Dead.* New York: Dover, 1967.

8. CAVENDISH, R. *Visions of Heaven and Hell.* New York: Harmony Books, 1977.

9. CLAIR, C. *Unnatural History: An Illustrated Bestiary.* London: Abelard-Schuman, 1967.

10. "Continuum." Exhibit. California Museum of Science and Industry, April 8, 1978–November 15, 1978.

11. DOMINO, E. F., and LUBY, E. D. "Abnormal Mental States Induced by PCP as a Model for Schizophrenia." In J. O. Cole, A. M. Freedman, and A. J. Friedhoff, eds. *Psychopathology and Psychopharmacology.* Baltimore: Johns Hopkins Press, 1973, pp. 37–50.

12. DOUGLAS-HAMILTON, I., and DOUGLAS-HAMILTON, O. *Among the Elephants.* New York: Viking Press, 1975.

13. EBON, M. *The Evidence for Life After Death.* New York: New American Library, 1977.

14. ELIADE, M. *Shamanism: Archaic Techniques of Ecstasy.* Princeton: Princeton University Press, 1964.

15. FARMER, P. J. *To Your Scattered Bodies Go.* New York: G. P. Putnam's Sons, 1971.

16. ———. *Traitor to the Living.* New York: Ballantine, 1973.

17. FISCHER, R. "Cartography of Inner Space." In R. K. Siegel and L. J. West, eds. *Hallucinations: Behavior, Experience, and Theory.* New York: Wiley, 1975, pp. 197–239.

18. FORD, A. *Unknown But Known.* New York, Signet, 1969.

19. ———. As told to J. Ellison. *The Life Beyond Death.* New York: Putnam's, 1971.

20. FRAZER, SIR J. G. *The Belief in Immortality and the Worship of the Dead.* London: Macmillan, 1913.

21. FULLER, J. *The Great Soul Trial.* New York: Macmillan, 1969.

22. GARDNER, M. *In the Name of Science.* New York: Putnam's, 1952.

23. GARFIELD, C. A. "Consciousness Alteration and Fear of Death." *Journal of Transpersonal Psychology,* 7 (2) [1975], 147–75.

24. GORDON, D. C. *Overcoming the Fear of Death.* New York: Macmillan, 1970.

25. GOULD, F. J. *Common-sense Thoughts on a Life Beyond.* London: Watts, 1919.

26. GROF, S., and HALIFAX, J. *The Human Encounter with Death.* New York: Dutton, 1977.

27. HARLOW, S. R. A. A Life After Death. New York: Manor Books, 1968.
28. HICK, J. H. Death and Eternal Life. New York: Harper and Row, 1976.
29. HOLZER, H. Beyond This Life. Los Angeles: Pinnacle Books, 1969.
30. HUXLEY, L. This Timeless Moment. Millbrae, California: Celestial Arts, 1968.
31. JACKSON, J. H. Selected Writings. London: Hodder and Stoughton, 1931.
32. JONAS, D. F. "Life, Death, Awareness, and Concern: A Progression." In A. Toynbee, A. Koestler, et al. Life After Death. London: Weidenfeld & Nicolson, 1976, pp. 169–81.
33. KALISH, R. A., and REYNOLDS D. K. "Phenomenological Reality and Post-death Contact." Journal for the Scientific Study of Religion, 12 (2) [1973], 209–21.
34. KOESTENBAUM, P. Is There an Answer to Death? Englewood Cliffs, N.J.: Prentice-Hall, 1976.
35. KOESTLER, A. "Whereof One Cannot Speak . . . ?" In A. Toynbee, A. Koestler, et al. Life After Death. London: Weidenfeld & Nicolson, 1976, pp. 238–59.
36. KÜBLER-ROSS, E. On Death and Dying. New York: Macmillan, 1969.
37. ———. Death: The Final Stage of Growth. Englewood Cliffs, N.J.: Prentice-Hall, 1975.
38. LA BARRE, W. The Ghost Dance: The Origins of Religion. New York: Dell, 1972.
39. ———. "Anthropological perspectives on Hallucination and Hallucinogens." In R. K. Siegel and L. J. West, eds. Hallucinations: Behavior, Experience, and Theory. New York: Wiley, 1975, pp. 9–52.
40. LESHAN, L. The Medium, the Mystic, and the Physicist. New York: Ballantine Books, 1975.
41. LOEHR, F. Diary After Death. Los Angeles: Religious Research Frontier Books, 1976.
42. MAC HOVEC, F. J. Life After Death: The Chances/The Choices. Mount Vernon, N.Y.: Peter Pauper, 1975.
43. MAC MILLAN, R. L., and BROWN, K. W. G. "Cardiac Arrest Remembered." The Candian Medical Association Journal, 104 (1971), p. 889.
44. MAETERLINCK, M. The Unknown Guest. Secaucus: University Books, 1975.

45. MARAIS, E. *The Soul of the Ape.* New York: Atheneum, 1969.

46. MASTERSON, L. *The Cricular Continuum.* Seattle: Scientific Progress Association, 1977.

47. MATHESON, R. *What Dreams May Come.* New York: G. P. Putnam's Sons, 1978.

48. MATSON, A. *Afterlife: Reports from the Threshold of Death.* New York: Harper and Row, 1975.

49. MAUDSLEY, H. *Natural Causes and Supernatural Seemings.* London: Watts, 1939.

50. MEHTA, R. *The Journey with Death.* Delhi: Motilal Banarsidass, 1977.

51. MILES, E. *Life After Life, or the Theory of Reincarnation.* London: Methuen, 1907.

52. MITCHELL, W. F. "Repeated Hallucinatory Experiences as a Part of the Mourning Process Among Hopi Indian Women." *Psychiatry*, 35 (2) [1972], 185–94.

53. MONTAGU, A. *Immortality, Religion, and Morals.* New York: Hawthorn, 1971.

54. MOODY, R. *Life After Life.* New York: Bantam/Mockingbird, 1975.

55. ———. *Reflections on Life After Life.* New York: Bantam/Mockingbird, 1977.

56. MOREAU (DE TOURS), J. J. *Hashish and Mental Illness*, 1845. New York: Raven, 1973.

57. MOSS, T. *The Probability of the Impossible.* New York: New American Library, 1974.

58. *National Enquirer.* "New Evidence of Life After Death." 52 (45) [June 20, 1978], p. 1.

59. NOLAN, W. F., and JOHNSON, G. C. *Logan's Run.* New York: Dell, 1967.

60. NOYES, R., and KLETTI, R. "Depersonalization in the Face of Life-threatening Danger: a Description." *Psychiatry*, 39 (1976), 19–27.

61. OSIS, K. *Deathbed Observations by Physicians and Nurses.* New York: Parapsychology Foundation, 1961.

62. ———, and HARALDSSON, E. *At the Hour of Death.* New York: Avon, 1977.

63. PRABHUPADA, A. C. *Beyond Birth and Death.* New York: The Bhaktivedanta Book Trust, 1972.

64. RITCHIE, G. G. *Return from Tomorrow.* Waco, Texas: Chosen Books, 1978.

65. ROGO, D. S. *The Welcoming Silence.* Secaucus: University Books, 1973.

66. ROGO, D. C. "Paranormal Tape-recorded Voices: A Paraphysical Breakthrough." In J. White and S. Krippner, eds. *Future Science: Life Energies and the Physics of Paranormal Phenomena.* Garden City, N.Y.: Anchor Press, 1977, pp. 451–64.

67. SIEGEL, R. K. "Cannabis-induced Visual Imagery." A report prepared for the Commission of Inquiry into the Non-medical Use of Drugs. Ottawa, Canada: December 1971.

68. ———. "An Ethologic Search for Self-administration of Hallucinogens." *The International Journal of the Addictions,* 8 (1973), 373–93.

69. ———, and JARVIK, M. E. "Drug-induced Hallucinations in Animals and Man." In R. K. Siegel and L. J. West, eds. *Hallucinations: Behavior, Experience, and Theory.* New York: Wiley, 1975, pp. 81–161.

70. SIEGEL, R. K. "Religious Behavior in Animals and Man: Drug-induced Effects." *Journal of Drug Issues,* 7 (3) [1977a], 219–36.

71. ———. "Normal Hallucinations of Imaginary Companions." *McLean Hospital Journal,* 2 (2) [1977b], 66–80.

72. ———. "Hallucinations." *Scientific American,* 237 (4) [1977c], 132–40.

73. ———. "Phencyclidine, Criminal Behavior, and the Defense of Diminished Capacity." In R. C. Petersen and R. C. Stillman, eds. *Phencyclidine (PCP) Abuse: An Appraisal.* NIDA Research Monograph 21. Washington, D.C.: National Institute on Drug Abuse, 1978, pp. 272–88.

74. ———. "The Psychology of Life After Death." *American Psychologist,* 35 (10) [1980], 911–31.

75. SLATER, P. *The Wayward Gate: Science and the Supernatural.* Boston: Beacon Press, 1977.

76. SPRAGGETT, A. *The Case for Immortality.* New York: New American Library, 1974.

77. STEARN, J. *A Matter of Immortality: Dramatic Evidence of Survival.* New York: Atheneum, 1976.

78. STEVENSON, I. "Research into the Evidence of Man's Survival after Death." *The Journal of Nervous and Mental Disease,* 165 (3) [1977], 152–70.

79. TAYLOR, R. M. Transcribed. *Witness from Beyond.* New York: Hawthorn, 1975.

80. Toynbee, A. "Man's Concern with Life after Death." In A. Toynbee, A. Koestler, *et al. Life After Death.* London: Weidenfeld & Nicolson, 1976, pp. 3–36.

81. Verwoerdt, A. *Communication with the Fatally Ill.* Springfield, Illinois: Charles C. Thomas, 1966.

82. Vidal, G. *Messiah.* New York: Dutton, 1954.

83. Weinberg, J. "Geriatric Psychiatry." In A. M. Freedman, H. I. Kaplan, and B. J. Sadock, eds. *Comprehensive Textbook of Psychiatry/II.* Vol. 2, 2nd ed. Baltimore: Williams & Wilkins, 1975.

84. Weinberger, J. "Apparatus Communication with Discarnate Persons." In J. White and S. Krippner, eds. *Future Science: Life Energies and the Physics of Paranormal Phenomena.* Garden City, N.Y.: Anchor Press, 1977, pp. 465–87.

85. Weisman, A. *Essays upon Heredity.* Vol. 2. Oxford: Clarendon Press, 1892.

86. Weiss, J. E. *The Vestibule.* New York: Ashley Books, 1972.

87. Weldon, J., and Levitt, Z. *Is There Life after Death?* Irvine, California: Harvest House, 1977.

88. West, L. J. "A Clinical and Theoretical Overview of Hallucinatory Phenomena." In R. K. Siegel and L. J. West, eds. *Hallucinations: Behavior, Experience, and Theory.* New York: Wiley, 1975, pp. 287–311.

89. Wetzl, J. Translation. *The Bridge Over the River.* Spring Valley, New York: The Anthroposophic Press, 1974.

90. Wheeler, D. R. *Journey to the Other Side.* New York: Ace Books, 1976.

91. White, S. E. *The Betty Book.* New York: Dutton, 1937.

92. ———. *The Unobstructed Universe.* New York: Dutton, 1940.

93. Wilson, E. O. *The Insect Societies.* Cambridge, Massachusetts: Belknap, 1971.

94. Winters, W. D. "The Continuum of CNS Excitatory States and Hallucinosis." In R. K. Siegel and L. J. West, eds. *Hallucinations: Behavior, Experience, and Theory.* New York: Wiley, 1975, pp. 53–70.

Kirlian Photography

1. Ostrander, S., and Schroeder, L. *Psychic Discoveries Behind the Iron Curtain.* Englewood Cliffs, N.J.: Prentice-Hall, 1970.

2. See, for example, *Time* and *Newsweek,* March 4, 1974.

3. Moss, T. *The Probability of the Impossible.* Los Angeles: Tarcher, 1974; Johnson, K. *The Living Aura.* New York: Hawthorn, 1975; Moss, T., and Johnson, K. "Radiation Field Photography." *Psychic Magazine,* July 1972, p. 50.

4. See note 3.

5. See Krippner, S., and Rubin, D. *The Kirlian Aura.* New York: Anchor, 1974; and Krippner, S., ed. *Energies of Consciousness.* New York: Gordon & Breach, 1975.

6. Johnson, *op. cit.,* p. 4.

7. Moss, *op. cit.,* p. 25.

8. Moss, T., and Johnson, K. "Bioplasma or Corona Discharge?" In Krippner, S., and Rubin, D., *op. cit.,* p. 70.

9. See Johnson, *op. cit.*

10. In Krippner and Rubin, *op. cit.*

11. Ostrander, S., and Schroeder, L. *Handbook of Psychic Discoveries.* New York: Putnam's, 1974, pp. 77–78.

12. Cooper, D. B., and Alt, R. L. Department of Physics, California State College, Dominguez Hills. Personal communication.

13. Prat, S., and Schlemmer, J. "Electrophotography." *Journal of the Biological Photography Association,* 7 (4) [1939], 145–48.

14. Pehek, J. O.; Kyler, H. J.; and Faust, D. L. "Image Modulation in Corona Discharge Photography." *Science,* 15 October 1976, 263–70; W. W. Eidson, D. L. Faust, H. J. Kyler, J. O. Pehek, G. K. Poock. "Kirlian Photography." *Proceedings of the Institute of Electrical and Electronic Engineers Conference,* Boston, 1978; W. W. Eidson and D. L. Faust. "Corona Discharge Photography." *Drexel University News,* Spring 1977, p. 7.

An Analysis of *Worlds in Collision*

Campbell, J. *The Mythic Image.* Princeton: Princeton University Press, 1974; 2nd printing, 1975.

Connes, P.; Connes, J.; Benedict, W. S.; and Kaplan, L. D. "Traces of HCl and HF in the Atmosphere of Venus." *Astrophysical Journal,* 147 (1967), pp. 1230–37.

Marov, M. Ya.; Avduersky, V.; Borodin, N.; Ekonomov, A.; Kershanovich, V.; Lysov, V.; Moshkin, B.; Rozhdestvensky, M.; and Ryabov, O. "Preliminary Results on the Venus Atmosphere from the Venera 8 Descent Module." *Icarus,* 20 (1973), pp. 407–21.

MAROV, M. YA. "Venus: A Perspective at the Beginning of Planetary Exploration." *Icarus*, 16 (1972), pp. 415–61.

OWEN, T. C., and SAGAN, C. "Minor Constituents in Planetary Atmospheres: Ultraviolet Spectroscopy from the Orbiting Astronomical Observatory." *Icarus*, 16 (1972), pp. 557–68.

POLLACK, J. B. "A Nongray CO_2-H_2O Greenhouse Model of Venus." *Icarus*, 10 (1969), pp. 314–41.

———; ERICKSON, E.; WITTEBORN, F.; CHACKERIAN, C.; SUMMERS, A.; AUGASON, G.; and CAROFF, L. "Aircraft Observation of Venus' Near-infrared Reflection Spectrum: Implications for Cloud Composition." *Icarus*, 23 (1974), pp. 8–26.

SAGAN, C. "Erosion of the Rocks of Venus." *Nature*, 261 (1976), p. 31.

———. *The Cosmic Connection*. Garden City, N.Y.: Doubleday, 1973.

———. "The Planet Venus." *Science*, 133 (1961), p. 849.

———. "An Analysis of *Worlds in Collision*." In *Scientists Confront Velikovsky* (ed., D. Goldsmith). Ithaca, New York: Cornell University Press, 1977, pp. 41–104.

———, and PAGE, T., eds. *UFOs: A Scientific Debate*. Ithaca, N.Y.: Cornell University Press, 1972; New York: W. W. Norton, 1973.

SILL, G. "Sulfuric Acid in the Venus Clouds." University of Arizona: Communications Lunar Planet Laboratory, 9 (1972), pp. 191–98.

VELIKOVSKY, I. *Worlds in Collision*. Garden City, N.Y.: Doubleday, 1950.

WILDT, R. "Note on the Surface Temperature of Venus." *Astrophysical Journal*, 91 (1940), pp. 266–68.

YOUNG, A. T. "Are the Clouds of Venus Sulfuric Acid?" *Icarus*, 18 (1973), pp. 564–82.

YOUNG, L. D. G., and YOUNG, A. T. "Comments on the Composition of the Venus Cloud Tops in Light of Recent Spectroscopic Data." *Astrophysical Journal*, 179 (1973), pp. 39–43.

Recasting the Past: Powerful Pyramids, Lost Continents, and Ancient Astronauts

Pyramids, Power, and Pi

BADAWY, ALEXANDER. "The Stellar Destiny of the Pharaoh and the So-Called Air-Shafts of Cheops' Pyramid." *Mitteilungen des Insti-*

tuts für Orientforschung, Band X (1964), pp. 189–206.

EDWARDS, I. E. S. *The Pyramids of Egypt.* Harmondsworth, England: Penguin Books Ltd., 1961.

FAKHRY, AHMED. *The Pyramids.* Chicago: The University of Chicago Press, 1961.

GARDNER, MARTIN. *Fads and Fallacies in the Name of Science.* New York: Dover Publications, 1957.

KRUPP, E. C. "Great Pyramid Astronomy." *The Griffith Observer,* Los Angeles, 42 (3) [March 1978], pp. 1–18.

———, ed. *In Search of Ancient Astronomies.* Garden City, New York: Doubleday and Co., 1978.

MENDELSSOHN, KURT. *The Riddle of the Pyramids.* New York: Praeger Publishers, 1974.

OSTRANDER, SHEILA, and SCHROEDER, LYNN. *Psychic Discoveries Behind the Iron Curtain.* New York: Bantam Books, 1971.

PROCTOR, RICHARD A. *The Great Pyramid: Observatory, Tomb, and Temple.* London: Longmans, Green, and Co., 1888.

SLADEK, JOHN. *The New Apocrypha.* New York: Stein and Day, 1973.

SMYTH, CHARLES PIAZZI. *On the Antiquity of Intellectual Man.* Edinburgh, Scotland: Edmonston and Douglas, 1868.

———. *Our Inheritance in the Great Pyramid.* London: Charles Burnet and Co., 1890 (5th edition).

TOMPKINS, PETER. *Secrets of the Great Pyramid.* New York: Harper and Row, 1971.

TRIMBLE, VIRGINIA. "Astronomical Investigation Concerning the So-Called Air-Shafts of Cheops' Pyramid." *Mitteilungen des Instituts für Orientforschung,* Band X (1969), pp. 183–87.

Continents: Lost and Found

CHURCHWARD, JAMES. *The Lost Continent of Mu.* New York: Crown Publishers, Xanadu Library, 1961. Reprint of 1931 edition.

COHEN, DANIEL. *Mysterious Places.* New York: Dodd, Mead, 1969.

DE CAMP, L. SPRAGUE. *Lost Continents.* New York: The Gnome Press, 1954.

———, and LEY, WILLY. *Lands Beyond.* New York: Rinehart & Co., 1952.

DONNELLY, IGNATIUS. *Atlantis: The Antedeluvian World.* New York: Dover Publications, 1976. Reprint of 1882 edition.

GALANOPOULOS, A. G., and BACON, EDWARD. *Atlantis: The Truth*

Behind the Legend. Indianapolis, Indiana: Bobbs-Merrill Co., 1969.

HARRISON, W. "Atlantis Undiscovered . . . Bimini, Bahamas." *Nature*, 230 (2 April 1971), pp. 287–89. In Corliss, William R., *Strange Artifacts*, vol. M2. Glen Arm, Md.: The Sourcebook Project, 1976.

LE PLONGEON, AUGUSTUS. *Queen Moo and the Egyptian Sphinx.* Blauvelt, N.Y.: Rudolf Steiner Publications, 1973. Reprint of 1896 edition.

LUCE, J. V. *Lost Atlantis: New Light on an Old Legend.* New York: McGraw-Hill Book Co., 1969.

MAVOR, JAMES W., JR. *Voyage to Atlantis.* New York: G. P. Putnam's Sons, 1969.

MUCK, OTTO. *The Secret of Atlantis.* New York: Quadrangle/The New York Times Book Co., 1978.

SHINN, E. A. "Atlantis: Bimini Hoax." *Sea Frontiers*, 24 (1978), pp. 130–41.

VELIKOVSKY, IMMANUEL. *Worlds in Collision.* Garden City, New York: Doubleday, 1950.

WAUCHOPE, ROBERT. *Lost Tribes and Sunken Continents.* Chicago: The University of Chicago Press, 1962.

ZINK, DR. DAVID. *The Stones of Atlantis.* Englewood Cliffs, N.J.: Prentice-Hall, 1978.

Twilight of the Gods

ASIMOV, ISAAC. "The Dark Companion." *The Magazine of Fantasy and Science Fiction*, 52 (4) [April 1977], pp. 144–54.

BRECHER, KENNETH. "Sirius Enigmas." *Technology Review*, 80 (4) [December 1977], pp. 52–63. This entire issue of the review, edited by Brecher, was devoted to archeoastronomy; also in *Astronomy of the Ancients*, Brecher and Michael Fiertag, eds. Cambridge, Mass.: MIT Press, 1979.

COHEN, DANIEL. *The Ancient Visitors.* Garden City, N.Y.: Doubleday and Company, 1976.

DÄNIKEN, ERICH VON. *Chariots of the Gods?* Translated by Michael Heron. New York: G. P. Putnam's Sons, 1970.

———. *Gods from Outer Space.* Tr. M. Heron. New York: G. P. Putnam's Sons, 1971.

———. *The Gold of the Gods.* Tr. M. Heron. New York: G. P. Putnam's Sons, 1973.

————. *In Search of Ancient Gods*. Tr. M. Heron. New York: G. P. Putnam's Sons, 1974.

————. *Miracles of the Gods*. Tr. M. Heron. London: Souvenir Press, 1976.

————. *Von Däniken's Proof*. New York: Bantam Books, 1978.

DILLON, JOHN, et al. "Lost Worlds and Golden Ages." Third Annual Division of Interdisciplinary and General Studies Interdisciplinary Symposium, University of California, Berkeley, May 30, 1974. Tapes available through University of California Extension Media Center, Berkeley, Cal. 94720.

FERRIS, TIMOTHY. "Interview with Erich von Däniken." *Playboy*, 21 (8) [August 1974], pp. 51 ff.

KRUPP, E. C. *In Search of Ancient Astronomies*. Garden City, New York: Doubleday and Co., 1978.

————. "On Not Taking It Seriously." *The Griffith Observer*, Los Angeles, 40 (9) [September 1976], pp. 16–17.

————. "The von Däniken Phenomenon." *The Griffith Observer*, Los Angeles, 38 (4) [April 1974], pp. 2–14. Reprinted in 41 (7) [July 1977].

LINGEMAN, RICHARD R. "Erich von Däniken's Genesis." *New York Times Book Review*, March 30, 1974, p. 6.

LUCKERMAN, MARVIN. "More Sirius Difficulties." *The Griffith Observer*, Los Angeles, 41 (10) [October 1977], pp. 14–17.

McCREA, W. H. "Sirius—a Conjecture and an Appeal." *Journal of the British Astronomical Association*, 83 (1973), pp. 63–64. Reprinted in Corliss, William R. *Ancient Man: A Handbook of Puzzling Artifacts*.

PESCH, PETER, and PESCH, ROLAND. "The Last Sirius Inquiry." *The Griffith Observer*, Los Angeles, 41 (12) [December 1977], pp. 15–17.

SAGAN, CARL, and SHKLOVSKII, I. S. *Intelligent Life in the Universe*. San Francisco: Holden-Day, 1966.

SCHELE, LINDA. "Palenque: the House of the Dying Sun," in *Native American Astronomy*, Anthony F. Aveni, ed. Austin, Tex.: University of Texas Press, 1977, pp. 42–56.

SEVER, TOM. "The Obsession with the Star Sirius." *The Griffith Observer*, Los Angeles, 40 (9) [September 1976], pp. 8–15.

STORY, RONALD. *The Space-Gods Revealed*. New York: Harper and Row, 1976.

TEMPLE, ROBERT. *The Sirius Mystery*. London: Sidgwick & Jackson, 1976.

THIERING, BARRY, and CASTLE, EDGAR. *Some Trust in Chariots*. New York: Popular Library, 1972.

THOMAS, ROY, and SEVERIN, MARIE. "Hot Rods of the Gods." *Crazy*, 3 (March 1974), pp. 29–34.

WHITE, PETER. *The Past Is Human*. New York: Taplinger Publishing Co., 1976.

WILSON, CLIFFORD. *Crash Go the Chariots*. New York: Lander Books, 1972.

———. *The Chariots Still Crash*. New York: Signet Books, 1975.

The Bermuda Triangle

Reputable References

Boston Globe, Aug. 20–31, 1881.

Boston Evening Transcript, Aug. 20–Oct. 15, 1881.

Boston Herald-American, Aug. 20–31, 1881.

Evening Telegram, St. John's, Newfoundland, 1881.

The Newfoundlander, St. John's, Newfoundland, 1881.

[*Suduffco*]. *New York Times*, 19 Mar. 1926, p. 23; 8 April, p. 2; 11 April, p. 3; 28 April, p. 27; 14 May, p. 17.

References of Doubtful Credibility

BERLITZ, CHARLES. *The Bermuda Triangle*. Garden City, N.Y.: Doubleday, 1974.

GADDIS, VINCENT H. "The Deadly Bermuda Triangle." *Argosy*, Feb. 1964, p. 29.

———. Chapter 13, "The Triangle of Death," *Invisible Horizons*. Philadelphia: Chilton, 1965.

GOULD, RUPERT T. *The Stargazer Talks*. London: Geoffrey Bles, 1944, p. 30.

SANDERSON, IVAN T. Chapter 8, "The Bermuda Triangle," *Invisible Residents*. New York: World, 1970; paperback, Avon, 1973.

SPENCER, JOHN WALLACE. *Limbo of the Lost*. Westfield, Mass.: Phillips, 1969; paperback, Bantam, 1973.

WINER, RICHARD. *The Devil's Triangle*. Garden City, N.Y.: Doubleday, 1974.

UFOs

1. STURROCK, P. A. "Report on a Survey of the Membership of the American Astronomical Society Concerning the UFO Problem." SUIPR Report No. 681, January 1977, Institute for Plasma Research, Stanford University, Stanford, Ca.

2. The following reports of UFO sightings are based on letters from the National Archives of the United States Air Force.

3. FAA Traffic Controller's account in "UFO Investigator," NICAP, February 1972.

4. HYNEK, J. ALLEN. "The Emerging Picture of the UFO Problem." American Institute of Aeronautics and Astronautics Paper 75-41, 1975.

5. ZEIDMAN, JENNIE, in "The MUFON UFO Journal," November 1977.

6. ———. "A Helicopter-UFO Encounter over Ohio." Report published by Center for UFO Studies, March 1979.

7. *Ibid.*

8. ———. "Major Coyne and the UFO—The True Story." *Fate* magazine, August 1978.

Intelligent Life in the Universe

DRAKE, FRANK. "On Hands and Knees in Search of Elysium." *Technology Review*, 78 (22) [1976], pp. 22–30.

MORRISON, PHILIP; BILLINGHAM, J.; and WOLFE, J. *The Search for Extraterrestrial Intelligence.* NASA Publication SP-419 (1977).

SAGAN, CARL, and DRAKE, FRANK. "The Search for Extraterrestrial Intelligence." *Scientific American*, 232 (80) [1975], p. 80.

SAGAN, CARL; DRAKE, FRANK; DRUYAN, ANN; FERRIS, TIMOTHY; LOMBERG, JON; and SAGAN, LINDA S. *Murmurs of Earth: The Story of the Voyager Record.* New York: Random House, 1978.

On the Causes of Wonderful Things: A Perspective

PORTA, JOHN BAPTISTA. *Natural Magick.* Derek J. Price, ed. New York: Basic Books, 1958.
This facsimile edition reproduces the anonymous English transla-

tion of 1658. Professor Price provides a very useful introduction to the work.

WELTFISH, GENE. *The Lost Universe: The Way of Life of the Pawnee.* New York: Basic Books, 1965.

This remarkable work of ethnography is as sympathetic as it is penetrating. The sleight-of-hand performances are described in some detail.

A recent review of the rabies vaccines by Martin M. Kaplan and Hilary Koprowski is found in the January 1980 issue of *Scientific American*, on pp. 120 ff.

Additional Readings

Introduction

GIERE, R. N. *Understanding Scientific Reasoning*. New York: Holt, Rinehart, and Winston, 1979.

Monsters

MEREDITH, D. *Search at Loch Ness*. New York: Quadrangle, 1977.

RINES, R. H. "Search for the the Loch Ness Monster." *MIT Technology Review*, March/April, 1976.

Astrology

DEAN, G., and MATHER, A. *Recent Advances in Natal Astrology*. The Astrological Association, 1977. Distributed by Para Research, Inc., Whistlestop Mall, Riverport, Mass. 01961.

RAWLINS, D. "What They Aren't Telling You." *Zetetic*, 2 (1977), pp. 62–84.

Moon Madness

ABELL, G. O., and GREENSPAN, B. "The Moon and the Maternity Ward." *The Skeptical Inquirer*, 4 (1979), p. 17.

Biorhythms

BAINBRIDGE, W. S. "Biorhythms." *The Skeptical Inquirer*, 2 (1978), pp. 40–57.

HINES, T. M. "Biorhythm Theory." *The Skeptical Inquirer*, 3 (1979), pp. 26–37.

LUCE, G. G. *Body Time*. New York: Random House, 1971.

Scientists and Psychics

CHRISTOPHER, M. *ESP, Seers, and Psychics*. New York: Crowell, 1970.

———. *Mediums, Mystics, and the Occult*. New York: Crowell, 1976.

HOUDINI, H. *Houdini: A Magician Among the Spirits*. Las Vegas: Gambler's Book Club, n.d.

———. *Houdini's Spirit World*. Portland, Maine: Tower, n.d.

KEENE, M. LAMAR. *The Psychic Mafia*. New York: Dell, 1976.

MARKS, D., and KAMMANN, R. *Psychology of the Psychic*. Buffalo, N.Y.: Prometheus Books, 1979.

The Subtlest Difference

ALCOCK, J. E. "Psychology and Near-death Experiences." *The Skeptical Inquirer*, 3 (1979), pp. 25–42.

Psychic Healing

FLAMMONDE, P. *The Mystic Healers*. New York: Stein & Day, 1975.

NOLEN, W. A. *Healing*. New York: Random House, 1974.

Science and the Chimera

RANDI, J. *The Magic of Uri Geller*. New York: Ballantine, 1975.

———. *Flim-Flam*. New York: Lippincott/Crowell, 1980.

An Analysis of *Worlds in Collision*

ASIMOV, I. "Worlds in Confusion," in I. ASIMOV, *The Stars in their Courses*. Garden City, N.Y.: Doubleday, 1971.

GOLDSMITH, D., ed. *Scientists Confront Velikovsky*. Ithaca; N.Y.: Cornell University Press, 1977.

The Bermuda Triangle

KUSCHE, L. *The Bermuda Triangle Mystery—Solved*. New York: Harper and Row, 1975.

UFOs

HAINES, R. F., ed. *UFO Phenomena and the Behavioral Scientist*. New Jersey: Scarecrow Press, 1979.

KLASS, P. J. *UFOs Explained*. New York: Random House, 1975.

MENZEL, D. H., and TAVES, E. H. *The UFO Enigma*. Garden City, N.Y.: Doubleday, 1977.

SAGAN, C., ed. *UFOs: A Scientific Debate*. Ithaca, N.Y.: Cornell University Press, 1972.

Intelligent Life in the Universe

ABELL, G. O. *Drama of the Universe*. New York: Holt, Rinehart, and Winston, 1978, pp. 372–93.

ASIMOV, I. *Extraterrestrial Civilizations*. New York: Crown, 1979.

BRACEWELL, R. N. *The Galactic Club*. San Francisco: Freeman, 1975.

SAGAN, C. *The Cosmic Connection*. Ithaca, N.Y.: Cornell University Press, 1974.

The Authors

GEORGE O. ABELL (*Introduction, Astrology, Moon Madness,* and editor) is a professor of astronomy at the University of California, Los Angeles. He was born and went to high school in the Los Angeles area and after a short period in the Army Air Corps entered the California Institute of Technology, where he obtained his bachelor's, master's, and doctor's degrees, the last in 1957. Subsequently he took a faculty position at UCLA, where he has been since, save for sabbatical leaves as guest at the Max-Planck-Institut für Physik und Astrophysik in Munich and as visiting professor at the Royal Observatory, Edinburgh. His research specialty is the study of rich clusters of galaxies, the large-scale structure of the universe, and problems related to observational cosmology. He is active in national and international scientific organizations as well as in the popularization of astronomy. In addition to his many research papers and general articles, Abell is the author of several widely used textbooks in astronomy, including *Exploration of the Universe,* and he has played a major role in the preparation of a television series dealing with relativity and cosmology. For many years he has been interested in the appeal of astrology and other pseudosciences and has been involved in many radio and television debates with well-known astrologers.

ISAAC ASIMOV (*The Subtlest Difference*) is one of the world's best known scientists and science writers. It is less well known that at the age of seven he taught his five-year-old sister to read. Asimov was born in Petrovichi, Russia, in 1920, came to the United States in 1923, and was naturalized in 1928. He received all of his advanced training at Columbia University, obtaining the Ph.D. in biochemistry in 1948. In 1949 he joined the Boston University School of Medicine—an association he still holds. He is recipient of the James T. Grady Award of the American Chemical Society (1965) and the American Association for the Advancement of Sciences Westinghouse Award for science writing in 1967. He is best known for his thousands of science fiction stories and popular-science articles, and has more than two hundred books to his credit. Asimov is a master of the limerick and is known to his friends and associates as a man of unparalleled wit and remarkable breadth of knowledge.

DANIEL COHEN (*Monsters*), born in Chicago in 1936, was educated in Chicago and at the University of Illinois School of Journalism. He served on the editorial staff of *Science Digest* for nine years before becoming a freelance writer. He has published more than sixty books (he forgets the exact number), many of which are on paranormal topics, attempting to give young readers a balanced and rational viewpoint of such subjects. His better-known books include *A Modern Look at Monsters, Monsters, Giants and Little Men From Mars,* and *The World of UFOs.* Cohen now lives in Port Jervis, New York.

FRANK D. DRAKE (*Intelligent Life in the Universe*), born in Chicago in 1930, earned his bachelor's degree with honors at Cornell University in 1952. After serving for three years in the navy as electronics officer he returned to graduate school at Harvard University. He received his Ph.D. in astronomy in 1958 and went to the National Radio Astronomy Observatory to become head of telescopic operations and scientific services. In 1964 he returned to Cornell as a faculty member and in 1971 became the first director of the National Astronomy and Ionosphere Center, which operates the world's largest radio telescope, at Arecibo, Puerto Rico. In 1976, Dr. Drake became the Goldwin Smith Professor of Astronomy at Cornell. He is very active in national and international astronomical organizations and is a member of the National Academy of Sciences. He has made important contributions to planetary radio astronomy. He is best known, however, for his pioneering work in the search for extraterrestrial intelligence, beginning with Project Ozma in 1960. He is an avid horticulturist and an accomplished lapidary.

ARTHUR W. GALSTON (co-author of *Plant Sensitivity and Sensation*) is a leading international authority on plant physiology. He was born in New York City in 1920 and studied at Cornell University, then at the University of Illinois, where he was awarded the Ph.D. in 1943. Subsequently he served in the navy, was on the faculty of the California Institute of Technology, and went to Yale in 1955 to become professor of plant physiology in the department of botany. Since 1973 he has been the Eaton Professor of Botany in the Department of Biology at Yale. Galston has received many national and international honors, including Guggenheim, Einstein, and Fulbright fellowships. The author of several successful textbooks, he is very highly regarded in national and international professional societies in botany, has held elective offices in several, and has served as president of both the American Society of Plant Physiologists and the Botanical Society of America. He has also been active in the role of a scientist in society, having testified before Congress on matters of ecological concern and having been the first American scientist to visit the People's Republic of China (in 1971). He has had interviews with Premiers Chou En-lai (China), Pham Van Dong (Vietnam), and Norodom Sihanouk (Cambodia).

MARTIN GARDNER (*Parapsychology and Quantum Mechanics*), born in Tulsa in 1914, majored in philosophy at the University of Chicago and received his B.A. degree in 1936. He did graduate work at Chicago with Rudolf Carnap and later edited Carnap's *Introduction to the Philosophy of Science*. Gardner has worked as a reporter for the *Tulsa Tribune*, with the public relations staff of the University of Chicago, and on the staff of *Humpty Dumpty's* magazine. Since 1957 he has written the monthly feature "Mathematical Games" for the *Scientific American* magazine, and these famous columns are now being collected in book form—nine volumes so far. Gardner's thirty-odd books also include *Fads and Fallacies in the Name of Science, The Relativity Explosion*, and *The Annotated Alice*. Gardner's principal hobby is conjuring, and he contributes regularly to journals for professional magicians. His many contributions to science and literature were recognized in 1978 with the award of an honorary doctorate from Bucknell University. His two sons now grown, Gardner lives with his wife, Charlotte, in Hastings-on-Hudson, New York.

RAY HYMAN *(Scientists and Psychics)* is a professor of psychology at the University of Oregon, where he has been on the faculty since 1961. He did his undergraduate work at Boston University, and received his master's and doctor's degrees at Johns Hopkins University, the latter in 1953. His specialty is experimental psychology, and he is author of books and many papers on thinking, perception, semantic memory, cognitive distortion, and related subjects. Hyman has also been a professional magician—he worked his way through high school and college by doing mind-reading and hypnotism shows. Because of this background he has frequently served as a consultant to granting agencies and journals in the investigation of paranormal claims of alleged psychics (among them, Uri Geller). Hyman is active in preparing teachers to detect fraud and to respond to their students' inquiries concerning pseudoscientific matters. Among his honors, he was awarded a Fulbright-Hays Scholarship to do research in Bologna, Italy, in 1967–68.

TAREK KHALIL (co-author of *Biorhythms*) is Professor of Industrial Engineering, Biomedical Engineering, and Epidemiology and Public Health at the University of Miami. He received the B.M.E. degree from Cairo University in 1964 and taught production engineering and industrial safety there for two years. Subsequently he studied at Texas Tech University, receiving the Ph.D. degree in 1969. He joined the University of Miami faculty in 1974. His research interests include biotechnology, biomechanics, production and health care delivery systems, and he currently directs the university's occupational safety and environmental health programs. He has consulted extensively to industrial, service, and educational organizations, and is recipient of the Jack A. Kraft Award for significant effort to extend the application of human factors and The American Institute of Industrial Engineers Award in Ergonomics. Khalil is the author of more than sixty publications, is multilingual, and is very active in professional and public service organizations.

PHILIP J. KLASS *(UFOs)* is the senior avionics editor for *Aviation Week & Space Technology* magazine—often called the bible of the aerospace field. A graduate electrical engineer (Iowa State University, 1941), he was named a Fellow in the Institute of Electrical and Electronics Engineers in 1973 in recognition of his contributions as a technical journalist. Since 1966, Klass has been actively involved, as a hobby, in investigating famous UFO incidents, drawing on both his technical background and probing journalistic skills. *Scientific American* magazine, in reviewing his second best-selling book on the subject, *UFOs Explained*, said: "There is no more explicit and insightful account of UFOs than this one." Mr. Klass also is a member of the American Association for the Advancement of Science, Aviation/Space Writers Association, and the National Press Club.

E. C. KRUPP *(Recasting the Past)* is director of the Griffith Observatory in Los Angeles, an institution he has been associated with since 1970. Born in 1944, he did his undergraduate work at Pomona College in Claremont, California, and his graduate work at UCLA, where he earned the Ph.D. in astronomy in 1972, with a study of the properties of clusters of galaxies. Subsequently Krupp became interested in archeoastronomy. He and his wife, Robin, have led field study expeditions to many archeoastronomical sites and have studied details and alignments in more than 250 ancient and prehistoric monuments throughout Britain, Brittany, Ireland, Mexico, Peru, Guatemala, Honduras, Malta, Egypt, and the American Midwest. Krupp has lectured widely on archeoastronomy as well as on fads, myths, and pseudoscience, which he has also studied extensively. One of his lecture series led to the book *In Search of Ancient Astronomies*, which won the American Institute of Physics–U.S. Steel Foundation Award for Best Science Writing in 1978. Krupp frequently appears on Los Angeles television and is the on-camera host for the highly successful astronomy series *Project: Universe*.

PAUL KURTZ *(Foreword)* is a professor of philosophy at the State University of New York at Buffalo. He was born in Newark, New Jersey, in 1925, and after serving in the army studied at New York University and Columbia University, where he earned his doctorate in 1952. He held several academic posts before going to Buffalo in 1965, among them a visiting professorship at the University of Besancon, France. Kurtz has been active on many national and international committees dealing with ethics and behavioral research. He has been especially active in the humanist movement, having served as a director of the American Humanist Association and as editor of the *Humanist* magazine from 1967 to 1978. Kurtz is author or editor of a score of books and is a frequent guest and moderator on television programs. In 1976 he was the driving force behind the formation of the Committee for the Scientific Investigation of Claims of the Paranormal (CSICOP) and has served as the committee's chairman since.

CHARLES KURUCZ (co-author of *Biorhythms*) is associate professor of Management Science and Industrial Engineering at the University of Miami. He was born in Buffalo, New York, in 1940 and studied at the State University of New York there, where he received the Ph.D. degree in 1969. He worked for the General Motors Corporation, the U.S. Army, and SUNY (Buffalo) before joining the faculty of the University of Miami in 1968. Kurucz's educational and teaching background includes mathematical modeling and applied statistics, but he has also done research and published papers in areas of traffic safety and accident prevention. His hobbies are music and boating, and he is often found sailing in Biscayne Bay on pleasant Miami weekends. Kurucz became interested in the investigation of biorhythms and whether they could possibly have any relation to human activity in work performance or accident occurrence, and has devoted a certain amount of his time to such questions since.

LARRY KUSCHE *(The Bermuda Triangle)*, a resident of Tempe, Arizona, has some 1,700 hours flying time, including commercial, flight instructor, instrument, instrument instructor, and flight engineer ratings. After becoming interested in the Bermuda Triangle, he researched it exhaustively, using reliable, original sources of information. His first book, *The Bermuda Triangle Mystery—Solved* (1975), contains the results of those investigations, and the conclusion that the Triangle is "a manufactured mystery." Published in many foreign countries, the book has been acclaimed by Lloyd's of London, the U.S. Coast Guard, and other groups and scientists as the most authoritative work on the subject. Kusche's most recent book, *The Disappearance of Flight 19* (1980), is a similarly thorough investigation of the most famous loss in the Triangle—the five Navy Avenger Torpedo bombers, and a search plane, that took off on December 5, 1945, and never returned. Part of Kusche's research for that book was to fly the route, himself, on which the planes were lost. He has appeared on hundreds of radio and television programs and has lectured at many colleges across the country.

PHILIP MORRISON (*On the Causes of Wonderful Things: A Perspective*) is Institute Professor at the Massachusetts Institute of Technology. He was born in Somerville, New Jersey, in 1915, and studied at the Carnegie Institute of Technology (B.S., 1936) and at the University of California, Berkeley, where he received his Ph.D. in 1940. Morrison held faculty appointments at San Francisco State College, the University of Illinois, the University of Chicago, and at Cornell before settling at MIT in 1965. During World War II he was a physicist and group leader at the Los Alamos Scientific Laboratory in New Mexico. He is the recipient of many prizes and honors, including the Oersted Medal in 1965 and the Priestley Award in 1980 and has been elected to the National Academy of Sciences. In recent years he has become increasingly interested in the challenging problems of modern astrophysics and has devoted considerable attention to the theoretical study of quasars, pulsars, and peculiar galaxies. Morrison is well known to the public through his frequent appearances on national and foreign television, and for his monthly book-review section in *Scientific American* magazine since 1965.

WILLIAM A. NOLEN (*Psychic Healing*), Chief of Surgery at Meeker County Hospital, Litchfield, Minnesota, was born in Holyoke, Massachusetts, in 1928. He received his M.D. degree at Tufts Medical College in 1953 and did his internship and residency at Bellevue Hospital. After a stint as captain in the U.S. Army Reserve Medical Corps from 1957 to 1959, he returned to Bellevue, where he remained until going to Litchfield in 1960. Nolen is very active in many professional societies, is a past president of the American College of Surgeons, and is internationally known and respected. In addition to publishing many papers in scientific journals, he has written many popular articles on medical subjects as well as six books. He is particularly concerned with public health and has traveled to the Philippines to witness firsthand and expose the alleged miracles of the psychic surgeons there who duped many hundreds of people into foregoing proper medical treatment in favor of quack cures.

JAMES RANDI (*Science and the Chimera*), known professionally as The Amazing Randi, has been ranked among the world's greatest magicians and is frequently seen on television in the United States and around the world. He also has been an investigator of paranormal claims for more than thirty-five years, is a founding member of the Committee for the Scientific Investigation of Claims of the Paranormal, and has a standing offer of ten thousand dollars for proof of any paranormal phenomenon under carefully controlled conditions. Randi's training gives him special expertise in detecting simple conjuring tricks in alleged paranormal feats, and he has spoken on the subject at many universities and institutions in the United States and abroad, including the Royal Institution in the United Kingdom. His book *The Magic of Uri Geller* is the definitive exposé of the Geller myth and the involvement of scientists with it. His new book, *Flim-Flam*, covers the field, from biorhythms to UFOs. Randi, a bachelor, iconoclast, and individualist, lives in Rumson, New Jersey, with an assortment of birds, cats, and itinerant magicians passing through.

CARL SAGAN (*An Analysis of* Worlds in Collision) is Professor of Astronomy and Space Sciences at Cornell University. Born in New York in 1934, he studied at the University of Chicago, where he received the Ph.D. in 1956. He has held academic appointments at the University of California (Berkeley), Stanford University, and Harvard before joining the faculty at Cornell and becoming director of the Laboratory of Planetary Studies there in 1968. Sagan is extremely active in research on planets and in the U.S. Space Program, as well as in international organizations. In addition to his prodigious number of technical papers and editorial services as editor of the planetary sciences journal *Icarus*, he has written a large number of popular articles and books, including the best-sellers *The Cosmic Connection*, *The Dragons of Eden*, and *Broca's Brain*. His very many honors include the David Duncan Professorship of Physical Science at Cornell and several honorary doctorates. His contributions to popular science through writing and television—including regular appearances on the Johnny Carson "Tonight Show," presentation in Public Broadcasting Service and British Broadcasting Corporation programs, and his own *Cosmos* series—have made him the world's most visible scientist.

RONALD K. SIEGEL (*Life After Death*) was born in 1943. He received his B.A. degree in sociology from Brandeis University and his M.A. and Ph.D. in psychology from Dalhousie University (Canada). After a postdoctoral fellowship in psychopharmacology at Albert Einstein College of Medicine in New York, he joined in 1970 the faculty at the University of California, Los Angeles, where he is now research psychologist in the Department of Psychiatry and Biobehavioral Sciences. Well known for his research on hallucinogens and hallucinations, Siegel has written numerous scientific works, including articles in *The American Journal of Psychiatry*, *The Journal of the American Medical Association*, and *Scientific American*, and co-edited *Hallucinations: Behavior, Experience and Theory* (Wiley, 1975). In addition to these academic pursuits, Siegel is an award-winning poet and published cartoonist. A serious marathon runner, he reports that "the only life after death I know of is when you cross the finish line after 26.2 miles."

BARRY SINGER (*Introduction, To Believe or Not to Believe, On Double Standards, Kirlian Photography*, and editor) is Professor of Psychology at the California State University, Long Beach. He received his bachelor's degree in psychology at Antioch in 1965 and his Ph.D. in experimental psychology at the University of California, Berkeley, three years later, and has been at Long Beach since, except for a year as a visiting professor at Massey University, Palmerston North, New Zealand (1978). Singer has published articles and books in the areas of human sexuality, alternative life-styles, learning theory, psychology of science, criminology, teaching methods, and occult belief. It was the latter interest that brought him into contact with George Abell (his co-editor), who had organized a series of lectures with invited speakers on various occult topics at UCLA. That meeting led to the collaboration that produced this volume.

CLIFFORD L. SLAYMAN (co-author of *Plant Sensitivity and Sensation*) is Associate Professor of Physiology at Yale University. He was born in Mount Vernon, Ohio, in 1936, and studied at Kenyon College and the Rockefeller University, receiving the Ph.D. in physiology at the latter in 1963. Subsequently, he was a National Sciences Foundation Postdoctoral Fellow in Cambridge, England, and then served on the faculty of Western Reserve University, Cleveland, before going to Yale in 1967. He is active in professional organizations and has carried out research and published papers in the physiology and biochemistry of energy conservation, and transplant in biological membranes, with emphasis on electrical processes. Slayman's principal hobby (other than helping to raise two young children) is restoring antique houses.

Index

Index

Note: Full chapters by contributors are not included with entries for those writers.

Abell, G. O., x, 395
abominable snowman, 31–34
Academy for Scientific Interrogation, 46
Adams, T., 281
Aerial Phenomena Research Organization (APRO), 313
Agel, J., 96
Agpoa, T., 190
Alexander, Mike. *See* Chen, N.
Ali, Muhammad, 115
alt, 204
American Association for the Advancement of Science (AAAS), 42, 224
American Astronomical Society, 216
American Polygraph Association, 46
American Society of Plant Physiologists (ASPP), 42
Andrews, E. J., 101–2
Ardrey, R., 170
Arecibo Observatory, Puerto Rico, 340ff
Argosy, article on Bermuda Triangle in, 298
Arigo, psychic healer, 190
Asimov, I., x, 120, 294–95
Assembly of Inspired Thought, The, 210
astral (bioplasma) body, 200
astrology, 70–94
  mundane, 73

astrology (*Continued*)
  natal, 75
  sidereal, 85
  tropical, 85
astronauts, ancient, 253, 282–95
Astrophysical Journal, 1–2, 246
Atlantis, 255, 270–82
aura, 197ff

Babylonia, 71, 73
Backster, C., 42ff
Bacon, Francis, 23
Badawy, A., 264
Barrett, W., 121
Bayless, R., 163
Beauregard, Costa de, 58, 68, 368
Beets, J. L., 101
Bell, J. S., 367–68
Bell's theorem, 60–61, 367–68
Berlitz, C., 281, 299ff
Bessel, F., 290
Beyond and Back (documentary
  film), 162
Bickman, L., 133
Bigfoot, 31, 34–39
Biocron Systems Company of Cal-
  ifornia, 116
biocycle, 107
biofeedback, 193
bioplasma (astral) body, 200
biorhythms, 105–18
  and industrial safety, 114, 116
Biorhythms and Industrial Safety
  (Thumann), 115
Bird, C., 42ff
Blackburn, psychic studies on, 131
Blavatsky, Madame, 278
Blondlot, R., 213
Bohm, D., 60–61
Borst, L. B., 102

Bose, J. C., 43
Bourbourg, Charles-Etienne Bras-
  seur de, 273ff
Bovis, Antoine, 267ff
Brahe, Tycho, 86
Brockopp, G. W., 100
Brown, F., 98
Brown, K. W. G., 163
Brownley, M. W., 114
Brugger, K., 289
Brush, R., 281
Budge, E. A. W., 170
Burns, J. W., 34
Burr, H. S., 44
Burt, C., 212
Byrne, R. J., 281

Campbell, A., 26
Campbell, D. E., 101
Cavendish, R., 170–71
Cayce, E., 281
celestial sphere, 73ff
Center for UFO Studies (CUFOS),
  327ff
Chen, N., 187, 193
chimera, 209–22
Churchward, J., 279
circadian rhythms, 106–8
circular continuum, 162
Clair, C., 171
clairvoyance, 12, 57, 63
Clark, A., 290
Clarke, A. C., 311
coelacanth, 38–39
Cohen, D., 396
coincidence, 14–17
Cole, J. H., 263
Coleman, S., 223
comet, Velikovsky's, 223, 230ff
Comité Para, 92

Committee for the Scientific Investigation of Claims of the Paranormal (SCICOP), viii–ix
Comte, A., 164
Connes, P., 243, 245
constellations, 72
Cook, F., 123ff
Cooper, D. B., 204
Copernicus, N., 66, 76
corona discharge, 200ff
Cortesianus Codex, 273ff
Coyne, L., 319ff
critical days, 108ff
Crookes, W., 121ff

Darwin, C., 167
Davey, S. J., 127
Dean, G., 89–90
Dicke, R., 60
Dieterlen, G., 290
Dinsdale, T., 28
diurnal rhythms, 106
Donnelly, I., 274ff, 289
Douglas-Hamilton, I., 168
Douglas-Hamilton, O., 168
Drake, F. D., 5, 396–97
Drbal, K., 268–69
dreams, 12

Ebon, M., 168, 172
ecliptic, 71, 74, 78
Edison, T., 160
Egyptian alphabet and grammar, 217–20
Eidson, W., 196ff
Einhorn, H. J., 363
Einstein, A., 59, 60, 338, 367
Eliade, M., 172

Ellen Austin, in Bermuda Triangle, 299ff
Ely, G., 324
energy body, 204
EPR (Einstein-Podolsky-Rosen) paradox, 59, 61, 367
Exodus, and Velikovsky hypothesis, 230ff
Experimental Investigation of the Spirit Manifestations, Demonstrating the Existence of Spirits and Their Communion with Mortals; Doctrine of the Spirit World Respecting Heaven, Hell, Morality, and God. . . . (Hare, 1855), 120
extrasensory perception (ESP), 56ff

Farmer, P. J., 160, 163
Faust, D., 196ff
Federal Aviation Administration, 112
Flammarion, C., 121
Fort, C. H., 37
Forteans, 37
Forwald, H., 65–66, 369
Fowles, J., 19
Freud, S., 164
Freya, 304
Frost, K. T., 179
Fuller, J., 164, 190

Gaddis, V., 298ff
Galanopoulos, A. G., 280
Galilei, Galileo, 1, 3
Galston, A. W., 397
Galvani, L., 43
Gamow, G., 67
Gardner, M., x, 165, 397–98

Garfield, C. A., 181
Gasteiger, E. L., 42, 49–50
Gauquelin, M., 88–93
Geller effect, 66
Geller Papers, The (Panati, ed.), 68
Geller, U., 58ff, 124ff, 216
Gimlin, R., 35–36
Gold, T., 223
Goldstein, R., 248
Goldstone Radio Observatory (Jet Propulsion Laboratory), 248
Gordon, D. C., 163
Gould, R., 300
Graham, J., 283
gravitation, 96ff
"graviton," 57
Greaves, J., 261
Greenspan, B., 103
Griaule, M., 290
Grof, S., 163, 166, 182
Guppy, Agnes. *See* Nichol, Agnes

Halifax, J., 163, 166, 182
Hall, T., 127
Halley's Comet, 250
Hanlon, J., 129
Haraldsson, E., 164, 174ff
Hare, R., 120ff
Harkrader, A., Jr., 315
Harrison, W., 281
Heisenberg, W., 213
Herne (alleged psychic), 125
Herschel, J., 263
Hillary, D., 33–34
Hipparchus, 85
Hirsh, R., 117
Home, D. D., 123ff
horoscopes, 75ff
Horowitz, K. A., 50

Humanist, The, statement on astrology, 70, 216
Huxley, L., 163
Hyman, R., x, 398
Hynek, J. A., 318ff

identified flying objects (IFOs), 312ff
intelligent life in the universe, 5
International Astronomical Union, 85
International Journal of Parapsychology, 49
Inverness Courier, 1933 popularization of Loch Ness monster, 26

Jachimezyk, J., 100
Jackson, H., 183
Jackson, Reggie, biorhythms of, 115
Jacobson, A., 143–44
James, W., 121, 166
Jarvik, M. E., 174, 176
Jastrow, J., 311
Jet Propulsion Laboratory, 244
Johnson, K., 163, 198ff
Jonas, D. F., 169
Jones, D. L., 278
Jones, Jimmy, 221
Josephson, B., 58
Journal of Parapsychology, 65
Jupiter, 223, 230ff, 333

Kahneman, D., 14–15
Kalish, R. A., 162
Kaplan, L. D., 244
Kelley, D., 283
Kepler, J., 3, 86
Khalil, T., 398

King, Billie Jean, 115
King, Katie, 123, 138
Kirlian, S. D., 197ff
Kirlian photography, 196–208
Klass, P., x, 399
Kmetz, J. M., 42, 50–52
Koestenbaum, P., 184
Koestler, A., 68, 162, 166–67
Kohoutek, comet, 241
Koumaris, J., 279
Krippner, S., 199
Krupp, E. C., 399
Kübler-Ross, E., 156, 171
Kurtz, P., 92, 399–400
Kurucz, C., 400
Kusche, L., x, 400–401
Kyler, H., 196ff

La Barre, W., 170–72
Landa, Diego de, 273ff
Laplace, P. S., 233
Lester, D., 100
Lewis, D. C., 50
Ley, Willy, 263, 280
Lichtenberg, G. C., 204
Lieber, A. L., 95–100
Loch Ness monster, 5, 25–31
Lodge, O., 121
Loehr, F., 172
Lombroso, C., 121
lost continents, 253, 270–82
Louis, A. M., 115
Lunar Effect, The (Lieber and Agel), 96ff
Lund, E. J., 44–45
Lundegaardh, H., 44
Luther, Martin, 66–67, 240
Lynch, M. P., 281

MacHovee, F. J., 170
Mackey, J., 26

MacLeer-CTV film, 214
MacMillan, R. L., 163
Maeterlinck, M., 163
magicians, 20–22
manna, 240–41
Marais, E., 169
Marbell, N., 70
Marinatos, S., 279
Marov, M. Ya., 246
Mars, 231ff, 333
Mars effect, 92
Mary Celeste, 15–16, 306
Masterson, L., 162
Matheson, R., 163
Mathews, P., 283
Matson, A., 184
Mattuck, R., 58
Maudsley, H., 172
McConnell, J. V., 142
McConnell, R. A., 65
McCrea, W. H., 295
medium, 160
Meisel, D. D., 325
membrane potential, 44
Menaker, A., 102
Menaker, W., 102
Mendelssohn, K., 263
Menzies, R., 260
Mercado, Joe, 190
meteorite, 211
Milky Way Galaxy, 342
"Miss Z," and astral projection, 145–47
Mitchell, P., 44
monsters, 24–39
Montagu, A., 167
Moody, R., 164, 173ff
moon, 74ff, 95–104
   craters on, 237ff
Moreau, J., 181

Moriez, J., 289
Morris, R. W., 102
Morrison, D., 223
Morrison, P., 401
Moss, T., 167, 198ff
Muck, O., 280

Nara, T., 289
National Enquirer, life-after-death
    advertisement, 162
Neil, D. E., 115
Nelson, J. H., 90–93
Nernst, W. H., 44
Nessiteras rhomboptery. See Loch
    Ness monster
neutrino, 57
Newcomb, B. L., 116
Newton, I., 73, 259, 311
New Zealand monster, 30–31
Nibley, H., 217
Nichol, Agnes (Guppy), 122ff
Nicklaus, J., 115
Nimoy, Leonard, 221
Nolan, W. F., 163
Nolen, W. A., xi, 401–2
N-rays, 213

observation
    powers of, 8–10
    tests of, 8–9
octopus, giant, 30
okapi, 39
Oliver, B. M., 337
Omarr, S., 70, 81, 91
Osborn, R. D., 101
Osis, K., 164, 174ff
Osley, M., 102
Osterhout, W. J., 44
Ostrander, S., 197, 268
Owen, T. C., 243

Palmer, A., 115
Panati, C., 68–69, 138
Parise, F., 66
Patterson, R., 35–36
Pauli, W., 67
Pehek, J. O., 196ff
Pesch, P., 292
Pesch, R., 292
Petiot, M., 88–89
Petrie, W. F., 261
phantom leaf effect, 199
photons, 57–60
Pickard, B. G., 42
Planck, M., 44
plant consciousness, 40–55
Plato, 270ff
plesiosaur theory, 31
Podolsky, B., 59, 367
Pokorny, A., 100–101
Pollack, J. B., 243
Poock, K., 206
Popper, K., 367
Prabhupada, A. C., 163
Pratt, J. G., 65, 215
precession, 85
precognition, 57, 63
Price, D. J., 390
Priebe, K., 100
probability, 12–23
problem solving, 18–23
Proctor, R., 264
Project Blue Book (USAF report
    on Bermuda Triangle), 222
Project Cyclops, 345
Project Ozma, 342
Project UFO, 222
Proskouriakoff, T., 283
psi powers, 57
psychic healing, 199
psychic phenomena, 121
psychics, 20–22, 119–41

psychic surgery, 187ff
psychogalvanic reflex, 46
psychokinesis (PK), 56–69
psychon, 58
Ptolemy, C., 76, 84
Putholf, H., 58, 124ff
pyramids, 253–70

quantum mechanics, 2–4, 56–69

Randi, J., x, 402
Rayleigh, Lord, 121
Recent Advances in Natal Astrology (Dean), 89
relativity theory, 4
representativeness fallacy, 15–16
Reynolds, C., 162
Rhind papyrus, 259, 263
Rhine, J. B., 57, 63
Richet, C., 121
Riggs, Bobby, 115
Righter, C., 70
Rippmann, E. T., 103
Ritchie, G., 173
Rogo, D. S., 163
Rosen, N., 59, 367

Sagan, C., x, 402
St. Columba, 26
St. Elmo's fire, 202
Salpeter, E. E., 223
Sanderson, I., 32, 302
Sandler, C. E., 114
Sanhein, J. M., 115
Sarfatti, J., 58
Sasquatch, 34–39
Saturn, 333
Schele, L., 283ff
Schliemann, H., 226
Schopf, J. W., 288
Schroeder, L., 197, 268

Science Unlimited Research Foundation, 50
Scott, P., 28
sea monsters, 29–31
Search for Bridey Murphy, The, 155
Secret Life of Plants, The (Tompkins, Bird), 40–55
Serios, T., 130, 140
Shackleton experiments, 215
Sherin, C., 97
Shinn, E. A., 281
Shipton, E., 33
Shklovskii, I. S., 282, 288
Showers, M., 127
sidereal time, 78
Siegel, R. K., 403
Sill, G., 243
Singer, B., 403
Sink, F. L., 115
Slade, H., 128
Slater, P., 184
Slayman, C. L., 403–4
sleep, stages and dreaming, 12
Smith, J., 220
Smith, psychic studies on, 131
Smith, S., 115
Smyth, C. P., 260–64, 270, 289
Soal, S. G., 215
Society for Psychical Research, ix, 131, 215
Soter, S., 223
Space Environmental Services Center, 91
Spencer, J. W., 299
spiritualistic phenomena, 121
Spiritualists, The (Hall), 127
Spitz, M., 114
squid, giant, 29
Stanford Research Institute, 124, 126

Stecchini, L., 265ff
Stevenson, I., 163
Sturrock, P. A., 327
Suduffco, disappearance of, 298ff
Summerville, D., 102
Swann, I., 68, 130

tachyons, 57–58
Targ, R., 58ff, 124ff
Tart, C., 145–47
Taylor, J., 258ff
Taylor, J. G., 136, 213, 216
telepathy, 57, 63
Temple, R. K. G., 289, 294
Tesla, N., 204
Tetrabiblos (Ptolemy), 84
Thumann, A., 114
tides, 96–101
Tobey, Carl Payne, 70
Tombazi, N. A., 32
Tompkins, P., 42ff, 265
Toynbee, Arnold, 165–66
Transcendental Meditators of the
    Mahareshi, The, publications
    of, 220
Trench, B. LePoer, 288
Trevino, L., 115
Trimble, V., 264
Troano Codex, 273ff
Truman, H. S., 115
Tversky, A., 14–15
Tyndall, J., 122

UFO Studies, Center for. *See*
    Center for UFO Studies
unidentified flying objects (UFOs),
    255, 310–28

Valentine, J. M., 281
Velikovsky, I., x, 223–52, 274
Venus, 231ff

vernal equinox, 76, 77, 85
Vidal, G., 163
Vogel, M., 55
von Däniken, E., 253ff
Vsekhsviatsky, V. S., 233

Walker, E. H., 58, 64, 369
Wallace, A. R., 121ff
Weaver, C. A., 114
Weinberger, J., 163
Weisman, A., 267
Weiss, J. E., 165
Wells, H. G., 235
West, L. J., 183
Western, R., 160
Wheeler, D. R., 175
Wigner, E., 368
Wildt, R., 246
Wilhelm, J. L., 140
William-Ellis, Lady, 127
Williams (alleged psychic), 125
Williamson, G. H., 288
Wilson, R. K., 27
Winer, R., 299, 305
Wittke, J., 60
Wolcott, J. H., 114
Worlds in Collision (Velikovsky),
    274

Yadin, Y., 226
yeti, 31–34
yoga, 193
Young, A. T., 243
Young, L. D. G., 243

Zelen, M., 92
Zink, D., 281–82
zodiac, 71ff
    Age of Aquarius, 85
Zoellner, J. C. F., 121, 128, 130,
    370

RENÉ DUBOS	Beast or Angel · $7.95
	So Human an Animal · $7.95
	The Wooing of Earth · $6.95
LOREN EISELEY	All the Strange Hours · $7.95
	The Innocent Assassins · $3.95
	The Invisible Pyramid · $6.95
	The Man Who Saw Through Time · $4.95
	The Night Country · $7.95
	Notes of an Alchemist · $7.95
F. SCOTT FITZGERALD	Afternoon of an Author · $2.95
	Babylon Revisited and Other Stories · $5.95
	The Beautiful and Damned · $7.95
	Flappers and Philosophers · $2.95
	The Great Gatsby · $4.95
	The Last Tycoon · $5.95
	Six Tales of the Jazz Age and Other Stories · $5.95
	Stories of F. Scott Fitzgerald · $9.95
	Tender Is the Night · $5.95
	This Side of Paradise · $5.95
	The Vegetable, or From President to Postman · $2.95
JOHN GALSWORTHY	The Forsyte Saga · $12.95
KENNETH GRAHAME	The Wind in the Willows · $6.95
ERNEST HEMINGWAY	Across the River and Into the Trees · $6.95
	By-Line: Ernest Hemingway · $12.95
	Death in the Afternoon · $9.95
	A Farewell to Arms · $7.95
	The Fifth Column and Four Stories of the Spanish Civil War · $4.95
	For Whom the Bell Tolls · $8.95
	Green Hills of Africa · $7.95
	In Our Time · $4.50
	Islands in the Stream · $7.95
	Men Without Women · $5.95
	A Moveable Feast · $6.95
	The Nick Adams Stories · $6.95
	The Old Man and the Sea · $4.95
	Selected Letters, edited by Carlos Baker · $12.95
	The Short Stories of Ernest Hemingway · $8.95
	The Snows of Kilimanjaro and Other Stories · $5.95
	The Sun Also Rises · $6.95
	To Have and Have Not · $8.95
	Winner Take Nothing · $4.95
WILL JAMES	Smoky the Cow Horse · $5.95

RING LARDNER	The Best Short Stories of Ring Lardner • $7.95
	Some Champions • $3.95
REINHOLD NIEBUHR	The Irony of American History • $6.95
	Moral Man and Immoral Society • $7.95
ALAN PATON	Cry, the Beloved Country • $5.95
	Tales From a Troubled Land • $8.95
	Too Late the Phalarope • $6.95
JANE PORTER	The Scottish Chiefs,
	illustrated by N. C. Wyeth • $6.95
MARJORIE KINNAN RAWLINGS	The Yearling • $8.95
C. P. SNOW	A Coat of Varnish • $7.95
	Death Under Sail • $5.95
	The Masters • $6.95
JESSE STUART	The Thread that Runs So True • $6.95
PAUL TILLICH	The Eternal Now • $5.95
	The New Being • $5.95
	The Shaking of the Foundations • $4.95
EDITH WHARTON	The Age of Innocence • $7.95
	A Backward Glance • $9.95
	The Custom of the Country • $10.95
	Ethan Frome • $4.95
	The Ghost Stories of Edith Wharton • $8.95
	The House of Mirth • $6.95
	Hudson River Bracketed • $9.95
	Madame de Treymes and Others:
	Four Novelettes • $7.95
	The Reef • $8.95
	Roman Fever and Other Stories • $5.95
THOMAS WOLFE	From Death to Morning • $4.95
	Look Homeward, Angel • $9.95
	Of Time and the River, one vol. • $14.95

All books listed are trade paperbacks, which are the same size as the original hardcover editions. If any of these titles are not available at your local bookstore, you can order them directly from Charles Scribner's Sons, 115 Fifth Avenue, New York, NY 10003. Enclose a check or money order for the price of the books ordered plus $1.50 for postage for the first book, 75¢ for each additional book. Prices are subject to change.